Conflict Prevention: Path to Peace or Grand Illusion?

Edited by David Carment and Albrecht Schnabel

**United Nations
University Press**

TOKYO · NEW YORK · PARIS

United Nations University Press
The United Nations University, 53-70, Jingumae 5-chome,
Shibuya-ku, Tokyo, 150-8925, Japan
Tel: +81-3-3499-2811   Fax: +81-3-3406-7345
E-mail: sales@hq.unu.edu (general enquiries): press@hq.unu.edu
http://www.unu.edu

United Nations University Office in North America
2 United Nations Plaza, Room DC2-1462-70, New York, NY 10017, USA
Tel: +1-212-963-6387   Fax: +1-212-371-9454
E-mail: unuona@ony.unu.edu

United Nations University Press is the publishing division of the United Nations University.

Cover design by Andrew Corbett

Printed in the United States of America

UNUP-1081
ISBN 92-808-1081-2

Library of Congress Cataloging-in-Publication Data

Conflict prevention : path to peace or grand illusion? / edited by
David Carment and Albrecht Schnabel.
    p.   cm.
Includes bibliographical references and index.
ISBN 92-808-1081-2
1. Pacific settlement of international disputes. 2. Conflict management.
3. North Atlantic Treaty Organization. 4. Security, International.
5. United Nations. 6. European Union. I. Carment, David.
Schnabel, Albrecht.
JZ6010 .C65 2003
341.5'23—dc21   2002151438

Conflict Prevention

Foundations of Peace

Note to the reader

The United Nations University Press series on the *Foundations of Peace* addresses themes that relate to the evolving agenda of peace and security within and between communities. Traditional or conventional conceptions of security, primarily military and inter-state, have been supplemented, or perhaps even surpassed, by a definition of security which rests upon much broader tenets, including human rights, cultural and communal rights, environmental and resource security, and economic security. To resolve the dialectic between state security and human security it is necessary to envision a wide agenda of international peace and security that embraces these tenets and the potential tensions that exist between them and the inter-state context. International actors, such as the UN and non-governmental organizations, are also increasingly playing a central role in building the foundations of sustainable peace. This series promotes theoretical as well as policy-relevant discussion on these crucial issues.

Titles currently available:

Peacekeepers, Politicians, and Warlords: The Liberian Peace Process by Abiodun Alao, John Mackinlay, and 'Funmi Olonisakin
Human Rights and Comparative Foreign Policy edited by David P. Forsythe
Asia's Emerging Regional Order: Reconciling Traditional and Human Security edited by William T. Tow, Ramesh Thakur, and In-Taek Hyun
Conflict Prevention: Path to Peace or Grand Illusion? edited by David Carment and Albrecht Schnabel

To Madeleine, Joseph, Rafael, and Daniel

Contents

Tables and figures

Acknowledgements

The idea for this book has its roots in a two-panel session on the state of the art and current challenges of conflict prevention that we organized for the 1999 Annual Meeting of the International Studies Association in Washington, D.C. The panels sparked exciting discussions and we decided to pursue this as a larger research project. It has, over time, evolved into the present, much more extensive, examination of conflict prevention as an academic debate and a policy tool. We are very pleased that we are now able to present the results of this work to a larger audience and hope that its timeliness will sharpen our understanding of the limits and opportunities inherent in preventive thought, talk, and action.

The writing of this book has been a rewarding and stimulating experience for the contributors and the editors, not least thanks to the support and assistance offered by a number of individuals and institutions. We would like to acknowledge them for their invaluable contributions. We extend our gratitude to Welmoet Wels and Monica Blagescu, both from UNU, for editorial and project assistance, and to Yoshie Sawada, also from UNU, for her diligent work in managing the project funds and various organizational matters. We are grateful for the support we received from UNU Press, particularly from Gareth Johnston. We thank Juliet Sydenham for carefully copyediting the book manuscript. We benefited greatly from the very helpful comments provided by the anonymous peer reviewers of the draft manuscript. We thank Thomas Weiss and Ben Fraenkel for comments on earlier drafts of the project outline and several draft chapters. We are particularly grateful for generous project funding provided by the United Nations University and the International Development Research Centre, Ottawa, Canada.

David Carment acknowledges the Security and Defence Forum of the Department of National Defence, Canada, and the Social Sciences and Humanities Research Council of Canada for their financial support of his research, Carleton University for a generous Research Achievement Award, and Harvard's Belfer Center where portions of this volume were written and edited. David Carment would also like to thank Susan Ampleford, Rasheed Draman, and Troy Joseph for their excellent research assistance. Albrecht Schnabel expresses his gratitude to the Peace and Governance Programme of the United Nations University for its support of his work on this project and volume, and for several opportunities to share its results with the wider academic and policy communities.

Finally, we are grateful to our families, who have invested many hours of family time into this project. The book is dedicated to our children.

David Carment
Albrecht Schnabel
Ottawa and Tokyo, March 2002

1

Introduction – Conflict prevention: A concept in search of a policy

David Carment and Albrecht Schnabel

... despite all the talk and activity in this field since the early 1990's, the basic argument and message of conflict prevention still has not 'stuck' in many critical policy quarters and levels of decision making. The quantity of policy doctrine, designated officials and offices, routinised decision procedures, public hearings, policy papers, political debates, appropriations, non-governmental organizations (NGO) network newsletters, programme regulations, job openings, field manuals, policy institutes, and other institutional infrastructure that is commonplace for other post-Cold War policy concerns such as humanitarianism, terrorism, development, democracy, peacekeeping, and arms control still vastly outweighs the counterpart activity in the sister field of conflict prevention.[1]

Introduction

In response to the recent record of traditional peacekeeping in conflict settlement and resolution, academics and policy makers have begun to re-examine conflict prevention as an ideal instrument for the creation of peace in a war-torn world. The main message of those involved in the study and practice of conflict prevention is as clear as it is obvious: compared to conflict management, it seems less costly in political, economic and human terms to develop institutional mechanisms that prevent tensions from escalating into violent conflict, to employ early warning mechanisms that allow the international community to monitor relations

1

between and within states, and to facilitate capacity building within conflict-prone societies.

While much has been written and said about the not-too-surprising logic and merits of conflict prevention in both its operational and structural forms, little has been said about the *feasibility* of conflict prevention. Moreover, only a few states and international organisations are moving towards working and useful conflict prevention systems. As Michael Lund's words, noted above, remind us, there is no lack of rhetoric on the necessity of conflict prevention, but serious attempts to give organizations the tools, procedures and means to put global and regional preventive systems into place are modest at best. Rhetorical commitment to conflict prevention continues to be high, while commitment to its implementation remains mixed.

Our primary purpose in writing this book is to evaluate the institutional record on conflict prevention and to identify current trends in conflict prevention practice. The focal points of this study are institutionalized conflict prevention structures within regional and global organizations.

Volume outline

Conflict prevention: Theory and evidence

For this volume we have brought together a diverse group of individuals involved in conflict prevention activities – scholars from developed and developing countries, and practitioners with insights on the work of regional organizations and the UN. Each contributor was asked to examine how scholarly discussions on conflict prevention are understood within the context of their own organizational framework and how this understanding can be translated into meaningful policy recommendations. Thus, the organizational structure of the volume reflects the comparative expertise of our contributors.

In chapter 2, Carment and Schnabel engage in a stocktaking exercise in order to identify common conceptual ground and identify common problems in the implementation of conflict prevention. Their chapter addresses some of the key deficiencies in current thinking on conflict prevention. In particular, they argue that too much emphasis is placed on narrowing the meaning and application of conflict prevention. Instead, they argue, conflict prevention should be broad in meaning and malleable as a policy. This approach, they suggest, has empirical validity – conflict prevention is applicable across a wide variety of cases and over different phases of a conflict. But it also has appeal for practitioners who perceive greater utility in conflict prevention as both an operational and structural response. The common underlying theme of all preventive approaches is that they are strategic as opposed to ad hoc responses to an anticipated problem.

In the remainder of this section, three scholars answer the question: What is successful conflict prevention? Their distinctive answers reflect an understanding of conflict prevention that is both analytically rigorous and useful to practitioners. Each provide extremely different – yet equally plausible – and policy relevant interpretations of successful conflict prevention. Conflict prevention can be understood as an important but understated element of statecraft and coercive diplomacy or as the physical presence of a deterrent force.

Chapter 3 of this volume, "The realism of preventive statecraft" by Bruce Jentleson, evaluates conflict prevention from the perspective of statecraft and preventive diplomacy as practised primarily by powerful and influential states. Jentleson argues that, despite belief to the contrary, examples of successful preventive diplomacy are well documented. Preventive diplomacy works best when the threat is real, opportunities for action exist, accurate early warning information is widely available and the potential for regional instability is palpable. The appropriate frame of reference for understanding many of today's conflicts focuses on the rational purposive behaviour of elites. Therefore, mixed strategies, combining both inducements and coercive measures that penalize and reward leaders are likely to work best under crisis conditions. Finally, Jentleson argues that military force and other coercive measures are essential elements within the repertoire of state-based preventive diplomacy. Indeed, more often than not, the diplomatic components of a preventive strategy need to be backed by a credible threat to act coercively through military force, economic sanctions or other coercive strategies.

Chapter 4, "Challenges to preventive action: The cases of Kosovo and Macedonia," by Raimo Väyrynen, evaluates preventive peacekeeping strategies intended to prevent the eruption of violence among groups in conflict. Väyrynen's assessment of preventive deployment in Macedonia (UNPREDEP) concludes that this kind of deterrent mechanism can succeed. Nevertheless, he also cautions against becoming overly optimistic. Optimism is to be tempered for two reasons. First, it remains unclear whether alternative efforts in Macedonia would have proven equally successful, and, second, the success of preventive deployment in Macedonia was reversed as a result of the vertical escalation of war in Kosovo in 1998–99.

Väyrynen argues that measures taken since 1992 to prevent the escalation of violence and humanitarian crisis in Kosovo were never very decisive and coordinated. The failure to push through a political settlement on autonomy and power sharing after the Dayton Accords in 1995 was a missed opportunity for long-term preventive action. Of course, such a settlement would have been difficult to accomplish and it might have cost Milosevic's support in Bosnia, but it would have, on the other hand, stemmed the vertical escalation of violence in Kosovo.

Chapter 5, by Andrea Talentino, titled "Evaluating success and failure: Conflict prevention in Cambodia and Bosnia" presents preventive action as a key ingredient in the life-cycle of a conflict. Like Lund, Talentino believes that a broad conceptual approach is justified by both theory and evidence. All conflicts both develop from the past and help shape the future. As a result, any attempt to measure success must also take account of this temporal continuum. Situating her comparison of four intrastate conflicts at different stages of intensity, Talentino provides convincing evidence that conflict prevention contains rehabilitative and transformative dimensions oriented to the past, a resolutive dimension focusing on the present, and a preventive dimension oriented to the present and future. She concludes by suggesting that failing to stop violence from breaking out today does not mean intermediaries should not stop trying to prevent the same for tomorrow.

The institutional record

In the second section we asked institutional experts to reflect on questions of how existing mechanisms and instruments for conflict prevention can be properly evaluated and improved. Their contributions consist of studies of institutions that are considered to be at the forefront of conflict prevention policy: the European Union, the North Atlantic Treaty Organization, and the Organization for Security and Cooperation in Europe.

In chapter 6, "Regional organizations and conflict prevention: CFSP and ESDI in Europe," Simon Duke argues that in the European context, conflict prevention consists of a number of reasonable but often half-hearted conflict prevention efforts. In particular, conflict prevention has often been associated with the lure of membership of the EU and NATO as well as their associated outreach programmes to Central and Eastern Europe. Duke argues that after Kosovo and Bosnia, there still remains the need to back up diplomacy and economic efforts with the ability to threaten or actually apply military force so that a seamless web of conflict prevention options is open to the EU and NATO member states. The possibility of the EU using NATO assets in "Europe-only" conflict prevention efforts is seen as, at best, a stop gap measure. ESDI remains attractive on paper but it relies too heavily on American willingness to act. Duke recommends that the EU should concentrate on developing an effective and indigenous conflict prevention capability. Until the EU possesses a seamless web of conflict prevention capabilities, it will remain an ineffective actor in the face of those who best understand diplomacy when backed by credible force.

By way of contrast Hans-Georg Ehrhart is more optimistic about the European Union's conflict prevention capabilities. His chapter, "A good idea, but a rocky road ahead: The EU and the Stability Pact for South Eastern Europe," argues that, if conflict prevention has received a new lease of life, this applies especially to the EU, whose record in the Balkans has been spotty at best. While it could not do much to stop escalating an ongoing conflicts, the EU should be in a better position to engage in normal and structural prevention or developmentalist diplomacy to prevent disputes from escalating into armed conflict (Jentleson, this volume). Moreover, in a new security environment, where not only military enemies, but also environmental, economic, political, and cultural threats pose significant danger to the survival of individuals, groups, and states, "new security providers" are needed. Ehrhart recommends that the EU continue with ongoing institutional reforms and procedural innovations. The impact of today's conflicts on the EU, its values, its economy, and its interests is such that there is no alternative but to cope with change on the periphery.

In the eighth chapter, "The OSCE and conflict prevention in the post-Soviet region," Natalie Mychajlyszyn argues that the Organization for Security and Cooperation in Europe (OSCE) is unique among European security institutions for the comprehensive participation of its 54-member states. Prominent among these features are the intrastate human dimension issue as a factor of security, and exclusively non-military approaches to dealing with security threats. Most importantly, the OSCE's uniqueness has been noted to stem from being the primary instrument in the region for early warning, conflict prevention, conflict settlement and post-conflict rehabilitation. Mychajlyszyn argues that the record of the OSCE's efforts to prevent conflict appears strong: goal incompatibility manifested as ethnic and national tensions have not escalated into violence after OSCE interventions. At the same time, its efforts have not been without challenges or complications, and caution should be raised before the OSCE record is enthusiastically presented as one demonstrating success and effectiveness.

Information and response

In the third section, contributors consider how informational and analytical needs can be used to improve both the quality of conflict analysis and its policy relevance. The premise of these arguments is that institutional capacity building must take into account the analysis side as much as the response part of conflict prevention.

In chapter 9, "Early warning and prevention of violent conflict: The role of multifunctional observer missions," David Last contributes a timely piece on peacekeeping and conflict prevention. Last argues that United Nations Military Observer (UNMO) missions and civilian fact-finding missions have been effectively deployed by the United Nations and by regional organizations at various stages in the escalation and de-escalation of conflicts. Last argues that UNMOs can do more than they have in the past if they go beyond diplomatic visits and simple military observation. If they incorporate effective analysis of all the dimensions of a conflict and communication in the broadest sense, then balanced multifunctional observer missions can help to prevent conflict. The limitations and strengths of traditional fact-finding and observation missions suggest that the concept of observer missions needs to be expanded to include political, social, economic, and psychological dimensions of the conflict. By collecting the right type of information and interpreting it accurately, it will be possible to link resulting knowledge of potential violence directly to the international community's ability and will to respond to it.

In chapter 10, "Early warning analysis and policy planning in UN preventive action," John Cockell places early warning and preventive action in the wider context of institutional transformation for the United Nations. He argues that there has been a significant gap between the global agenda on conflict prevention and the institutional capacity of the UN to mobilize rapid responses to conflict. The current reform process established by Secretary-General Kofi Annan has both reflected this wider normative agenda as well as created new opportunities for capacity-building efforts within the UN to respond to this agenda.

Building from this discussion of UN capacity and needs, the chapter outlines an alternative approach to close the gap between warning and response, based on policy planning methods. This planning approach links early warning analysis and the strategic deployment of preventive measures into a single, integrated process. Each element of the process is discussed in brief, with emphasis being placed on early warning analysis and preventive action. Cockell calls for a practical and action-oriented method for early warning analysis and places particular focus on the nature of such early warning as a form of decision support within the UN. He notes that this approach to early warning is an innovative yet practical answer to the warning-response gap in preventive action. Of course, its success will be measured by the extent to which it may act as the basis for shared analysis and planning between those departments and agencies within the UN system that are responsible for responding to the global agenda of intra-state conflict.

In chapter 11, "The International Monetary Fund and conflict prevention," Dane Rowlands and Troy Joseph examine the role of the International Monetary Fund in countries with civil conflict. In addition to laying out a framework for analysing the IMF in the context of conflict, they present a statistical analysis and offer policy and research suggestions. They argue that there appear to be sufficient grounds for recommending that the IMF routinely incorporate an evaluation of the conflict potential of member states in their country review process. In terms of implementation, the IMF needs to align itself with the more traditional conflict-management institutions in order to gain expertise in conflict risk assessment, and in order to contribute to the effort by providing data and analytical capacity. The fact that civil disturbances and tension may well compromise the effectiveness of IMF programmes means that such efforts are entirely consistent with its current mandate. Exposure to these other institutions will provide the Fund with additional information on what policy adjustments might be useful from the perspective of conflict management, and vice versa.

Building capacity at the regional level

In the fourth and concluding section, two practitioners from regional organizations consider how their particular organization contributes to conflict prevention. Their frank assessments of the limitations on existing capacity both increase our understanding of the main impediments facing organizations in the developing world and the specific measures required for their improvement.

In chapter 12, Rasheed Draman writes on the African experience. Draman's chapter provides an analytical overview of current African capabilities. This exercise conclusively shows that the formation of sub-regional conflict prevention mechanisms represents a positive step in capacity building. However, Draman warns of undue optimism, as basic limitations – both financial and political – are likely to inhibit effectiveness over the short run. Financial and other resource constraints, compounded by the rivalries of foreign powers, will continue to degrade the effective functioning of Africa's conflict prevention mechanisms.

In chapter 13, entitled "Conflict prevention in the Americas: The Organization of American States (OAS)," Osvaldo Kreimer shows that conflict prevention in the Americas has been a relatively successful effort in the last decade, basically because of the work of the inter-American system, in conjunction with sub-regional systems (such as Caricom and MERCOSUR) and non-governmental organizations. In an incremental way they have developed and improved their mechanisms and capacities to prevent or at least reduce the intensity of confrontations. Principal amongst the diverse mechanisms are those working within the general framework of the OAS, mainly (a) the system for regional security; (b) the mechanism defined by Resolution 1080 of the General Assembly to defend democracy and constitutional regimes; (c) the good offices of the Secretary-General; (d) the work of the Unit for the Promotion of Democracy in the areas of conflict prevention and electoral observation; and (e) the system for the defence and promotion of human rights, where the principal organs are the Inter-American Commission and the Inter-American Court of Human Rights. In his discussions Kreimer shows that the operations of the different tools of this system (similar to other regional human rights systems) de facto operate as a conflict prevention mechanism and are able to anticipate and channel tensions arising from human rights violations before they escalate into more violent conflicts.

Note

1. Michael Lund, "Introduction and Overview," *The Impact of Conflict Prevention Policy: Cases, Measures, Assessments: Conflict Prevention Network Yearbook*, Baden-Baden: Nomos Verlagsgesellschaft, 1999/2000, p. 14.

Part One

Conflict prevention: Theory and evidence

2

Conflict prevention – Taking stock

David Carment and Albrecht Schnabel

Conceptual issues

Were it as simple as relying on a definition in order to *describe* the process of conflict prevention, our task would be relatively straightforward. Our focus would be on the sources of conflicts and the processes associated with their prevention. However, contributors to our study were faced with a much larger problem – how to render the analyses of effective/ineffective conflict prevention and capacity building meaningful and practicable to practitioners and policy makers alike.

For the purposes of this study, we define conflict prevention as an evolving concept and innovative set of policy recommendations comprising fundamental attitudinal change among its end users. In short, conflict prevention is not a transitory ad hoc reaction to emerging and potential problems.[1] It is *a medium and long-term proactive operational or structural strategy undertaken by a variety of actors, intended to identify and create the enabling conditions for a stable and more predictable international security environment.* The key assumptions in our definition that merit attention are:

- Conflict prevention involves attitudinal change;
- Conflict prevention is malleable as a concept and as a policy;
- Conflict prevention can be multisectoral;
- Conflict prevention can be applied at different phases of conflict;

- Conflict prevention can be implemented by a range of actors acting independently or in concert.[2]

We recognise that our definition and assumptions are somewhat broad.[3] However, they have their basis in the conceptual ground work and theoretical brush-clearing that has been conducted over the years by a number of scholars in Europe and North America. Recent research has focused on the phases of conflict, tools, and techniques for monitoring conflict, political will issues, and response strategies.[4] Much of this work culminated in the 1998 contribution to conflict prevention undertaken by the Carnegie Commission on Preventing Deadly Conflict. According to the Carnegie Commission, conflict prevention as a strategy has the potential to establish a more stable international environment through effective response to emergent, ongoing and escalating conflicts by means of economic, political, and military techniques by states, NGOs, and other international organizations. We are particularly sympathetic to the approach advocated by the Commission that conflict prevention connotes a way of thinking; a state of mind, perhaps even a culture that permeates the activities of all those engaged in the implementation of preventive policy – be they NGOs, states, or regional and global organizations.

More concretely, in order to be productive, prevention needs to be part of a policy maker's overall policy planning process. A key question is: to what extent can prevention be integrated into the policy frameworks of individual states, NGOs and regional and global organizations? In answering this question, the contributors to this volume offer two different but not necessarily contradictory views. On the one hand, there are good reasons to favour a more *short-term* interplay between states and institutions. On the other hand, there is a need to square this approach with a desire for more long-term structural approaches to prevention and the institutionalization of conflict prevention through capacity building and training. There are simply not enough resources available to meet every potentially violent conflict with an operational response in every instance. From a realistic and cost-effective perspective, structural prevention and long-term attitudinal change may be preferable.

This attitudinal shift among practitioners can be traced to Boutros Boutros-Ghali's *An Agenda for Peace* (1992). To be sure, Boutros-Ghali chose to reflect only on preventive diplomacy within a range of conflict management techniques that include peacebuilding, peacemaking, and peacekeeping and essentially on those activities that usually, but not always, fall under the purview of the United Nations, such as confidence building measures, arms control, and preventive deployment.

Ten years after *An Agenda for Peace* was published, preventive diplomacy has now come to refer to a response generated by a state, a coalition of states, or a multilateral organization intended to address the rapid escalation of emergent crises, disputes, and interstate hostilities. Preventive diplomacy entails primarily, but not exclusively, *short and medium-term* consultations using non-compartmentalized and non-hierarchical forms of information gathering, contingency planning, and operational response mechanisms. The risks are proximate and analysis and action are combined at once in rapid succession.[5]

Despite its post-Cold War faddishness, popular usage of this kind of conflict prevention can be traced to the activities of UNSG Dag Hammarskjöld (although its underlying logic has existed at least since the emergence of the modern state system; the Westphalian Treaty at its birth was an attempt to prevent the continuation of interstate warfare of the early seventeenth century; and indeed, its rationale is deeply imbedded in such fundamentals of statecraft as deterrence, reassurance, and compellence).[6] Hammarskjöld realized that early engagement of the global organization could act to forestall the destructiveness of conflict created by external military intervention and arms transfers. According to Väyrynen, "preventive action stemmed from the more general reasoning that external interventions can be avoided or tempered if a region is made more autonomous in terms of security" (this volume). The underlying rationale was expressed in Hammarskjöld's introduction to the 1959–60 annual report of the United Nations: preventive action "must in the first place aim at filling the vacuum so that it will not provoke action from any of the major parties."[7] When crisis threatens, traditional diplomacy continues, but more urgent preventive efforts are required – through unilateral and multilateral channels – to arbitrate, mediate, or lend "good offices" to encourage dialogue.

Today, preventive diplomacy is considered important, due in part to the evolving nature of conflict. The shift from inter-state to intra-state conflict is well documented. However, this change in itself is not sufficient to generate a call for revised thinking on preventive action. It is the surrounding circumstances, the ability of such complex conflicts to spread vertically and horizontally – in essence the potential of such conflicts to do harm to others, ordinary citizens, neighbouring states, refugees, and minorities – that generate preventive diplomacy efforts.[8]

Moreover, official diplomacy can be greatly strengthened by private sector activity. Long used in international negotiations by leaders to take informal soundings of adversaries' intentions, so-called track-two diplomacy is increasingly the strategy of choice for dealing with problems beyond the reach of official efforts. Some governments have found NGOs very useful in brokering political agreements and supplementing governmental roles. In recent years, many groups in the United States and Europe, such as the Institute for Multi-Track Diplomacy, International Alert, the Carter Center's International Negotiation Network, the International Crisis Group, the Forum on Early Warning and Early Response, the Project on Ethnic Relations and the Conflict Management Group, have developed models for multi-track diplomacy and conflict resolution. These organizations have played active roles in building relationships between conflicting parties and interested governments, offering training in diplomacy and conflict resolution, and providing good offices to parties that are committed to the peaceful resolution of conflict.

Kalypso Nicolaides provides a useful conceptual framework for determining how preventive diplomacy relates to conflict prevention.[9] Preventive diplomacy is principally an operational response. It is premised on incentive structures provided by outside actors to change specific kinds of undesirable behaviour. Preventive diplomacy is therefore, targeted and short-term and the preventive action taken relates directly to changes in conflict escalation and conflict dynamics (see Jentleson, this volume).[10] In this regard outside actors can seek to influence the course of events and try to alter or induce specific behaviour through coercive and operational threats and deterrents (see Väyrynen, this volume) or through less coercive strategies of persuasion and inducement (see Jentleson, this volume).[11]

Ultimately though, while outside actors can work to influence the incentives of the relevant parties engaged in conflict, they cannot change the initial conditions that led to conflict in the first place. That process has to take place within. Thus, structural approaches emphasize capacity building to provide conflict-prone societies with the means to address root causes of conflict. In this sense, structural conflict prevention strategies, such as those focusing on human security, conflict transformation and development cast a much broader net. They tend to be long term and are generally applied across a range of countries, issues, and actors.[12] The goal is to transform conflictual behaviour over time. This change in behaviour can be dependent on institutional inducements – such as conditionality for membership in international institutions, arms control agreements and stability pacts or on the promotion of sustainable development, support for human security, and regional confidence building mechanisms.[13]

An analogy of clinical and environmental approaches to health care highlights the difference between operational and structural approaches. Clinical and environmental health care may both be preventively oriented. However, the former focuses on the treatment of sick individuals whereas the latter emphasizes a public health model that aims to prevent illness by focusing on its associated environmental factors.[14] Of course, operational and structural approaches are not mutually exclusive activities. Shifting attitudinal change necessarily entails, in our opinion, a concerted movement toward, and investment in, both strategic operational responses and long-term approaches.[15] This view is shared, for instance, by the Swedish Ministry of Foreign Affairs, whose report on *Preventing Violent Conflict* proposes early conflict prevention strategies as the corner stone of Sweden's developmental assistance programmes.[16] Among its recommendations are: the call for a strengthening of a secretariat or "task force" within the Swedish Foreign Ministry whose activities would be to establish methods for preventive measures through development cooperation, the development of security mechanisms within troubled regions, and the establishment of regional early warning networks.

Analytical needs

A key concern in ensuring effective conflict prevention is how to ensure that the practitioner is equipped with the best available analytical skills to ensure valid and reliable evaluations of potential problems. To be sure, the increasing role of academics, private organizations, and non-governmental organizations in providing risk assessments, analyses and early warning information points to a fundamental change in the way in which potential threats to security are assessed and acted upon. Nevertheless, understanding the root causes of conflict, identifying the point at which a conflict is likely to become violent and deciding what to do about them is more akin to "solving mysteries" (e.g. group problem-solving) than it is to "breaking secrets" (e.g. spying).

The impetus for current UN-based approaches to risk assessment and early warning came from UN Secretary-General Javier Perez de Cuellar's first Annual Report to the General Assembly in 1982. In the report, he called for "more systematic," less last-minute use of the Security Council, and urged that "if the Council were to keep an active watch on dangerous situations and, if necessary, initiate discussions with the parties before they reach the point of crisis, it might otherwise be possible to defuse them at an early stage before they degenerate into violence."[17] Since the call for preventive diplomacy by former UN Secretary-General Boutros-Ghali in 1992, the UN inter-agency arrangement for humanitarian early warning (HEWS) was created to assist humanitarian operations. However, it has not succeeded. It was never properly equipped to detect or analyse political and military warning signals and the UN lost whatever capacity it had to analyse political early warning information when it disbanded the Office for Research and Collection of Information (ORCI).

A more fundamental deficiency is that the early warning currently required to respond to human-generated disasters is often late warning; a response to crises that are already at an advanced stage of escalation and violence, that are well known and where causes are proximate. The inherent risk for decision makers in this approach is that, at the height of a crisis, policy options are rapidly and significantly constrained and significantly narrowed to operational responses (usually military and humanitarian) such as those detailed in our volume. Late response, with the attendant likelihood that a strategy will be less than successful, is the strongest impediment to developing more coherent forward-looking approaches. Critics are quick to claim that early warning rarely succeeds, but the evidence they cite to support this argument are situations where action is taken to treat the symptoms rather than the underlying causes.[18]

It is a truism to say that effective conflict prevention entails a substantial understanding of conflict dynamics, their structural consequences, the processes by which they become violent, and what well-meaning leaders, NGOs, and governments can do about them. Unfortunately, while the bulk of research is useful for understanding why, when and how some conflicts originate, it is less useful in explaining or predicting when or how violent interactions will occur in a way that is directly consumable by policy makers. One response to this problem has been to ensure that policy makers are better equipped to do their own in-field analyses (as suggested by Cockell in this volume).[19]

As a result, many organizations, such as the European Union, have developed an in-house capacity for conducting their own risk assessments and are developing independent procedures for conducting early warning, monitoring, and response. One of the obvious dangers in creating independent analytical tools of this sort is that these "lenses" can and do point to fundamentally different causes of conflict. For example, some may rely on the monitoring of background factors and enabling conditions that are associated with the risk of conflict while others only provide information on the probability of specific events leading to conflict.[20] Ideally, both approaches should be pursued simultaneously. However, it is obvious that analytical capacity alone will never be sufficient for generating effective response.[21] There is also a need for field monitoring of indicators of specific types of behaviour, monitoring of indicators of related factors and proximate causes or systematic analysis of events through predictive models.[22] Collectively, their objective is to combine monitoring of indicators with diagnosis, using theoretical findings and index construction to develop knowledge of certain causes that produce specific effects.[23] The effect can be either a danger, such as a crisis, war or genocide, or an opportunity, such as economic investment or the victory of a democratic government. Risk assessments precede and complement early warning. Therefore, accurate diagnosis has implications for strategic planning. Assessments identify background and intervening conditions that establish the risk for potential crisis and conflict. They focus monitoring and analytical attention on high-risk situations before they are fully developed and they provide a framework for interpreting the results of real-time monitoring.[24]

Once information is weighed for its relative importance, there still remains a significant gap between analysing the information and developing a strategy to deal with the problem. Analysis by itself does not generate an immediate solution. At best, monitoring of indicators helps in regulating the flow of information to policy makers.[25] Thus, early warning systems are not confined just to analysing a conflict, but also relate to and, indeed, see their raison d'être in the capacities and response strategies for dealing with a conflict.

Several problems arise in translating analysis into action. First, there is a need to know what to look for, and what, specifically, should be warned about. Ethnic warfare, regime failure, massive human rights violations and refugee flows are the results of different combinations of factors, hence require somewhat different models, explanations, strategies, and responses. Second, there is a need for specificity in the combinations of risk factors and sequences of events that are likely to lead to crises. Lists of variables or indicators are only a starting point. Explanations should identify which measurable conditions, in what combination or sequence, establish a potential for certain types and kinds of crises.

The question of how to actually bring early warning into the process of policy planning also needs to be considered (Cockell, this volume; Rowlands and Joseph, this volume). There are two complementary approaches. The first is primarily an array of decentralized early warning networks for the analysis of impending humanitarian crises and complex emergencies. This option would see states and NGOs rely to some extent on global networks for their information analysis.

A second option is to pursue the integration of risk assessments into the strategic planning processes of states, NGOs and regional organizations – beginning with developmental aid – in order to develop coherent, sustainable, and long-term policies on conflict prevention (see Cockell, this volume; Duke, this volume). This is a five-step process: first, because risk assessment data and information must satisfy the needs of different agencies, there is a need to integrate them more closely into routinized foreign policy activities of the various departments engaged in foreign and security policy. Second, integration means that assessments are used to identify not only future risks but also to identify links between conflict processes and identifiable focal points of activity in which the end user is engaged. Assessments should be able to identify a sequence of events that are logically consistent with operational responses. Third, end users should be able to use the information in a way that helps them plan for contingencies. In essence, the goal is to establish a risk assessment chain that is multi-departmental, multi-purpose and multi-directional.

Fourth, measurements of effectiveness need to be harmonized across states. As structured databases will continue to be an important tool despite their imperfections, the current situation of decentralized data holding will only be able to function if the information handling systems – including indicators – in the different countries are harmonized. Fifth and finally, an essential step would be to establish conflict prevention secretariats and councils within states and organizations.

Political will

According to Jentleson (this volume) one of the main reasons why leaders have been so reluctant to take on comprehensive conflict prevention is that they have held to the conventional wisdom that the costs to be borne and risks to be run are too high, and the interests at stake are too low. In recent years states have not always fared well in mustering the necessary response to an emerging problem. This is because the essence of statecraft is to develop and manage relationships with other states in ways that will protect and enhance one's own security and welfare.

In a perfect world there would be a clear undivided link between information and action. In an ideal world there would be a healthy synergy between particularist and universalist interests that would in fact consider global humanitarian interests, for instance, as an inherent part of one's own national interest. And in an ideal world the average citizen in country A would be aware of his/her responsibility to participate in meeting the human needs of his/her counterpart in country Z. But constructing and "selling" effective policy is always more complicated. For example, Jentleson shows that political will is not an insurmountable problem: political constraints do have a degree of malleability. Jentleson's claim is especially pertinent to institutionalized approaches to conflict prevention. Institutions are most likely to be the lead actors in specific activities that advance human security, alleviate poverty, increase respect for human rights, foster good and stable governance and contribute in one way or another to long-term stability and the prevention of disintegration and violence.

Regional organizations also offer several advantages in pursuit of effective conflict prevention. Most notable is their familiarity with the history of the locale and parties to an impending dispute (see Ehrhart, this volume). These organizations often have the most at stake and therefore they are generally more willing to get involved. By their proximity to a conflict, regional organizations almost inevitably are involved because their members must deal with refugee-related problems and other consequences. Finally, states that hesitate to refer a local dispute to the United Nations – for fear that it will no longer be under their control – may be more willing to see the matter addressed at a regional level.

Unfortunately, regional organizations are extremely hesitant in engaging in costly prevention strategies at the outset, as they lack either the necessary resources or consensus to fulfil their commitments. The inherent problem is that not only do quick terminations of escalating violence require the military backing and political support of major powers, they also require long-term post-conflict commitments. It is no longer sufficient to stop the violence – refugees must be protected and returned, political control must be reinstated, and economic development pursued. If preventive actions at the early stages of a conflict demand close coordination of military, diplomatic, and non-governmental assets, then the post-conflict phase requires an even more complex coordinated operation plan; one that engages global organizations and cuts across civilian and military control. In sum, considerable resources are required to foster development, inter-communal interdependence and attitude change over a long time – perhaps generations.[26]

Capacity building

It is important that institutions obtain a better understanding of both long-term structural and operational strategies. More importantly, individuals within these institutions must understand how they can best use the array of political instruments available to them to create more effective responses. Such an approach requires that organizations have a better sense of their own institutional needs and capabilities – far more than they do now.

Capacity building is central to the strengthening of conflict prevention in four ways. First, there is an important long-term *investment* in conflict prevention through the publication of policy reports/handbooks on methods in risk assessment, conflict analysis, and conflict prevention policy. Second, field workers and desk officers engaged in the analysis of conflict-prone societies need specific analytical skills and risk assessment techniques. Most successful monitoring and preventive efforts have been training programmes that introduce people who live in conflict areas to the theory and practice of conflict management, and that provide training in negotiation, facilitation, mediation, and consensus building. An important objective of such efforts is to improve future preventive efforts by analysing the consequences of different policies that improve conflict prevention effectiveness (peace and conflict impact assessment).

Third, conflict prevention practitioners are ultimately responsible for their own evaluation and impact assessment of their prevention methods.

Such evaluation includes the systematic documentation of conflict interventions and post-conflict assessments; improved information exchange
among conflict prevention practitioners and with parties outside the conflict management field; assessment and evaluation of conflict prevention
interventions; and improved coordination of conflict prevention activities.
Fourth, there is the need to create a network of local conflict prevention
specialists who will be able to run conflict prevention training seminars
at their organizations and institutions.

It is also important that the link between early warning and preventive measures be a direct function of the proximity of the analyst to
senior decision makers. As Tapio Kanninen has argued, "[e]arly warning is linked to possible immediate action by an actor who is close to
one giving the early warning, e.g. belonging to the same organization."
This, he asserts, calls for early warning to be "practice-oriented, dynamic,
and geared to the possibilities of the actor to intervene purposefully."[27]
Such close interaction between different parts of an organization can only
result from successful mainstreaming efforts of conflict prevention strategies within the organization.

Conclusion

To recapitulate, conflict prevention is an evolving concept and innovative set of policy recommendations comprising fundamental attitudinal
change among its end users. In short, conflict prevention is not a transitory ad hoc reaction to emerging and potential problems. It is a medium
and long-term proactive strategy intended to identify and create the
enabling conditions for a stable and more predictable international security environment. The former point highlights the main weakness of past
thinking among practitioners that prevention was regarded primarily as
a "technical" issue that encompasses early warning, arms control, preventive deployment of peacekeepers, fact-finding, and related matters.
Structural factors create several problems that contribute to conflict, such
as reconciling multicultural reality with the principle of national self-
determination; the pursuit of a stable, democratic society in a tumultuous
regional system; uneven economic development; and coping with fundamental changes brought about by the outbreak of violent conflict.
Greater understanding of these deeper problems will be needed if effective structural prevention becomes a possibility. Only then can a comprehensive and balanced approach to alleviate the pressures that trigger
violent conflict through elemental aid, developmental assistance, and the
work of NGOs be developed. Over the long run, structural prevention
strategies include the creation and strengthening of international legal

systems, dispute resolution mechanisms, and cooperative arrangements at the regional level, as well as meeting people's basic economic, social, cultural, and humanitarian needs.

Notes

1. According to Michael Lund, "conflict prevention entails any structural or interactive means to keep intrastate and interstate tensions and disputes from escalating into significant violence and to strengthen the capabilities to resolve such disputes peacefully as well as alleviating the underlying problems that produce them, including forestalling the spread of hostilities into new places. It comes into play both in places where conflicts have not occurred recently and where recent largely terminated conflicts could recur. Depending on how they are applied, it can include the particular methods and means of any policy sector, whether labelled prevention or not (e.g. sanctions, conditional aid, mediation, structural adjustment, democratic institution building etc.), and they might be carried out by global, regional, national or local levels by any governmental or non-governmental actor." Michael Lund, "Improving Conflict Prevention by Learning from Experience: Context, Issues, Approaches and Findings," paper presented at the Conflict Prevention Network Annual Conference, Berlin, 31 October 1999.
2. For a precise and exhaustive list of conflict prevention terms, see Alex Schmid, *Thesaurus and Glossary of Early Warning and Conflict Prevention Terms*, London: Synthesis Books and FEWER Publications, 1998. In applying these assumptions to the objectives of this book it is obvious that a broad conceptual base has several advantages. For example, in some instances the term conflict prevention is qualified by the antecedents "violent" or "deadly," suggesting that some conflicts may be constructive and are not in need of immediate attention or are at least less threatening. Others have taken conflict prevention to mean the task of addressing latent, underlying, or non-violent behaviour, which, under certain conditions, has the potential to become deadly. Still others equate preventive diplomacy with conflict prevention (see Jentleson, this volume), which carries with it connotations of crisis management, statecraft, and the use of force in order to prevent the escalation of organized and wide-scale violence.
3. Recent findings and research focus, for example, on the phases of conflict, tools and techniques for monitoring conflict, political will issues, and response strategies. For analyses of analytical and informational prerequisites for success, see for example, S. Schmeidl and H. Adelman, eds., *Early Warning and Early Response*, Columbia International Affairs Online, Columbia University Press, 1998; John Davies and Ted Gurr, eds., *Preventive Measures: Building Risk Assessment and Crisis Early Warning Systems*, Lanham, MD: Rowman & Littlefield, 1998. For evaluations of operational response strategies, see Bruce Jentleson, ed., *Opportunities Missed, Opportunities Seized: Preventive Diplomacy in the Post-Cold War World*, Lanham, MD: Rowman & Littlefield, 1999; and Janie Leatherman, William Demars, Patrick Gaffney, and Raimo Väyrynen, *Breaking Cycles of Violence: Conflict Prevention in Intrastate Crises*, Bloomfield, CT: Kumarian Press, 1999. On tools and instruments for implementing structural conflict prevention, see Michael Lund's book, *Preventing Violent Conflict*, Washington, D.C.: USIP Press, 1996; Robert Rotberg, ed., *Vigilance and Vengeance: NGOs Preventing Ethnic Conflict in Divided Societies*, Washington, D.C.: Brookings Institution, 1996. Institutional policy and capacity building is evaluated by Abram Chayes and Antonia Handler Chayes, eds., *Preventing Conflict in the Post-Communist World: Mobilizing International and Regional Organizations*, Washington, D.C.: Brookings Institution,

1996; and Nat Colletta and Michael Cullen, *Violent Conflict and the Transformation of Social Capital: Lessons from Cambodia, Rwanda, Guatemala, and Somalia*, Washington, D.C.: World Bank 2000. Impact assessment and lessons learned are considered in Astri Suhrke and Howard Adelman's *The International Response to Conflict and Genocide; Lessons from the Rwanda experience*, http://www.um.dk/danida/evalueringsrapporter/ 1997_rwanda/ and the Conflict Prevention Network's 1999/2000 Yearbook, *The Impact of Conflict Prevention Policy*, Baden-Baden: Nomos Verlagsgesellschaft, 1999/2000.

4. Analytical and informational prerequisites for success (see for example *Early Warning and Early Response*, edited by Adelman and Schmeidl; and *Preventive Measures: Building Risk Assessment and Crisis Early Warning Systems*, edited by John Davies and Ted Gurr (1998). For operational response strategies, see *Opportunities Missed, Opportunities Seized: Preventive Diplomacy in the Post-Cold War World*, edited by Jentleson; and *Breaking Cycles of Violence: Conflict Prevention in Intrastate Crises*, edited by Leatherman et al. For tools and instruments for implementing structural conflict prevention, see Michael Lund's book *Preventing Violent Conflict*; and *Vigilance and Vengeance: NGOs Preventing Ethnic Conflict in Divided Societies*, edited by Rotberg. For institutional policy and capacity building, see Chayes and Chayes, eds., *Preventing Conflict in the Post-Communist World: Mobilizing International and Regional Organizations*; and *Violent Conflict and the Transformation of Social Capital: Lessons from Cambodia, Rwanda, Guatemala, and Somalia* by Colletta and Cullen. Impact assessment and lessons learned: Suhrke and Adelman's *Joint Evaluation of Emergency Assistance to Rwanda*, Copenhagen: Danida, 1996 and the Conflict Prevention Network's 1999/2000 Yearbook, *The Impact of Conflict Prevention Policy* (2000).

5. The form of such interventions is best seen as a continuum. Different third party techniques are set in motion at different points within a conflict (Lund, *Preventing Violent Conflict*). At one end of the intervention spectrum is pure mediation – the facilitation of a negotiated settlement through persuasion, control of information and identification of alternatives by a party who is perceived to be impartial. Further along the spectrum of preventive strategies is "mediation with muscle," or the deliberate and strategic use of rewards and punishments to bring the belligerents to the negotiating table. Finally, where consent is absent, third parties are likely to be required to take on a multiplicity of functions, including peacekeeping, humanitarian assistance, and possibly peace enforcement. See David Carment and Frank Harvey, *Using Force to Prevent Ethnic Violence*, Westport, CT: Praeger Press, 2000. At this end of the spectrum, preventive efforts involve the exercise of force to either deter or, possibly, subdue intransigent combatants. Thus the forms of prevention range from traditional preventive diplomacy to its more forceful descendants. The specific tactics and strategies associated with these third-party efforts are examined elsewhere, for example in I. William Zartman, *Ripe for Resolution: Conflict and Intervention in Africa*, 2nd ed., New York: Oxford University Press, 1989; William J. Durch, *The Evolution of UN Peacekeeping: Case Studies and Comparative Analysis*, New York: St. Martin's Press, 1993; John G. Ruggie, "The New US Peacekeeping Doctrine," *Washington Quarterly*, Vol. 17, No. 4, pp. 175–84, 1994; David Carment and Patrick James, eds., *Peace in the Midst of Wars: Preventing and Managing International Ethnic Conflicts*, Columbus, SC: University of South Carolina Press, 1998. Recent international developments have led to fundamental changes in the nature of conflict prevention (Jentleson, this volume). Before the end of the Cold War, preventive efforts were generally performed to monitor cease-fire arrangements between two warring states. The superpowers of the Cold War period could either block formal United Nations missions or deter most unilateral efforts on the part of their rival. David Carment and Dane Rowlands, "Three's Company: Evaluating Third Party Intervention into Intrastate Conflict," *Journal of Conflict Resolution*, Vol. 42, No. 6, October,

1998, pp. 572–99. With the reduced importance of traditional ideologically based rivalry, the ability for individual states or state coalitions to intervene in the conflicts of others has increased dramatically. Furthermore, with the loosening of ideological bonds and the erosion of strong state centres backed by foreign governments, the likelihood of intrastate conflict has risen, especially conflict over territory and identity.

6. For other definitions of conflict prevention, see Carment and Harvey, *Using Force To Prevent Ethnic Violence* and David Carment and Karen Garner, "Conflict Prevention and Early Warning: Problems, Pitfalls and Avenues for Success," *Canadian Foreign Policy Journal*, Winter, 1999, pp. 103–17. For distinctions between operational and structural prevention see Jentleson, ed., *Opportunities Missed, Opportunities Seized: Preventive Diplomacy in the Post-Cold War World*; *The Carnegie Commission on Preventing Deadly Conflict: Final Report*; Lund, *Preventing Violent Conflict*; Jacob Bercovitch, "Understanding Mediation's Role in Preventive Diplomacy," *Negotiation Journal*, Vol. 12, No. 3, 1996; Stephen J. Stedman, "Alchemy for a New World Disorder: Overselling Preventive Diplomacy," *Foreign Affairs*, May/June, 1995; Diana Chigas, "Preventive Diplomacy and the Organization for Security and Cooperation in Europe: Creating Incentives for Dialogue and Cooperation," in Chayes and Handler Chayes, eds., *Preventing Conflict in the Post-Communist World*.

7. Hammarskjöld's approach covers, however, only one type of conflict action, i.e. the horizontal, cross-border escalation of violence. In addition, escalation can also be vertical when the destructiveness of violence increases within a given political unit without spilling over boundaries to other units. A critical difference between these two processes of escalation lies in their relationship with the principle of sovereignty. In the former case, national sovereignty is violated and thus the offence-defence cycle is set in motion.

8. According to the Carnegie Commission's *Report*, in declining situations a number of steps may help manage the crisis and prevent the emergence of violence. First, states should resist the traditional urge to suspend diplomatic relations as a substitute for action and instead maintain open, high fidelity lines of communication with leaders and groups in crisis. Second, governments and international organizations must express in a clear and compelling way the interests being affected. Third, the crisis should immediately be put on the agenda of the UN Security Council or of the relevant international organization, or both, early enough to permit preventive action. At the same time, a means should be established to track developments in the crisis, to provide regular updates, and to include a mechanism to incorporate information from NGOs and other non-governmental actors to support high-level deliberations on unfolding events. Fourth, and notwithstanding the foregoing imperative to broaden the multilateral context of an unfolding crisis, governments should be attentive to opportunities to support quiet diplomacy and dialogue with and between moderate leaders in the crisis. Special envoys and representatives of key states or regional organizations or on behalf of the UN have time and again demonstrated their value, particularly in the early stages of a crisis. Diplomatic and political strategies to avert a looming crisis demand creative ways of defusing tensions and facilitating mutual accommodation among potential belligerents.

9. Kalypso Nicolaides, "International Preventive Action: Developing a Strategic Framework," in *Vigilance and Vengeance: NGOs Preventing Ethnic Conflict in Divided Societies*, Washington, D.C.: Brookings Press, 1996, pp. 23–72.

10. For similar approaches linking prevention to response using an overarching framework see David Lake and Donald Rothchild, eds., *The International Spread of Ethnic Conflict: Fear Diffusion and Escalation*, Princeton: Princeton University Press, 1998; David Carment and Patrick James, eds., *Peace in the Midst of Wars: Preventing and Managing International Ethnic Conflicts*, Columbus, SC: University of South Carolina

Press, 1998; A. J. Tellis, Thomas S. Szayan and James A. Winnefeld, *Anticipating Ethnic Conflict*, Rand Corporation, 1998; Gerald Schneider and Patricia A. Weitsman, eds., *Enforcing Cooperation: Risky States and Intergovernmental Management of Conflict*, London: Macmillan, 1997.

11. In this respect the behaviour and actions of the outside actors is contingent on a specific and usually pre-specified desired behaviour of the internal parties, or they can do so through support for a more "hands on" approach which seeks transformation or changes in the initial conditions which precipitated the conflict. Nicolaides, "International Preventive Action: Developing a Strategic Framework," pp. 23–72.

12. Capacity building is the process by which outside actors provide the means to address root causes through blueprints and resources – for local stakeholders through such activities often associated with development, support for human rights and democratization, but not exclusively.

13. Nicolaides, "International Preventive Action: Developing a Strategic Framework."

14. Stephen Ryan, "Preventive Diplomacy, Conflict Prevention and Ethnic Conflict," in Carment and James, *Peace in the Midst of Wars*, pp. 63–92.

15. Margaretha Af Ugglas, a former Chairman in Office of the OSCE and former Swedish Foreign Minister contends that success in conflict prevention is related to the following five key factors: the degree of political support from the parties concerned; the prudent selection of political and diplomatic instruments to be applied; a careful balance between public and quiet diplomacy; the adoption of a long-term approach; the extent of cooperation with other international organizations.

16. Swedish Ministry of Foreign Affairs, *Preventing Violent Conflict: A Study*, Stockholm: Norstedts Tryckeri AB, 1997. Key recommendations include: strengthening civil society, strengthening of regional security arrangements, efforts to address religious and cultural conflicts and strengthening of early warning mechanisms such as FEWER.

17. See UN Secretary-General Javier Perez de Cuellar's first Annual Report to the General Assembly, 1982. http://www.un.org.

18. See for example Stedman, "Alchemy for a New World Disorder: Overselling Preventive Diplomacy."

19. Here the distinction between risk assessment and early warning is important. The policy relevance of early warning stems directly from the fact early warning systems are not restricted to analysing a crisis, but also assess the capacities, needs, and responses for dealing with a crisis. Second, early warning is essentially networks – states, intergovernmental organizations and NGOs – conducting their analyses together in order to prevent likely events from occurring. According to the Forum on Early Warning and Early Response (FEWER) early warning is "the communication of information on a crisis area, analysis of that information and development of potential strategic responses to respond to the crisis in a timely manner. The central purpose of early warning is not only to identify potential problems but also to create the necessary political will for preventive action to be taken", www.fewer.org.

20. Schmeidl and Adelman, eds., *Early Warning and Early Response*, https://wwwc.cc.columbia.edu/sec/dlc/ciao/bookfrm.html. See also FEWER reports (various) available at www.fewer.org.

21. Indeed, to convince themselves that action is necessary, strategists must have knowledge about the costs of not being involved coupled with the likelihood that a conflict will escalate. Early warning is necessary only if decision makers can be persuaded that accurate information is useful for finding an appropriate fit between strategy, the problem at hand and the resources available (Jentleson, this volume). Such an approach has two implications. First, it means that the analysis of events and intelligence gathering do not fit neatly into compartmentalized and modular frameworks of responsibilities

(if they ever did). Second, it means that in order to cope with events as they unfold "just in time," strategies of information gathering and analysis become crucial. Long-term planning tends to take a back seat to more medium and short-term contingency planning.

22. Ted Robert Gurr, "Early Warning Systems: From Surveillance to Assessment to Action" in Kevin, M. Cahill, ed., *Preventive Diplomacy: The Therapeutics of Mediation*, Proceedings of a conference at the United Nations, New York, April, 1996, pp. 23–4.
23. Gurr, "Early Warning Systems."
24. Will Moore and Ted R. Gurr, "Assessing Risks of Ethnopolitical Rebellion in the Year 2000: Three Empirical Approaches," in Schmeidl and Adelman, eds., *Early Warning and Early Response*.
25. Gurr, "Early Warning Systems."
26. For a powerful and authoritative statement on these and related issues, see International Commission on Intervention and State Sovereignty (ICISS), *The Reponsibility to Protect: Report of the International Commission on Intervention and State Sovereignty*, Ottawa: International Development Research Centre, 2001. See also the so-called "Brahimi Report:" *Report of the Panel on United Nations Peace Operations*, A/55/305-S/2000/809, New York: General Assembly/Security Council, 21 August 2000.
27. Tapio Kanninen, "The Future of Early Warning and Preventive Action in the United Nations," Occasional Paper No. 5, Ralph Bunche Institute on the United Nations, New York: CUNY, May 1991, p. 2.

3

The realism of preventive statecraft

Bruce W. Jentleson

Introduction

An often heard criticism of conflict prevention is that it is unrealistic.[1] Self-styled "realists" do not dispute the desirability of preventing ethnic cleansing, genocide, and other deadly conflicts, but they question both the viability and the value of priority efforts to do so. Are not many of these conflicts just the playing out of history – of "Balkan ghosts" that still haunt the region, of pre-colonial African tribal hatreds, of other decades and historical animosities? Is it in the interests of major powers such as the United States to get involved in these complex conflicts at an early stage? Why not just wait and see, and if needed resort to conflict management at a later stage?

For all its self-styled realism, this line of reasoning is flawed. It is wrong about both the viability and the value of conflict prevention. It underestimates the interests at stake and overestimates the costs and risks, especially compared to the costs and risks incurred by waiting or not acting. There is a realism, not just idealism, to preventive statecraft.[2]

This chapter is organized in four sections. First, I present the empirical and analytic bases supporting the claim that preventive statecraft is possible. I then turn to an explanation of the strategic logic of preventive statecraft. This is followed by an evaluation of the problems related to "political will." The final section concludes with some specific policy recommendations.

The viability of preventive statecraft

The claim that preventive statecraft is not just a noble idea but a viable, real world strategy has four principal bases. They are: the purposiveness of conflict interactions, the availability of early warning, opportunities for meaningful response strategies and, the unavoidability of international action. Each is considered in turn.

Purposive, not primordialist, sources of conflict

The question of the viability of preventive statecraft in its essence is a debate over historical determinism. The assumption of an overwhelming inevitability to current conflicts that is inherent to their characterization is indicative of what is called the "primordialist view," in which ethnic conflicts are seen primarily as manifestations of fixed, inherited, deeply antagonistic historical identities.[3] In this analysis the end of the Cold War stripped away the constraining effects of the strategic overlay of bipolar geopolitics, releasing the "Balkan ghosts" and other historical hatreds to their "natural" states of conflict.[4]

If the primordialist theory were valid, then it truly would be hard to hold out much prospect for preventive statecraft. Yet as a number of studies have shown, ethnic identities are much less fixed over time, and the frequency and intensity of ethnic conflict is much more varying over time than primordialist theory would have it. The point is made, albeit with some hyperbole, in a statement by a Bosnian Muslim schoolteacher that "we never, until the war, thought of ourselves as Muslims. We were Yugoslavs. But when we began to be murdered because we are Muslims things changed. The definition of who we are today has been determined by our killing."[5]

Michael Brown delineates other variables such as political institutions and socio-economic factors as possible "underlying" sources of ethnic as well as other internal conflicts.[6] However, while these underlying factors are helpful in identifying dispositions towards political instability, they almost always end up both over-determined and under-determined in explaining the fundamental reasons why violence actually occurs in any particular case.[7]

The optimal analytic approach both for avoiding the historical determinism fallacy and for getting beyond underlying factors to proximate, violence-triggering factors is through a "purposive" view of what the key sources of deadly conflict are. This approach acknowledges the deep-seated nature of ethnic identifications and the corresponding inter-group tensions, animosities, and unfinished agendas of vengeance and retribution that carry forward as historical legacies. But it takes a much less deterministic view of how, why, and if these identity-rooted tensions become deadly conflicts. The dominant dynamic is not the playing out of historical inevitability, but rather the consequences of calculations by parties to the conflict of the purposes served by political violence. It is in seeking to influence this calculus that preventive statecraft has its potential viability.

Early warning availability but the warning-response gap

Even more than the traditional problem of the "signal-to-noise" ratio of such classical intelligence problems as an impending surprise attack or major advances in an adversary's military capabilities, the question of what constitutes early warning of ethnic and other post-Cold War conflicts is more difficult to ascertain in a number of respects. The "challenge for early warning systems," as put in another study, "is not so much in identifying societies at risk, in general, but in recognising patterns of change that will lead to the acceleration of conflicts."[8] Nevertheless, the evidence in all the cases presented in *Opportunities Missed, Opportunities Seized: Preventive Diplomacy in the Post-Cold War World* showed that timely and reliable intelligence and other information was available to policy makers. This is not to go so far as to claim that any of these warnings were strictly unequivocal or self-evident. The "signal-to-noise" problem raised by Alexander George and Jane Holl was evident in a number of cases.[9] Still, the cases clearly show that early warning was less the problem than was the response to those warnings.

It is in this sense that early warning is not just an informational problem but also an analytic one. Both the "under-warning" problem of missing developing conflicts, and the "over-warning" problem of ending up "predicting" eight of the next three coming deadly conflicts have to be avoided. But this too is a problem that, while difficult, can be viably addressed.

The opportunities were there

In all of the cases in the *Opportunities Missed, Opportunities Seized* volume there were specific and identifiable opportunities for the international community to limit, if not prevent, the conflicts. For example, in the Somalia case Ken Menkhaus and Louis Ortmayer acknowledge that no amount of preventive diplomacy could have completely pre-empted some level of conflict, but trace a virtual litany of missed opportunities, presenting solid evidence that timely diplomatic interventions at several key junctures might have significantly reduced, defused, and contained that violence. In the Rwanda case Astri Suhrke and Bruce Jones are also able to substantiate a series of missed opportunities, including that a more determined international response against the extremists would have found allies in the military. As to Croatia and Bosnia-Herzegovina, Susan Woodward is clear and unequivocal. There are few, if any, deadly conflicts in recent history that have provided more opportunity for prevention than the wars that engulfed the Balkan peninsula with the disintegration of Yugoslavia in 1991.[10] In these and other cases the assessment of missed opportunities is made conscious of and consistent with the caveats concerning counterfactual analysis.[11]

The counterfactual works back in the other direction as well, to show why the avoidance of major conflict in cases like Macedonia, Ukraine, the Baltics, North Korea and at least initially in the Congo-Brazzaville was not a given. Any or all of these could have become quite deadly in their own right, but did not become so in significant part because of effective preventive statecraft.

Unavoidability of a role for international actors

Another important conclusion is that, notwithstanding claims to neutrality or non-involvement, there is no non-position for international actors. While international actors may profess neutrality, be it by limiting their involvement to humanitarian rescue or simply staying out, there simply is no "non-position" for the international community. When one party to the conflict concludes that it has the advantage in military and other means of violence over the other (so long as the other cannot count on international assistance to balance and buttress) it should be no wonder that the former chooses war. In some instances the choice of war is at least a pre-emptive one, less out of outright aggressive intentions than as a manifestation of the "security dilemma," in which warfare breaks out from mutual insecurities and fears of vulnerabilities, which credible international action could have assuaged. In this regard, to cite two other cases from the *Opportunities Missed, Opportunities Seized* study, Gail Lapidus stresses that all along Yeltsin still had a considerable repertoire of tools and strategies for Chechnya other than military intervention, but made his choices in part based on knowing that the United States and others in the international community were not going to impose significant costs for using force. In Congo-Brazzaville 1997 William Zartman shows how the conflicting parties exploited the unwillingness of the international community to get involved in any serious way.

In sum, there is ample basis for the viability of preventive statecraft. To be sure preventive statecraft is *hard* to do. But it is *possible* to do. Both points are integral to a genuine realism. The claim is not that some policy *X* surely would have prevented ethnic cleansing in Bosnia, or some policy *Y* smoothly rebuilt the Somali state, or some policy *Z* prevented genocide in Rwanda. But it is also not to accept the assertion that nothing else could have been done, or that different strategies weren't more viable than the policies pursued.

The strategic value of prevention

Even if preventive statecraft is doable, is it worth doing? It may be viable, but does it have sufficient value to international actors for them to run the risks and incur the costs of undertaking it? The argument here is twofold: the need to reassess the basic interests/costs calculus, and an analysis of how the dynamics of these conflicts contradict the assumed preference of waiting to see if and when concerted action is necessary.

Reassessing the interests/costs calculus

If it were the case that the fires of ethnic and intrastate conflicts, however intense, would just burn upon themselves and not have significant potential to spread regionally or destabilise more systematically, or if the options for later action had the presumed pragmatic preference, then in strict realist terms one could argue that, even if there still were to be a humanitarian concern, major powers could afford just to let them be. But that is not always or even frequently the case. As numerous cases have shown and as much of the literature substantiates, the spread of ethnic conflicts is much more common than self-containment. This occurs through various combinations of direct "contagion" from the actual physical movement of refugees and weapons to other countries in the region, "demonstration effects" that even without direct contact activate and escalate other conflicts, and other modes of conflict diffusion.[12] As a result, even though many of these conflicts did not initially involve inherently strategic locales, the damage to major power and other international interests proved greater than anticipated.

   A related point concerns the basic fallacy in the dichotomy so often drawn between realism and idealism. In the most fundamental sense "the distinction between interests and values," as Stanley Hoffmann argues, "is largely fallacious ... a great power has an 'interest' in world order that goes beyond strict national security concerns and its definition of world order is largely shaped by its values."[13] Moreover, it is worth pondering whether in such a globalist age we want to become a people that does not feel a moral imperative to seek to prevent genocide and other mass violence and destruction just because it may be on a geopolitically unimportant piece of real estate. This too is both a moral question and a pragmatic one, as it bears upon how such hardening can affect domestic intersocietal relations. The central point, however, is that *these are assessments to be made, not assumptions to be set.*

Furthermore, whereas waiting is often assumed to be less costly than acting early, waiting has proven to be much more costly than expected, and is arguably more costly than preventive action would have been.

In a sense policy makers are no different from most people in putting greater weight on immediate costs compared to anticipated ones. It always seems easier to pay tomorrow rather than today – thus the success of credit cards, thus the failures of preventive statecraft. There is the added probability calculus that perhaps the costs will not have to be paid, that the bill will not come due if the issue disappears or loses its urgency. But in the 1990s, the bills did come due, and when they did it was with the equivalent of exorbitant interest and late fees. One study estimated that the costs of conflict prevention to outside powers in the Bosnia case would have been US$33.3 billion, compared to the estimated US$53.7 billion that it actually cost. Similar disproportions were extrapolated for other cases: e.g., US$5 billion costs for the Haiti conflict compared to US$2.3 billion estimate for conflict prevention; US$7.3 billion/US$1.5 billion for Somalia; and in a cases of successful prevention like Macedonia, US$0.3 billion costs for prevention compared to US$15 billion had the conflict even reached intermediate intensity, let alone larger levels.[14]

The less quantifiable aspect of costs goes to the credibility of major powers and international institutions. There is a point to be made that credibility is not just about resolve but also about judgement and the capacity to discern when major interests are at stake and when they are not. But so too does credibility incur costs when international actors appear to lack the judgement to discern that their interests are at stake and/or to lack the will to act when this is the case.

Conflict dynamics

A former Croatian militiaman who later turned himself in reflected on his own killing of 72 civilians and command of a death camp. "The most difficult thing is to ignite a house or kill a man for the first time," he stated, "but afterwards even this becomes routine."[15] The addition of revenge and retribution to other sources of tension plunges a conflict situation down to a fundamentally different and more difficult depth. Certain international strategies that might have been effective at lower levels of conflict are less likely to be so amidst intensified violence. When that happens, a "Rubicon" gets crossed, and on the other side resolution and even limitation of the conflict become much more difficult.

Part of this is the classic problem for statecraft: the more extensive the objectives, the greater and usually more coercive are the strategies needed to achieve them. Consistent with both Thomas Schelling's deterrence/compellence distinction and Alexander George's work on coercive diplomacy, preventing a conflict from escalating to violence is a more limited objective than ending violence once it has begun.[16] Another aspect is that the capacity of domestic leaders who see their interests well served by the conflict to expand and maintain constituencies is that much greater when they have retribution and revenge to invoke. Moreover, the offence has the advantage, as it is easier to attack than to hold, feeding the incentive to act pre-emptively.[17]

Thus, options do *not* necessarily stay open over time; a problem can get harder down that road to where it has been kicked. Related literature shows a similar dynamic. For example, Jacob Bercovitch and Jeffrey Langley, in their study of 97 disputes of various types involving 364 separate mediation attempts, found a declining success rate for mediation as fatalities increased. David Carment and Frank Harvey show that there is a much greater chance for third parties to help achieve "definitive" rather than "ambiguous" outcomes to civil wars and other internal conflicts when they intervene at an early rather than a middle stage.[18]

This insight has implications for the theory of "ripeness." As developed by Zartman in his other work, as well as by others, this is an important and powerful theory.[19] The central idea is that there are points in the life-cycle of conflicts at which they are more conducive to possible resolution than others. When a situation is not "ripe," as determined in large part by the extent to which the parties to the conflict are disposed even to seriously consider an agreement, international strategies have much less chance of succeeding than others. But while ripeness theory is helpful in counselling prudent assessments of when and where to engage so as not to overestimate the chances of success, it sometimes gets interpreted and applied in ways that underestimate the risks and costs of waiting. Natural processes do not only work in one direction; they can move toward ripening, but also toward "rotting." The crops can be left in the fields too long, as well as harvested too early; the conflict may be intervened in too early, but it also can deteriorate over time, grow worse, become too far gone.

Moreover, putting such severely shattered societies back together again is enormously difficult, hugely expensive, very risky – and, very possibly, just not possible. One of the key tenets of the argument for not acting early has been that when the time comes, what could be done, was done. Yet experience has been that ending the conflicts has been one thing, putting these societies back together quite another. It is a problem, to draw again on work by Zartman, of "putting humpty-dumpty together again."[20] Even providing the basic relief of humanitarian aid to societies once they are war-torn has been difficult and dangerous. The Rwandan case illustrates how food distribution and other humanitarian assistance risks ending up getting politicized, feeding the conflict as it tries to feed the people. Moreover, the very safety of relief workers has been precarious. The most glaring case was the murder of six International Red Cross workers in Chechnya, sleeping in their beds, in a hospital – the worst atrocity against the Red Cross in its 130+ year history.

The dilemma of political will: How fixed, how malleable are political constraints?

Almost every study of preventive statecraft concludes that when all is said and done, the main obstacle is the problem of political will. As an explanatory statement, this is largely true. Governments have not acted because they have not had the political will to do so. But the analytic question that follows is whether this is to be just accepted as a fixed parameter or acknowledged as a severe constraint but a potentially and partially malleable one?

To be sure, there should be no illusions about the difficulties of mustering political will for the kinds of action in the kinds of situation required by preventive statecraft. Inertia and inaction are much more natural states for democratic governments not confronted by clear and present dangers than mobilization and action. Some point to the modern media as a major factor. As a study by veteran BBC foreign correspondent Nik Gowing shows, the media can be more of a hindrance than a help to conflict prevention.[21]

Even so, there is more room for manoeuvre, more potential malleability and basis for the political will to act in these ways and for these situations than often assumed. I cite the US case here as an example I know well, and as one that many see as having especially difficult domestic politics.

First of all, poll after poll shows the American public to be much more internationalist than isolationist. This does not mean that it will support every international commitment made, but it does mean that there is a basic understanding of the need and desirability of maintaining an active role in the world. Public support for the UN has recovered from the post-Somalia fallout and generally runs at over 60 per cent. Even on foreign aid one study showed that much of the opposition was based on the misperception of how much was spent.[22]

Second, my own studies of public opinion on the use of military force show a "pretty prudent public," that is neither gun-shy nor trigger-happy but rather makes distinctions according to the principal purposes military force is to serve and supports or opposes accordingly.[23] The tolerance for casualties is not very high, but it is not as low as often gets assumed, especially when the Somalia political firestorm is the case from which generalizations are made.

The data from Kosovo are especially interesting in this regard.[24] While well short of overwhelming levels, the public was much more inclined to support the use of force, *including ground troops and despite possible casualties*, than the Clinton administration kept assuming it was. Support for air strikes averaged about 57 per cent in public opinion polls and stayed pretty steady despite the ups and downs and uncertainties of daily news on the war effort. Support for ground troops showed more ambivalence but still averaged a plurality in favour over 12 polls, 48 per cent to 47 per cent. This was despite the Clinton administration's own statements about ground troops being unnecessary and the consequent absence of the kind of presidential cue that tends to prompt an additional 5–10 per cent "rally round the flag" effect. Moreover, in four out of five polls that posed questions about whether the Kosovo conflict was "worth" some American casualties, the majority answered yes.

This is not to say that the American public will be eager to use force and risk casualties. But it is to say that there is no enduring Somalia syndrome among the public.[25] Indeed, the image is of more deliberative and less reactive processes. This is despite other studies showing the low levels of information the public has, and despite the low levels of attention it pays to foreign affairs. Yet it still comes across as quite prudent in its judgements about when, where, and why to use military force.

Some of this also bears on the problem of congressional resistance to the use of force. Indeed, it is not just in the flaws in the casualty aversion assumption that the public is being "misread," especially on Capitol Hill.[26] Much other data shows the public to be much more internationalist than typically presumed. While not the huge margin of the middle of the Cold War, and slightly narrower than in the late Cold War, a strong majority (65 per cent) still comes out internationalist. The public essentially understands that the United States has come to be so interconnected in so many ways with the rest of the world, that isolationism is not just undesirable – it simply is not possible.

Yet while this may register in polls, it does not become a significant political force unless it is mobilized. A president willing to pursue a sustained dialogue with the American public as a priority effort could provide this mobilization. To the extent that there is a genuine misreading of the public by some in Congress, this would help correct misperceptions.[27] To the extent that the problem is more one of manipulation with the ostensible lack of will of the American people more as cover story than cause, the cover can be blown. A president who makes this case on a sustained basis can reshape the political context in ways that make the domestic constraints less constraining.

Policy recommendations

My intent here is to provide a broad sense of guidelines which have sufficient generality to constitute the parameters of a strategy, but also are to be adapted for specific application on a case-by-case basis.[28]

Diplomatic strategies

Other studies have provided quite comprehensive inventories of the range of diplomatic strategies that can be used for conflict prevention. One of the points I want to emphasize is the importance of mixed strategies, combining both inducements and coercive measures, offering carrots and wielding sticks. This is never strictly a reflexive Skinnerian-like combination, but the general point is the need to avoid the dichotomies that so often get drawn between coercive threat-based strategies on the one hand, and positively inducing strategies of cooperation on the other. A "viable theory of deterrence," as Alexander George and Richard Smoke argued back in the 1970s in the Cold War context, requires less of an "exclusive preoccupation with threats of punishment" as the sole means for influencing an adversary's behaviour, and more of "a broader theory of processes by which nations influence each other, one that encompasses the utility of positive inducements as well as, or in lieu of, threats of negative sanctions."[29] Similarly, post-Cold War theories of cooperation that focus too exclusively on positive inducements and fail to encompass the utility that threats and negative action can have on facilitating cooperation also lack the necessary complexity and dynamism.[30]

Within this overarching dynamic a number of factors are key to an effective negotiating strategy. One is the importance that the terms of negotiation allow all sides to derive and to be able to show their domestic constituencies' gains from cooperation and conflict management. Those leaders and groups that are more prone to non-violent and cooperative measures – cooperation constituencies – need to be strengthened. The particular domestic political constitutive formula will vary, power-sharing in some situations and majority rule or other structures in others.[31] The key is to gauge diplomatic efforts so as to reinforce and be reinforced by the cooperation over the conflict constituencies.

Another important point is the key role played by special envoys and other lead diplomats as negotiators and mediators. In many of the successes in the *Opportunities Lost, Opportunities Seized* volume substantial credit is attributed to key individuals. Gabonese President Bongo, with his "patient listening and avuncular counsel" and personal and familial ties to key protagonists, as well as OAU special envoy Mahmoud Sahnoun, played key roles in the Congo in 1993. A Carnegie Commission study by Cyrus Vance and David Hamburg stresses the role that UN special representatives and personal envoys have played, and calls for "a more activist approach" in their use for preventive statecraft.[32] In Bosnia-Herzegovina, for ending albeit not preventing the war, Richard Holbrooke generally is acknowledged to have played a key role in the Dayton Accords.[33] Other studies are corroborative on this point as well. A series of US Institute of Peace studies affirmed that the "credibility and character of the mediator are even more critical in internal conflicts than in inter-state conflicts."[34]

Our study also showed how the "lure of membership" in major international and regional organizations is an increasingly influential instrument. In her study of Croatia and Bosnia and Herzegovina Susan Woodward stresses the too early and too unconditional offering of diplomatic recognition, the most basic form of membership in the international community, to the former Yugoslav states, as a key problem. Conversely, the Council of Europe postponed Latvia's admission until the Russian minority issue was worked out. Another example is the March 1995 agreement between Hungary and Slovakia on minority rights for the greater than half a million ethnic Hungarians in Slovakia, which was in part facilitated by the lure of membership in the EU and NATO.

Another general point is that no one international actor is singularly key to preventive statecraft. While it might be easier if we could point to one international actor as the optimal key player, neither the literature nor our cases support this.[35] Different cases involve different international actors playing different roles.

With regard to the United States, its role continues to be an essential one much more often than not. Its optimal role is as the leader of multi-lateral action. Both because of the nature of many of these issues and the structure of power in the post-Cold War era, unilateralism is more the exception than the rule. Yet multilateralism on its own lacks reliable capacity for proactive diplomacy. Whether through international institutions and organizations, or on a more *ad hoc* basis, leadership is needed, and that leadership needs to come from the United States as the major power. A more concerted commitment to preventive statecraft also is needed from the Western European powers. The aspirations to a Common Foreign and Security Policy as proclaimed at Maastricht in 1991 were severely damaged by the national interest-based approaches to Yugoslavia. Hopes for greater cohesiveness were refostered in 1999 by a number of developments including the appointment of former NATO secretary-general Javier Solana as EU foreign and security policy coordinator.

The United Nations brings two great strengths to preventive statecraft. One is its unique normative role for "collective legitimation."[36] No other body can claim comparable legitimacy for establishing global norms and for authorizing actions in the name of the international community, be it diplomatic intermediation or military intervention. The other is its network of agencies, which provide it with significant institutional capacity to help cope with refugee flows, help relieve starvation and perform other humanitarian tasks. Yet the ambitious role outlined in Boutros-Ghali's 1992 *An Agenda for Peace* has proven too far-reaching in a number of respects, politically and strategically. One of the lessons from recent cases is that the UN has its own inherent institutional limitations. It is also true that at times the UN has ended up being blamed as an institution for problems for which deeper responsibility lies with its major members. Each in its own way on its own issues has been reluctant to endow the UN Security Council with needed capacity to act decisively.

Regional organizations have an increasingly important role to play, which can be complementary to the UN and at times have a comparative advantage. Recent studies show successes and failures for both the Organization for Security and Cooperation in Europe (OSCE) and the Organization of African Unity (OAU). One of the keys to success was the establishment of a normative basis for preventive action to an extent including intrastate issues. The OSCE has gone the furthest in this regard, starting with the 1990 Charter of Paris declaration "that in order to strengthen peace and security among our states, the advancement of democracy, and respect for and effective exercise of human rights, are indispensable" and as furthered in its 1999 Charter for European Security affirming the commitment "to preventing the outbreak of violent conflicts wherever possible."[37] The OSCE has also made significant headway in operationalizing a range of instruments for preventive statecraft, such as the High Commissioner on National Minorities and the missions of "long" and "short" duration to more than 12 countries that provide first-hand information gathering for early warning, and increasing transparency and accountability in ways that can help deter greater repression and escalation to violence (see Mychajlyszyn, this volume).

The OAU made some advances with its June 1993 creation of a "Mechanism for Conflict Prevention, Management and Resolution." While still working within significant qualifiers about "the respect of sovereignty" and "consent and cooperation of the parties to a conflict," the undeniability of regional security consequences of conflicts traditionally considered domestic had reached the point that, as Edmond Keller puts it, African leaders felt it necessary "to seriously reconsider the norms of external intervention for the purpose of settling domestic disputes."[38] Clearly the OAU has a long way to go to fulfil such normative shifts in its actions, but the point nevertheless is that the normative shifts are occurring (see Draman, this volume).

While not always in an explicitly coordinated fashion, NGOs can play key roles, often achieving what governments cannot. This is a delicate relationship in a number of ways. NGOs need be careful about becoming or even being perceived as being too close to governments and the UN as well. Yet they have a number of advantages both inherent in their nongovernmental status and also as manifestations of their capacity to be "more flexible and creative."[39] Their role in track-two diplomacy encompasses a number of aspects, including the ongoing preventive work of developing inter-ethnic and other understanding and cooperation, the facilitating of unofficial talks when official ones are stymied, and the building of the structures and practices of civil society that ultimately are crucial to long-term peaceful conflict prevention and resolution.

Credible preventive military force

I stressed earlier the fallacy of excluding military force and other coercive measures from the realm of preventive statecraft instruments and strategies. Indeed, more often than not, the diplomatic components of a preventive strategy need to be backed by a credible threat to act coercively through military force, economic sanctions, or other coercive strategies. As a matter of deterrence, given the purposive nature of these conflicts and the deliberate calculations made by certain parties to them that they can prevail militarily at acceptable cost, the credibility of the international community's threat to respond coercively is a crucial factor. As a matter of reassurance, with regard to the ways in which the parties may be driven to military action less out of strict aggression than the uncertainty inherent in the security dilemma and "commitment" problem, the protection that only international actors can provide is key for the parties to feel secure in restraint and agreements.

The guiding requisites for seeking this balance should be along the lines of a *fair-but-firm strategy*. On the one hand the parties to the conflict must have confidence in the fairness of international third parties, with fairness defined as a fundamental commitment to peaceful and just resolution of the conflict rather than partisanship for or sponsorship of one or the other party to the conflict. But fairness is not necessarily to be equated with impartiality if the latter is defined as strict neutrality even if one side engages in gross and wanton acts of violence or other violations of efforts to prevent the intensification or spread of the conflict. The parties to the conflict must know both that cooperation has its benefits and that those benefits will be fully equitable, and that non-cooperation has its consequences and that the international parties are prepared to enforce those consequences differentially as warranted by who does and does not do what. In this regard fairness and firmness go together quite symmetrically.

Macedonia is the most often cited example of a successful preventive deployment (see Väyrynen, this volume). Like all cases, however, its generalizability must be conditional. Different situations always have to be assessed as to whether preventive military action or the threat thereof is likely to have positive effects as deterrence and/or reassurance, or to be exacerbants to the conflict. However, the usual assumption of using force only as a last resort does need to be questioned. "Preserving force as a last resort implies a lockstep sequencing of the means to achieve foreign policy objectives," Jane Holl argues, "that is unduly inflexible and relegates the use of force to *in extremis* efforts to salvage a faltering foreign policy."[40] Force rarely if ever should be a first resort, but it often needs to be more of an early resort.

Any such forces must be given a robust mission and appropriate training, equipment, and organization to carry out such a mission. The characterization of many of the interventions undertaken as humanitarian accurately describes the consequences of the conflicts more than their causes. Back in April 1991, when a deadly cyclone hit Bangladesh, killing 139,000 people and doing $2 billion worth of damage to this already impoverished country, and American military forces were sent to help provide relief and reconstruction, this genuinely was a humanitarian mission. But the starvation in Somalia, the massive refugee flows in Rwanda and Croatia and Bosnia-Herzegovina, all were politically precipitated humanitarian crises. To be successful, and indeed to be credible, given the nature of the instability they had to deal with, military action needed to have been sufficiently strong and assertive in terms of the scope of the mandate authorizing military action, the size of the forces, and the rules of engagement to overcome the reluctance of the target to comply.

Proposals for a standing UN rapid reaction force need to be given serious attention.[41] By that I mean that we need to get beyond the rhetorical dimension of the debate in which opponents rail against black helicopters and the like, while proponents pay less attention to the difficult operational details than to the value of such a force as the embodiment of the will of the international community. The latter are quite significant, perhaps not necessarily prohibitive of some UN standing force but sufficient that such a force is unlikely to be more than supplemental to other coalitions, such as NATO. Even before the 1999 Kosovo war post-Cold War NATO doctrine had begun to change, explicitly recognizing that security threats are less likely to come from calculated aggression against the territory of its allies than from the risks of the adverse consequences that may arise from serious difficulties which are faced by many countries in Central and Eastern Europe. Africa is the region other than Europe in which there has been the most effort to develop regional capacity for preventive military intervention. The Liberia intervention by ECOMOG (Economic Community of West African States Cease-fire Monitoring Group), with regional power Nigeria in the lead, was too late to be considered preventive but rather was more about conflict management; and it was not very successful.[42] More along the preventive lines has been the US-sponsored African Crisis Response Initiative (ACRI), although it remains to be seen, however, whether this initiative can overcome the obstacles it faces and dispel the doubts about its potential efficacy.

In sum, the difficulties in establishing the modes and mechanisms for more credible preventive military threats and action must not be underestimated. But unless these difficulties can be better managed and overcome, preventive statecraft will lack the coercive component essential to success in most cases.

Sanctions can also be an effective coercive preventive strategy. In the North Korea and Russia-Baltics cases the threat of sanctions was an important part of the mixed strategy, the stick accompanying the carrot of other incentives and inducements. In cases such as Somalia, Rwanda, and Haiti the sanctions were ineffective if not counterproductive. Nevertheless, for reasons that I develop more extensively elsewhere, the question remains whether some of these findings are "false negatives" in which the policy failures may have been more attributable to flaws in other parts of the strategy (e.g. lack of a credible military threat) or in which sanctions might have worked had they been done more effectively.[43] One of the main findings in the sanctions literature is that for reasons both of disruptive economic impact and conveying credibility, sanctions are more likely to be effective if imposed comprehensively and decisively and enforced tightly rather than imposed partially and incrementally with limited real effort at enforcement.[44] Yet partial-incremental sanctions with lax enforcement have been much more common than comprehensive-decisive and tightly enforced ones.[45]

Establishing the norm of sovereignty as responsibility

Norms matter. They provide an internationally recognized standard against which policies are measured and to which behaviour is held. They legitimize international action against states or other offenders whose actions violate those standards. As such, norms have power.

The crucial normative issue is the tension between conceptions of sovereignty as states' rights and as state responsibilities. The sovereignty as rights norm recognises each state as having its own jurisdictional exclusivity and giving very limited and narrowly construed bases of legitimacy for some other actor, whether another state or an international institution, to seek to insert itself in the domestic affairs of a state. Yet the need is increasingly apparent, given the intrastate nature (in whole or in part) of the vast majority of post-Cold War conflicts, to value sovereignty less as strictly a right and more as a "responsibility."[46]

State sovereignty's strict interpretation as prevailed for the 1945–90 period was geared to the two principal factors that defined the international system of that era: anti-colonialism and the Cold War. In these contexts the affirmation of the rights of states was largely consistent with the rights of the individuals within those states to self-determination and to living free from external repression or worse. Now, anti-colonialism and major power geopolitics no longer define the international system. Moreover, it is the actions of state governments against their own people, much more than foreign powers, that pose the major threats to the rights of individuals.

The conception of responsible sovereignty as advanced by Francis Deng, William Zartman, Donald Rothchild, and colleagues requires states "at the very least ensuring a certain level of protection for and providing the basic needs of the people."[47] Neither Deng *et al.* nor others are necessarily arguing for international trusteeships, protectorates, or other such extreme measures. The concept of sovereignty, as James Rosenau makes the point, allows for gradations, conditionalities, and other combinations.[48] Moreover, any abridgements on state sovereignty would need to avoid becoming guises for power politics and to maintain the utmost consistency with their normative bases. But the key point is that the scope of a state's right to sovereign authority is not unconditional or normatively superior to the right to security of the polity.

Strict constructionists are quick to cite Article 2(7) of the UN Charter – "nothing contained in the present Charter shall authorise the United Nations to intervene in matters which are essentially within the domestic jurisdiction of any state." Yet numerous other portions of the UN Charter provide normative and legal basis for the individual as the "right and duty bearing unit" in international society. Article 3 affirms that "everyone has the right to life, liberty and the security of person;" Article 55 commits the UN to "promote ... universal respect for, and observance of, human rights and fundamental freedoms;" Article 56 pledges all members "to take joint and separate action" toward this end. Further affirmations of the inalienability of basic human rights are ensconced in the Genocide Convention, the Universal Declaration of Human Rights, and other international covenants that make no distinction as to whether the offender is a foreign invader or one's own government. UN Secretary-

General Kofi Annan reminds us that "the [UN] Charter was issued in the name of 'the peoples,' not the governments of the United Nations ... The Charter protects the sovereignty of peoples. It was never meant as a license for governments to trample on human rights and human dignity. Sovereignty implies responsibility, not just power."[49]

Annan goes on to stress the legitimacy of interventions based on the Chapter VII provision for preserving international peace and security even when the locus of the conflict is intrastate. Similar duality pertains to the macro level of regional and international security. Even Article 2(7) is qualified with "the important rider that 'this principle shall not prejudice the application of enforcement measures under Chapter VII.' In other words, even national sovereignty can be set aside if it stands in the way of the Security Council's overriding duty to preserve international peace and security."[50]

In fact some important precedents have been set in the 1990s of UN Security Council authorized interventions abridging sovereignty's narrow interpretation, such as with UNSC 688 (1991) authorizing a peacekeeping mission protecting the Kurds in Northern Iraq, and the "all necessary means" authorization (1994) of the US military intervention in Haiti. Most cases have been to protect refugees and for other humanitarian purposes. Indeed the doctrines of refugee protection and other humanitarian intervention have been taking on increasing legitimacy.[51]

However, with regard to preventive statecraft, the norm remains much weaker. In cases like the Baltics, as well as Macedonia and Congo 1993, the international involvement was at the invitation of the host government and thus the normative constraint was more avoided than overcome. Requiring an invitation, however, also means that such an invitation often will not come forward, with the consequence that intrastate conflicts get "protected" from international action. The norm of sovereignty as responsibility as it pertains to preventing intrastate violence needs to be strengthened sufficiently to legitimize early action to prevent, and not just respond to, genocides and other deadly violence and humanitarian crises.

Conclusion

One of the main reasons why leaders have been so reluctant to take on preventive statecraft is that they have held to the conventional wisdom that the costs to be borne and risks to be run are too high and the interests at stake are too low. In challenging this conventional wisdom and showing the realism of preventive statecraft as a strategic calculation, we address this crucial aspect of the political will. We have also shown that political will is not an insurmountable problem, that political constraints have a degree of malleability. This is not just deciding against inaction on moral grounds. It is not just trying to place policy over politics. Rather, it is to argue that politics and policy are more complementary than assumed. It also suggests that the reason that there can and should be political will for preventive statecraft is that both political and policy interests are better served.

All this speaks to what is possible. Whether it becomes actual requires sustained efforts, both intellectual and political. As we seek to do this, we should bear in mind some other lessons to be learned from the early post-World War II era. When Bernard Brodie and others first began developing the theories on which the dominant deterrence paradigm was to be based, the basic idea was relatively simple and straightforward. Preserve the peace through fear of retaliation. That core idea was further developed, refined, elaborated, modified, adapted, extended – indeed it became a major component of an entire paradigm that dominated US foreign policy and most of international affairs for a generation. So, too, in this post-Cold War era we need to work with the core idea of preventive statecraft. Act early to stop disputes from escalating or problems from worsening. Reduce tensions that, if intensified, could lead to war. Deal with today's conflicts before they become tomorrow's crises. Much more development, refinement, elaboration, modification, adaptation, and extension are needed. For if we know one thing for sure, it is that the need for prevention is not going to subside at any time soon.

Notes

1. Parts of this chapter are based on a project I led for the Carnegie Commission on Preventing Deadly Conflict, and the recently published book of which I am editor, *Opportunities Missed, Opportunities Seized: Preventive Diplomacy in the Post-Cold War World*, Lanham, MD: Rowman and Littlefield, 1999. The book includes 10 1990s case studies: Croatia-Bosnia, Rwanda, Somalia, Nagorno-Karabakh, Chechnya, Macedonia, Congo (Brazzaville), Russia-Latvia/Estonia, Russia-Ukraine, North Korea. These represent different types of conflicts that characterize the post-Cold War world, as well as a mix of successes and failures – i.e. opportunities missed and opportunities seized. Each case study is written by a noted expert. There are also additional chapters by Alexander George and Jane Holl on the problem of the "warning-response gap" and by this author laying out a conceptual and analytic framework and then drawing analytic conclusions and policy lessons. It is from these latter chapters that this chapter is drawn.
2. I intentionally use the term "preventive statecraft" as a shift from preventive diplomacy. I have come to prefer this as better conveying the importance of thinking in terms of "mixed strategies," not just confined to negotiation and other classical forms of diplomacy but also encompassing preventive uses of military force and other more coercive components.
3. Crawford Young, ed., *The Rising Tide of Cultural Pluralism: The Nation-State at Bay?*, Madison: University of Wisconsin Press, 1993; David Lake and Donald Rothchild,

"Spreading Fear: The Genesis of Transnational Ethnic Conflict," in David Lake and Donald Rothchild, eds., *International Spread of Ethnic Conflict: Fear, Diffusion and Escalation*, Princeton, NJ: Princeton University Press, 1998, pp. 5–7; Harold Isaacs, *Idols of the Tribe: Group Identity and Political Change*, New York: Harper and Row, 1975; Robert D. Kaplan, *Balkan Ghosts: A Journey Through History*, New York: St. Martin's Press, 1993.

4. *Ibid.*, Kaplan, *Balkan Ghosts*.

5. Chris Hedges, "War Turns Sarajevo Away from Europe," *New York Times*, 29 July 1995.

6. Michael E. Brown, "The Causes of Internal Conflict: An Overview," in Michael E. Brown, Owen R. Cote Jr, Sean M. Lynn-Jones and Steven E. Miller, eds., *Nationalism and Ethnic Conflict*, Cambridge, MA: MIT Press, 1997, pp. 4–12. See also I. William Zartman, ed., *Collapsed States: The Disintegration and Restoration of Legitimate Authority*, Boulder, CO: Lynne Rienner, 1995; Brown, ed., *Ethnic Conflict and International Security*, Princeton, NJ: Princeton University Press, 1993; Samuel P. Huntington, *Political Order in Changing Societies*, New Haven: Yale University Press, 1968; Ted Robert Gurr, *Why Men Rebel*, Princeton, NJ: Princeton University Press, 1970.

7. See also David Carment, "The Ethnic Dimension in World Politics: Theory, Policy and Early Warning," *Third World Quarterly*, No. 4, 1994, p. 557.

8. Kalypso Nicolaidis, "Preventive Action: Developing A Strategic Framework," in Robert Rotberg, ed., *Vigilance and Vengeance: NGOs Preventing Ethnic Conflict in Divided Societies*, Washington, D.C., Brookings Institution Press, 1996, p. 34.

9. Alexander L. George and Jane E. Holl, "The Warning-Response Problem and Missed Opportunities in Preventive Diplomacy," in Jentleson, *Opportunities Missed, Opportunities Seized*, note 1 above.

10. See also the study convened by the Carnegie Commission on Preventing Deadly Conflict, the Georgetown University Institute for the Study of Diplomacy and the United States Army, involving an international panel of senior military leaders which, while stressing the requisites such a force would have had to meet, generally concurred; Scott R. Feil, *Preventing Genocide: How the Early Use of Force Might Have Succeeded in Rwanda*, Washington, D.C.: Carnegie Commission on Preventing Deadly Conflict, 1998. See also reports on General Dallaire's testimony to the UN International Criminal Tribunal for Rwanda, such as Stephen Buckley, "Mass Slaughter Was Avoidable, General Says," *Washington Post*, 26 February 1998, pp. A17, A22.

11. Five key methodological criteria – specificity, minimal historical rewrite, plausible causal logic, knowability, doability – are elaborated in Jentleson, the first chapter of the study. See also Philip E. Tetlock and Aaron Belkin, eds., *Counterfactual Thought Experiments in World Politics: Logical, Methodological and Psychological Perspectives*, Princeton, NJ: Princeton University Press, 1997.

12. Stuart Hill and Donald Rothchild, "The Contagion of Political Conflict in Africa and the World," *Journal of Conflict Resolution*, Vol. 30, December 1986, pp. 716–35; Stuart Hill, Donald Rothchild and Colin Cameron, "Tactical Information and the Diffusion of Peaceful Protests," in Lake and Rothchild, *International Spread of Ethnic Conflict*, note 3 above, pp. 61–88.

13. Stanley Hoffmann, "In Defense of Mother Theresa: Morality in Foreign Policy," *Foreign Affairs*, Vol. 75, March/April 1994, p. 172; see also Hoffmann, "The Politics and Ethics of Military Intervention," *Survival*, Winter 1995–96, pp. 29–51.

14. Michael E. Brown and Richard N. Rosecrance, eds., *The Costs of Conflict: Prevention and Cure in the Global Arena*, Lanham, MD: Rowman and Littlefield, 1999, p. 225.

15. Chris Hedges, "Croatian's Confession Describes Torture and Killing on a Vast Scale," *New York Times*, 5 September 1997, p. A1.

16. Thomas C. Schelling, *Arms and Influence*, pp. 69–74; Alexander L. George and William E. Simons, eds., *The Limits of Coercive Diplomacy*, 2nd ed., Boulder, CO: Westview Press, 1994; Alexander L. George, *Forceful Persuasion*, Washington, D.C.: U.S. Institute of Peace Press.
17. Barry Posen, "Military Responses to Refugee Disasters," *International Security*, Vol. 21, Summer 1996, pp. 342–3.
18. Jacob Bercovitch and Jeffrey Langley, "The Nature of the Dispute and the Effectiveness of International Mediation," *Journal of Conflict Resolution*, Vol. 37, 1993, pp. 670–91; David Carment and Frank Harvey, *Using Force to Prevent Ethnic Violence*, Westport, CT: Praeger, 2000; see also David R. Smock, ed., *Creative Approaches to Managing Conflict in Africa: Findings from USIP-Funded Projects*, Peaceworks No. 15, Washington, D.C.: U.S. Institute of Peace, 1997, pp. 1–4; Roy Licklider, *Stopping the Killing: How Civil Wars End*, New York: New York University Press, 1993.
19. I. William Zartman, *Ripe for Resolution: Conflict and Intervention in Africa*, New York: Oxford University Press, 1989: Richard N. Haass, *Conflicts Unending: The United States and Regional Disputes*, New Haven: Yale University Press, 1990.
20. I. William Zartman, "Putting Humpty-Dumpty Together Again," in Lake and Rothchild, *International Spread of Ethnic Conflict*, note 3 above.
21. Nik Gowing, *Media Coverage: Help or Hindrance in Conflict Prevention?* Washington, D.C.: Carnegie Commission on Preventing Deadly Conflict, 1997.
22. Steven Kull and I. M. Destler, *Misreading the Public: The Myth of a New Isolationism*, Washington, D.C.: Brookings Institution Press, 1999.
23. Bruce W. Jentleson and Rebecca Britton, "Still Pretty Prudent: Post-Cold War American Public Opinion on the Use of Military Force," *Journal of Conflict Resolution*, Vol. 42, August 1998, pp. 395–417, and Bruce W. Jentleson, "The Pretty Prudent Public: Post Post-Vietnam American Opinion on the Use of Military Force," *International Studies Quarterly*, Vol. 36, March 1992, pp. 49–74.
24. For elaboration of this argument and further details on the data, see Bruce W. Jentleson, "Coercive Prevention: Normative, Political and Policy Dilemmas," *Peaceworks* series, U.S. Institute of Peace, 2000.
25. See also the findings in the study by the Triangle Institute for Security Studies (Duke-UNC Chapel Hill), as discussed in Peter D. Feaver and Christopher Gelpi, "A Look at Casualty Aversion," *Washington Post*, 7 November 1999, p. B3.
26. Kull and Destler, *Misreading the Public*, note 22 above.
27. The Kull-Destler study found that 74 per cent of policy makers believed that the public favoured "disengagement," only 32 per cent believed that the public wanted the United States to be an international leader and only 15 per cent believed that the public could be convinced to support engagement.
28. Consistent with Alexander L. George, *Bridging the Gap: Theory and Practice in Foreign Policy*, Washington, D.C.: U.S. Institute of Peace, 1993, p. xxv and *passim*.
29. Alexander George and Richard Smoke, "Deterrence and Foreign Policy," *World Politics*, Vol. 41, January 1989, p. 182, and their award-winning study *Deterrence in American Foreign Policy: Theory and Practice*, New York: Colombia University Press, 1974, especially chapter 21.
30. For a similar argument, see Bruce W. Jentleson, *With Friends Like These: Reagan, Bush, and Saddam, 1982–1990*, New York: W.W. Norton, 1994, especially chapter 5.
31. Timothy Sisk, *Power Sharing and International Mediation in Ethnic Conflicts*, Washington, D.C.: U.S. Institute of Peace Press, 1996.
32. Cyrus R. Vance and David A. Hamburg, *Pathfinders for Peace: A Report to the UN Secretary-General on the Role of Special Representatives and Personal Envoys*, A Report of the Carnegie Commission on Preventing Deadly Conflict, September 1997.

33. A balanced assessment is David Rieff, "Almost Justice" (Review of Holbrooke's book, *To End A War*), *The New Republic*, 6 July 1998, pp. 29–38.

34. Smock, *Creative Approaches to Managing Conflict in Africa*, note 18 above, p. 4.

35. See, for example, Carment and Harvey, "Effectiveness of Third Party Mediation," in *Using Force to Prevent Ethnic Violence*, note 18 above.

36. The term is from Gene M. Lyons and Michael Mastanduno, "Introduction: International Intervention, State Sovereignty and the Future of International Society," in their book *Beyond Westphalia: State Sovereignty and International Intervention*, Baltimore, MD: Johns Hopkins University Press, 1995.

37. "Charter for European Security," Organization for Security and Cooperation in Europe, Istanbul summit, November 1999, http://www.osce.org, accessed 27 January 2000. See also P. Terrence Hopmann, *Building Security in Post-Cold War Eurasia*, United States Institute of Peace, *Peaceworks*, No. 31, September 1999.

38. Edmond Keller, "Transnational Ethnic Conflict in Africa," in Lake and Rothchild, *International Spread of Ethnic Conflict*, note 12 above.

39. Larry Minear and Thomas G. Weiss, *Mercy Under Fire: War and the Global Humanitarian Community*, Boulder, CO: Westview Press, 1995, p. 49; Rotberg, *Vigilance and Vengeance*, note 8 above.

40. Jane E. Holl, "We the People Here Don't Want No War: Executive Branch Perspectives on the Use of Force," in Aspen Strategy Group, *U.S. and the Use of Force*, p. 124 and *passim*.

41. Carnegie Commission, *Final Report*, pp. 65–67; Brian Urquhart, "Who Can Police the World?" *New York Review of Books*, 12 May 1994, and "For a UN Volunteer Military Force," *New York Review of Books*, 10 June 1993.

42. Herbert House, "Lessons of Liberia: ECOMOG and Regional Peacekeeping," *International Security*, Vol. 21, Winter 1996/97, pp. 145–76.

43. Bruce W. Jentleson, "Economic Sanctions and Post-Cold War Conflicts: Challenges for Theory and Policy," study prepared for the Committee on International Conflict Resolution, Commission on Behavioral and Social Sciences, National Research Council, National Academy of Sciences, 2000.

44. *Ibid.*, and Gary Clyde Hufbauer, Jeffrey J. Schott and Kimberly Ann Elliott, *Economic Sanctions Reconsidered*, Washington, D.C.: Institute of International Economics, 1990; David Cartwright and George Lopez, eds., *Economic Sanctions: Panacea or Peacebuilding in a Post-Cold War World*, Boulder, CO: Westview Press, 1995.

45. David and Frank Harvey, *Using Force to Prevent Ethnic Violence*, Westport, CT: Praeger, 2000.

46. Francis M. Deng, Sadikiel Kimaro, Terrence Lyons, Donald Rothchild, and I. William Zartman, *Sovereignty as Responsibility: Conflict Management in Africa*, Washington, D.C.: Brookings Institution, 1996.

47. *Ibid.*, p. 28.

48. James N. Rosenau, "Sovereignty in a Turbulent World," in Lyons and Mastanduno, eds., *Beyond Westphalia: State Sovereignty and International Intervention*, note 36 above, p. 195.

49. Kofi Annan, "Intervention," Ditchley Foundation Lecture XXXV, 1998, p. 2 (reprinted).

50. *Ibid.* See also Annan, *Report of the Secretary-General*, September 1999.

51. See, for example, Jarat Chopra and Thomas G. Weiss, "Sovereignty is No Longer Sacrosanct: Codifying Humanitarian Intervention," *Ethics and International Affairs*, 1992, Vol. 6, pp. 95–117; and Dowty and Loescher, "Refugee Flows as Grounds for International Action," pp. 43–71.

4

Challenges to preventive action: The cases of Kosovo and Macedonia

Raimo Väyrynen

Basic features of preventive action

The origins of modern preventive diplomacy can be traced to the 1950s when Dag Hammarskjöld as the UN Secretary-General made great efforts to strengthen the preventive role of the world organization. The tenet of his policy was to keep great powers out of regional conflicts and thus forestall the increase in their destructiveness through external military intervention and arms transfers. Preventive action stemmed from the more general reasoning that external interventions could be avoided or tempered if a region is made more autonomous in terms of security.[1]

The underlying rationale was expressed in Hammarskjöld's introduction to the 1959–60 annual report of the United Nations: preventive action "must in the first place aim at filling the vacuum so that it will not provoke action from any of the major parties." Neutralization of the conflict zone – as in Gaza in 1956–57 and Laos in 1962 – was the principal tool of preventing the future involvement of great powers in local crises. Neutralization meant that the external powers agreed to keep a region as a sphere of absence in their mutual relations.

Hammarskjöld's approach covers, however, only one type of conflict action, i.e. the horizontal, cross-border escalation of violence. In addition, escalation can also be vertical when the destructiveness of violence increases within a given political unit without spilling over boundaries to other units. A critical difference between these two processes of escalation lies in their relationship with the principle of sovereignty. In the former case, national sovereignty is violated and thus an interstate offence-defence cycle is set in motion. In such a situation the threshold of external intervention tends to be lowered as we can see in the Gulf War example. If the escalation process is encapsulated within the borders of a country, third parties may be tempted to let the parties fight out their war despite major humanitarian costs.

The policy aim in preventive action, after violence has started, is to forestall its vertical and/or horizontal escalation. In both cases, escalation means that conflict actions cross salient boundaries, which transforms, in turn, the nature and intensity of the conflict.[2] It seems that the salient thresholds are, in vertical escalation, primarily humanitarian and, in horizontal escalation, territorial. The distinction between the humanitarian and territorial dimensions of preventive diplomacy harks back to their diverging relationship with the principle of sovereignty and, therefore, of intervention. Humanitarian intervention is, under specific conditions, permitted, and perhaps increasingly so, while the interference with the territorial integrity of states is almost always off limits. In general, the feasibility of preventive diplomacy hinges on the complex and dynamic interactions between humanitarian norms, sovereignty, and intervention.[3]

As a rule, preventive diplomacy is thought to focus on the phase preceding the active resort to violence. Preventive action in the pre-war phase of the conflict cycle can be divided into indirect, structuralist and direct, action-oriented components; in the former, preventive action aims to eliminate or mitigate causes that fuel violence over a long term, while in the latter, strategic actions are carried out to forestall the imminent outbreak of war.[4] The focus of this chapter is on direct, action-oriented policies to prevent the outbreak and escalation of violence in intrastate and interstate situations. Such policies may also be needed after the conclusion of the peace agreement to make sure that the situation does not relapse back to fighting, as has happened, for example, in Angola and the Democratic Republic of Congo.

The goals, instruments, and outcomes of preventive action vary considerably between the three stages of the conflict cycle; i.e. pre-war prevention, escalation prevention, and post-war prevention. The success of preventive action seems to depend critically on the political context and the ability of policy makers to read it correctly, the appropriate choice and coordination of the instruments used, and the effective combination of incentives and punishments. To be successful, preventive diplomacy has to become a form of goal-oriented, strategic action.[5]

Practical experiences, however, indicate that incentives alone are not enough to stop recalcitrant actors from continuing their misdeeds. Promises and rewards must be backed up by threats and, if they fail, even by punishments. Alexander L. George has made this vital point over and over again, and most recently in the following words: successful preventive action requires that "one makes threats of *sufficient credibility* and *sufficient potency* to persuade an adversary to cease or desist from an objectionable course of action."[6]

Obviously, for humanitarian, economic, and political reasons, it is desirable to forestall violence before it breaks out. Recent empirical work, necessarily tentative in nature, indicates that the opportunity costs of non-action in crises are high and the costs of failed prevention are seldom excessive.[7] However, in reality, the success stories of pre-violence prevention are few and far between. In the 1990s, possibly Macedonia, the relations between Hungary and Slovakia, the Baltic countries, Burundi, and, by some criteria, Montenegro during the Milosevic era can be considered partial successes. Due to the cautious, inertial, and often selfish policies of the major powers, preventive action tends be placed on the political agenda only after violence has broken out, public pressure to act mounts, and the benefits of preventing its escalation are realized.

In international politics there is a strong bias in favour of preventing horizontal escalation of violence. Much less attention is given to its vertical escalation.[8] This is mostly due to the fact that the horizontal spillover of conflict violates the sovereignty of other states. It also threatens the escalation of a limited intranational conflict into a regional and possibly a global confrontation. Thus, horizontal escalation is a bigger risk to the territorial and statist principles of international relations than the vertical escalation which threatens "only" the domestic order and human life within a single state.

This chapter focuses on two interdependent case studies, Macedonia and Kosovo, in an effort to determine which factors contribute to the success and failure of conflict prevention. The chapter also makes an effort to find out how horizontal and vertical prevention interact and how this interaction is shaped by the different phases of the conflict, and the different modes of intervention by the third parties. The relevance of the Macedonian case is increased by it being the testing ground for a new type of preventive action, i.e. the preventive deployment of international forces with the express purpose of forestalling horizontal escalation of conflict with its neighbouring countries. Recent developments also highlight the mutual dependence of the internal conflicts in Kosovo and Macedonia.

UNPREDEP in Macedonia

It has been often pointed out that an early preventive deployment of multilateral forces is one of the most cost-effective measures to stop the spread of violence and instability. Preventive deployment requires a more active role for international organizations and coordination among the great powers. Peacekeepers must also establish a stable and secure environment to create conditions for a lasting peace. Gareth Evans, now with the International Crisis Group and previously a long-time Foreign Minister of Australia, was an early advocate of preventive deployment. He emphasized that, to be successful, the international presence must be more than symbolic, it must have a specific mandate based on the host-country consent, this mandate must be embedded in a more comprehensive preventive strategy, and the goals of deployment must be clearly defined.[9]

Preventive deployment and national security

The purpose of preventive deployment is to curtail the spread of violence, especially horizontal escalation, but it can also have other functions, especially to provide humanitarian assistance, to help solve local conflicts, and to create preconditions for the maintenance of public order and political stability in a vulnerable country. The politics of internal stabilization may also help external aspects of prevention to succeed by reducing the risk that a violent conflict in a neighbouring country will spread across the border. Such horizontal escalation can be due either to strategic moves made by an external or internal actor, or inadvertent contagion through ethnic, political, or other links (see Jentleson, this volume).

The deployment of UN troops in Macedonia has been construed as a paradigmatic case of successful preventive deployment.[10] The United Nations Preventive Deployment Force (UNPREDEP) was comprised mainly of Finnish and US troops and smaller contingents from other Nordic countries and Indonesia. The Nordic forces formed a composite battalion (NORDBAT) and the task of Force Commander rotated among them. The troops were deployed from 1992–99 to forestall the use of force by Macedonia's neighbours and to stabilize the internal conditions of the country. The force may also have had a reverse function to prevent any Albanian-Macedonian involvement in Kosovo.[11] The potentially troublesome neighbours were Albania, Bulgaria, Greece, and Serbia which all could, in different ways, have threatened Macedonia's security or destabilized it internally. The reasons for their actions could have been historical, ethnic, and territorial.

Preventive deployment was initiated under UN Security Council Resolution 795 as the local command of UNPROFOR in December 1992, at the request of Macedonia's president, Kiro Gligorov. Gligorov's main objectives were to legitimize Macedonia's sovereignty and to assure its internal stability in the face of potential external pressures. In Macedonia, UNPROFOR had been preceded by an OSCE monitoring mission ("Spill-Over Mission") in September 1992 to alleviate ethnic tensions in the country and to prevent clashes between Serbia and Macedonia over their poorly demarcated joint border.[12]

In June 1993, the United States decided to send, on the basis of Security Council authorization (Res. 842), its troops to Macedonia as a part of the UNPROFOR mission. The move was a part of the policy by the Clinton administration to prevent, by its presence, the spread of the war in Bosnia to other parts of Southeast Europe. In March 1995, the Macedonian component of UNPROFOR was converted into UNPREDEP.[13]

UNPREDEP operated in three areas: political, military, and socioeconomic. The political pillar included reconciliation and mediation between the Macedonian and Albanian communities, the military pillar rested on the deployment of international troops at the northern and western borders of the country, and the socio-economic pillar was intended to assist the local communities. During its lifetime, UNPREDEP monitored Macedonia's 240-kilometre long border with Serbia and 182-kilometre long border with Albania. UNPREDEP succeeded in demarcating a *de facto* border between Serbia and Macedonia by defining its observation posts along the so-called Northern Limit Line.[14]

The success of UNPREDEP seems to have been due to its comprehensive, yet clear and flexible mandate. Success also depended on the right timing and good conduct of the operation. It is difficult to find any major fault in the operation itself, partly because the number of troop-sending countries was small and their political and bureaucratic cultures quite similar.

UNPREDEP's operation was helped by local consent and a sense of political ownership that developed in Macedonia. Macedonia's government had requested the troops in the first place both as an assurance against external threats and as a sign of Western support for its sovereign status. The US presence in particular was seen in Skopje to contain a promise to include Macedonia in Western institutions, which would avoid the marginalization of the new country's international position. In fact, the United States recognized Macedonia in 1994 and in the following year the country became a member of NATO's Partnership for Peace. However, the United States and NATO did not approach Macedonia only for altruistic reasons. As the crisis in Kosovo started to re-escalate in 1998, Macedonia (and Albania) became a base for NATO forces (the Extraction Force).[15] Some analysts consider NATO deployments in Macedonia, and in Albania, to have been crucial for NATO's Kosovo strategy.[16]

For their part, Macedonians were concerned about some domestic aspects of UNPREDEP's operations, especially the role of the civilian police, which the majority feared would favour the Albanian minority. The concerns over sovereignty did not hamper the government, however, from inviting on several occasions the presence of NATO forces, obviously to strengthen political relations with the West. However, the alliance turned down these suggestions until after UNPREDEP's dissolution when there was no other option to exercise its influence. It seems that the Albanians were somewhat more apprehensive of UNPREDEP than the titular Macedonians, but they were even more critical of the possibility of NATO forces arriving in the country.[17]

The meticulous study on UNPREDEP by Brad Thayer concluded that by July 1997 the total costs of conflict prevention in Macedonia had amounted to US$255 million. On the other hand, the costs of an intermediate two-year conflict were estimated by him at US$15 billion and those of a large one-year conflict at US$143.94 (sic!) billion.[18] The inevitable conclusion to be drawn from these figures is that preventive deployment in Macedonia was relatively inexpensive.

Obviously, the validity of this counterfactual reasoning depends critically on the threat scenarios used as the basis of the estimates. In other words, in estimating the costs of a potential war as an alternative to successful preventive action, the probability of war must be considered. In general, one should keep in mind that this kind of application of counterfactual reasoning is primarily an actuarial exercise rather than a policy analysis. In a true counterfactual analysis, one should specify the connecting principles of antecedents (preventive action or the lack of it) and consequences (peace or war) and ensure that they are theoretically, logically, and empirically consistent.[19] Thayer concludes that the risk of the Serbian attack on Macedonia was rather low and he seems to be right in this.[20] On the other hand, he seems to overestimate the military threat from Greece where the tough line towards Macedonia reflected mostly the victory of one domestic political faction over another; both of them cutting, to some extent, across the traditional party lines.[21] Moreover, it is clear that NATO and the European Union would never have permitted Greece, their member state, to use military force against Macedonia. This is evidenced by the critical international reaction to the trade embargo that Greece imposed on Macedonia in February 1994. In fact, the Greek intervention into Macedonia would have jeopardized the entire Western strategy in the region and would have hence been averted. Thayer should also have taken into account the fact that a transnational crisis involving ethnic Albanians in Macedonia would have required the outbreak of a larger war in the region. In other words, a major crisis involving Macedonia could hardly have started as an isolated, bilateral event with Albania, Bulgaria, Greece, or Serbia.[22]

Thayer's assessment of the risk of instability due to the position of the Albanian minority in Macedonia and its links with the ethnic brethren in Albania and Kosovo is clearly on the right track. The simmering war in Kosovo and the decline of Albania into political and economic turmoil

have posed direct threats to Macedonia's stability and even its independence.[23] The perceived threat of Kosovo Albanians mounting an attack
on Macedonia became a reality in 2001 when a splinter group of the
UCK/KLA made military inroads to the Tanusevci region, prompting the
Macedonian army and police to respond by a counterattack. NATO and
the EU have refused to become militarily engaged in the prevention of
the escalation of the dispute, but especially the EU member states have
lent strong political support to the Macedonian government, urging it at
the same time to undertake major reforms to improve the social position
and political rights of the Albanian minority in the country.

The Kosovar attack on Macedonia showed that they do not harbour
resentment only against the Serbs, but that some of them are also ready
to act on behalf of their brethren in Macedonia. This threat has created a
tacit but unconsummated alliance between the Serbs and the titular
Macedonians, although they are obviously at odds in many other issues.
On the other hand, the crisis in March 2001 showed in a positive way that
the Albanian government is opposed to the destabilization of Macedonia
from outside. In addition, the two Albanian parties in Macedonia's government have asked its supporters to be calm and continue work for social
and political reforms by peaceful means.

Preventive deployment and deterrence

The establishment and impact of UNPREDEP can obviously be interpreted from different theoretical vantage points. One possibility is to
consider it a form of expanded peacekeeping, which does not only aim to
separate the adversaries from each other, but also pays attention to conflict resolution, reconciliation, and social welfare. Along these lines, Clive
Archer has suggested that the Nordic contribution to UNPREDEP reflected their liberal-institutional policies of curtailing and controlling
intra- and international conflict. Instead of balance of power, the Nordics
pursued a community-building effort.[24]

However, for long-term conflict prevention and peacebuilding to succeed, innovation, flexibility, and pragmatism rather than specific political
principles are required.[25] This criticism may not apply, however, to the
Macedonian case, as liberal peace building had some success there. If we
are to identify a reason for UNPREDEP's success, attention must be
given to other factors, especially the link with the United States and the
prevention of domestic and transnational ethnic instability. The former
issue harks back to conventional military deterrence and the latter to the
separation of the internal and external aspects of the crisis from each
other. Each is considered in turn.

The presence of US forces had considerable influence on the success of UNPREDEP as they created a trip wire leading to Washington. The US contingent sent, in effect, the political message that if Serbian or Albanian forces tried to violate the territorial integrity of Macedonia, the action would have serious political and possibly military consequences. In so doing, UNPREDEP was linked to Western policy in Bosnia, which tried to prevent Serbia from escalating the war to new theatres. The West wanted to deal with the war in Bosnia separately from any other potential military confrontation in the region (as any territorial expansion of the war would have brought about untold consequences). Milosevic understood Western preferences well and used that knowledge skilfully to construct his own policy, especially in Kosovo, but this required that he left Macedonia alone.

Partly for this reason, the political linkage between preventive action in Macedonia and Bosnia (where it largely failed until August 1995) was never extended to Kosovo. There, Belgrade, stressing Kosovo's internal sovereignty, had a rather free hand. The main reason for the differential treatment seems simply to be that Bosnia and Macedonia were internationally recognized sovereign states, while Kosovo was not. In addition, Kosovo had a quite different historical and political meaning for Serbia.

The success in protecting Macedonia's borders was made easier by the fact that Greece and Serbia probably did not have any serious plans to attack it. I tend to agree with Michael Ignatieff that Slobodan Milosevic had divided in his mind the former Yugoslavia into three zones. The first zone consisted of Macedonia and Slovenia, which, having only a very tiny Serb minority, were let go without major confrontation. In the second zone, comprising Bosnia and Croatia, there were enough Serbs to be armed to grab land to be annexed to Greater Serbia. As is known, both of these campaigns failed badly and Milosevic blithely abandoned the Croatian and Bosnian Serbs when the military defeats of 1992 of 1995, respectively, became apparent. Finally, the third zone – including Serbia, Kosovo, and parts of Montenegro – is the Serb homeland where control would be defended to the bitter end.[26] If this geopolitical blueprint is correct, then the prevention of the Serbian (and Greek) attack did not require particular resolve. Yet, there was enough volatility in the region that an unexpected event or a major mistake could have led to the collapse of the house of cards and thus to violence.

During the war over Kosovo in spring 1999 such diffusion took place as refugees fled from Kosovo to Albania, Macedonia, and Montenegro to escape ethnic cleansing by the Milosevic government and the NATO bombing. Horizontal escalation was not manifested, however, in an armed attack across the borders (except for some Serbian raids to the Albanian border areas and, of course, the NATO bombing of Serbia). The political and military consequences of such non-military escalation are not any less real, though. In fact, it has been suggested that Milosevic used refugee flows from Kosovo to deliberately destabilize neighbouring countries, and to burden NATO's logistics.[27] In practice, non-military escalation requires different responses from those of a military invasion.

For now many ethnic Macedonians remain fearful of the creeping dominance of the Albanian minority, which accounts, according to various estimates, for 25–30 per cent of the total population. Local observers like to point out that Macedonian insecurity originates from the ethnic characteristics of the country. This claim suggests that the external and internal dimensions of Macedonia's security are closely intertwined. The ethnic Albanian factor (rather than the Serbian one) is the common denominator of these two dimensions of insecurity. The key political objective is the preservation of the newly independent country as a coherent Macedonian nation state. This objective is under fire from the Albanian minority and the political demands by Bulgaria and Greece (rather than Serbia).[28]

Against this backdrop, it is clear that for the ethnic Macedonians, the goal of preventive deployment was as much to keep the country internally coherent as to deter an external military attack against it. Yet, the risks involved in inter-ethnic relations seem to be exaggerated as the Macedonian and Albanian elites have on several occasions shared political power. These elites are pragmatic and calculate their costs and benefits of being a part of Macedonia rather than pushing single-mindedly for secession.[29] A central question is to what extent the cooperative inter-ethnic relations have been due to the balancing effects of Kiro Gligorov, who served as the President in 1991–99. Gligorov's personal stabilizing effect is indicated by the politicking in which the presidential election in the fall of 1999 became engulfed. These elections showed the depth of disagreement between the Macedonian parties in which the ethnic Albanian leaders became involved.[30] In general, the Macedonian case suggests that one cannot dismiss the domestic dimensions of preventive deployment as unimportant; on the contrary, their effective and balanced management is a key to successful prevention.[31]

Nevertheless, an important function of the UNPREDEP mission was to contribute to Macedonia's internal political stability. This goal was, in effect, consistent with the Western "grand strategy" in the region which aimed to reduce the risk of a regional conflagration that could draw Albania, Bulgaria, Greece, Serbia, Turkey, and, possibly, other countries into a mutual confrontation. The possibility of such a regional crisis continuously informed cautious Western decision makers.[32] A regional crisis would not just have produced problems for NATO, it would have had devastating regional and global consequences.

Thus, UNPREDEP reflected a number of mutually compatible and reinforcing goals. The Macedonian government tried to underpin this linkage of external and internal security by pursuing the policy of "equidistant" bilateral relations with its neighbours.[33] The purpose of this policy was to eliminate any reason that any neighbouring country would interfere in Macedonia's internal affairs. NATO's logistical need of Macedonia further underpinned the Western commitment. This approach could have become a mixed blessing. If prevention failed for any reason, the conflict in the region would escalate beyond what was experienced in the preceding five years.

Kosovo

A polarized and stalemated conflict

For the purposes of this volume, it is useful to contrast the cases of Macedonia and Kosovo. Until 1989 their positions within the Yugoslavian Federation were roughly similar. However, the abolition of Kosovo's autonomous status, in abrogation of the 1974 constitution, made it ineligible for the wave of diplomatic recognitions that swept the former Yugoslavia in 1991–92. Instead, Kosovo was considered by the international community to be a member of the rump Yugoslavian Federation and, thus, subject to Serbian domination. In practice, the respect for the principle of state sovereignty at the expense of national self-determination meant in Kosovo's case that the West undertook no far-reaching measures to contain Belgrade's policy of suppression, but was content to issue verbal warnings of limited practical consequence.

One of the reasons for the submissive policy was that the West and especially the United States needed Slobodan Milosevic in brokering the Dayton Agreement in 1995. Therefore, his grip on Kosovo was not challenged in any fundamental way; Milosevic's acquiescence in the outer zone of conflict bought him the control of the inner zone. On the one hand, had the West accepted the secession of the Kosovars from Serbia, and thus Kosovo's division, its policy to keep Bosnia united would have been vitiated. In such a situation, the likelihood that the Bosnian Serbs would join Serbia proper would have considerably increased. On the other hand, the neglect of Kosovo contributed heavily to the subsequent failure of the international prevention of violence there.[34]

The situation in Kosovo was more complicated that it appeared on the surface. On one level, Kosovars, in the early 1990s, were happy that the turmoil in other parts of Yugoslavia had mostly passed them by. However, this sullen satisfaction was shattered after the neglect of the Kosovo issue in Dayton; the ethnic Albanian society started to mobilize politically and then divided. Radical Kosovars demanded more. Others were unsure what to do. Over time, a firm line was drawn between political and military options to increase Kosovo's autonomy.[35]

Looking at the situation in 1998, it was clear that Macedonia's territorial integrity remained untouched. Despite inter-ethnic tensions, the country was relatively stable internally and the risk of external aggression was declining over time. By these standards, the preventive deployment in Macedonia to forestall the horizontal escalation of violence was an undeniable success. But, it was equally clear that in Kosovo the prevention of vertical escalation was rapidly failing; the Serbian military and police units were becoming more aggressive, partly as a response to the increasing violence by the units of the Kosovo Liberation Army (KLA or UCK if the Albanian acronym is used). Except for a brief period in summer 1998, the KLA was unable to extend its control outside the mountain areas. This left the urban population open to the repression of Serbian paramilitary forces. In September 1998, there were as many as 241,000 refugees or internally displaced persons (IDPs) in Kosovo. Moreover, the situation continued to deteriorate and the risk of a humanitarian crisis had become real.

By late 1998, Kosovo had become a deeply divided society in which the Albanian majority and the Serbian minority were organized in opposition. Even worse, both ethnic communities had fixed, stereotyped images of each other. The Serbs controlled the administrative and coercive organs of the state, while the Albanians had created, under Ibrahim Rugova, the leader of the Democratic League of Kosovo (LDK), a parallel society and a shadow state, complete with education and health care. While the parallel state structures uplifted the Kosovar morale and pointed a way to non-violent resistance, it was unable to create normal societal institutions. Moreover, the parallel state had hardly any control over the means of violence in the province. Ultimately, in the Albanian community, the struggle for power and money by Rugova and the KLA became increasingly clear.[36]

There was no remedy in sight to reconcile the Albanian and Serb communities in Kosovo. As a result, the province came to feature a "conflict between two fully mobilized, deeply divided, and completely segmented ethnic communities, with a potential for far higher – and more tragic – levels of violence." In such a situation, an integrationist approach, applicable in Macedonia, was impossible. Only a significant deal on power sharing between the parties could have prevented the outbreak of major violence in Kosovo.[37]

The recognition by third parties that power sharing, in conjunction with the return of autonomy to Kosovo, was the only feasible option to avoid large-scale violence prompted various efforts to pressure the Serbs and Kosovars to seek a compromise. For example, in late 1992 the Bush administration issued a stern warning to Belgrade to avoid the use of violence in Kosovo. In his letter to Milosevic, Bush went so far as to say that "in the event of conflict in Kosovo caused by Serbian action, the United States will be prepared to employ military force against the Serbs in Kosovo and in Serbia proper."[38] However, this ultimatum was not followed by any concrete commitments or follow-up action. In addition, the US policy on Kosovo remained badly coordinated between different agencies. Gradually, the Clinton administration came to accept tacitly that Kosovo was an internal Serb affair (as Chechnya was Russia's).[39]

Several NGOs, most notably the Italian Catholic Community of St. Egidio, tried to mediate between Belgrade and the Kosovars on cooperation in the fields of education and health care. Also other international NGOs, such as Search for Common Ground, tried to mediate between the Serbs and the Kosovars.[40] As late as 1996, St. Egidio was able to persuade Milosevic and Rugova to sign an education agreement that supported public Albanian schools. The agreement was not, however, adequate to lead to any breakthrough; incompatible political demands on status and power structure, and repression, remained the main facts of life in Kosovo. Belgrade's ability to control Kosovo militarily, albeit at a high cost, reduced its incentives to make any substantial concessions to the Albanian community there.

In sum, the conflict in Kosovo was polarized and stalemated. The constructive solution, power sharing, did not get much of a chance as neither Serbs nor radical Kosovars wanted it. Even fewer were the opportunities for the peaceful implementation of more radical solutions which included, theoretically, independence for Kosovo, merger with Albania, and the division of the province between the Serbs and the Albanians.[41] In reality, any solution in Kosovo required the structural transformation of the conflict. That transformation was, however, an unlikely development without a war and/or forcible external intervention.

In fact, the process of conflict transformation started with the strengthening of the KLA in 1997 and with its new-found ability to punish Serbian police forces. This change created a rift between the LDK's accommodating and peaceful policy on the one hand and the KLA's political and military radicalism on the other. The rift also meant that Western policy to encourage a compromise between LDK and the Milosevic regime on the basis of Kosovo's negotiated self-determination in the framework of the Yugoslavian federation had become largely irrelevant. Now the task had become preventing the further deterioration of the Kosovo situation.

The road to war

By summer 1998, the KLA had gained the capability to fight effectively against the Serb forces and to capture control of mountainous parts of Kosovo. The military success of the KLA, however limited, emboldened its leaders politically and its popularity increased at the expense of Rugova's non-violent strategy.[42] Originally, Belgrade had tolerated Rugova and his campaign as he served Serbia's primary interest: to keep Kosovo stable enough to allow Serb forces to go after radical opposition to the Serbian rule.[43] However, by 1998, the situation on the ground had changed so fundamentally that Rugova could not, from the Serbian point of view, deliver stability any more; therefore, more forceful measures were needed.

As a result, the conflict in Kosovo moved to a more intense level in which military attacks followed each other. This created a new and more serious risk of escalation to which the international community had to react. As early as 1992–93, the OSCE had sent a long-term mission to Kosovo (and Sandjak and Vojvodina as well) to monitor the conflict there, but it was recalled after the suspension of Yugoslav's membership of the OSCE.[44]

In 1998, several international organizations sprang into action to prevent the further escalation of violence. Members of the Contact Group, a concert of major powers and international organizations, were in constant consultation and tried to arrange diplomatic mediation between the parties. Since fall 1997, the Contact Group had issued statements in which parties were warned not to escalate the conflict further. The main reason for the Western reliance on the Contact Group was the political need to keep Russia on board. This arrangement slowed and narrowed the search for viable Western options. Milosevic sought to exploit this weakness. For example, in June 1998, Milosevic visited Moscow and was able to extract a commitment from Russia. He was told that Kosovo was Yugoslavia's internal affair which made both its independence and the multilateral use of military force against Belgrade impossible.[45]

For its part the Contact Group yielded few solutions and none better than previous efforts at power sharing. To add insult to injury, Milosevic refused to meet the designated mediator, the former Spanish Prime Minister, Felipe Gonzalez. Instead of providing comprehensive and effective diplomatic services, the Contact Group increasingly focused on keeping Russia on board in an effort to block an informal Russo-Serb alliance.[46]

The need to accommodate Russia required rejection of the option to intervene militarily, as Moscow was unprepared to accept such a move. As a result, the work of the Contact Group became increasingly complicated, as some consultations were open only to Western members, while others involved bridge building with Russia. This approach was further complicated by the belief that it had to strengthen Rugova's political position rather than support the KLA as this was believed to be the only avenue for a compromise with Belgrade.[47]

Similar reasoning dominated the UN Security Council, which, in March 1998, imposed an arms embargo on both parties to the crisis (Res. 1160). The embargo had only a very limited effect as Serbia had plenty of weapons in its possession and the KLA could obtain them through the porous border with Albania. In response, the Security Council condemned the growing repression of the civilian populations and demanded that the parties stop the violence. It did not go further than that, however, as Russia was unwilling to agree on any enforcement actions against Serbia. In June 1998, NATO took a different turn and started preparing for military action by organizing military manoeuvres in Albania and mobilizing its aircraft in the area. Various military options were prepared by NATO to prevent the increasing use of force by the Milosevic regime in Kosovo.[48]

Thus, the use of force against Serbia was becoming an inevitable move, as no other preventive measures seemed to work. Preparations faced political difficulties, though; in addition to Russian resistance and hesitation among the members of NATO, there was genuine concern that a military operation could end up strengthening the KLA's hand. Diplomacy was given one more chance when Richard Holbrooke, armed by a NATO "activation order" and an ultimatum on the use of military force, started yet another round of discussions with Milosevic. In October 1998, the two parties struck a bilateral deal in which they agreed on a cease-fire and a cutback in the size of Serbian army and police units in Kosovo. To monitor the implementation of these provisions, the OSCE was asked to send 2,000 unarmed monitors to the province (although, in reality, the number of monitors never exceeded 1,400).[49] The Holbrooke-Milosevic cease-fire agreement was essentially a holding operation which few expected to produce permanent results.

In hindsight, it has been argued that the agreement was fundamentally flawed in nature. Its provisions were deemed inadequate and lacked a credible means of enforcement, a result of the fact that armed (NATO) units were barred from Kosovo. The reliance on OSCE observers and their vulnerability to Serbian countermeasures emasculated NATO's options as its military moves would have jeopardized the security of observation teams (as had happened in Bosnia in 1994–95). Equally serious, the agreement did not provide the means to contain the KLA (a non-signatory). In sum, "not only was there no way to punish Serb noncompliance, there was also no way to prevent the KLA from exploiting Serb compliance and provoking a possibly violent Serb retort."[50]

Once the failure of the Holbrooke-Milosevic agreement became obvious by early 1999, the Contact Group once again entered centre stage.

Threatening military strikes in the case of non-compliance, the Contact Group's Western members pushed Serbia to make concessions to the Kosovars. These concessions were expected to be ratified in the talks held in February–March 1999 at the Rambouillet castle in France. To a large extent, the shift to a harder-line policy towards Belgrade reflected the victory of Madeleine Albright in Washington's inter-agency battles. Albright's hand in these battles was further strengthened by the massacre in Racak in January 1999 when over 40 people, practically all civilians, were killed by the Serb paramilitary troops.

The original purpose of the Rambouillet talks was to create confidence among the belligerents. For example, there would be continuing recognition of Serbia's sovereignty over the province for an interim period of three years, after which a referendum would be held on the future status of Kosovo. By taking the Serbian yoke off the back of the Kosovars, these measures were expected to reduce the popularity of the KLA and perhaps create an opportunity to disarm it. The Rambouillet conference was the first genuine recognition of the fact that peace in Kosovo was impossible without the involvement of the KLA.

From Belgrade's perspective, the draft Rambouillet Accord included demands that were unpalatable to the Serbs. After initial passivity, they rewrote in the conference most of the key provisions. In addition to challenging the need for a referendum after three years on Kosovo's independence, Belgrade was strongly opposed to the deployment of NATO forces on Yugoslav territory. No doubt Milosevic resented the strong arm tactics of NATO. He was deeply critical of some asymmetric provisions in the accord and refused to sign. In hindsight it is doubtful whether it would have been, under any conditions, possible to pressure Belgrade to accept the main provisions of the Rambouillet agreement. Belgrade was committed to continue its control of Kosovo, and it did not expect Russia and the NATO allies to give consent to any major military operations by the United States against Serb forces there.[51]

Realizing that major concessions in the Kosovo issue would probably result in his undoing at home, Milosevic started to prepare a large-scale military operation to suppress the KLA and to eliminate other strata within the Albanian leadership. The ultimate aim was to weaken Kosovar society to such an extent that Serb control could be restored. Preparations for the operation coincided with Belgrade's refusal to support the Rambouillet accord. Milosevic adopted a defiant posture signalling his commitment to defend Serbia's national interests. When the KLA agreed, after strong US pressure, to the main points regarding a political framework in the accord, this gave Western leaders a chance to identify Milosevic as the party responsible for torpedoing the peace process. When the NATO bombing began on 25 March, the aim was to convince Milosevic to give up after some surgical strikes; few people expected the war to last until 3 June 1999.

Why did coercive diplomacy fail to prevent the outbreak of violence in Kosovo? To answer this question it is necessary to examine preventive action designed to deter widespread conflict in Kosovo as well as preventive action during the crisis stage when violence had already broken out and the goal was to compel Milosevic's withdrawal from Kosovo. The main reason for the failure of pre-conflict deterrence was the unwavering commitment by Belgrade to keep Kosovo both legally and militarily under Serbian control. Political appeals, economic sanctions, and military threats were not enough to convince Milosevic and his supporters of the wisdom of concessions. Kosovo belonged historically and metaphorically to Serbia's inner core.

From the Western perspective, to take it from Serbia would have required heavily arming the KLA and NATO, starting a major ground war against the Serbian forces in Kosovo. In reality, there was, in NATO, only very limited interest in either of these policy options. After all, Milosevic was half-right in that NATO was not prepared to use ground forces to challenge Serbia's territorial control of Kosovo. For its part, some within NATO believed that a short bombing, as a signal of political resolve, would produce a quick diplomatic victory.[52] Over the long run, Belgrade expected the unity of NATO to crumble (and perhaps Russia to come to its rescue). The likely consequence would, then, have been a compromise along the lines of the Holbrooke-Milosevic agreement of October 1998. In such a scenario, the United Nations or the OSCE would have established a thin presence in Kosovo which would remain under Serbia's sovereign control. A NATO presence would require ground forces, especially from the United States, although a political agreement to send them could have been a hard sell in Washington.[53]

To recapitulate, the recalcitrance of the Milosevic government, the headstrong policies of the KLA, and deep divisions in Kosovo society rendered preventive strategies practically ineffective. Milosevic had few incentives to change his mind and much to lose. I think that Michael Ignatieff is right in stressing that Belgrade (and NATO) miscalculated the situation; Milosevic doubted NATO's political resolve to act decisively, while Washington could not believe that he was foolish enough to submit Serbia to the devastation of sustained aerial bombing.[54] In retrospect an effective strategy should have involved an earlier and more decisive political and military commitment to the region. Military pressure on Belgrade should have been applied at the turning points of the negotiations to remove any doubt that NATO was very serious.[55]

However, the nature of multilateral decision making and political divisions within NATO, and even more so within the Contact Group, made the pursuit of such a policy difficult. Ultimately, the failure of preventive diplomacy, and continuing ethnic cleansing in Kosovo, stiffened, in the absence of other options, NATO's resolve and permitted the use of extensive military force. This resolve came too late, though, to convince Milosevic to capitulate. Perhaps he would not have been ready for a compromise under any circumstances; or rather on one condition only – that for Milosevic, the alternative to concessions would have been the loss of power at home. It is ironic that in March 1999, Milosevic was convinced that a conflict with NATO would prop up his standing as the indispensable leader of the Serbian nation. Since October 2000 history has proved otherwise.

Conclusion: Success and failure?

Preventive deployment is intended primarily to deter external attacks and, secondarily, promote internal stability in the host country. There is no dispute that the policy succeeded in Macedonia after 1992. The only debate concerns the degree of and reasons for success; i.e. whether there were real external security threats and risks of internal stability in Macedonia, which the deployment helped to avert, or whether they were so limited that other policies would have produced similar results. In addition, one has to ask why the measures taken produced, more or less, the expected results.

My judgement is that the main reasons for success included the consistent nature of UN policies which were carried out by multinational, especially Nordic, troops that were well trained and equipped for such a mission (including conflict resolution tasks). On the one hand, for the US troops in Macedonia, force protection was too dominant an objective to make their operations versatile enough. On the other hand, they served larger political purposes, convincing the Macedonian government that its sovereignty had Western support and, by creating a tripwire, deterred any efforts by external powers to attack the country. At the time, deterrence was perhaps not too demanding as few neighbours had serious plans to violate Macedonia's sovereignty. Therefore, it is open to debate whether Macedonia can be used as a critical case to demonstrate the value of preventive deployment. It seems that the most serious threat was, after all, the risks of cross-border spill-over from neighbouring areas, especially Kosovo, and the ensuing domestic instability in Macedonia. As these risks did not materialize in any significant way during UNPREDEP's deployment, this may be reason enough to conclude that in this particular case preventive deployment was a wise policy.

Unfortunately the early success of preventive deployment in Macedonia was reversed as a result of the war in Kosovo and its aftermath. As has been shown above, there were various efforts since 1992 to prevent the escalation of violence and a humanitarian crisis in Kosovo, but the measures taken were never very decisive and coordinated. The failure to push through a political settlement on autonomy and power sharing after the Dayton accord in 1995 was a missed opportunity for long-term preventive action. Of course, such a settlement would have been difficult to accomplish and it might have cost Milosevic's support in Bosnia, but it could have, on the other hand, stemmed the vertical escalation of violence in Kosovo.

It seems that the chances of preventive diplomacy in Kosovo ran out by late 1997 or so. After that, decisive international support for the non-violent Kosovar struggle for greater autonomy against the Serbian harassment would have been necessary to win the support of KLA moderates and to dampen down the violence. The subsequent political and military mobilization of the KLA diminished the prospects of a peaceful solution between Kosovo and Serbia (see Jentleson, this volume, on coercive diplomacy).[56]

There are those who argue that external intervention to prevent the outbreak of war or mitigate its horizontal or vertical escalation is counterproductive. This is because prevention, and peacekeeping, easily freeze the conflict without resolving it. Therefore, it is better to let the parties fight the war and create, in that way, a new distribution of power. This Darwinistic advice has been offered both as a general remedy and as an argument in the debate about the crisis in Kosovo. Thus, Edward Luttwak wonders "whether the Kosovars would have been better off had NATO simply done nothing."[57] Such views underestimate, however, the severity of the humanitarian crisis in Kosovo and overestimate the possibility of creating a new political reality by the force of arms in situations like Kosovo. A much more likely alternative in Kosovo would have been a protracted and deadly civil war in which neither side would have emerged as an undisputed military winner. External intervention can be justified, despite the costs, by the human lives saved.

It is useful to remember that intensification of the linkage between vertical escalation in Kosovo and the horizontal spread of the conflict to Macedonia coincided with the departure of UN forces from the country and their replacement by NATO troops. It should be noted that NATO troops in Macedonia served a larger logistical purpose in the region and were not there primarily for the purpose of preventive deployment. However, the deterrent effect of the preventive deployment may have continued to function in Macedonia even after 1999, as its borders were not violated in any major way by the Serbian forces.

A bigger risk was the potential vertical escalation of ethnic tensions in the country as a consequence of the huge inflow of Albanian refugees that continued to pour into Macedonia, Montenegro, and Albania. These flows were thought to tilt the ethnic balance irreparably in favour of the Albanians. In Macedonia, fears were further fuelled by worsening socio-economic conditions for which much of the blame was put on the refugees.[58] Despite these concerns, there were no signs that ethnic Albanian leaders either from Kosovo or Macedonia tried to benefit politically from the refugee problem. The situation in Kosovo was grave enough to warrant such tactical ploys, which would have undoubtedly failed and worsened the humanitarian crisis further.

To conclude, the ability to incorporate the lessons learned from Macedonia and Kosovo will have a direct impact on the probability of success in other regions and to some degree by other organizations in other parts of the world. In order to establish a strong and credible preventive response it is first necessary to respond to protect ordinary citizens and to control the escalation of violence. Macedonia was an important test case in this regard. If Kosovo showed how a failure to develop credible and consistent response to conflict can lead to even more conflict, then Macedonia shows how organizations need to establish and maintain a stable and long-term deterrent threat to prevent potential vertical and horizontal escalation.

Notes

1. Richard Rosecrance and Peter Schott, "Concerts and Regional Intervention," in David A. Lake and Patrick M. Morgan, eds., *Regional Orders: Building Security in a New World*, University Park, PA: The Pennsylvania State University Press, 1997, pp. 155–6.
2. For a useful discussion and definition of escalation, see Richard Smoke, *War: Controlling Escalation*, Cambridge, MA: Harvard University Press, 1977.
3. For related reflections see Thomas G. Weiss and Jarat Chopra, "Sovereignty Under Siege: From Intervention to Humanitarian Space," in Gene M. Lyons and Michael Mastanduno, eds., *Beyond Westphalia? State Sovereignty and International Intervention*, Baltimore: Johns Hopkins University Press, 1995, pp. 87–114.
4. These two approaches are discussed in greater detail by Michael S. Lund, *Preventing Violent Conflicts: A Strategy for Preventive Diplomacy*, Washington, D.C.: U.S. Institute of Peace Press, 1996; Jentleson, this volume, and Peter Wallensteen, "Preventive Security: Direct and Structural Prevention of Violent Conflicts," in Peter Wallensteen, ed., *Preventing Violent Conflicts: Past Record and Future Challenges*, Uppsala: Department of Peace and Conflict Research, Uppsala University, 1998, Report No. 48, pp. 9–38.
5. I have developed these points in more detail in Raimo Väyrynen, "The Failure of Preventive Action in Yugoslavia," *International Peacekeeping*, Vol. 3, No. 4, 1997, pp. 21–42; and Raimo Väyrynen, "Toward Effective Conflict Prevention: A Comparison of Different Instruments," *International Journal of Peace Studies*, Vol. 2, No. 1, 1997, pp. 1–18. The need to combine sanctions and incentives to reach desired goals has been stressed

by David Cortright, "Incentives and Cooperation in International Affairs," in David Cortright, ed., *The Price of Peace, Incentives and International Conflict Prevention*, Lanham, MD: Rowman and Littlefield, 1997, pp. 3–20.

6. Alexander L. George, "Strategies for Preventive Diplomacy and Conflict Resolution. Scholarship for Policy-Making," *Cooperation and Conflict*, Vol. 34, No. 1, 1999, pp. 12–13 (emphases in the original). For an empirical study along the same lines, see Peter Viggo Jakobsen, *Western Use of Coercive Diplomacy after the Cold War: A Challenge for Theory and Practice*, London: Macmillan, 1998.

7. Michael E. Brown and Richard N. Rosecrance, eds., *The Costs of Conflict: Prevention and Cure in the Global Arena*, Lanham, MD: Rowman and Littlefield, 1999.

8. This point is elaborated in Raimo Väyrynen, "Preventing Deadly Conflicts: Failures in Iraq and Yugoslavia," *Global Society*, Vol. 14, No. 1, 2000, pp. 5–33.

9. Gareth Evans, *Cooperating for Peace. The Global Agenda for the 1990s and Beyond*, St. Leonards, Australia: Allen and Unwin, 1993, pp. 81–5.

10. UNPREDEP as a positive example of preventive deployment has been stressed, in particular, by Alice Ackermann, *Make Peace Prevail. Preventing Violent Conflict in Macedonia*, Syracuse, NY: Syracuse University Press, 2000. In a study conducted in 1997, Macedonian public opinion evaluated UNPREDEP positively, although a large share of the respondents did not have any specific opinion on the matter. The UN operation was deemed largely a success and there was only limited interest in bringing in NATO and Russian troops. One-fifth of the respondents wanted to broaden the present mission more to economic and social areas, while another one-fifth was in favour of its termination. See Lidija Georgieva, "Preventive Deployment: Missing Link between Conflict Prevention and Peacebuilding," paper prepared for the 40th Annual Convention of the International Studies Association, Washington, D.C., 16–20 February 1999.

11. For a detailed study of various strategies of conflict prevention and an assessment of their outcomes in Macedonia, see Janie Leatherman, "Preventing Conflict in Macedonia: A Lasting Peace or a Line in the Sand," in Janie Leatherman, William DeMars, Patrick Gaffney and Raimo Väyrynen, *Breaking the Cycles of Violence: Conflict Prevention in Intrastate Crises*, West Hartford, CT: Kumarian Press, 1999, pp. 149–78.

12. On the OSCE mission, see Ackermann, note 13 above, pp. 134–9, Carsten Giersch, *Konfliktregulierung in Jugoslawien 1991–1995: Die Rolle von OSZE, EU, UNO und NATO*, Baden-Baden: Nomos Verlag, 1998, pp. 96–100; and Berthold Meyer, "In der Endsschleife? Die OSZE-Langzeitsmissionen auf dem Prüfstand," *HSFK-Report 3, 1998*, Frankfurt am Main: Hessische Stiftung Friedens- und Konfliktforschung, 1998, pp. 9–11. The existence of two separate missions on the Macedonian soil alone could not but mean that the tasks of the UN preventive deployment and the OSCE monitoring overlapped to some degree and resulted in mutual tensions. The problems were resolved in April 1993 by an Agreement on the Principles of Coordination between the UN and the OSCE.

13. Thereafter, its mandate was renewed several times for longer or shorter periods, and the forces were also occasionally restructured. The mission ended abruptly in February 1999 because of China's Security Council veto on its renewal. The use of the veto resulted from the politically short-sighted exchange of Macedonia's security and stability for US$1.8 billion from Taiwan (which helped to line the pockets of a few individuals in Skopje) in return for Skopje's diplomatic recognition of Taipei.

14. Giersch, *ibid.*, pp. 241–3. For a detailed study of UNPREDEP and its operations in Macedonia, see Abiodun Williams, *Preventing War: The United Nations in Macedonia*, Lanham, MD: Rowman and Littlefield, 2000.

15. Stefan Troebst, "Feuertaufe – Der Kosovo-Krieg und die Republik Macedonien," in Jens Reuter and Konrad Clewing, eds., *Der Kosovo Konflikt: Ursachen – Verlauf – Perspektiven*, Klagenfurt: Wieser Verlag, 2000, pp. 239–40.

16. Ivo H. Daalder and Michael E. O'Hanlon, *Winning Ugly: NATO's War to Save Kosovo*, Washington, D.C.: Brookings Institution Press, 2000, p. 5.

17. For assessments of UNPREDEP and its operations, see Sophia Clément, "Former Yugoslav Macedonia, the Regional Setting and European Security: Towards Balkan Stability?," in James Pettifer, ed., *The New Macedonian Question*, London: Macmillan, 1999, pp. 285–302; and Biljana Vankovska-Cvetkovska, "UNPREDEP in Macedonia. New Approach to the Concept of Modern Diplomacy," paper prepared for the 39th Annual Convention of the International Studies Association, Minneapolis, 17–21 March 1998, pp. 10–14.

18. Bradley Thayer, "Macedonia," in Brown and Rosecrance, eds., *The Costs of Conflict: Prevention and Cure in the Global Arena*, note 7 above, pp. 131–45.

19. Philip E. Tetlock and Aaron Belkin, "Counterfactual Thought Experiments in World Politics. Logical, Methodological, and Psychological Perspectives," in Philip E. Tetlock and Aaron Belkin, eds., *Counterfactual Thought Experiments in World Politics: Logical, Methodological, and Psychological Perspectives*, Princeton, NJ: Princeton University Press, 1996, pp. 3–38.

20. This stance can be explained by the fact that the Serbs in Macedonia accounted for only 2 per cent of the total population that harboured resentments against the Serbian domination before the break-up of Yugoslavia. Therefore, Macedonia would have been a hard bite for Serbia to digest as it was already overextended in Croatia and Bosnia; see Stefan Troebst, "An Ethnic War that Did Not Take Place: Macedonia, Its Minorities and Its Neighbours in the 1990s," in David Turton, ed., *War and Ethnicity. Global Connections and Local Violence*, Rochester, NY: University of Rochester Press, 1997, pp. 82–4. The Serbs thought, on the other hand, that Macedonia was not a viable state and it would in any case become a satellite of Serbia. As the flawed privatization process in Macedonia benefited some Serbian entrepreneurs and as it could be used as a conduit for smuggling, there was no material reason to kill the "milking cow;" see Nina Dobrkovi, "Yugoslavia and Macedonia in the Years 1991–6: From Brotherhood to Neighbourhood," in James Pettifer, ed., *The New Macedonian Question*, note 17 above, pp. 88–90.

21. For a detailed analysis, see Evangelos Kofos, "Greek Policy Considerations over FYROM Independence and Recognition," in James Pettifer, ed., *ibid.*, pp. 226–67.

22. For the threat estimates discussed above, see Thayer, "Macedonia," note 18 above, pp. 132–7.

23. The crisis in Albania and its national and regional consequences are well analysed by Daniel Vaughan-Whitehead, *Albania in Crisis: The Predictable Fall of the Shining Star*, Cheltenham, UK: Edward Elgar, 1999.

24. Clive Archer, "Conflict Prevention in Europe: The Case of Nordic States and Macedonia," *Cooperation and Conflict*, Vol. 29, No. 4, 1994, pp. 376–8.

25. This kind of criticism is developed by Roland Paris, "Peacebuilding and the Limits of Liberal Internationalism," *International Security*, Vol. 22, No. 2, 1997, pp. 54–89.

26. Michael Ignatieff, "Balkan Physics," *The New Yorker*, 10 May 1999, pp. 74–5. The article has been republished in Michael Ignatieff, *Virtual War: Kosovo and Beyond*, New York: Henry Holt, 2000, pp. 49–50.

27. Ignatieff, "Balkan Physics," p. 41 and Timothy Garton Ash, *History of the Present: Essays, Sketches, and Dispatches from Europe in the 1990s*, New York, Random House, 2000, p. 329.

28. Bilyana Vankovska-Cvetkovska, "Between Preventive Diplomacy and Conflict Resolution: The Macedonian Perspective of the Kosovo Crisis," paper prepared for the 40th Annual Convention of the International Studies Association, Washington, D.C., 16–20 February 1999.

29. Troebst, "An Ethnic War that Did Not Take Place," note 20 above, pp. 88–92; and *Unfinished Peace: Report of the International Commission on the Balkans*, Washington,

D.C.: Carnegie Endowment for International Peace/The Brookings Institution Press, 1996, pp. 127–30.

30. On the other hand, it has been pointed out that the real political conflict is as much between the leading Macedonian parties (SDSM and VMRO) as the Albanian minority and Macedonian majority. See Troebst, "Feuertaufe – Der Kosovo-Krieg und die Republik Macedonien," note 15 above, pp. 242–3.

31. On the domestic politics of preventive deployment in Macedonia, see Ackermann, *Making Peace Prevail*, note 10 above, pp. 76–100.

32. David Owen, *Balkan Odyssey*, New York: Harcourt Brace and Co., 1995, pp. 11–12.

33. Clément, "Former Yugoslav Macedonia, the Regional Setting and European Security," note 17 above, p. 287.

34. Hugh Miall, "Kosovo in Crisis: Conflict Prevention and Intervention in the Southern Balkans," *Peace and Security* (Vienna), Vol. 30, No. 2, 1998, pp. 9–10.

35. Tim Judah, *Kosovo: War and Revenge*, New Haven, CT: Yale University Press 2000, pp. 91–98.

36. Tim Judah, "Inside the KLA," *The New York Review of Books*, Vol. 46, No. 10, 1999, pp. 19–23; and Ariane Barth *et al.*, "Sprache der Morde," *Der Spiegel*, 2 August 1999, pp. 42–59. On the parallel society in Kosovo, see Denisa Kostovicova, "Kosovo's Parallel Society: The Successes and Failures of Nonviolence," in William Joseph Buckley, ed., *Kosovo: Contending Voices on Balkan Interventions*, Grand Rapids, MI: William B. Eerdmans Publishing Co., 2000, pp. 142–8.

37. Steven L. Burg, "Nationalism and Civic Identity: Ethnic Models for Macedonia and Kosovo," in Barnett R. Rubin, ed., *Cases and Strategies for Preventive Action*, New York: The Century Foundation Press, 1998, pp. 23–45 (the quotation is on p. 38); and Alexis Heraclides, "The Kosovo Conflict and Its Resolution: In Pursuit of Ariadne's Thread," *Security Dialogue*, Vol. 28, No. 3, 1997, pp. 325–6.

38. Daalder and O'Hanlon, *Winning Ugly*, note 16 above, pp. 9–10.

39. Susan L. Woodward, *Balkan Tragedy: Chaos and Dissolution after the Cold War*, Washington, D.C.: The Brookings Institution, 1995, pp. 398–9.

40. On the role of international NGOs in Macedonia, see Ackermann, *Making Peace Prevail*, note 14 above, pp. 147–61.

41. On these solutions, see Heraclides, "The Kosovo Conflict and Its Resolution," note 37 above, pp. 326–7. John J. Mearsheimer and Stephen van Evera have consistently argued for the partitioning of conflict-ridden countries. On their case for Kosovo's partitioning, see Mearsheimer and Van Evera, "Redraw the Map, Stop the Killing," *The New York Times*, 19 April 1999, p. A27. For a similar suggestion, see David Owen, "To Secure Balkan Peace, Redraw the Map," *Wall Street Journal*, 13 March 2001, p. A26.

42. On the political and military situation in 1998, see "Kosovo's Long Hot Summer: Briefing on Military, Humanitarian and Political Developments in Kosovo," International Crisis Group; http://www.crisis...rg/projects/abalkansa/reports/kosrep05.htm, 2 September 1998.

43. Judah, *Kosovo: War and Revenge*, note 35 above, p. 84.

44. Meyer, "In der Endsschleife?" note 12 above, pp. 7–9.

45. Jens Reuter, "Die Kosovo-Politik der internationalen Gemeinschaft in den neunziger Jahren," pp. 324–26 and Carsten Giersch, "NATO und militärische Diplomatie im Kosovo-Konflikt," in Jens Reuter and Konrad Clewing, eds., *Der Kosovo Konflikt: Ursachen, Verlauf, Perspektiven*, Klagenfurt: Wieser Verlag, 2000, pp. 447–9.

46. Victor-Yves Ghebali, "Totem et tabou dans le conflit du Kosovo: remarques sur les limites naturelles d'un mediation internationale," *Cultures et Conflicts*, No. 37, 2000, pp. 5–22.

47. Gunter Hofman, "Wie Deutschland in den Krieg geriet," *Die Zeit*, 12 May 1999, pp. 17–20.

48. Daalder and O'Hanlon, *Winning Ugly*, note 16 above, pp. 31–7 and Berthold Meyer, "Die westliche Staatenwelt im Strudel der Kosovo-Kriege," in Bruno Schoch, Ulrika Ratsch, and Reinhard Mutz, eds., *Friedensgutachten 1999*, Münster: LIT Verlag, 1999, pp. 62–4.

49. Daalder and O'Hanlon, *Winning Ugly*, note 16 above, pp. 45–9 and Giersch, "NATO und militärische Diplomatie im Kosovo-Konflikt," note 45 above, pp. 449–53.

50. *Ibid.*, Daalder and O'Hanlon, pp. 49–59 (the quotation is on p. 50).

51. On the details of the Rambouillet talks and their outcomes, see Judah, *Kosovo: War and Revenge*, note 40 above, pp. 197–226; Daalder and O'Hanlon, *Winning Ugly*, *ibid.*, pp. 63–89; Giersch, "NATO und militärische Diplomatie im Kosovo-Konflikt," note 45 above, pp. 453–55; Meyer, "Die westliche Staatenwelt im Strudel der Kosovo-Kriege," note 48 above, pp. 64–67; and Paul-Marie de la Gorge, "Histoire secerète des négociations de Rambouillet, *Le Monde diplomatique*, May 1999, pp. 4–5.

52. The quick-war assumption has been criticized as a "strategic blunder," which almost resulted in a defeat in the war, by Daalder and O'Hanlon, *Winning Ugly*, note 16 above, pp. 84–100.

53. See Dana Priest, "A Decisive Battle That Never Was," *The Washington Post*, 19 September 1999, pp. A1 and A30; and Steven Erlanger, "With Milosevic Unyielding on Kosovo, NATO Moved Toward Invasion," *The New York Times*, 7 November 1999, p. A4.

54. Ignatieff, "Balkan Physics," note 26 above, pp. 59–65.

55. It has been quite common in various commentaries to argue for earlier and more robust NATO reaction; see, e.g., Leon Wieseltier, "Saving NATO, Losing Kosovo: Force Without Force," *The New Republic*, 3 May 1999, pp. 27–9.

56. Agon Demjaha, "The Kosovo Conflict: A Perspective from Inside," in Albrecht Schnabel and Ramesh Thakur, eds., *Kosovo and the Challenge of Humanitarian Intervention: Selective Indignation, Collective Action, and International Citizenship*, Tokyo: United Nations University Press, 2000, pp. 34–5.

57. Edward Luttwak, "Give War a Chance," in Buckley, ed., *Kosovo: Contending Voices on Balkan Interventions*, note 36 above, pp. 349–55 (the quotation is on p. 353).

58. "The Kosovo Crisis Takes Its Toll on Macedonia," International Crisis Group, 17 May 1999; see http://www.icg.org/projects/sbalkan/reports/mac08rep.htm.

5

Evaluating success and failure: Conflict prevention in Cambodia and Bosnia

Andrea Kathryn Talentino

Introduction

As the preceding chapters demonstrate, evaluating conflict prevention success is easier said than done. There are two reasons for this. First there is the problem of conceptual ambiguity. Sometimes the term conflict prevention means, as it implies, efforts to stop violent conflict before it occurs (see chapter 1 and Jentleson, in this volume). Conflict prevention can, in this case, refer to early and pre-emptive attempts to stop violence through mediation, negotiations, coercion, promises, and perhaps threats (see Väyrynen for an interpretation of preventive deployment, in this volume).

Conflict prevention can also mean action taken in cases where violent conflict has already broken out. In the latter instance the same techniques may be used but they may also be accompanied by more forceful methods that are not strictly "preventive" in design (see Jentleson and Väyrynen, this volume). Since the idea of prevention would seem to suggest that action must occur *prior to* the outbreak of violence, this latter category seems at first glance to cloud the meaning of the term and by extension constrain our ability to evaluate success. The evaluation of success, therefore, must take careful *account of the circumstances* in which preventive efforts are applied.

The second point is that though we could demand a strict interpretation of conflict prevention and use the term only to describe actions intended to stop something that has not yet happened, in reality a broader interpretation of conflict prevention is far more relevant. Conflict prevention means not only trying to stop imminent violent conflict from occurring but also attempting to ameliorate past or actual conflicts that may have been in a violent stage for some time. As a result, any attempt to measure success must also take into *account the temporal continuum* in which conflict prevention is applied.

In this chapter I argue that prevention is a worthwhile objective *even in the midst of ongoing protracted conflict*, since history shows, all too well, that each war is rooted in the grievances of the past and carries the seeds of violence for the future. Conflict prevention thus contains a *rehabilitative dimension* oriented to the past, *a resolutive dimension* focusing on the present, and *a preventive dimension* oriented to the future.[1] Failing to stop violence from breaking out today does not mean intermediaries should stop trying to prevent the same for tomorrow.[2]

The obvious consequence of this tripartite interpretation is to make assessments of conflict prevention very complex. Citizens and policy makers want to judge the efficacy of conflict prevention efforts by their immediate effect on a situation, but as the broad-based meaning of the term suggests that may be a very restrictive view. Instead, conflict prevention efforts must be judged by the breadth of their objectives, including not only their ability to resolve or lessen tensions at a specific time (which is the most common interpretation of conflict prevention) but also on their ability to mitigate grievances of the past and to create more stable and less conflictual means of interaction for the future. In some cases this may be accomplished by encouraging and sponsoring negotiations and interactions that introduce new means of cooperation. In other cases, however, conflict prevention may require far more complex and potentially long-lasting efforts to redress structural inequalities in economic, political, or social systems. It is a protracted process requiring long-term political and socioeconomic reforms which may take decades to complete.[3]

Secondarily, there is a tendency to judge the absence of a speedy solution as failure. In many cases, however, a quick fix is either not available or not possible (see Jentleson, this volume). This is particularly true in cases when preventive efforts are to be undertaken where violence is already taking place. Reversing the effects of bloodshed and revenge-based animosity is very challenging, and requires, at its most fundamental level, changing the "hearts and minds" of the citizens (see David Last, this volume). Attitudinal change is obviously a protracted and indeterminant undertaking, the eventual success of which will be known only over time. Long-term efforts should not be unfairly judged if the processes of change move incrementally.

This broader perspective means that peacebuilding and nation building efforts are essential elements of conflict prevention. Most analyses of conflict prevention do not include peacebuilding, since it occurs once a conflict has been resolved through the signing of peace agreements. However, it is perhaps the only strategy that can remove the sources of conflict from society and/or create alternative means of resolving tension. Though peacebuilding takes place in the immediate sense to complete the resolution of one conflict, it also seeks to address the social and political grievances that could lead again to violence. It looks at once both backwards and forwards, and encourages societal reconstruction along consensual, inclusive, and liberal lines. Peacebuilding thus includes all three dimensions of conflict prevention, encompassing past and future sources of tension.

In sum, conflict prevention success and failure are highly relative terms. That does not mean we cannot reasonably evaluate outcomes, merely that we must be careful about how we do so. An apparent success may in fact be a failure if it does not address the problems that gave rise to the original conflict. Likewise, what seems a failure could over time demonstrate cautious yet solid progress towards a new and stable society. Conflict prevention can only be considered successful when it prevents or ends conflict in the short term *and* undertakes, through development and rehabilitation programmes, efforts to alter the relationships and inequalities that produced the tendencies toward violence. Durable prevention must resolve current problems and build upon that resolution into the future.

Obviously, without an understanding of the societal dimensions of a conflict there is little possibility of providing the appropriate means of changing that society's dynamics. Successful conflict prevention, therefore, must be informed by an understanding of local context, structures, and power dynamics.[4] Just as important, those attempting conflict prevention activities must think through their objectives carefully, clearly identifying their goals as well as their plans for achieving them. The most important point is that practitioners should attempt only what local realities will allow. As Bruce Jentleson has argued, realism rather than idealism must be the guide. This is because the structures of governance and the idea of compromise so familiar in the West are unfamiliar to people in some parts of the world. Therefore the methods of conflict prevention must incorporate the established structures of a society and seek to exert influence from within in order to change the likelihood of violence. Success also requires flexibility and a willingness to adjust and compromise in mid-course.

Judging success will always be a matter of reconciling ideals with realities. Failure is easy to assess. It is easily observed, while success is likely to be an outcome neither as good as observers might wish, nor as bad as they might have feared. How then can we measure a successful outcome? Returning to the threefold meaning of conflict prevention noted above, it is clear that there are several indices of success. By posing four questions it is possible to develop a better feel for whether specific efforts of conflict prevention have had a positive impact:

1. Have the adversaries engaged in negotiations, truce talks, or any head-to-head meetings?
2. Has an effort been made to reduce violence and prevent its re-escalation?
3. Have conflict-generating structures been identified and is there a plan to alter conflict dynamics?
4. Has the salience of group identity been decreased in the political and economic realms?

Answers to these questions are crucial in developing meaningful measures of success. The first two indicate a short-term, if limited, understanding of success. Negotiations and truce talks do not themselves indicate long-term resolution, but they do indicate the beginning of a process that may in time yield positive developments. And the way to make talks more likely to be productive is to deal with old or ongoing sources of tension. Talks are unlikely to be sustained where violence continues or reignites, so resolution efforts must focus on making the use of violence unterable.

The latter two questions reflect concerns over the impact of long-term structurally oriented efforts. Question 2 is also relevant here, functioning in both the short and long term to create a climate for political resolution and then improve the prospects for its durability. Recent history demonstrates that some conflicts are not limited to political groups but infiltrate the citizenry, spreading quickly once violence is initiated. These conflicts tend to be among the most vicious and intractable because they create long-term and entrenched hatreds that subsist on notions of revenge and victimization. Attempts to contain a conflict by insulating the citizenry from its most pernicious effects is important. As Väyrynen points out in chapter 3, containment is critical to eventual resolution – limiting the spread of violence and the ferocity with which it is waged. Few conflicts are as simple as the popular ethnic hatred explanations so often offered in the media (and taken up by Jentleson in detail). Instead, intrastate violence generally develops from grievances about tangible inequalities such as the distribution of economic or political power and access. Groups that feel slighted can develop a sense of ethnic or racial crusade, but the underlying sources of conflict are derived from real inequalities in the structure of the society. Treating those structures is a critical part of conflict prevention. Unless the problem dynamic is altered, the conflict is likely to flare up again, and perhaps more viciously. Thus the success of any conflict prevention effort must be judged not only for its immediate effect, but also for how well it identifies the underlying sources of conflict and lays the groundwork for altering the cycles that lead to conflict. This is where peacebuilding can play a critical preventive role. Without a long-term perspective any efforts made today are mere band-aids, hastily applied dressings to immediate problems with no concern for the underlying deep-rooted sources of conflict in the society. Changing such internal structures is obviously a difficult and long-term task, but this objective must form the crux of serious conflict prevention efforts.

One of the most difficult tasks of successful conflict prevention is identifying the moment, or moments, for appropriate action. The conflict prevention literature places a lot of emphasis on the need for early warning, but evidence suggests that, more often than not, outside observers have understood the potential for violence, yet failed to act on it (see Duke, this volume). Problem definition may thus be less critical than possessing the resolution for action, but in either case it is important to monitor closely violence-prone societies and prepare for the possibility of acting. Indeed, if there is no commitment to working in a preventive capacity, monitoring may be a wasted effort, since even sending observers implies a potential interest in acting. One of the most difficult scenarios for action occurs in the case of ongoing violence. Involvement in intense conflict is by definition far more complex and potentially dangerous. Mid-course preventive efforts deserve intensive analysis due to the challenges they pose and the risks they present.

In an evaluation of these approaches to conflict prevention, this chapter examines two cases, representing both success and failure. The cases were chosen not only because of their different outcomes, but also because they demonstrate the different hazards present in prevention efforts undertaken at different stages of conflict. Cambodia, proposed here as an example of success, is a case of mid-course prevention undertaken only after decades of war. Bosnia, presented as an example of failure, allows analysis of prevention possibilities at the onset of conflict, and the costs of failure to take action at an early stage. Both cases, however, also demonstrate the ambiguous nature of success or failure, highlighting the extent to which outcomes do not always fit clearly into one category.

Cambodia

Cambodia's history has been marked by invasion, civil war, and turbulence. Racked by violent conflict since the 1960s and held prisoner by the rivalries of the Cold War's bipolar structure, Cambodia's future changed, however, when the world changed. Vietnam, long pilloried by the West for its invasion of Cambodia and its support for the PRK government, decided to seek a settlement of the issue in order to avoid diplomatic isolation in the rapidly changing post-Cold War world. Its 1989 decision to remove all its troops from Cambodian territory provided the first real possibility of long-term peace. The constellation of factions, relatively static since 1979, pitted the sitting government against a coalition of groups, including followers of former rulers Prince Sihanouk and the Khmer Rouge, operating as a government in exile.

After Vietnam's withdrawal the Phnom Penh government proved to have considerable staying power even without Vietnamese backing. Pressured by their international backers, the local parties acquiesced in a long and often bitter negotiating process. Signed in October 1991, the Paris Agreement brought an end to the conflict and provided for a political transition to be overseen by the UN. The accords left many difficult problems unaddressed, however, and did not remove the sitting regime. This last decision proved to be of considerable importance, and led to continual tensions in the process of reconstruction.

The United Nations Transitional Authority for Cambodia (UNTAC) was deployed in March 1992 with the objective of building a foundation for democracy. This task reflected the greatest flaw of the peace agreement. Many political issues could not be agreed upon in Paris, most importantly, what to do with the present regime. As a result the settlement circumvented the problem by attempting to start afresh with democratic elections. Thus UNTAC's principal responsibility was conducting the national election, including organizing and monitoring the entire set-up from the creation of electoral laws to managing the ballot boxes. At the same time UNTAC was occupied with training and supervising a new civilian police force and the repatriation of refugees.

Cambodia's transition was not simply a political enterprise but was intended to operate in the economic and social structures of the country as well. A comprehensive approach was rooted in the need to find a graceful means of removing the sitting government. Democratic elections were identified as the easiest and most defensible means of installing a new government. The interim administration, the Supreme National Council (SNC) was composed of six members of the Phnom Penh regime and two representatives from each of the opposition factions. The SNC was subject to oversight from the UN special envoy who could veto decisions unilaterally. The most radical element in UNTAC's mandate was its direct supervision of various areas of civil administration.

In order to demonstrate success we should return to the questions posed earlier. To what extent were those objectives achieved? Questions 1 through 3 we can answer in the affirmative. The adversaries did engage in talks, beginning in 1987. Negotiations began initially because Prince Sihanouk's faction, the National United Front for an Independent, Neutral, Peaceful, and Cooperative Cambodia (FUNCINPEC) was tired of fighting and did not foresee a positive military outcome. These self-motivated talks soon fell apart, but third parties then worked hard to sustain negotiations and continue discussion of issues even if resolution remained difficult. Once Vietnam offered its unconditional withdrawal the talks moved to more high profile venues, with France and Indonesia chairing a Paris Conference in July 1989. The ability of the PRK to sustain itself without direct Vietnamese support actually hastened the possibility of agreement by convincing the government in exile that military victory was unlikely and giving all participants an incentive to continue negotiations.

The signing of the Paris Agreement led directly to realization of the second goal of resolution, reducing the likelihood and value of violence. UN forces served as guarantor of the peace agreement, raising the stakes by putting offenders in opposition to a global organization, not simply a belligerent political group. UNTAC's mandate was to provide security and stability during the transition period. The military elements of that mandate consisted of cantonment and demobilization of the various factions, with a target of 70 per cent completion expected by September 1992. It was here that cracks in the "success" first began to show. The operation was too small and the task too large to allow for completion. Fighting continued throughout UNTAC's tenure, although it remained far below previous levels and those who engaged in it were delegitimized in the eyes of the population. The Khmer Rouge was particularly difficult in this regard, refusing to allow UNTAC entry into areas under its control or provide information on its forces and equipment. Eventually it withdrew from the entire process. It is important to note, however, that the organization's influence waned significantly as a result of its intransigence. This was most clearly demonstrated by the high turnout for the general election in spite of Khmer Rouge intimidation, and the continued decline of the party to total collapse in 1998. Though UNTAC did not root out all violence it succeeded in demobilizing most of the other groups and created a secure environment for the election.

In spite of the Khmer Rouge's defection from the peace process the reduction in violence has remained relatively stable. The election was successful, installing a constitutional monarchy headed by Prince Sihanouk and run by two prime ministers. A flare up occurred in 1997 when Hun Sen ousted his co-prime minister, Prince Ranariddh, from government, but this lasted only briefly. Elections have continued in form, although Hun Sen now functions essentially as a constitutional dictator and often shows little respect for the rules of democracy introduced in 1993. Matters improved when a coalition government was formed after national elections in 1998, leading to greater stability and the surrender of the Khmer Rouge. The political process is gaining legitimacy, and violence is used less frequently to settle political differences.

In terms of question 3, conflict-generating structures were identified and a plan developed to change them. The main sources of conflict were the factionalism of politics, the easy recourse to coup as a means of generating political change, and the opposition forces such tactics created. The plan for change rested largely in the creation of democratic rule, since the belligerent groups could agree on few other ways to reach compromises on power and because the holding of elections was the only viable strategy for removing the sitting government. Introducing democracy was seen as the best way to prevent the fragmentation and personalization of political parties. Attempted changes have been difficult to implement, however.

Democracy was a notion unheard of in Cambodia, where deference to elders, distaste for debate, and acquiescence to "wise" men were inherent parts of the culture. Indeed, consensus is a word that has no translation in Cambodian.[5] The first task was to convince political leaders that there were enough government portfolios to share. Creating the dual prime ministers was part of this approach. The second task was to educate the populace to the changes in society and the importance of the election. This was done successfully, and courageously, by international volunteers who braved violence and intimidation by the Khmer Rouge to educate Cambodian citizens, particularly those in the more remote parts of the country. Their success is evident in the 90 per cent turnout for the May 1993 elections, despite a Khmer Rouge campaign to prevent polling from taking place by public threats, some of which were carried out. The importance of the elections was understood by Cambodians, even if they did not understand quite what they were voting for, and the citizens dressed in their finest clothes, such as they would wear for only the most sacred religious occasions, and waited in tremendous lines to cast their votes.[6] Though democracy remains limited, citizens are more involved in the process, government has some accountability, and some issues garner nationwide debate. One example is the prospect of creating an international war crimes tribunal, which thus far has been demanded by the populace but stymied by the government.

This success, however, carried in it elements of failure. UNTAC had too many duties and not enough personnel or time to fulfil its objectives properly. The Khmer Rouge opted out of the peace process early on, claiming manipulation by the sitting Phnom Penh government. The dispute turned particularly on demobilization efforts, since the Khmer Rouge contended that the government was not participating fully, thereby justifying its own refusal to disarm.

Demobilization for all parties was incomplete, eroding the basis of trust UNTAC so wanted, and needed, to build. The Khmer Rouge returned to the bush, derided the peace process, and continued its campaign of violence, which it directed against the election process. The high turnout demonstrated that Cambodians refused to be intimidated, and fortunately, the Khmer Rouge's weakness led to near total collapse in 1998. But its defection undermined the success of the new government and encouraged others to use violent channels when events went against them. The Hun Sen-led coup and resulting violence is one example. This lasted only briefly, and Cambodia has now returned to relative stability. However, the potential for violence exists and remains very close to the surface, since the emphasis on achieving influence through strong arm tactics rather than institutionalized practices remains.

Finally, the salience of group identity was reduced in politics, although this was much easier in Cambodia than in other places. Cambodia did not experience divisive ethnic or clan conflict, or mass nationalism. Its belligerent groups tended to be ousted political parties or leaders looking for a way back into power, and their sympathizers. To a large degree the population remained outside the conflict, a victim rather than an active participant. Even so, efforts have been made to reduce identities that might have been hardened through the decades of violence by incorporating parties into the political structure and relying on process to air grievances and express opposition. The desire for a tribunal to prosecute members of the Khmer Rouge for its brutal rule is part of this, though as noted, remains unfulfilled. Many citizens are now calling for a truth and reconciliation commission modelled after that in South Africa as a means of moving the society forward. That such possibilities can even be discussed suggests that government and society have both changed significantly since 1990.

Though the road was quite bumpy, Cambodia represents an example of success. For some time that appeared uncertain, with Khmer Rouge violence increasing in the mid-1990s and then the coup in 1997. And there are still significant criticisms we could make. The reforms implemented were obviously incomplete. Demobilization was never entirely finished, the Khmer Rouge's defection undermined the success of the new government, and the possibility of reversion remains salient. However, negotiations were begun, violence was reduced and remains low, the sources of conflict were addressed, and steps taken to change them. Citizens began to view their political structure in a different way, and legitimacy, though limited, is now a relevant concern for government. With every year that passes, and we are now a decade from UNTAC, the prospects look brighter. We must acknowledge, however, that success is precarious. The government is characterized at least in part by strongman rule, which means that the potential remains for frustration to build into violence.

Bosnia

Bosnia by contrast represents the failure of conflict prevention efforts, yet that failure also holds the potential for success. The conflict in Bosnia was preceded by the Croatian and Slovenian declarations of independence, the European recognition of those countries, and the short but vicious Serbo-Croatian War. People knowledgeable about the area predicted that the crisis accompanying Bosnia independence would be far worse because of the large Serb minority in the republic. Violence erupted in April 1992 when Bosnian Serbs responded to the Bosnian vote for independence, as they had promised they would, by attacking Sarajevo and other predominately Muslim towns that they claimed for incorporation into Serbia. The war quickly took on an ethnic cast, with Bosnian Muslims, Serbs, and Croats pitted against each other for control of the fledgling nation's territory. The United Nations Protection Force (UNPROFOR), already established in Croatia to maintain the settlement ending the earlier Serbo-Croatian war, was expanded and deployed into Bosnia, with the intent of preventing further Serb aggression. Limited to light arms and the use of force only in self-defence, UNPROFOR units had little effect on the violence, which produced enormous refugee counts, deportations, and wholesale massacres.

As the years dragged on, Serbian disdain for the UN force grew. Every strategy UNPROFOR tried proved ineffective, primarily because it lacked a robust means of attack or even self-protection. Reluctant to have UN forces become a party to the conflict, the Security Council refused to make UNPROFOR's mandate more robust, despite the fact that international personnel were subject to more attacks and perhaps greater danger because of their known weakness. Midway through the conflict, NATO airstrikes against Serb forces were introduced under UN request but were severely restricted out of concern for the safety of the peacekeeping force, which was subject to reprisal. The UN's lowest point was when it became a silent collaborator in the 1995 Bosnian Serb drive to take over the misnamed safe areas and the notable massacre at Srebrenica.[7] The situation changed significantly when NATO took control of the military process in mid-1995. By late 1995 a peace agreement was concluded at Dayton, Ohio. The NATO Implementation Force (IFOR) and a follow on Stabilization Force (SFOR) replaced UNPROFOR in December 1995, and the painful process of settlement began.

The collapse of Yugoslavia highlights the importance of international will in pursuing conflict prevention. There was clear foreknowledge of the potential violence (just as there would be in Rwanda two years later, another notable failure), yet no will to act. For example, the Serbo-Croatian war of 1991 demonstrated Serbia's intent to protect Serbs in other republics (see Väyrynen, this volume). Moreover, Serbian President Slobodan Milosevic had been quoted more than once as saying that he would fight for Bosnia.[8] Such clues had been evident since the early stages of Yugoslavia's break-up in 1990, when observers predicted that Bosnia, with its complex mix of ethnicities, would become a battleground for ethnic control of territory. While European nations had begun addressing the problem of Yugoslavia's dissolution in 1991, the US stayed out of the proceedings, initially at European behest. The early stages of attempted conflict prevention were thus left largely to the UN, an organization constrained in properly structuring its peacekeeping force by the reluctance of its member states to countenance anything more than a self-defence mandate for UNPROFOR. The expectation that the Serbs would back down with a show of Western interest was quickly disabused, and Western resolve was revealed for what it was, a weak and uncertain attempt to stop the violence without the necessary commitment to the means of making this possible.

Some observers have suggested that prior to and even as late as April 1992 the Serbs would have backed down if confronted with a Western force fully equipped with offensive capabilities and committed to preserving peace. Composed mainly of thugs and criminals in pursuit of self-aggrandizement, the Serbian militias knew they were not entitled to much of the land they were claiming.[9] At that point the international community missed (avoided?) the opportunity to put the first two objectives of prevention efforts into motion – to get the belligerent parties engaged in talks and to impose costs on the use of violence. Without international restraint the violence only increased, and to the Serbs's advantage, making the possibility of productive talks more remote. Even when the international community got the various groups to negotiate, resolution was impossible because the Bosnian Serbs had no incentive to give up their military gains at the conference table. A critical window of opportunity thus passed in late 1991 and early 1992 when the West could have, with a relatively small show of force and a great deal of resolve, forced negotiation, controlled the violence, and changed the course of events. At this early juncture critical actors ignored warnings and missed a clear opportunity to act before violence broke out, when, as Lund points out, preventive intervention might have had a greater chance of success.[10]

This is significant because it was during this window that real prevention could have occurred. Forcing negotiation and imposing limits on violence might have lessened the conflict, if not prevented it altogether.

Just as importantly, action at this point would have prevented nationalist fervor from spreading to the citizenry and creating the cycle of mass suspicion and revenge that followed. By failing to apply the first two criteria of conflict prevention the international community missed the opportunity to prevent, instead essentially fanning the flames, ensuring even more difficult.

The fundamental problem was that UN member states tried to do the minimum possible, and thus constructed a wholly ineffective strategy for dealing with the unfolding crisis. UNPROFOR was too lightly armed, too spread out, and too restricted in its possible use of force to make a difference. It was designed to be a peacekeeping force that would form a buffer between parties, but those parties were already engaged in all out warfare before it arrived and gained confidence in their mission as time went on. Without aggressive action UNPROFOR could not make a difference, and aggressive action was exactly what UN members hoped to avoid. Thus UNPROFOR was sent as a minimalist force into a complex situation. And as problems mounted UNPROFOR's troop contributors wavered; advocating a less aggressive stance even as it became increasingly necessary.

Demonstrating little flexibility to adapt to the changing situation or violent realities, UN members persisted in maintaining UNPROFOR's weak mandate until the costs, financial, human, and reputational, became too great to bear. Ultimately the conflict was settled, or at least reduced to a simmer, by the Dayton Peace Accords and the deployment of NATO troops in December 1995.[11]

In part the failure here may be attributed to the fact that policy makers may not have genuinely understood how they could alter events in Bosnia. The dissolution of a major state was a significant and poorly understood problem and its handling was largely a process of trial and error. Germany's recognition of Bosnia in 1991 is a case in point – designed to defuse the crisis, it instead pushed Yugoslavia more certainly towards war. Thus, while foreknowledge was not a constraint, a clear and effective plan of action was.[12]

But this description characterizes only the early months of the conflict. After UNPROFOR was in place the problem was very different. Contributing nations persisted in continuing an inappropriate and dangerous mission that merely emboldened the Serbs through its impotence. UNPROFOR troops had no real capacity to lessen or control violence, and in fact only contributed to it. Bosnian Serb forces kidnapped and besieged UN troops with impunity, often taking their weapons and equipment as at Srebrenica. This impotence in the field led to weakness in negotiations, where the international community lacked any ability to force agreement or guarantee the terms. The Serbs were clearly the most

powerful actor, calling the shots in both military and verbal confrontations. The problem here was twofold: first, the involved nations
refused to revise their conventional strategies; second, they sought easy
solutions rather than accepting the need for tough preventive and coercive efforts. The result was a long tenure of an ineffective UNPROFOR
(the unseemly spectacle of UN personnel handcuffed to potential NATO
bombing targets is a prominent example) rendered helpless in the face of
executions, and forced to stand idly by as the belligerents broke every
agreement the international organization had put on the table.

That said, the last stages of international involvement in Bosnia could
tentatively be ranked among the successes in this chapter. When NATO
and the Organization of Security and Co-operation in Europe (OSCE)
established a firm response strategy, international commitment and effort
changed dramatically. Beginning in 1995 the international community,
particularly NATO, did begin imposing costs on the use of violence and
was able to force and for the first time control substantive negotiations.
Once that happened the third and fourth questions posed above could
begin to be addressed. The international community sought to identify
and eliminate conflict-generating structures, focusing on the desire of the
belligerent groups to determine their own political future. A major cause
of conflict was the ability of elites to create a fear of minority status and
then use that to incite nationalist hatred. In recognition of this concern,
the US and NATO sought to develop structures that could accommodate
the three ethnic groups equally, which accounts for the creation of the
two entities and the tripartite form of the federal government. The comprehensive agreements signed at Dayton sought to reform politics, economics, and society in such a way as to allow for ethnic affiliation but to
harness it within a unified state. The first component was military, since
stability had to be restored, but the greater part of the Dayton Accords
and the subsequent international operation has been the civilian reforms.
IFOR took an aggressive military stance and had succeeded in achieving
most of its objectives by the end of 1996. SFOR, a scaled-down version of
IFOR, continues to provide the secure environment in Bosnia necessary
to ensure that the OSCE's civilian rehabilitation mission succeeds. This
mission is responsible for changing conflict dynamics on a long-term
basis. The OSCE's task is no less than building consensual political, economic, and social structures to form the foundation of a cooperative and
stable Bosnian state. In conjunction with the United Nations Mission in
Bosnia and Herzegovina (UNMIBH) it is undertaking a wholesale re-
building of Bosnia. Progress on the civilian front was marginal until late
1997, when SFOR became fully committed to facilitating the implementation of civilian reform. After that significant albeit incremental progress
was made. With solid SFOR backing the High Representative has been

able to play a more decisive role. SFOR and the OSCE now work in tandem on civilian reform, with the focus currently on refugee and property issues and building central institutions. However, the plan to change nationalist antipathies has not matched realities, in part because separation and integration are simultaneously part of the effort. Thus success must be measured not only by how well conflict prevention efforts worked, but by how quickly and effectively international and regional organizations learned to work together. The most positive sign of success in Bosnia is the sporadic but increasing number of spontaneous refugee returns in both the Federation and the Republika Srpska (RS), indicating increasing but still tentative confidence in the social and political environment. Citizens in both entities express confidence in the role and effect of the International Police Task Force (IPTF), tasked with training and monitoring the civilian police, and this has helped keep violence low while encouraging refugee returns. While tensions remain they are now focused on economic issues rather than ethnic ones.[13]

In answer to the fourth question, reducing the salience of group identity, there are some successes, but also notable failures. The most recent and biggest success was the creation of a unified border service that began operation in June. UNMIBH hoped to have the multiethnic force deployed around the country by the end of 2000. This is part of UNMIBH and OSCE's effort to reduce the salience of entity boundaries and increase the commitment to the central state, even if political expression continues to come through largely ethnically oriented organizations and parties.[14]

They are also undertaking a process to vet and certify the judiciary, as was done with the police, to ensure even application of the law. However, the very structure of government reinforces group relevance. The national government has no revenue base of its own and must rely on transfers from the ethnically based entities. The entity governments also enjoy independent army and police forces, judicial systems, and taxing rights, thus easily overshadowing the national government. Though recent elections (2000) indicated that moderates were gaining strength, the RS remains dominated by more extreme leaders and this creates significant pressures for other political elites.

Deeply divisive problems still exist, particularly the still unsettled problem, six years later, of repatriating refugees. Property laws are proving effective but work slowly, and the size of the displaced population means that the problems are quite complex.[15] The RS is also less accepting of returnees than the Federation, which does not help erase the divisions in society. The small successes to date, such as establishing a common currency, common licence plates, a common border service, and cooperative economic zones, are not likely to capture Western imaginations but represent critical stepping stones on the road to reconciliation. All workers in Bosnia agree that there is a long-term need for an international presence.

The failure in Bosnia is thus clear, while success remains uncertain. Initially the international community did not act credibly to decrease the violence or guarantee peace agreements, ensuring that attempts to negotiate were futile. With the first two criteria for prevention answered negatively, the remaining criteria were impossible to contemplate. The chance to prevent violence existed, but was not taken. The tide turned when NATO took over the resolution process in 1995. The first two criteria could be answered affirmatively with the Dayton Agreements and the NATO deployment, even though they required substantial arm-twisting. The presence of NATO troops created a stable environment allowing prevention efforts to proceed. There assessment becomes more difficult, however. The conflict generating nature of ethnic rivalry was identified, but the plan to change interactions carried a paradox at its heart. The international community sought security through separation, but that was detrimental to the goal of integration also proclaimed at Dayton. The goals of the reforms – stability and unity – are thus in some ways mutually constraining.

As a result, the salience of group identity has not been markedly decreased in either the political or economic realms. One problem is the international community's inability to induce reform in the RS. Another is the lack of economic opportunity and presence of widespread corruption. A third is the weakness of the central state. In the face of these flaws Bosnians, whether Serb, Croat, or Bosniac, have little reason to believe that unity will triumph, and even less to respect the structures of the national state.

Conclusions

The two cases discussed above highlight several lessons and implications for conflict prevention. Most of all, they emphasize the point that a responsible analysis must address the aftermath of the conflict as a prevention challenge in itself. That conclusion may seem counter-intuitive: to suggest that undoing the effects of conflict constitutes prevention. But resolution cannot last unless it changes the patterns that create violence. "Preventive peacebuilding" is essential to long-term success. Cambodia fits this point nicely, as in spite of some flaws it seems to have reached a point of durable peace.

Three lessons clearly emerge from consideration of the four criteria posed at the start of this chapter. The first is that although the questions posed related to external actions, internal circumstances matter. One significant difference between Cambodia and Bosnia was the depth of the divisions in society. Cambodia had weak divisions, primarily focused around political regimes, and large sections of society remained outside the conflict. Bosnia, on the other hand, had a society rent by intensely perceived ethnic differences, which led to the mobilization of mass nationalism. The former situation is far more propitious for realization of the criteria external actors must achieve for successful prevention. In cases such as Cambodia we can postulate that the limited nature of division in society makes it easier first to promote negotiation, and then to reduce the salience of those divisions once structures have been created to mitigate them. The argument is strengthened by the fact that other examples of successful outcomes, such as El Salvador and Mozambique, had similar political rather than ethnic divisions. In cases such as Bosnia conflict prevention efforts will have to seek creative solutions to overcome those divisions, a task which has not been achieved successfully for the Balkan nation. The complexity of the problem, however, is something that the international community should be aware of, and prepared for, before involvement.

A second lesson is that the commitment of the domestic parties matters to success. In the case of Cambodia the warring parties were already tired and saw little prospect of victory. Conversely, in Bosnia the conflict was young and the Serbs had every hope of success. Having a group willing to enter negotiations, as in Cambodia, certainly makes the way easier. However, we should not take that to mean that external actors cannot influence willingness to negotiate. Indeed, this was a central failing in the first months of the Bosnian conflict. Part of conflict prevention must include creating the circumstances that induce groups to seek negotiation. Success will remain elusive unless and until external parties make violence more costly than potential compromise. This is the lesson that Dayton clearly shows. Prior to 1995 the international community gave the Serbs no reason to negotiate. After 1995 the international community changed several factors – undertaking sustained bombing, supporting the Croatian offensive, providing incentives for the sponsors of the Bosnian Serbs to seek resolution – that made continued pursuit of violence untenable. The notion of ripeness is therefore relevant, but it is a condition that can be created, not necessarily a moment one must wait for. Rather than counselling patience, the issue of readiness suggests that external actors should become more active when the willingness is absent rather than less.

Finally, these cases show that successful conflict prevention efforts are long term. We cannot think of this as a quick fix. The effort in Cambodia was too short and could not achieve some of its more important goals. This led to problems in implementation and a very shaky start. Reforms seem to have succeeded in spite of the problems, but it would have been far better to commit more time and more money to make them sustainable rather than waiting and hoping that the effort would take root. Participants in conflict prevention efforts must come prepared for the long haul and not seek to remove their personnel or resources at the earliest possible moment. The fragility of the societies where such efforts take place demands long-term and incremental reform. Change and rehabilitation will not come overnight, and participating nations should understand the nature of their commitment before they begin. This lesson should be communicated to citizens and policy makers alike, in order to reduce the controversy that often attends such operations.

The protracted efforts ongoing in Bosnia show the relevance of this point. Though conflict prevention efforts came late in the game, the international community has maintained the commitment it established. The rehabilitation project is now in its seventh year, and aid workers suggest it may take decades more. The successes remain small, and precarious, but there is evidence that the perceptions of citizens and politicians are beginning to change. The long-term commitment could be avoided, however, if the international community began to focus on acting earlier to prevent violence from breaking out. Efforts should centre on true prevention, in the traditional meaning of the word, especially now that we know the costs of not acting. That is obviously not possible in all cases. However, the key to future success lies in the speed of response and the willingness to take action before the problems are so entrenched. Again, Bosnia highlights this lesson well.

Notes

1. For a discussion on the wide meaning of conflict prevention see Janie Leatherman, William DeMars, Patrick D. Gaffney, and Raimo Väyrynen, *Breaking Cycles of Violence, Conflict Prevention in Intrastate Crises*, West Hartford, CT: Kumarian Press, 1999, pp. 7–9.
2. Stockholm International Peace Research Institute, *Peace, Security and Conflict Prevention, a SIPRI-UNESCO Handbook*, Oxford: Oxford University Press, 1998, p. 37.
3. See John Paul Lederach, *Building Peace: Sustainable Reconciliation in Directed Societies*, Washington, D.C.: United States Institute of Peace Press, 1997; Elizabeth M. Consens and Chetan Kumar, eds., *Peacebuilding as Politics: Cultivating Peace in Fragile Societies*, Boulder, CO: Lynne Rienner, 2001.
4. This and other methods for identifying when conflict prevention should take place are discussed in Janie Leatherman *et al.*, *Breaking Cycles of Violence*, note 1 above, as well as Helene Grandvoinnet and Hartmut Schneider, *Conflict Management in Africa: A Permanent Challenge*, Paris: Development Centre of the Organization for Economic Co-operation and Development, 1998.
5. Cooperative politics was truly something that ran directly contrary to Cambodian culture and traditions, and proved very difficult to overcome.

6. A wonderful film detailing the lead up to the elections and then election day itself has been made by William Shawcross, entitled "Fear and Hope in Cambodia."

7. The Dutch peacekeepers protecting the safe area of Srebrenica were disarmed by the Serbs and forced to hand over their Armored Personnel Carriers (APCs), jeeps, rifles, and even their bulletproof vests. They did not protect the city's desperate citizens but allowed them to be rounded up and deported practically from the gates of the UN compound. Humiliated and held hostage, the Dutch both saw and heard direct evidence of the massacre of 7,000 men and boys from Srebrenica, but were powerless to provide assistance or prevent the slaughter. The story of Srebrenica is told in moving detail in the Pulitzer Prize winning book by David Rohde, *Endgame*, Boulder, CO: Westview Press, 1997.

8. Milosevic had based his initial appeal on the slogan "all Serbs in one state," and warned that he would fight to keep Bosnia within Serbia. See Warren Zimmerman, *Origins of a Catastrophe*, New York: Times Books, 1996, and Laura Silber and Alan Little, *Yugoslavia, Death of a Nation*, New York: TV Books, Inc., 1996.

9. See Zimmermann, *ibid.*, David Owen, *Balkan Odyssey*, London: V. Gollancz, 1995, and John Mueller, "The Rise, Decline, and Shallowness of Militant Nationalism in Europe," presented at the Rochester-Jagiellonian Conference, Krakow, Poland, 30–31 May 1997.

10. Lund, *Preventing Deadly Conflict*, pp. 14–15.

11. Bosnia is now divided into two units, a Bosniac-Croat federation and a Serbian republic, which live in uneasy coexistence. The central state is weak, and the individual entities retain their own security forces, indicating to many that Dayton codified the partition of Bosnia and the rewarding of Serbian aggression with the substantial control and territory that the Bosnian Serbs had sought.

12. External observers and policy makers were caught in the grip of Hegel's observation that Minerva's owl flies at dusk, realizing only in the evening what they should have done during the day.

13. Interviews with Andy Bearpark, Deputy High Representative for Reconstruction and Return, Office of the High Representative, Sarajevo, 26 June 2000; Jonathan Stonestreet, Political Analyst, OSCE, Sarajevo, 22 June 2000; Barbara Smith, Public Information Office, United Nations High Commissioner for Refugees, Sarajevo, 23 June 2000.

14. For more on the possibilities of this effort see Susan Woodward, "Implementing Peace in Bosnia and Herzegovina: A Post-Dayton Primer and Memoranda of Warning," *Brookings Discussion Papers*, The Brookings Institution, May 1996, and Jane M. O. Sharp, "Dayton Report Card," *International Security*, Vol. 22, No. 3, Winter 1997/98, pp. 101–37.

15. Take for example the plight of a Muslim woman from Brcko. She fled to Germany during the war, leaving her house in the care of a Serb couple she knew. She returned two years ago but could not go home because the Serbs' house had been destroyed and they remained in her home. She leased an apartment but filed in January to reclaim her home. The Serbs bought a new house which was also occupied by refugees. By purchasing the house they violated their temporary occupancy permit for the Muslim woman's house and now face eviction, but cannot go to their house because the refugees there have no other accommodation. Whatever house the third party is eventually removed to is likely to be also occupied, and so on. This author attended mediation sessions between the Muslim and Serb parties with members of the UN International Police Task Force and Human Rights Officers in Brcko, 28 June 2000.

Part Two

The institutional record

6

Regional organizations and conflict prevention: CFSP and ESDI in Europe

Simon Duke

An overview of European conflict

The incidence of major armed conflict in Europe has been relatively low compared to, for example, Africa and Asia. Until the eruption of the recent Kosovo crisis the only notable armed conflict in Europe (excluding the CIS) was that in Bosnia-Herzegovina. NATO's Stabilization Force (SFOR) in Bosnia with 35,000 personnel far outnumbers any UN mission in spite of the fact that the scale of the conflict and the casualties involved pale in comparison with those in, for example, the border clashes between Ethiopia and Eritrea. The size of the NATO-led post-conflict force in Kosovo (KFOR) is around 46,000 personnel. Europe is, when it comes to peacekeeping in its various forms, a privileged region since it is generally more peaceable but, when conflict does erupt, it is more likely to elicit robust efforts.

There are, however, three characteristics of conflict prevention that Europe shares with other regions of the world. First, broadly speaking, the constraints applying to conflict prevention in Europe are those that apply elsewhere. These can be listed as:

- The legal prohibition against intervention in the domestic affairs of a nation state in most circumstances;
- Overuse of the humanitarian pretext for intervention with the absence of any "end game" for involvement;

- Lack of accurate intelligence and resources to monitor potential trouble spots (this often includes the lack of personnel with intimate knowledge of the cultural, linguistic, and historical factors involved);
- "Donor fatigue" and a general reluctance to become involved.

Second, the post-Cold War years have seen an increasing emphasis on conflict prevention although neither the UN nor regional security organizations have developed a cohesive approach to conflict prevention. Indeed, there is general disagreement about which level is most appropriate for such an approach. Regional approaches to conflict prevention may demonstrate both strengths and weaknesses over their international counterparts. On the plus side, the regional body will have a vested interest in stability in the region and will probably have a more detailed "local" knowledge of the matter in dispute, its history, parties, and cultures. The proximity to a conflict may also, importantly, translate more easily into material and financial support for conflict prevention measures. There are however weaknesses. Regional organizations vary enormously in their size (the OSCE and OAU for instance have more members now than the UN did at its founding), wealth and resources, and their willingness to be impartial. The suspicion of vested interests on the part of a regional organization in a crisis may not only fan the flames of conflict but may complicate efforts by international bodies to reach a settlement. If it comes to measures beyond conflict prevention, such as peace enforcement, few regional organizations have sufficient resources and military force to intervene and, if necessary, monitor a prolonged cease-fire. When measures beyond conflict prevention fall to regional organizations, the need for close international supervision of the organization is paramount, as is the observance of UN peacekeeping principles.[1]

Finally, effective conflict prevention for intrastate disputes calls for a reconceptualization of many of the basic building blocks of the international system, especially statehood, sovereignty, and self-determination. The prohibition against the non-interference by any state or the international community in the internal affairs of another state, as enshrined in Chapter 1 of the UN Charter, looks particularly dated. There are indications (Bosnia-Herzegovina, Kosovo, Rwanda, and Somalia) that there is a greater willingness to intervene on humanitarian grounds. Although it should be noted that NATO's Operation Allied Force, which consisted of multiple air strikes against targets in Serbia and Kosovo between 26 March and 10 June, has stretched the meaning of humanitarian intervention to its limits. The willingness to disregard the normal prohibitions on intervention in the domestic affairs of the nation state is not however a global phenomenon. The international community's willingness to intervene with the same vigour in the Great Lakes region of Africa suggests that Europe is, to paraphrase George Orwell, more equal than others when it comes to the willingness to defend humanitarian principles.

Europe and conflict prevention

Europe or, to use the geographic term Eurasia, is not subject to any one conflict prevention structure. NATO's air campaign in Kosovo, executed in spite of objections from Russia, may carry negative connotations for trans-European conflict prevention. It should, however, be noted that "preventive diplomacy and approaches to conflict prevention" have been mentioned as areas for enhanced NATO-Russia dialogue and cooperation.[2] There are four principal reasons that suggest a rather pessimistic outlook for regional conflict prevention.

First, the CIS is subject to Russian "peacekeeping" and, with the sole exception of the OSCE, there are few effective external conflict prevention mechanisms. Conflicts in Chechnya, Dagestan, and Moldova fell within Russia's self-declared "near-abroad" and were therefore subject to Russian mediating efforts or, in the case of Chechnya, bloody military intervention. Such cases illustrate some of the pitfalls of regional crisis management arrangements, since Russia's capacity to be dispassionate was clearly in doubt. Indeed, regional mediation may even exacerbate the situation. For instance, the Foreign Affairs Minister of Moldova, Nicolae Tabacaru, commented that "the withdrawal of troops of the Russian Federation and especially of the munitions and armaments from the Transdniester region, would be a considerable impulse for the conflict settlement."[3]

Second, the lack of parallel membership of the various organizations has hindered the creation of a coherent conflict prevention and resolution mechanism. Although something of a cliché, the structures that have emerged are indeed often interblocking rather than interlinking. Until recently NATO considered the OSCE to be a four-letter word and this was reciprocated. There is little indication that potentially useful institutions, such as the OSCE's Conflict Prevention Centre in Vienna, have any impact upon NATO or CFSP contingency planning (see Mychajlyszyn, this volume). Ties between NATO and the now almost defunct WEU have improved but collaboration in critical areas, such as intelligence, leaves much to be desired. Even within organizations coordination of efforts is not only difficult, but also ultimately a matter of national priority-setting, especially when the use of force is considered.[4]

Third, in spite of the construction or modification of organizations, there has been a marked preference for ad hoc arrangements, such as the six-member Contact Group established for Bosnia and Kosovo. Ad hoc arrangements reflect a profound ambiguity on the part of the regional powers about their degrees of responsibility in crisis prevention scenarios. The direct and indirect challenges resulting from the actual eruption and internationalization of conflict tend to elicit a less ambiguous response.

Lastly, the continued reliance upon the US for initiative and resources in many areas relevant to conflict prediction, prevention, and peace-keeping has slowed the European allies in developing a self-reliant pan-European conflict prevention strategy and capability. Though with the creation of a EU rapid reaction capability that too may change. There is nothing intrinsically wrong with such reliance provided there is a strong congruence of transatlantic interests. Transatlantic differences over fundamental issues such as the Middle East peace process, trade policy or agriculture, should provoke concern at the lack of any truly indigenous regional conflict prevention capacity.

If comprehensive conflict prevention mechanisms are to become more meaningful, they will do so in the context of the EU's second pillar (Common Foreign and Security Policy, or CFSP) and NATO's ESDI (European Security and Defence Identity) frameworks. Ideally, any such developments should not compete with the conflict prevention of the OSCE but support it. It is equally important that an active dialogue develops between those with a conflict prevention role and those with peacekeeping or enforcement capabilities since, at times, conflict prevention may well rest upon conflict deterrence.

CFSP and ESDI: Do they have a conflict prevention role?

At the outset it should be noted that ESDI is still primarily a concept, like much in contemporary European security. It represents, along with CFSP, an attempt to build greater European autonomy and responsibility in security and defence matters. Progression from the conceptual stage towards practical arrangements for conflict prevention depends in part upon the willingness of EU and NATO member states to give substance to related concepts, such as CJTFs, as well as upon visible political-level agreement that priority should be accorded to conflict prevention.

The experience of ESDI and CFSP with conflict prevention is extremely limited. Until Kosovo, it was not immediately apparent to many observers that there should even be a conflict prevention role for CFSP or ESDI. Official documents and specialist academic literature on European security rarely mention conflict prevention in this context. In the EU context conflict prevention, as such, finds its expression in the belief that democratization and the development of market economies are essential elements of stability. This is reflected in the PHARE, TACIS, EU Democracy Programs, the Royaumont Process,[5] as well as the 1994 Stability Pact (the latter being declared a joint action).[6] The supporting academic debates in the late 1980s and early 1990s, suggesting that democracies do not fight democracies and that democratic states are more likely to resort to arbitration when disputes arise, supports the EU's emphasis upon economic and political stability as conflict suppressers.[7] The late consideration of the military aspects of CFSP has made the EU's reliance on economic and political tools for conflict prevention a matter of necessity rather than choice.

Under NATO's aegis the Partnership for Peace (PfP), the North Atlantic Cooperation Council and its successor, the Euro-Atlantic Partnership Council (EAPC), were designed with a general stabilization role in mind. NATO has also made a commitment to "prevent conflict" as part of a general effort with other organizations.[8] The prospect of EU and NATO membership has also played an extremely important role since it has encouraged interested parties to modify their behaviour to attain this goal. It has also encouraged rapid solutions to numerous cross border or regional disputes in Central and Eastern Europe. The 1993 Copenhagen conditions for membership, the 1994 Stability Pact and the Europe Agreements are all useful in the sense that they codify what is expected from aspirant members across a variety of activities (see Ehrhart, this volume).[9]

It would however be a mistaken assumption that conflict prevention can be addressed exclusively through economic, social, and political inducements. On occasion, as Kosovo has illustrated and as previous chapters have argued, there is need for a military element to complement other areas of conflict prevention. The arguments in favour of an effective military contribution to conflict prevention are fourfold. First, the credible threat of force can play a valuable role in supporting other forms of conflict prevention. Some, like Yugoslav President Slobodan Milosevic, may only respond when diplomacy is backed by force (this point is taken up by Jentleson in his chapter). Second, the prepositioning of military forces can contribute to conflict containment, as was the case with UNPREDEP in Macedonia (see Väyrynen this volume). Third, there may be occasions where it is necessary to separate physically two or more protagonists, as was the case in Bosnia. Fourth, military forces can be used in a variety of roles as was illustrated by the Military Advisory Police Element (MAPE) in Albania. The objective of conflict prevention in the European context should therefore be to create a seamless web of conflict prevention capabilities, ranging from the economic to the political and military, where CFSP and ESDI are the expressions of the latter two.

CFSP and conflict prevention

Given the emphasis placed upon conflict management and resolution by CFSP's predecessor, European Political Cooperation (EPC), the EU has had to start virtually from scratch to design conflict prevention mechanisms. Several factors that became apparent in the late 1980s shaped the EU's conflict prevention strategy:

- The European Community aimed to provide not only economic growth but also stability to Western Europe and to make war between member states unthinkable. The dissolution of the iron curtain dividing Eastern and Western Europe led to the same logic being applied eastward (how far, however, was not agreed upon);
- The European Community could not remain isolated either from the direct results of insecurity on its borders or from the secondary effects of conflict elsewhere;
- The EC had been preoccupied with economic affairs and had developed a weak external political dimension. The changes introduced by the end of the Cold War made the assumption by the Community of an active political dimension (in other words, the move towards union) a matter of necessity not choice;
- The assumption by NATO of the Community's external defence responsibilities during the Cold War period (notwithstanding somewhat cosmetic Euro-options) left the Community with no conflict management capabilities and per force the emphasis was put upon conflict prevention.

More pragmatic considerations also pushed some EU members, especially the small states, in the direction of conflict prevention. For instance, during the Dutch presidency of the EU in the first half of 1997, emphasis was placed on conflict prevention with a conference in Amsterdam for NGOs to coincide with the EU Development Minister's Informal Council meeting. The outcome of the conference was the European Platform on Conflict Prevention and Transformation hosted by the Centre for Conflict Prevention in Utrecht. The objective of the platform is to facilitate networking and the exchange of information amongst lobbying groups, governments, and NGOs. The Amsterdam Platform was launched at almost the same time as the Conflict Prevention Network[10] backed by Michel Rocard, which was designed to provide the Commission with analyses of potential crises and trouble spots.[11] These complementary NGO activities, as well as those of the EC in the economic realm, were designed to establish conflict prevention as part of the Union's general activities. Larger EU states however appeared to be heavily oriented toward crisis management in an effort to maximize the use of existing funds, hardware, and personnel by preserving traditional missions.

In spite of the initiatives referred to, the Treaty on European Union does not specifically mention conflict prevention, although the general objectives contained in the preambles to both treaties could certainly extend to conflict prevention. For instance, the general provision that the Union shall "preserve peace and strengthen international security, in accordance with the principles of the United Nations Charter, as well as the principles of the Helsinki Final Act and the objectives of the Paris Charter," implies that conflict prevention is a legitimate concern of the EU. It is also the task of the European Council to "define the principles of and general guidelines for the common foreign and security policy," which again could include conflict prevention.[12] Similarly the general definitions accorded to joint actions and common positions[13] could also include conflict prevention tasks.

The Amsterdam Treaty also makes reference to the WEU's 1992 Petersberg tasks in the context of the WEU's prime responsibility to support the "Union in the framing of the defense aspects of the common foreign and security policy."[14] Superficially the emphasis would therefore appear to be on crisis management.[15] However, the WEU Council's three-part Petersberg declaration did actually mention crisis prevention in the first section:

As WEU develops its operational capabilities in accordance with the Maastricht Declaration, we are prepared to support, on a case-by-case basis and in accordance with our own procedures, the effective implementation of conflict-prevention and crisis-management measures, including peacekeeping activities of the CSCE or the United Nations Security Council. This will be done without prejudice to possible contributions by other CSCE countries and other organizations to these activities.[16]

A subsequent section of the declaration mentioned a number of activities that military units of WEU member states, operating under the authority of the WEU, could be employed for. The list, which was referred to in the Amsterdam Treaty, did not include specific mention of crisis prevention.[17] Crisis prevention was explicitly mentioned in the St. Malo declaration, signed by President Jacques Chirac and Prime Minister Tony Blair, in December 1998. The Cologne Presidency conclusions of 3–4 June 1999 contained *verbatim* the St. Malo references to conflict prevention and conflict management:

... [the European Council is] convinced that the Council should have the ability to take decisions on the full range of conflict prevention and crisis management tasks defined in the Treaty of European Union, the "Petersberg Tasks." To this end, the Union must have the capacity for autonomous action, backed up by credible military forces, the means to decide to use them, and a readiness to do so, in order to respond to international crises without prejudice to actions by NATO ... we are convinced that to fully assume its tasks in the field of conflict prevention and crisis management the European Union must have at its disposal the appropriate capabilities and instruments.[18]

The specifics of how to actually implement conflict prevention measures are only addressed in the broadest sense in the Cologne European Council's conclusions. Three areas were identified as in special need of reinforcement in terms of military capacity building: intelligence, strategic transport, command and control.[19] Of the three identified, intelligence is a vital prerequisite (conflict prediction) for conflict prevention. The CFSP's underlying intelligence problem is not merely a matter of technical shortcomings but a matter of competing pressures on dwindling defence budgets where investment in satellites may compete with the need for a new generation jet fighter. These were exactly the pressures that led Germany to withdraw from the Horus satellite project. Effective strategic transport is also vital to the ability to move military forces from place to place and to sustain them for a prolonged period of time if required. Making good these and other shortcomings will demand additional expenditure and it is far from clear that the EU publics are willing to sanction the necessary investment for the mitigation of conflict. Ironically, it may well be the high costs of post-conflict stabilization and reconstruction efforts in Kosovo that hamper attempts to enhance the CFSP's conflict prevention capability.

The entry into force of the Amsterdam Treaty on 1 May 1999 introduced two new institutional modifications that may have significant consequences for the CFSP's conflict prevention capabilities. First, the Amsterdam Treaty created the new post of High Representative for the CFSP. It remains the role of the Presidency to "represent the Union in matters coming within the [CFSP]"[20] but the presidency shall be assisted by a "High Representative," who is the Secretary-General of the Council of Ministers.[21] The High Representative's duties are broad and, aside from assisting the Council in matters falling within the scope of the CFSP, he shall contribute to the "formulation, preparation and implementation of policy decisions" and, at the request of the Presidency, act "on behalf of the Council."[22] In June 1999 Javier Solana, NATO's former Secretary-General, was invited to become the first High Representative. Solana's past role when combined with his new one could provide a potent force for shaping conflict prevention, especially the organizational questions. It remains to be seen how the presidency will react to such a well-known and high-profile Monsieur PESC. Some of the neutral and non-aligned EU members (Austria, Finland, and Sweden) may have difficulties working with someone who was so closely connected to NATO and some of the larger members may possibly view his role as intrusive.

Second, amongst his various duties, the High Representative will oversee the Policy Planning and Early Warning Unit (PPEWU) which could have positive connotations for conflict prediction.[23] The pre-Amsterdam intergovernmental conference agreed that the PPEWU should be made up of specialists drawn from the General Secretariat, the Member States, the Commission, and the WEU. The tasks include:

- Monitoring and analysing developments in areas relevant to CFSP;
- Providing assessments of the Union's foreign and security policy interests and identifying areas on which the CFSP could focus in future;
- Providing timely assessment and early warning of events, potential political crises, and situations that might have significant repercussions for the CFSP;
- Producing, at the request of either the Council or the presidency, or on its own initiative, reasoned policy option papers for the Council.

The envisaged tasks of the PPEWU could point to a more active conflict prevention role on the part of the CFSP. Although the respective powers of the High Representative, the PPEWU, the Council, and the presidency are all defined in the CTEU, the relations between the constituents remain unclear. Nevertheless, the advent of the High Representative and PPEWU has the potential to enhance significantly the CFSP's conflict prevention abilities. Parties are more likely to listen to an appointed representative of the EU and a recognizable face who is not in office only for six months. The PPEWU, although it promises to be modest, is similarly important since conflict prevention rests upon the ability to identify potential trouble spots before they erupt.

A succession of EU presidencies has built upon the December 1998 St. Malo Declaration.[24] The development of what has become known as the Common European Security and Defence Policy (CESDP) is still very much a work in the making. The efforts of Sweden and Finland, the latter using its EU Presidency in the last half of 1999 to good effect, to stress not only crisis management but the non-military aspects of crisis management came to fruition under the Portuguese Presidency. In the European Council's Feira summit, in June 2000, the EU member states undertook that by 2003 they would be able to provide 5,000 police officers for international missions (1,000 available within 30 days) either for autonomous EU missions or to support UN, OSCE.

This brief *tour d'horizon* of conflict prevention in the CFSP context suggests the following conclusions. First, the bulk of EU conflict prevention measures, such as they are, have been undertaken by the Community. Conflict prevention, *per se*, has not been an area of high priority for the CFSP until relatively recently. The Kosovo crisis has done more than anything to change the focus.

The knock-on effects of the Kosovo crisis and, in particular, Operation Joint Guardian which commenced on 11 June 1999 with 39 contributing countries, have focused attention not only upon post-conflict reconstruction but also the high costs (in all senses) of crisis management. Within the EU conflict prevention has, as has been indicated, been portrayed as a *Community* preserve. In particular the Commission and its Commissioner for External Relations, Chris Patten, has claimed competence. Since the first pillar is *communautaire* in its working practices it is not yet apparent how the conflict prevention aspects of the EU's activities will complement the military aspects of crisis management being developed under the CESDP label in the staunchly intergovernmental second pillar. Even within the second pillar, it is unclear how the civil/police international missions will be coordinated with the peacemaking aspects of crisis management outlined in the Petersberg tasks.

Second, grass roots conflict prevention, such as SECI or the Royaumont process, PHARE, the Amsterdam Platform and the efforts of NGOs may well have a positive effect, but they do not go far enough. One of the lessons that may well surface from the Kosovo crisis is that conflict prevention will sometimes require the ability to tread lightly but also to carry a big stick. There is a need therefore either to develop a "capacity for autonomous action," as recommended by the European Council in Cologne, or to weave the different institutional components of conflict prevention within the EU and NATO into a coherent conflict prevention tool. The extent to which CESDP should be autonomous will be a matter of ongoing dispute between those with Europeanist or Atlanticist persuasions. Suffice it to note that, for the moment, it is the British view of 'autonomy' that has prevailed (in other words, that CESDP should support the European pillar of the Atlantic Alliance) over the more exclusive French interpretation of autonomy. The linkage between the EU and NATO also means that any effective crisis prevention or crisis management will depend upon the ability of the EU to develop closer relations not only with the non-EU European NATO members (EU+6) but also the EU candidate countries (of which there are 12, but since three are also NATO members, the collective group is referred to as the six plus nine which equals the EU+15).[4]

Third, effective conflict prevention depends upon a number of factors, including conflict risk assessment. The intelligence shortcomings of the CFSP have already been noted but they will not be easy to address given the immense sensitivity surrounding issues of intelligence sharing. In the meantime the US remains the main purveyor of strategic intelligence to which Britain has preferential access amongst the European allies as indicated by the 2000 Echelon affair (although they lack neither the technological know-how nor the analytical capability to develop and deploy indigenous facilities). The allies do, however, lack the will to commit resources to such a capability, although the case might be easier to make post-Kosovo, given the misgivings regarding US intelligence that, amongst other incidents, led to the mistaken bombing of the Chinese Embassy in Belgrade.

Any assessment of the EU's conflict prevention capacity is necessarily tentative at this juncture. The development of CESDP is still in its early stages, commencing only in December 1998 with the Anglo-French St. Malo declaration. The significance of conflict prevention has certainly been recognised by the EU or, more specifically, the Community, where the Commission legitimately claims to have a critical role. The rapid developments in CESDP, which include the establishment of permanent crisis management structures such as the Political and Security Committee, the Military Committee and Military Staff, as well as support structures within the Council Secretariat, such as the Situation Centre and the incorporation of the Petersberg-relevant aspects of the WEU, holds the potential for a serious European crisis management capability. These developments will lose much of their impact if the EU is unable to link the diplomatic and economic forms of crisis prevention with the credible threat of military force and, *in extremis*, the ability to use military force. The EU's main priority must be to create a seamless web of tools within which to address crises.

The frequently noted gaps in EU military and support capabilities also need to be addressed. The St. Malo declaration noted the need for "appropriate structures and a capacity for analysis of situations, sources of intelligence and a capability for relevant strategic planning, without unnecessary duplication ..." The EU will, as noted at St. Malo, need to have "recourse to suitable military means" (European capabilities pre-designated within NATO's European pillar or national or multinational European means outside the NATO framework). The extent to which access to NATO assets can be guaranteed is very much in question due to Turkey's perceived exclusion from the CESDP decision-making process and its subsequent willingness to block EU access to NATO planning facilities.

The issue of early warning and intelligence is of enormous, if understated importance. Its significance for conflict prevention is of particular significance since, as has been argued, effective conflict prevention depends upon *conflict prediction*. A number of early warning mechanisms have been established within the Council Secretariat and the Commission but it is unclear upon what sources of information these mechanisms will base an early warning upon. The transfer of the Torrejon Satellite Centre from the WEU to the EU, as an agency, will provide CESDP with its only indigenous intelligence capability. This may though prove to be of limited value since much of the imagery it provides is for non-military applications and is not of particularly high resolution. The willingness of the EU member states or other organisations, such as NATO, to share intelligence with the early-warning units or even with the main EU institutions, is severely limited by the porous nature of the EU (due in part to treaty-based commitments to openness and transparency) and the fact that until very recently it was a 'civilian power' with no security culture.

NATO, ESDI, and conflict prevention

NATO's conflict prevention role is twofold. First, NATO is more than a military alliance and its attraction to potential members allows it to ensure compliance with a set of standards consistent with stability and avoidance of aggression. In this regard NATO's Partnership for Peace (PfP) and the Euro-Atlantic Partnership Council (EAPC) are important.

Second, until a few years ago OSCE was regarded as the focus of the region's conflict prevention effort. Traditionally, the OSCE has stressed its preventive diplomacy role, but conflict prevention requires a "comprehensive strategy for the OSCE and much better coordination with other international organizations."[25] The concept of "interlocking institutions," adopted by the 1992 CSCE Helsinki Summit therefore has considerable importance for conflict prevention and the development of good working relations between the OSCE and other international organizations, such as NATO. The Alliance's contribution to the institutional architecture was outlined in 1994 in Brussels. NATO offered to "support on a case-by-case basis in accordance with its own procedures, peacekeeping and other operations under the authority of the UN Security Council or the responsibility of the OSCE, including by making available Alliance resources and expertise."[26]

NATO, in collaboration with other organizations, could therefore play a valuable conflict prevention role. It has already been argued that, in order to do so, it may be necessary on occasion to match efforts aimed at preventive diplomacy with military force, such as preventive deployment. The aim should therefore be to establish what has been described as a "politico-military" framework for crisis prevention.[27] Since the focus of this chapter is upon the regional dimensions of conflict prevention, the ability of the European Security and Defence Identity (ESDI) to become the "military" complement to the "politico" element (CFSP) is of central concern.

The ministerial meeting of the North Atlantic Council (NAC) at

NATO headquarters in Brussels on 10–11 January 1994 saw the first explicit references to ESDI when the NAC noted the

... enduring validity and indispensability of our Alliance. It is based on a strong transatlantic link, the expression of a shared destiny. It reflects a European Security and Defense Identity gradually emerging as the expression of a mature Europe. It is reaching out to establish new patterns of cooperation throughout Europe.[28]

The development of ESDI should be viewed in light of a number of decisions taken in London and Rome in the early 1990s. ESDI was unambiguously framed in the context of the transatlantic security and defence ties but it was also portrayed as a complementary activity to CFSP with the overall objective of strengthening the European pillar of the Atlantic Alliance. In the wording of the Brussels Declaration:

We give our full support to the development of a European Security and Defence Identity which, as called for in the Maastricht Treaty, in the longer term perspective of a common defence policy within the European Union, might in time lead to a common defence compatible with that of the Atlantic Alliance. The emergence of a European Security and Defence Identity will strengthen the European pillar of the Alliance while reinforcing the transatlantic link and will enable European allies to take greater responsibility for their common security and defence. The Alliance and the European Union share common strategic interests.[29]

The intent of ESDI is therefore quite clear, it is to strengthen the European pillar of the Alliance and to reflect a greater European responsibility for its common security and defence. However, a statement on paper is hardly sufficient by itself. What was required was a mechanism whereby the "indispensability" of the Alliance could be confirmed while at the same time allowing the CFSP's defence aspects to be operationalized in support of the move towards greater responsibility on the part of the European allies. The mechanism to accomplish this involves the introduction of a further important concept, that of the Combined Joint Task Force (CJTF) concept, with the intent of providing the operational link between CFSP and ESDI.

The CJTF concept was first proposed by Les Aspin during an informal meeting in Travemunde on 19–21 October 1993. American advocacy of the CJTF concept was based on the acceptance that, in some situations, American interests may not be as directly engaged, and that American capabilities may not be essential to the success of low-intensity operations. Thus, according to Ambassador Alexander Vershbow, US Permanent

Representative on the North Atlantic Council, "[i]n such cases, it made sense to enhance the potential for the European members of the Alliance to act – using the vehicle of the revitalized Western European Union – with the US in a largely supporting role."[30]

The CJTF concept was approved at the Brussels summit. Its key component was the offer to "make collective assets of the Alliance available, on the basis of consultations in the North Atlantic Council for WEU operations undertaken by the European Allies in pursuit of their Common Foreign and Security Policy."[31] Essential to the implementation of the concept was the development of "separable but not separate capabilities which could respond to European requirements and contribute to Alliance security."[32] Reference was also made to other emerging security structures, such as the Eurobrigade (later expanded to the Eurocorps), which "will also have a similarly important role to play in enhancing the Allies' ability to work together in the common defence and other tasks."[33]

Importantly, from the conflict prevention perspective, NATO also announced the Partnership for Peace (PfP) at its Brussels summit. PfP was the first of a number of chambers created for aspirant members from Central and Eastern Europe. More importantly, PfP cooperation came to be seen as a potent tool for promoting confidence-building and conflict prevention.[34] Although the EU and NATO soon proved that on enlargement they would not move in parallel, as had first been assumed, PfP nevertheless provided a complementary mechanism to the EU's Europe Agreements for ensuring non-aggressive behaviour and addressing a number of cross-border problems. NATO membership was also reinforced by Edouard Balladur's Stability Pact and its untarnished image as a victorious, albeit unproven, military alliance. Specific goals for membership were outlined in a number of individual dialogues between NATO and its recently admitted members the Czech Republic, Poland, and Hungary.

NAC's Berlin meeting, held on 3 June, recognized that NATO had become "an integral part of the emerging, broadly based, cooperative European security structure."[35] ESDI was seen as "an essential part" of the general adaptation to meet new security challenges. More specifically ESDI was regarded as a mechanism for all European allies:

- To make a more coherent and effective contribution to the missions and activities of the Alliance;
- To act as an expression of shared responsibilities;
- To enable the European allies to act themselves as required; and
- To reinforce the transatlantic partnership.

An explicit linkage between ESDI and the CJTF concept was made in the Berlin Final Communiqué when it was made clear that the CJTF concept is

... central to [the Council's] approach for assembling forces for contingency operations and organising their command within the Alliance. Consistent with the goal of building the European Security and Defence Identity within NATO, these arrangements should permit all European Allies to play a larger role in NATO's military and command structures and, as appropriate, in contingency operations undertaken by the Alliance.[36]

The Berlin Communiqué therefore provided an ad hoc procedure to mount non-Article 5 operations. The CJTF concept was intended to be "one system capable of performing multiple functions." It was however also clear that non-Article 5 operations "may differ from one another in contributions by Allies and, as a result of Council decision on a case-by-case basis, aspects of military command and control."[37] ESDI was furthermore to be "grounded on sound military principles and supported by appropriate military planning and permit the creation of military coherent and effective forces capable of operating under the political control and strategic direction of the WEU."[38] Rather confusingly the communiqué continues that the North Atlantic Council will prepare, with the involvement of NATO and the WEU, "for WEU led operations (including planning and exercising of command elements and forces)." However, the emphasis placed on the WEU to exercise political control left open the question of who actually exercises military control.

In spite of the existence of a "Europe-only" option, on paper if not in fact, many conceivable operations will nevertheless rely upon US assets. The Chairman of the WEU Assembly observed that, "[t]he US has unparalleled means for satellite and remote observation, intelligence-gathering, communications, transport, logistics, nuclear deterrence and effective air-land action, all which have ensured the Alliance's effectiveness in the past and are essential to action on any scale today."[39] For its part, Washington recognized since at least May 1994 (when President Clinton unveiled Presidential Decision Directive 25), that there were circumstances in which the US would not contribute to multilateral operations if no vital national interests were involved.[40] Henceforth, US involvement was to be more selective and effective. However, the resources that the WEU might draw upon in a CJTF operation would in most circumstances involve a request for the use of key US assets. This underlying point was referred to in the European Council's June 1999 Cologne Summit where demands were made for "assured access to NATO planning capabilities" and the "presumption of availability to the EU of pre-identified NATO capabilities and common assets for use in EU-led operations."[41]

The Alliance's Strategic Concept, which was unveiled at the Washington

Summit of 23–24 April 1999, makes a general commitment to preventing crises and, "should they arise to defusing them at an early stage."[42] Within the NATO structure the successor to the North Atlantic Cooperation Council, the Euro-Atlantic Partnership Council (EAPC), became an influential network for Alliance cooperation with its partners. EAPC activities include increased transparency and confidence-building activities that contribute to conflict prevention and crisis management. In association with EAPC activities the Membership Action Plan (MAP) which builds upon the Individual Dialogues established with some non-members and provides for a number of practical commitments as a condition for membership consideration, is also forwarded as another conflict prevention tool.[43] However, there is the danger that MAP could be seen as yet another chamber for Europe's select club, and frustration or ever higher and perhaps unattainable standards may dilute NATO's appeal.

The Strategic Concept recognized that the promise of membership or various partnership arrangements might not be sufficient to curb conflict and the importance of maintaining adequate military means to respond. Accordingly priority was accorded "[t]o protect peace and to prevent war or any kind of coercion." In order to meet this goal, alongside the non-military aspects of NATO's mission, "the Alliance will maintain for the foreseeable future an appropriate mix of nuclear and conventional forces based in Europe and kept up to date where necessary, although at a minimum sufficient level."[44]

Although NATO will continue to be the focus of the military elements of conflict prevention, with or without the North American allies, there are a number of other potentially useful developments that deserve brief mention in the conflict prevention context. The Baltic states, along with Denmark, Norway, Poland, and Sweden joined in creating a NORDPOL brigade for duty in Bosnia while also fielding a BALTBAT battalion. In the South, Bulgaria, Greece, Romania, and Turkey established a multinational Balkan force. Security collaboration even spread to central Asia for peacekeeping purposes. Although none of the above mechanisms proved sufficient to stem the tide of violence in Kosovo, the changes in Europe's security map, complete with the burial of a number of what had been portrayed as intractable problems, paint a more optimistic note for conflict prevention. Even Ireland, reacting to the changes in European security and the greater emphasis on peacekeeping, quietly applied to NATO's PfP. An active role in conflict prevention by such sub-regional groupings, especially those mentioned, is desirable, since they may carry a less burdensome political message than full NATO involvement. However, this has to be balanced against relatively slim resources.

The discussions about what contributions CFSP and ESDI might make to conflict prevention assumed a somewhat academic air in light of the crisis in Kosovo. The unfolding crisis in Kosovo and the humanitarian crisis during 1998 put conflict prevention at the forefront of Europe's security agenda.

Kosovo: Avoiding the issue?

Two sets of issues arose from the conflict prevention measures undertaken in Kosovo. First, the relationship between the European efforts and international ones may not be complementary. The debate over the legal basis for NATO's threatened air strikes opened up much deeper questions of the need for international endorsement for regional conflict prevention efforts. In the European context this was already an issue that had been considerably complicated by the open frictions between the UN and NATO in the Bosnian (UNPROFOR) context.

Second, the objective of the EU is to speak with "a single voice." However, they have not only failed to do so in nearly every post-Cold War crisis, but there is a marked preference to work outside the evolving conflict prevention and management mechanisms. The six-nation Contact Group, active in both Bosnia and Kosovo, marks the most notable failure to speak with a single voice. It was also apparent that the EU's inability to match its diplomatic and economic clout with military muscle could limit the EU as an effective tool for conflict prevention for an indefinite future.

The Kosovo crisis would seem to mark a watershed in the sense that aside from official pronouncements, NATO emerged from the crisis still standing but battered while the CFSP proved largely irrelevant since much of the diplomatic and military initiative and force were provided by the US and not Europe. Even the European contribution exhibited many differences, kept in check by Washington and punctuated with acrimonious exchanges. The watershed could therefore either condemn the EU and Europe Agreement countries to more of the same, depending on whether and when the US may feel like becoming involved. Alternatively, the nagging guilt that the EU countries might have done more to actually halt the humanitarian crisis, instead of turning it into a humanitarian catastrophe, will spur on efforts to actually create an autonomous conflict prevention capability. Similarly, as the considerable costs of post-conflict reconstruction and policing (for an unknown period of time) become evident, investing in and training for conflict prevention may appear to be an attractive option. It has to be hoped that the costs of reconstruction do not effectively freeze initiative or investment in conflict prevention.

Operation Allied Force underlined the fact that in some circumstances diplomacy needs to be backed by the threat or actual use of military power. It is all too apparent that the CFSP lacks a credible military option to be able to do this. NATO, on the other hand, is a blunt instrument and is primarily suited to be a crisis management tool. The EU's strengths are to be found in the lure of membership as well as its considerable economic leverage. The inability of the EU to offer a seamless web of conflict prevention options was all too apparent in Kosovo. It was the US that assumed the initiative and leadership. Yet it was the US's stalwart ally, Britain, who forced the pace of Operation Allied Force and was willing to take the risks associated with a ground operation in Kosovo.[45] Britain's role in the Kosovo conflict, when combined with the call at St. Malo for an "autonomous" European military capability may yet lead to the creation of a seamless web of CFSP peacekeeping options. In order to achieve this end the EU will have to find the necessary unity and sense of purpose to pull together, even in the intergovernmental second pillar.

Conclusions

Within Europe much of the emphasis has been placed on conflict resolution and management. In part this is due to the historical vestiges of the Cold War years, which not only stressed defence, but also shaped ministries, armed forces and, more importantly, minds around reactive approaches to crises. The general prohibition on intervention in the domestic matters of sovereign states meant that a conflict had to demonstrate regional or international consequences, by which time the crisis was normally well advanced and beyond the conflict prevention stage.

The crisis in Kosovo has underlined the need for less emphasis on conflict management and more on conflict prevention. In political terms, conflict prevention now features prominently within the CFSP and ESDI contexts. This also signifies recognition of the need for a comprehensive approach to conflict prevention that goes beyond the more traditional economic and political approaches. The question of who or what entity should assume responsibility for the military element of regional conflict prevention is less important than the need for such a capability. The call for "autonomous capabilities" may also encourage the development of less reliance upon the US in certain critical areas, not the least of which is an effective conflict prediction capability, with a possible downgrading of the importance of ESDI as a consequence. However, there are a worrying number of "ifs" and "buts" along the road to any indigenous European conflict prevention capability, especially the role of Russia and whether there is the necessary will amongst the participants to create the necessary defence industrial underpinning to plug the capability gaps. The $5 billion costs of reconstruction and financial assistance to Kosovo, the bulk of which the EU will foot, may concentrate minds wonderfully on the affordability of conflict prevention and the costs of conflict management.

What does the twenty-first century hold in store for CFSP and ESDI and conflict prevention? Javier Solana, former Secretary General of NATO, reminded NATO members that they "cannot remain aloof or indifferent to [the] potential for conflict, whether it exists in the more remote regions of this continent or closer to home, as in the Balkans."[46] The challenges of the twenty-first century also suggested to Solana that NATO's security policies must become "increasingly proactive." He noted that "many problems and potential conflicts can be anticipated, and many solutions can be devised before it is too late. From preventive military deployments to economic assistance – there are many tools at our disposal."[47] There could not be a more hopeful or ambitious statement coming from a man who shortly after was appointed as the EU's High Representative.

Notes

1. It could be argued that these principles themselves are under challenge with the rejection by some of the "traditional" or classical peacekeeping with its emphasis upon interpositionary forces, to more muscular forms of peacekeeping such as "peace enforcement."
2. "Areas for Pursuance of a Broad, Enhanced NATO/Russia Dialogue and Cooperation," *Noordwijk*, 31 May 1995.
3. Nicolae Tabacaru, Minister of Foreign Affairs of the Republic of Moldova. Statement at the meeting of the EAPC at the level of Foreign Ministers, 29 May 1998, at http://www.nato.int/docu/speech/1998/s980529o.htm.
4. Notorious examples of the breakdown of such cooperation were Belgium's refusal to sell ammunition to the United Kingdom during the Gulf War and Austria's refusal to allow NATO access to its airspace during Operation Allied Force (Kosovo).
5. See Hans-Georg Ehrhart's contribution to this volume.
6. For a good overview of the EU and conflict prevention, see Reinhardt Rummel, "The CFSP's Conflict Prevention Policy," in Martin Holland, ed., *Common Foreign and Security Policy: The Record and Reforms*, London: Pinter, 1996, pp. 105–20.
7. See for example, William Dixon, "Democracy and the Management of International Conflict," *Journal of Conflict Resolution*, Vol. 37, No. 1, 1993, pp. 42–68.
8. Strategic Concept, NATO Press Communiqué NAC-S(99)65, *The Alliance's Strategic Concept*, 24 April 1999, para. 31.
9. Codification of behaviour also requires the capacity to monitor errant behaviour and, on occasion, the capacity to intervene at an early stage.
10. The Conflict Prevention Network is a network of independent research institutes, think tanks and NGOs that assists the Commission to tap, rapidly and systematically, existing information and analysis on specific countries or issues.
11. See João de Deus Pinheiro, "Can EU Development Assistance Contribute to Peace?" Contribution to CESD/ISIS Conference on "The Future of the EU's Security Policy," Brussels, 24 September 1999, at http://europa.eu.int/comm/speeches/en/980924.htm.

12. CTEU, *Consolidated Version of the Treaty on European Union*, Luxembourg: Office for Official Publications of the European Communities, 1997, Title V, Art. 13.
13. *Ibid.*, Arts 14, 15 and 17.
14. The Petersberg tasks are humanitarian and rescue tasks, peacekeeping tasks and tasks of combat forces in crisis management, including peacemaking.
15. For an interesting discussion of the EU's relations with the WEU see Antonio Missiroli, "Flexibility and Enhanced Cooperation After Amsterdam – Prospects for CFSP and the WEU," *The International Spectator*, Vol. XXXIII, No. 3, Aug–Sept. 1998, pp. 101–18.
16. Petersberg Declaration, WEU Council of Ministers Petersberg Declaration, Bonn, 19 June 1992, s. I, para. 2.
17. *Ibid.*, s. II, para. 4.
18. Cologne European Council, Presidency Conclusions, Annex III, European Council Declaration on Strengthening the Common European Policy on Security and Defence, 3–4 June 1999, paras 1–2.
19. *Ibid.*, para. 3.
20. CTEU, Art. 18, para. 1.
21. CTEU, Art. 18, para. 3.
22. CTEU, Art. 26.
23. Treaty of Amsterdam, Declarations adopted by the Conference, Declaration 6 on the establishment of a policy planning and early warning unit, 2 October 1997.
24. St. Malo, Franco-British Summit, Joint Statement on European Defence, Saint-Malo, 4 December 1998.
25. Bohdan Lupiy, "Ukraine and European Security – International Mechanisms as Non-Military Options for National Security of Ukraine," Individual Democratic Institutions NATO Research Fellowship, 1994–96; ch. 4, s. 2.5.
26. Strategic Concept, 1999, note 8 above, para. 31.
27. Jaakko Blomberg, "Confidence-Building and Conflict-Prevention in the Euro-Atlantic Area," Statement by Under-Secretary of State for Political Affairs, Finland, Luxembourg, 29 May 1998.
28. Brussels Declaration, Press Communiqué M-1 (94)3, Declaration of the Heads of State and Government, Ministerial Meeting of the North Atlantic Council/North Atlantic Cooperation Council, NATO Headquarters, Brussels, 10–11 January 1994.
29. *Ibid.*
30. Alexander Vershbow, "Confidence-Building and Conflict-Prevention in the Euro-Atlantic area," US Permanent Representative on the North Atlantic Council, Madrid, 4 May 1998.
31. Brussels Declaration, 1994, note 28 above, para. 6.
32. *Ibid.*
33. *Ibid.*
34. See for instance Jan Eliasson, Speech by State Secretary for Foreign Affairs of Sweden, at a meeting of the EAPC, Luxembourg, 29 May 1998.
35. Berlin Declaration. 1996, NATO Press Communiqué M-NAC-1 (96)63, Ministerial Meeting of the North Atlantic Council, Final Communiqué, Berlin, 3 June 1996; para. 3.
36. *Ibid.*, para. 7.
37. *Ibid.*
38. *Ibid.*
39. Luis Maria De Puig, "The European Security and Defence Identity within NATO," *NATO Review*, No. 2, Summer 1998, p. 7.
40. Dispatch, "The Clinton Administration's Policy on Reforming Multilateral Peace Operations," (PDD-25), released by the White House, 5 May 1994. Text in US Department of State, *Dispatch*, 16 May 1994, Vol. 5, No. 20, p. 321.

41. Cologne European Council, 1999, note 18 above, s. 4.
42. Strategic Concept, 1999, note 8 above, para. 32.
43. MAP, Membership Action, NATO Press Communiqué NAC-S(99)66, 24 April 1999.
44. Strategic Concept, 1999, note 8 above, para. 46.
45. Patrick Wintour and Peter Beaumont, "Revealed: The Secret Plan to Invade Kosovo," *The Observer*, 18 July 1999.
46. Javier Solana, Keynote address, "Preparing NATO for the 21st Century," at the Maritime Symposium, Lisbon, 4 September 1998.
47. *Ibid.*

7

A good idea, but a rocky road ahead: The EU and the Stability Pact for South Eastern Europe

Hans-Georg Ehrhart

Introduction

If conflict prevention has received a new lease on life, this applies as well to those actors and organizations that have found themselves unable to be effective peacemakers, peace-enforcers and peacekeepers. The EU belongs in this category of actors. As Simon Duke argues in the preceding chapter, while it could not do much to stop escalating and ongoing conflicts, the EU should be in a better position to engage in normal and preventive diplomacy, to use Jentleson's terms, to prevent disputes from escalating into armed conflict. Moreover, in a new security environment, where not only military enemies, but environmental, economic, political, and cultural threats pose significant danger to the survival of individuals, groups, and states, "new security providers," i.e. those actors who can prevent what has hitherto been called "soft security threats" from escalating into hard security challenges, have another chance and, often, comparative advantage, to offer solutions to disputes before they escalate into war.

Although the EU is struggling to obtain military conflict management capabilities in the framework of its evolving Common Foreign and Security Policy (CFSP) as Duke shows in the preceding chapter, the main emphasis is to improve the EU's internal and external cooperative power through ongoing institutional reforms and procedural innovations.[1] The impact of today's conflicts on the EU, its values, its economy, and its in-

112

terests is such that there is no alternative but to cope. Ongoing tensions in the Balkans and elsewhere in Europe "challenge the long-term goal of enlarging the European zone of stability, prosperity and democracy toward Eastern and South Eastern Europe. It is essential that violent conflict is prevented from erupting in these regions if a stable, undivided, and peaceful European environment is to be achieved."[2] Conflict prevention is here meant in a broad sense to cover not only preventive diplomacy, but also the promotion of human rights, democratic institutions, and socio-economic development. In this sense, the ongoing process of a step-by-step EU widening starting with technical and economic assistance over trade and cooperation agreements to association agreements with the prospect of EU membership is little else than structural or early conflict prevention.[3]

I argue that there is a place for the EU in contributing to future security and stability of not only the core of Europe, but also its peripheries, including the region of South Eastern Europe. Thus, not only the European Stability Pact for Central and Eastern Europe, but also the Royaumont Process on Stability and Good Neighbourliness in South Eastern Europe as well as the Stability Pact for South Eastern Europe, targeting the Balkans as Europe's most volatile and conflict-prone region, are considered as useful and crucial initiatives in supporting the evolution of peace, stability, and prosperity throughout the region.

The key tasks of the EU are promotion of regional cooperation, support for economic development and democratic transition, and the manifestation of a regional and civil society in which citizens, state, and non-state actors interact with a sense of responsibility, purpose, and vision – in preparation for regional and intergroup cooperation for the sake of peace, cultural tolerance, and economic development. These may be high-flying goals, but the inability to meet them has led and will probably lead to further war, displacement, and bloodshed, as experienced in the Balkan region. This can be accomplished in the long run through a Stability Pact embracing all relevant players from inside and outside the region, by providing top-down assistance in coordination of sub-regional and regional initiatives and programmes, and by fostering bottom-up assistance in the creation of a working civil society within and between countries of the region.

The first part of the chapter discusses the EU Stability Pact for Central and Eastern Europe as a precursor of the Royaumont Initiative. The second part introduces the Royaumont Process as a conflict prevention instrument for South Eastern Europe. The next two parts deal with the Stability Pact for South Eastern Europe and the effort to use it for a lasting solution for the war-torn Balkan region. I will conclude with an evaluation of the lessons of the two first mentioned approaches and ask to what extent they have been applied in the third one.[4]

The Pact for Stability as a forerunner of Royaumont

The Pact for Stability for Europe goes back to an initiative by French Prime Minister Edouard Balladur in 1993, which was implemented in a modified form by the foreign ministers of the EU as the first "Joint Action" within the framework of the CFSP.[5] In view of the dramatic events in Yugoslavia, this initiative was aimed at making a preventive contribution toward the stabilization of Europe by strengthening the democratic process, expanding regional cooperation, regulating minority issues and guaranteeing the inviolability of frontiers. In particular, those countries that had not yet entered into agreements on cooperation and good-neighbourly relations were encouraged to do so. The main targets of this initiative were associated members of the EU from Central and Eastern Europe.[6]

The project began in Spring 1994 with an opening conference in Paris. It was attended by EU and OSCE member states, as well as representatives from NATO, WEU, UN, and the Council of Europe. Two "round tables" were created, at which "interested states" discussed problems of regional stability with the assistance of third parties. The participants of the round table for the Baltic region were the three Baltic states, the members of the Baltic Council, the USA, Canada, Iceland, Belarus, and representatives of both the OSCE and the Council of Europe. The Central Eastern European round table featured Bulgaria, Poland, Romania, Slovakia, the Czech Republic, Hungary, and the neighbouring states of Slovenia, Ukraine, Moldova and Turkey, as well as the USA, Canada, Switzerland and representatives of the OSCE and the Council of Europe. The EU chaired both round tables. Within one year, the project was supposed to result in a Pact for Stability for Europe, at which point it was to be transferred to the OSCE.

The Pact for Stability was adopted in March 1995. It consists of three parts. The principles of good neighbourliness and European stability are reinforced in a declaration. The OSCE is assigned the task of functioning as a collection point ("depository") for the agreements that are implemented by participants on a voluntary basis. The second part contains a list of more than 120 agreements, arrangements, and declarations which, for the most part, were signed prior to the beginning of the conference process. By the closing of the conference, the only new agreement was the Hungarian-Slovak Treaty. The third part consists of an annex, which contains project suggestions from the nine interested countries and financial commitments by the EU. These projects, ranging from a wide variety of issues such as language courses for the Russian population in the Baltic, the improvement of the communications infrastructure, or cross-border environmental projects, are intended to give substance to the objectives of the Pact.

Four months later the Permanent Council of the OSCE created guidelines for the continuation of the Pact for Stability: the majority of the resolutions are concerned with the regional tables which were considered to be a sensible method to deal with regional questions and to promote the objectives of the Pact. The instruments and procedures of the OSCE are available to verify the implementation of the agreements. The Chairman of the OSCE has to report regularly to the Permanent Council with regard to the two initial tables and any future ones. Project participants are invited to report periodically on their progress to the Permanent Council.

Since then, little has been heard about the Pact for Stability. Neither of the round tables met again and the OSCE confined itself to dedicating a working group to the subject at the Monitoring Conference on 18 November 1996. In addition, the EU Presidency presented the OSCE with a report on the implementation of accompanying measures financed with funds from the PHARE Program. According to the report, 38 measures had been started or were being assessed for approval.[7] Finally, the OSCE compiled a register of Agreements and Arrangements, which had been deposited by 25 October 1996.[8]

It would be wrong to dismiss the political effects of the Pact for Stability. It should be given at least partial credit for improving cooperation between its participants. One and a half years after its adoption, Romania and Hungary were able to ratify a basic agreement. The relationship between the Baltic states and Russia improved. Other initiatives for the promotion of good-neighbourly relations were prompted.[9] Networking in Central and Eastern Europe as well as between various international organizations was brought a step further and channels for dialogue were developed. NATO assumed the logic upon which the Pact for Stability was based, namely that minority and border conflicts have to be resolved before a country can join the Alliance. As a result, the main addressees of the Pact behaved cooperatively and resolved many of their problems bilaterally.

The Royaumont Initiative

After the acceptance of the Pact for Stability for Central and Eastern Europe and its transfer to the OSCE, the EU member states attempted to devote themselves to the question of medium and long-term stabilization in the region of the former Yugoslavia. Initially, the conflict was explicitly excluded from the application of the (preventive) Pact for Stability, as the conflict had already escalated to open violence. While the Pact for Stability was the first attempt to conduct preventive diplomacy within the framework of the CFSP, this initial experience was then to be applied to post-conflict efforts to stabilize the precarious peace in Bosnia-Herzegovina.

Following bilateral German-French consultations, the idea of a new Pact for Stability was discussed within the EU. Thus, on 11 December 1995, the Council provisionally resolved a Joint Action for the Participation of the Union in the Implementation of the Peace Treaty for Bosnia-Herzegovina.[10] The proposal was to be included into the context of the larger peace process in Bosnia. On 13 December 1995, shortly before the ceremonial signing of the Dayton Agreement, the Foreign Ministers of the 15 EU member states, representatives of the five Yugoslav successor states, their four non-EU neighbouring states, the USA, Russia, the Council of Europe and the OSCE (represented by the Chairman in Office, the Secretary General, and the High Commissioner for National Minorities) all met in Royaumont near Paris. The EU was represented by Italy, which held the Presidency at that time.[11] Based on a platform submitted by the EU,[12] the "Declaration on the Process of Stability and Good Neighbourliness" was adopted by the participants and started the so-called Royaumont Process – established within the framework of the Paris Peace Conference.

The objective of Royaumont is to make a contribution towards long-term stability and good neighbourliness in South Eastern Europe, and thus towards the building of a "new Europe, a Europe of democracy, peace, unity, stability and good-neighbourliness."[13] This was to be done in tune with the implementation of the Dayton Agreement. Worries that the Dayton process could be harmed by the EU's initiative were clearly addressed in the Royaumont Declaration, which describes its process as a "joint and continuous effort" that complements Dayton in terms of arms control and security arrangements. Moreover, its focus is the "progressive restoration of dialogue and confidence, the prevention of tension and crises, reconciliation, regional cooperation, economic reconstruction and good-neighbourliness." The Royaumont Process covers the same geographic region as the Dayton Peace Plan. Every state and every organization is called upon to "make a contribution ... depending on its wishes and its possibilities." As with the Stability Pact, accompanying measures to finance transborder projects were initially excluded, to be discussed at "Identification Conferences." It should be noted that the Royaumont Initiative does not wish to provide any economic reconstruction aid. It is meant to be a political process that, following the EU's regional approach[14] and in cooperation with other regional initiatives,[15] aims at the normalization of interstate relations and the support of civil societies in South Eastern Europe. These aims, already expressed by the Pact for Stability for Europe, were to take place within the framework of the OSCE, following the establishment of a "Regional Table for Stability and Good Neighbourliness in South Eastern Europe," at which all states in the region would participate with equal rights.

While the implementation of the civilian parts of the Dayton Agreement proceeded extremely slowly, the simultaneous Royaumont Process did not even get off the ground. Following the adoption of the Royaumont Declaration in December 1995, only four meetings had taken place by Spring 1997. At the first of these meetings, on 24 April 1996 in Vienna, the participants noted that the initiative had nothing to do with programmes for reconstruction or cooperation in security matters, but that it should be seen as a comprehensive process of stabilization concerned with political, civilian, cultural, and information-related aspects to foster good-neighbourly relations and sub-regional cooperation. Further regular meetings were approved, and the Presidency of the EU provisionally became the contact office for the Royaumont Initiative.[16]

The first four follow-up meetings of the Royaumont Process were rather futile: the significance of the process was emphasized, there were reports on other regional initiatives and activities towards regional stability, the work of the Royaumont Process towards a new round table for stability in South Eastern Europe within the framework of the OSCE was noted, and, of course, the next meeting was announced. Although these "accomplishments" were disappointing, at least the meetings offered a forum to discuss the various bilateral and multilateral initiatives in the region. Moreover, projects and ideas to promote stability in the region could be discussed in an atmosphere of equality by *all* interested parties involved, including the Federal Republic of Yugoslavia (FRY). Contacts were made and information was exchanged between the various regional and sub-regional initiatives that often worked on very similar projects and towards very similar aims and goals. It seemed that greater appreciation developed in all parties for the potential of regional cooperation – a not-so-small accomplishment in the conflict-ridden Balkans. Nevertheless, there was still plenty of room for improvement: There was no real coordination to speak of, and, as a consequence, forces for creative and effective synergy remained unleashed.[17]

The fifth follow-up meeting, which took place in Turkey on 27 October 1997, brought some progress. First, the participants agreed to institutionalize the Royaumont Process with the establishment of the position of a coordinator and the creation of a small secretariat. However, the EU states were unable to agree on a person to take up the position of coordinator. Busek, the Austrian Coordinator of the Southeast European Cooperative Initiative (SECI) had been discussed as a potential candidate. However, France objected to the appointment of a person that already chaired the "American Initiative" SECI, and it was agreed to postpone the appointment of a coordinator.

It was agreed that the coordinator should be the key representative of the Royaumont Process, be responsible for its progress, and be a person of international standing, who could dedicate himself/herself to the task "on site." He/she should furthermore draft the provisional agenda and assure the implementation of resolutions and guidelines. In addition, the coordinator should serve as the key contact person for all state and non-state participants in the Royaumont Process, and serve as a liaison person to other regional and sub-regional initiatives. He/she also had the task to identify, plan, and organize projects or programmes in the areas of culture, religion, sport, information, education, science and technology, to mobilize sources of financing, and bring together those social forces which can contribute to the evolution of a civil society in the region. Lastly, the coordinator would not only establish contacts between sponsors and local projects, but also with those persons in the OSCE responsible for regional confidence building and disarmament initiatives in accordance with Article V, Annex IB of the Dayton Agreement.[18] Eventually, the alternative candidate to Busek, the Greek Roumeliotis, was appointed before the sixth follow-up meeting took place in Athens in early 1998.

A further accomplishment of this meeting was that, for the first time, possible support programmes were outlined by a representative of the European Commission. It was clear from the very beginning that the Royaumont Process would primarily be a political venture, for which no special funding would be made available. Thus, support programmes had to draw on PHARE Programs that were already in place, such as those for the encouragement of transborder cooperation, for democratization, or for the reconstruction of Bosnia-Herzegovina, as long as allocation criteria could be met. As Croatia and the FRY had not yet complied with the political requirements established for PHARE aid, only very modest funds were available to them.[19]

The process continued to make some progress in the sixth follow-up meeting, which took place in Athens from 31 March to 1 April 1998. For the first time the top-down approach was combined with a bottom-up element. Before the official start of the conference a meeting of journalists from the 18 participating countries in the Royaumont initiative took place and a "Media Action Plan for Peace, Understanding and Tolerance in Southeast Europe" was adopted and later on welcomed by the Royaumont follow-up conference. There was much interest in a new formula that would envision meetings of representatives of civil society as participants of future Royaumont conferences. Further, for the first time the coordinator of SECI and a Member of the European Parliament participated in a Royaumont meeting. Finally, 45 projects were submitted, from which 36 fulfilled the Royaumont criteria (which are regional networking, cross-border cooperation, continuity, small or medium size of individual projects).[20] NGOs from Greece, the FRY, and Macedonia were especially engaged, while Luxembourg, Greece, and the Netherlands offered some funding for the first projects. It is worth noting that an invitation from Belgrade to host the next meeting was declined because of the FRY's policy on Kosovo.[21]

Instead, the participants met again in Graz. This seventh follow-up meeting confirmed two important innovations of the Athens meeting: the involvement of the European Parliament and the combination with a bottom-up element. This time a joint plenary session was held together with the Conference on Education Cooperation for Peace, Stability and Democracy. The Coordinator gave his first activity report in which he stressed the importance of the Royaumont Initiative's approach of promoting social dialogue and cross-border cooperation. Thus far 13 projects with the total amount of 2,250,000 ECU could be financed.[22] After having initiated several meetings and networks during the first year as Coordinator, Roumeliotis noted the growing support of EU institutions and the fact that the Royaumont Process was entering a new phase.

The most important step in this context was the EU's adoption of a common position on the basis of Article J.2 of the Treaty on European Union, concerning the "Process on Stability and Good Neighbourliness in Southeast Europe." The activity aimed at consolidating support for the Royaumont Process at a time of growing tensions in Kosovo and its neighbourhood. It did so in two ways: first, the common position gave the Royaumont Process a legal basis inside the EU. Second, the EU promised to support projects as accompanying measures to the Process.[23] In December 1998 the heads of state and government of the EU recalled the EU's strong interest in stability and prosperity in South East Europe and announced the passing of a Common Strategy for the Western Balkans once the Amsterdam Treaty had entered into force.[24]

Towards a South East European Stability Pact

Six months later another conflict had taken place in the Balkans, this time between NATO and the FRY, causing loss of thousands of human lives, uncounted injured people, several hundred thousand (mainly ethnic Albanian) refugees and a partly devastated country.[25] While the drafting of a common strategy remained in limbo, the German government pressed for the launching of a Stability Pact on South Eastern Europe under the auspices of the OSCE.[26]

The basic idea is that, given its particular interests, the EU should lead the effort towards a medium and long-term strategy that would take into account the results of existing regional initiatives such as SECI or the Royaumont Initiative. The EU and the OSCE are supposed to be main players in the field. While the EU is the most important political and economic point of orientation, the OSCE has an all-European approach and can involve important players such as the USA and Russia in a stabilization strategy for South Eastern Europe. NATO (which has developed a political-military regional approach in the framework of the Euro-Atlantic Cooperation Council and the Partnership for Peace initiative[27]), the Council of Europe, the United Nations, the OECD, the WEU, and the international financial institutions are also deemed to be crucial for such a complex stabilization effort.

In a Common Position of 17 May 1999 the Council of the EU stated that "a political solution to the Kosovo crisis must be embedded in a determined effort geared towards stabilising the region as a whole" and that therefore "a Stability Pact for South Eastern Europe should be prepared." The EU expressed the will to play "the leading role in establishing a Stability Pact for South Eastern Europe." Then the Council defined the aim "to help ensure cooperation among the countries in the region towards comprehensive measures for long-term stabilization, security, democratization, and economic reconstruction and development in the region, and for the establishment of durable good-neighbourly relations among them, and the international community." Furthermore the EU committed itself to the creation of a "South Eastern Europe Regional Table" to carry forward the Stability Pact. Finally, the whole process was to be kick-started by a foreign minister conference in July 1999.[28]

In order to set the pace the EU decided to go beyond the current instruments such as the regional approach for Croatia, Bosnia-Herzegovina, the FRY, FYROM, and Albania or reconstruction aid for Bosnia by offering these countries a new stabilization and association process with the goal of concluding Stabilization and Association Agreements (SAAs). These agreements are to provide a new kind of contractual relations with the countries concerned, including the perspective of closer integration into the EU structures. The conditions for the start of negotiations on such agreements are defined as follows:

- Rule of law, democracy, compliance with human rights and minority rights;
- Free and fair elections, full implementation of results;
- Absence of discriminatory treatment;
- Implementation of first steps of economic reform;
- Proven readiness of good neighbourly relations; and
- Compliance with the Dayton Agreement.

The conditions for concluding negotiations are:
- Substantial progress in the achievement of the objectives of the conditions for the opening of negotiations;
- Substantial results in the field of political and economic reforms; and
- Proven cooperation and good-neighbourly relations.

The EU Commission is starting with feasibility studies on the initiation of such negotiations with Albania and FYROM. Bosnia-Herzegovina and Croatia are not yet considered to be appropriate negotiation partners, and the FRY meets the least conditions. The EU offers other elements of the stabilization process regardless of the conditions for the Stabilization and Association Agreement, such as:
- The development of economic and trade relations,
- Economic and financial assistance,
- Increased assistance for democratization, civil society, education, and institution-building,
- New opportunities for cooperation in various fields; and
- The development of a political dialogue, including at the regional level.

The Commission is preparing regular reports on compliance by the five countries, as it has already done since 1996 with the conditionality criteria of the regional approach.[29]

Following the EU's call, the Stability Pact for South Eastern Europe was adopted by a foreign ministers' conference on 10 June in Cologne. It took place in the so-called "Royaumont format," i.e. the 15 EU member states, the EU Commission, the South East European countries except the FRY, the USA, Russia, Canada, and Japan as well as all relevant international organizations and the representatives of all regional initiatives. The participants reconfirmed the basic principles and norms enshrined in various international documents and expressed their will to seek the conclusion of bilateral and multilateral agreements on good-neighbourly relations.

As to the objectives, the participants underlined the general aim of strengthening the efforts of the countries of the region to foster peace, democracy, respect for human rights, and economic prosperity, in order to achieve prosperity in the whole region. To this end international efforts must focus on consolidating and linking areas of stability in the region to lay a firm foundation for the transition towards a peaceful and democratic future. The FRY was welcomed as a full and equal participant in the Stability Pact, provided the political requirements are fulfilled. At the same time, and in order to draw the FRY closer to the Pact, the participants expressed their intention to consider ways of making the Yugoslav Republic of Montenegro an early beneficiary.[30]

The mechanisms of this Stability Pact and the one of 1995 are similar, but not identical. A South Eastern Europe Regional Table reviews the progress and provides guidance for advancing the Pact's objectives. A Special Coordinator appointed by the EU and endorsed by the OSCE Chairman in Office chairs the Regional Table.[31] He is responsible for promoting achievement of the Pact's objectives within and between the individual countries. He will provide periodical progress reports to the OSCE and ensure coordination of activities of and among three working tables on democratization and human rights, on economic reconstruction, development, and cooperation as well as on security issues. As the Royaumont Process has established a framework for cooperation in the area of democracy and civil society, it is supposed to play a key role in the first Working Table.[32]

On 30 July 1999 the first Stability Pact summit took place in Sarajevo. It ended with the adoption of a Declaration of the Heads of State of the participating and facilitating countries of the Stability Pact that confirmed the principles already mentioned above. The first meeting of the Regional Table was convened in September, and the Working Tables began their work one month later.[33]

Conclusions

The Royaumont Initiative could be considered a good idea that unfortunately did not effectively get off the ground until the war in Yugoslav began. It is tragic that at the very moment when the initiative started to work the situation in Kosovo deteriorated. Thus, the basic idea of a Stability Pact for South Eastern Europe as a tool to prevent crisis escalation could only be put into effect after the war had started. Only then the EU and the international community showed the necessary commitment. At least, the EU has had a concept that could be adapted to the requirements of the new situation after the war. In summary, the lack of success of the Royaumont Process of stability and good-neighbourly relations has a number of reasons:

- First, utmost priority was given to the implementation of the Dayton Agreement and the extremely laborious progress in the implementation of its civilian aspects. The slow implementation progress was in part due to teething problems, bureaucratic inefficiencies, and a lack of coordination on the part of donor countries and international organizations.
- Much more serious, however, was the fact that those directly affected did not cope with their responsibility. The political leadership of the "patronage states", Croatia and FRY, only very reluctantly fulfilled their responsibilities under the civilian components of Dayton. In Bosnia-Herzegovina, the cooperation of the traumatized population was ten-

tative, and the political leadership in Bosnia, burdened by the war, lacked the will, faith, and confidence to cooperate in joint institutions.

- Third, the Royaumont Process was lacking the necessary political support from the Western capitals. Despite the highly problematic situation in Bosnia and later on in Kosovo, events in the former Soviet Union, the Middle East, and elsewhere required the attention and limited personnel resources in the major capitals' foreign ministries. The EU Council of Ministers, in particular, did not show serious commitment until October 1998, whereas the European Commission was not allowed to play a significant role in the Royaumont Process. To make matters worse, it took an entire two years to decide on the appointment of a Coordinator.
- Fourth, as the Initiative had no financial resources of its own, direct financial incentives were missing. Weak financial endowments of the projects and complicated application procedures for EU funds reduced incentives for cooperation and limited the effectiveness of the Royaumont Process.

Conflict prevention is a thankless business. If it is successful, hardly anybody notices, as was the case with the Pact for Stability of 1995. If it fails, the conflict may escalate uncontrolled as in Bosnia-Herzegovina and in Kosovo. The Pact for Stability for Central and Eastern Europe was a successful contribution towards long-term conflict prevention, as it allowed for multilateral approaches to potential centres of conflict – both at an early stage of the conflict and in a committed manner. It was not aimed at managing acute tensions, but at the improvement of "civic security" through the strengthening of democracy, the improvement of the rights of minorities and individuals, and the strengthening of economic and social conditions. In addition, it supported cooperation between individual states and international organizations. The Royaumont Initiative pursued similar objectives, but it had to develop in a completely different environment from Central Eastern Europe. Following the dreadful wars in the former Yugoslavia, the first priority of security providers was to manage and end conflicts, and then work towards the consolidating of peace in Bosnia-Herzegovina.

There are other important differences between the Pact for Stability for Central and Eastern Europe and the Royaumont Initiative. The addressees of the former had already been associated with the EU when the Pact was initiated. They were also aware of reasonable prospects to join the EU, based on their political and economic performance. In contrast, those addressed by the Royaumont Initiative either have great trouble fulfilling even minimum requirements for constructive relations with the EU, or they have no intention of doing so. The Pact for Stability for Central and Eastern Europe was pursued with great diplomatic commitment, and the overlapping interests of the main protagonists France and Germany were as significant to its success as the pressure created by the tight timeframe of only ten months between the inaugural and the final conference. In contrast, the Royaumont Process lacked the diplomatic initiative and political clout necessary to make it an influential instrument of regional security building and conflict prevention. Finally, while it was not difficult to transfer the Stability Pact for Central and Eastern Europe to the OSCE, a round table for South Eastern Europe within the framework of the OSCE was seen as not feasible until the FRY has fulfilled the requirements necessary to be readmitted to the Organization. In view of these differences, it is not surprising that the Royaumont Initiative has been caught in the starting blocks for so long. The experience with the Pact for Stability for Central and Eastern Europe shows that at least the following five conditions need to be fulfilled if the Stability Pact for South Eastern Europe is to become a functioning conflict prevention instrument:

1. The Pact must be supported by a core group of countries. Special responsibility falls to the EU, whereas Germany, France, Austria, Greece, and Italy would have to show particular commitment because of their specific interests in South East European stability and security. Closer collaboration with the USA, Russia, and Turkey is also necessary.
2. Adequate instruments and finances have to be available. They should be used primarily to assist in the evolution of civil society throughout the region. Consequently, a "top-down" approach that aims at the conclusion of treaties on good-neighbourly relations and political, economic, and cultural cooperation, should be supplemented by an intensive "bottom-up" approach which aims to soften dividing lines between intrastate and interstate divisions (often along ethnic lines) "from below." Since established elites can only overcome their concept (or vision) of the enemy with great difficulty, alternative social forces have to be given increasing support. However, to be able to do this requires appropriate funding, flexible instruments, and decentralized project management.
3. The willingness to cooperate on the part of *all* players is indispensable as a crucial prerequisite for the creation of regional networks and for improved coordination of the various existing regional initiatives. Effective coordination allows for a better flow of information, enhanced transparency, as well as an appreciation for the value of inter-organizational divisions of labour and burden-sharing.
4. The principle of sustainability must be considered vis-à-vis the conflicting parties as well as in the context of interconnected civil societies. If effective cooperation is to be achieved, participating states, international organizations, regional initiatives, NGOs, and other civil players have to be networked. In order to promote the willingness to

cooperate between these actors, a more consistent approach should be pursued. This concerns positive and negative incentives, as well as the need to hand over indicted war criminals to the International War Crimes Tribunal. If words and actions drift too far apart, credibility and, in extension, the success of conflict prevention will be undermined.

5. Preventive diplomacy must be incorporated into a comprehensive strategy of conflict resolution and peace consolidation. As the various meetings of representatives of South East European countries in recent times have shown, the political readiness to engage in regional cooperation is on the increase. The various opportunities and platforms for dialogue need to be consolidated. Furthermore, the various different versions of the "mental map" of the target region need to be brought in line from organization to organization, and from initiative to initiative.

If one evaluates the Stability Pact for South Eastern Europe with respect to these five lessons one could come to the positive conclusion that the right path has been chosen. However, in its present state, it is more a political statement that requires a great deal of work. The July 1999 conference gave the necessary political push and the March 2000 funding conference did the same in the financial field. The main challenge is now to maintain momentum. It should be clear from the very beginning that there is no quick fix solution but that the Pact is oriented to the medium and long term. The first task is to make the institutional structure of the Pact work. While the first donor conference is over and with others to come, the difficult question of "Who pays the bill?" is on the table and thus the quarrelling for short financial resources has started. The EU Commission estimates that a "Marshall Plan" for the Balkans would cost US$30 billion over the next five years, not to speak of the costs for the approximately 100,000 peacekeepers stationed in the region. Nevertheless, bearing in mind the costs of one B2 bomber (US$2 billion) the conventional wisdom remains valid that investing in prevention is much less expensive than dealing with war.

By embracing all countries concerned, all relevant international organizations, regional initiatives, and NGOs, the Pact offers the right framework for a multilevel approach. But it has to resolve the tricky problem of coordination of all these disparate players and to bind their different agendas, capabilities, and requirements into a common, focused purpose. In principle it responds to an important lesson from previous conflicts and represents a crucial condition of conflict prevention.[34] It remains to be seen how the bottom-up component will evolve.

Another lesson of conflict prevention has been taken into account. Although the long-term goal – in this case the integration of the Euro-Atlantic structures – is important as it gives direction to the various activities, the main emphasis of the Pact lies in the stabilization process, fostering a concrete step-by-step approach that leaves aside abstract and less fruitful debates on what seems to be desirable.[35] Translating the goal into concrete steps creates a strategy that is indispensable for a fruitful outcome. But again, it is crucial to keep the political momentum alive.

When dealing with actual or potential conflicts it is necessary to address both direct causes and the background or structural conditions favouring the outbreak of violence, such as political-military, socio-economic, and external dimensions.[36] The three Working Tables address the first two aspects, while the Pact's general approach attempts to change the external environment by favouring regional cooperation and European integration.

This leads to the last lesson, which is admittedly not very encouraging. The EU launched the 1995 Stability Pact *inter alia* in reaction to the violent conflict in Bosnia-Herzegovina. The Royaumont Process on Stability and Good Neighbourliness in South Eastern Europe was initiated after this war in order to prevent other ones, but the Stability Pact for this region could only be put on the rails after the Yugoslav war. The EU did not act successfully before the outbreaks of these violent conflicts, partly because of the lack of both capacity and political will to act preventively. This means that the EU's and all other players' institutional capacities and response systems have to be evaluated and adapted constantly in order to become more responsive to the prevention of violent conflict (see Duke, this volume).

The first Funding Conference for the Stability Pact for South Eastern Europe that was held in March 2000 went beyond all expectations. Representatives from 47 countries and from 36 international organizations took part. Instead of the 1.8 billion Euros originally targeted, 2.4 billion were granted for quick-start projects.[37] The major part of the 1.83 billion Euros was naturally pledged to projects from Working Table II; investments in infrastructure alone were 1.4 billion. Working Table I was accorded 430 million Euros, Working Table III was granted 81 million and the cross-table initiatives received 5.2 million Euros.

By the end of the Funding Conference, the fundamental institutional and financial prerequisites for the implementation of the Stability Pact had been established for the following 12 months. Thus the Pact entered a new phase: on the one hand, it is now a matter of utilizing the allocated funding in the most efficient manner in order to achieve the strategic goals for stabilization in the region. In addition, applications for new funds are to be initiated to ensure continuity after the quick-start phase. At the second meeting of the Regional Table on 8 June 2000, the necessity for clear priorities was emphasized and the establishment of a donor network was announced. This network is to serve as a flexible information and coordination forum.[38] On the other hand, there has been a necessity to re-examine the structure of the Pact and if necessary adapt it to changing situations and optimize it functionally. Finally, reforms have to be mobilized in the field. The countries of the region therefore have to be prepared to provide something in return for the active involvement of the international community and to make more of a commitment to the Stability Pact.[39]

There have been great expectations placed in the Stability Pact since it was adopted. After all, it is the first time a comprehensive peace project, which raises hopes for the sustainable regulation of the conflict potential in South Eastern Europe, has been launched. It has re-emphasized civil diplomacy in a war phase and thus contributed to a higher acceptance of the policies of the international community as well as having enhanced the value of the EU, OSCE, and the Council of Europe. Thus after the earlier failures in the Balkans, it offers the chance of gradually placing a prevention culture in position rather than using reactive crisis intervention.

However, an adequate policy requires time, courage to deal with complex situations, and stamina. These are very scarce resources in our breathless electronic media age. Accordingly the Stability Pact and the Special Coordinator were criticized in a seldom differentiated manner even before the Funding Conference. The Sarajevo Summit was publicly degraded as being expensive film footage or there were complaints about the allegedly belated date of the Funding Conference. However, the trite criticism "too little too late" can be countered with several arguments. First, it was necessary to establish a time-consuming broad consensus for smooth project implementation. Second, the success of the Conference was more important than its date. Third, a series of activities had already been embarked upon before the Funding Conference so that afterwards project implementation could be effected without disruption. According to Bodo Hombach, of the approximately 200 projects that had been at the starting line, 20 per cent had already begun by the end of June 2000.[40]

If one considers that, for example, in Bosnia and Herzegovina there was a lot of talk about coordination, but that at the end of the day everyone acted on their own initiative, the success and potential successes of the Stability Pact are by no means small. For the first time, the three international funding institutions, the World Bank, EBRD and the EIB are cooperating by sharing tasks. For the first time NATO and the World Bank are pursuing a joint project (professional training for former Romanian and Bulgarian officers). And for the first time specialists, who have dealt with a particular area of expertise, have come together at the same table to deal e.g. with problems like de-mining or the quantity and transfer of light arms and small weapons. Moreover the Stability Pact is based on an approach that includes several innovations. These are the emphasis on "public-private partnership" in project promotion, integrating non-governmental organizations in project implementation, and the development of plans of action with clear-cut benchmarks and timetables to evaluate projects. Finally the Stability Pact has contributed in many areas to the creation of regional cooperation.

Naturally it would have been desirable for the Stability Pact to be poured into a mould with less complicated structures. However, the present design has the advantage that it is flexible. The frequent lamentations about the "Balkanization" of the international Balkan policy[41] have found an ear, with the result that within the framework of the Stability Pact as well as within the EU, efforts have become visible to adapt instruments and structures to each specific situation. Thus the Royaumont Initiative was officially integrated into Working Table I on 8 June 2000. The Coordinator, the Greek diplomat Panagiotis Roumeliotis, had already taken over the Chair from Max van der Stoel at the beginning of the year.[42] Whether the regional initiative SECI will be integrated into the Stability Pact is under discussion. Finally, the designation facilitating state has been eliminated. Japan and Canada are thus full members of the Stability Pact. This is also true of Switzerland and Norway, who after persistent demands, were raised from the status of non-voting observers to full members entitled to vote.[43]

Furthermore, the criticism of the complexity of Balkan aid is directed primarily at the EU itself.[44] On the one hand, the EU claims a leading role in the Stability Pact, but on the other its organization suffers from being excessively complex. Moreover, when the office of a Special Coordinator was created, a hidden power struggle began between the Commissioner for External Relations and the High Representative for CFSP on who would have the most influence in a political area, which is considered to be the choice morsel of foreign and security policy in the EU. Let us take a quick look at its role: the EU is the initiator of the Pact and its biggest sponsor for the region. Like the UN, it has several Balkan representatives including Hombach. It runs a Reconstruction Agency for Kosovo and implements numerous promotional programmes for the whole region, which are administered by very diverse offices. The Council jealously guards its foreign-policy authority, the Commission its influence on funding and the High Representative for CFSP is also looking for an entrée into the internal EU scramble for authority.

By the end of March 2000, the Council of Europe self-critically realized that the financial, administrative, and political involvement of the Union was so complex that operational effectiveness was a problem. Too many political actors impaired efficiency and long-winded decision-making processes made quick reactions unfeasible. As a result, they gave Javier Solana and Chris Patten a mandate to secure coherency in EU Balkan policies and to strengthen coordination with the Stability Pact. At the same time they strengthened Hombach's role and thus rejected efforts to weaken his position.

Despite all the inadequacies of the Stability Pact and EU policies one must keep in mind that external aid can only be implemented in a manner that helps these countries help themselves. Past EU experience has shown that material and political incentives do not necessarily lead to the desired reforms. The most decisive point here is the political will, occurring in varying degrees in the countries affected, to put reforms into practice. However, this necessitates certain structural prerequisites. The basic economic principle "strategy follows structure" is also valid for South Eastern Europe. Certain basic structures must be established to implement a comprehensive development strategy. These include a legitimate political order, functional administrative structures, a minimal standard of legal security, basic equipment for an infrastructure, an adequate educational level and not least a certain awareness of the issues. That is, one must resolve no greater dilemma than that although economic development should lead to political stability, a certain amount of political stability is also a necessary prerequisite for economic development. For the moment it would be a great success if the quick-start packages led to a positive prevailing mood based on the justified hope for a better future.

Only if these lessons of conflict prevention are constantly observed, will the Stability Pact evolve as a road to peace for the whole Balkan region. If it turns out to be a "grand illusion," new bloodshed can be expected. Hopefully, EU countries understand what is at stake: it is not only the stability at the EU's South Eastern fringe, but also its very credibility as a cooperative security organization and its future international role.

Notes

1. Reinhardt Rummel, *Common Foreign and Security Policy and Conflict Prevention*, London: International Alert and Saferworld, 1996.
2. Marie-Janine Calic, "Introduction and Summary," in Peter Cross and Guenola Rasamoelina, eds., *Conflict Prevention Policy of the European Union. Recent Engagements, Future Instruments*, CPN-Yearbook 1998/99, Baden-Baden: Nomos, 1999, p. 11.
3. For a definition of long-term and short-term prevention or of "early" and "late" prevention, see Cockell, Jentleson, and Väyrynen, this volume and Max Van der Stoel, "Key-Note Speech to the Seminar on Early Warning and Preventive Diplomacy," in OSCE/ODIHR, *Bulletin*, Spring/Summer 1994, Vol. 2, No. 2, pp. 7–13; and Gareth Evans, *Cooperating for Peace*, St. Leonards: Allen and Unwin, 1993, pp. 65–70.
4. For earlier versions of this ongoing study please see the following previous publications by the author: "Prevention and Regional Security: The Royaumont Process and the Stabilization of South-Eastern Europe," in Institute for Peace Research and Security Policy at the University of Hamburg, ed., *OSCE Yearbook 1998, Yearbook on the Organization for Security and Cooperation in Europe*, Baden-Baden: Nomos, 1999, pp. 327–46; "Preventive Diplomacy or Neglected Initiative: The Royaumont Process and the

Stabilization of Southeastern Europe," in Hans-Georg Ehrhart and Albrecht Schnabel, eds., *The Southeast European Challenge: Ethnic Conflict and the International Response*, Baden-Baden: Nomos, 1999, pp. 177–95; and "EU Conflict Prevention in the Balkans: the Royaumont Process and Beyond" (with Albrecht Schnabel), in Peter Cross and Guenola Rasamoelina, eds., *Conflict Prevention Policy of the European Union: Recent Engagements, Future Instruments*, Yearbook 1998/99, Baden-Baden: Nomos, 1999, pp. 55–69.

5. Hans-Georg Ehrhart, "EU, OSZE und der Stabilitätspakt für Europa: Präventive Politik als gemeinsame Aufgabe," *Integration*, No. 1, 1996, pp. 37–48. See also Pàl Dunay and Wolfgang Zellner, "The Pact on Stability in Europe. A Diplomatic Episode or a Lasting Success?" in Institute for Peace Research and Security Policy at the University of Hamburg/IFSH, ed., *OSCE-Yearbook 1995/96*, Baden-Baden: Nomos, 1996, pp. 319–33.

6. Bulgaria, Czech Republic, Hungary, Poland, Romania, Slovakia, Estonia, Latvia, and Lithuania. Slovenia joined later.

7. These measures are distributed across the fields of "Regional Transborder Cooperation" (15), "Questions Relating to Minorities" (4), "Cultural Cooperation, Including Language Training" (7), "Economic Cooperation in the Region" (3), "Legal Cooperation and Administrative Training" (4), and "Environmental Problems" (5). See OSCE, REF. PC/96, 25 June 1996.

8. See OSCE, Register of Agreements/Arrangements Deposited with the OSCE Pursuant to the Pact of Stability in Europe, Status as of 25 October 1996.

9. See, for instance, "Final Statement by the President of the Republic of Lithuania and the President of the Republic of Poland at the Vilnius Conference 'Co-existence of Nations and Good Neighbourly Relations – the Guarantee of Security and Stability in Europe'," in OSCE, PC.DEL/16/97, 10 September 1997; or Contribution of the Delegation of Malta to the Discussion of a Pact for Stability in the Mediterranean, REF. PC/290/96, 7 May 1996.

10. See Joint Action 95/545/CFSP, Bulletin 12/1995, 1.4.80-82. In addition, the scope of the PHARE Program was extended to include Bosnia and a crash programme amounting to 62.5 million ECU for imports in favour of Bosnia was resolved.

11. The European Commission was not represented.

12. See European Union, Process of Stability and Good Neighbourliness in South-East Europe: Platform for the Development of the Process, unpublished document (quoted as "Platform.")

13. See "Declaration sur le Processus de Stabilité et de Bon Voisinage," Royaumont, 13 December 1995, unpublished document.

14. At its meeting of 29 April 1997, the EU Foreign Ministers agreed to adopt a coherent policy towards South Eastern Europe. It is directed at four of the successor republics of former Yugoslavia and Albania. The policy lays out clear conditions that these countries must fulfil in order to qualify for trade, aid, and deepening of relations with the EU.

15. See for these initiatives Ehrhart, "Preventive Diplomacy or Neglected Initiative," note 4 above, pp. 177–95.

16. See "Process of Stability and Good-Neighbourliness in South East Europe, Identification Meeting," Vienna, 24 April 1996, Chairman's summary, unpublished document, pp. 1–2.

17. See here also Presidency of the European Union, "Stability Pact, Stability and Good Neighbourliness in South East Europe, Regional and Sub-Regional Cooperation," OSCE Review Meeting, Working Group 2(a), 18 November 1996.

18. See "Description of Tasks of Royaumont Process Coordinator," DG E, PESC IV, No. 11629/97, pp. 2–3.

19. See "Intervention by the Representative of the European Commission, EU Assistance in South Eastern Europe," Istanbul, 27 October 1997.
20. Updated Description of Programs Submitted to the Royaumont Process, April 1998, unpublished document. The proposals deal with Media (6), Inter-Ethnic Dialogue (3), Dialogue Between Political Leaders (2), Academic Cooperation and Education (7), Cooperation in Science and Technology (7), Cooperation Between Women's Organizations (3), Cooperation and Partnership Between Cities (1), Cooperation Between Trade Unions (1), Youth Cooperation (1), Cultural Cooperation (6), Cooperation Between Business and Legal Matters (2), Inter-Parliamentary Dialogue (1), Cooperation in Public Administration (2), Cooperation for the Environment (3).
21. "Process on Stability and Good-Neighbourliness in Southeast Europe, Follow-up meeting," Athens, 31 March–1 April 1998, Chairman's summary, unpublished document.
22. The bulk of the funds came from member countries (Luxembourg, Great Britain, France, Greece, Netherlands, and Austria) wheras the rest was provided by private organizations and the European Commission. For more information see Processus de Stabilité et de Bon Voisinage dans le Sudest de l'Europe, Réunion de suivi, Graz, 17 November 1998, Rapport d'Activités du Docteur Roumeliotis.
23. Common Position 98/633/CFSP.
24. See Europäischer Rat, "Tagung am 11. und 12. Dezember 1998 in Wien, Schlußfolgerungen des Vorsitzes," *EU-Nachrichten (Dokumentation)*, No. 8, 1998, pp. 3 and 17.
25. See Hans-Georg Ehrhart and Matthias Z. Karádi, "Krieg auf dem Balkan: Lage, Interessen, Optionen, Lehren und Perspektiven," *Hamburger Informationen zur Friedensforschung und Sicherheitspolitik*, No. 27, 1999.
26. See Foreign Office, "Preparing a Stability Pact for South Eastern Europe," 9 April 1999, http://www.auswärtiges-amt.de/6_archiv/inf-kos/hintergr/stabeng.htm, from 24 June 1999.
27. See "Kommuniqué der Staats- und Regierungschefs anläßlich des 50. Jahrestages der NATO," Washington, 23 and 24 April 1999, in Presse- und Informationsamt der Bundesregierung, *Bulletin*, No. 24, 1999, p. 236.
28. Common Position, Annex to Council Conclusions, Brussels, 17 May 1999, http://europa.eu.int/comm/dg1a, from 6 July 1999.
29. European Commission – DG1a, The Stabilization and Association Process for Countries of South-Eastern Europe, http://europa.eu.int/comm/dg1a/see/intro/index.htm, from 6 July 1999.
30. The peaceful change in Yugoslavia and the overwhelming victory of the democratic movement DOS in the parliament elections of December 2000 have opened up new perspectives to the country, which was granted member status of the Stability Pact two months before. See *International Herald Tribune*, 27 October 2000, p. 5.
31. The former German minister Bodo Hombach has been appointed Special Coordinator. See *Frankfurter Allgemeine Zeitung*, 30 June 1999.
32. "Stability Pact for South Eastern Europe," Cologne, 10 June 1999, http://www.auswaertiges-amt.de/6_ARCHIV/inf-kos/hintergr/stabpact.htm.
33. See "Sarajevo Summit Declaration," www.summit-sarajevo-99.ba.
34. See for example Paul van Tongeren, "European Platform for Prevention and Transformation: Organising Support for a Plausible Idea," in Peter Cross, ed., *Contributing to Preventive Action*, CPN-Yearbook 1997/98, Ebenhausen: Stiftung Wissenschaft und Politik, 1998, pp. 61–73.
35. See Mark Salter, "Balkan Endgame: The Kosovo Conflict in a Southern Balkan Context," in Peter Cross, ed., *Contributing to Preventive Action*, p. 248.
36. See Pyt Douma, Luc van de Goor, and Klaus van Walraven, "Research Methologies and Practice: A Comparative Perspective on Methods for Assessing the Outbreak of

Conflict and the Implementation in Practice by International Organisations," in Peter Cross, ed., *Contributing to Preventive Action*, pp. 75–90.

37. Detailed information on individual projects can be obtained from the annex of the report given by the Special Coordinator for the Funding Conference. See Special Coordinator of the Stability Pact for South Eastern Europe, *Report of the Special Coordinator for the Regional Funding Conference for South East Europe*, Brussels, 23 March 2000, 29–30 March 2000.

38. Agenda for Stability, Regional Table, 8 June 2000, Thessaloniki, pp. 5f.

39. See corresponding Declaration of Intent of the informal meeting of the foreign ministers of the South Eastern European States on 7 June 2000, www.stabilitypact.org/ Regional%...20 report_on_the_informal_meeting_o.htm.

40. *Frankfurter Allgemeine Zeitung*, 30 June 2000, p. 4; see also Statement by Mr. Bodo Hombach to the OSCE Permanent Council, Vienna, 20 January 1999, www.stabilitypact. org/Speeches/Speech%20Vienna%20Jan%2000.htm.

41. See, for example, Erhard Busek, "Balkanisierung als politische Strategie?," in *Europäische Rundschau*, 1/2000, pp. 41–3.

42. Déclaration sur le Processus de Royaumont, www.stabilitypact.org/Regional%...%20le& 20Processus%20de%20Royaumont.htm.

43. To give support to their demands to become full members, Switzerland threatened to cut its lump-sum payments to finance administrative and organizational expenses of the Pact. *Neue Züricher Zeitung*, 30 March 2000, p. 1.

44. Romano Prodi, "EU Must Bring Peace to the Balkans," *International Herald Tribune*, 21 March 2000, p. 6.

8

The OSCE and conflict prevention in the post-Soviet region[1]

Natalie Mychajlyszyn

Introduction

At the Copenhagen Council meeting in 1997, the Organization for Security and Cooperation in Europe (OSCE) was designated by its 54 participating states as the primary instrument in the region for conflict prevention.[2] This designation reflected in large part an emerging OSCE tradition for involvement in this vital area of activity as well as the confidence of the participating states in the OSCE's efforts to prevent conflict in post-Cold War Europe.[3] Indeed, OSCE supporters point to the absence of violent ethno-national conflict in Estonia, Latvia, and Ukraine as testament to the OSCE's strong record in its application of conflict prevention, primarily through the OSCE field mission and the activities of the High Commissioner on National Minorities (HCNM). Notwithstanding this enthusiastic support, the application of the field mission and the HCNM as tools of conflict prevention have not been without difficulty. While these three cases may lend themselves to illustrate the strengths of the OSCE experience in preventing conflict, they are equally valuable to advancing our understanding of the challenges encountered by the field mission and the HCNM as tools of conflict prevention.

Accordingly, this chapter focuses on the experience of the OSCE in the prevention of conflict in Estonia, Latvia, and Ukraine as a crucial study of lessons learned, both positive and negative, about the application of conflict prevention by regional organizations. It furthermore reflects on the strengths and weaknesses of the OSCE's efforts and suggests recommendations to refine its application of conflict prevention.

The chapter begins with a description of the OSCE's conception of conflict and conflict prevention. This is followed by a brief examination of the post-Soviet situations in Estonia, Latvia, and Ukraine as illustrations of potential ethnic conflict with which the OSCE is concerned and to which it applies its tools of conflict prevention. The next section outlines the two most prominent tools applied by the OSCE to prevent conflict, the field mission and the HCNM.[4] The lessons learned from these applications will be interspersed throughout this section. The chapter will conclude with a short assessment of the OSCE's application of conflict prevention, followed by a list of recommendations for improving areas of weakness in the OSCE.

The OSCE's approach to conflict prevention

Although the participating states have not explicitly defined conflict prevention, OSCE documents indicate that its conception closely follows a general definition from the literature: "efforts to avoid the development of contentious issues and the incompatibility of goals" and/or "measures which contribute to the prevention of undesirable conflict behaviour once some situation involving goal incompatibility has arisen."[5] In the first instance, the OSCE is concerned with the elimination of the root causes of conflict as a means of avoiding the development of incompatible goals. In the second instance, the "undesirable conflict behaviour" for the OSCE entails violent expressions of mutually incompatible differences. It follows that, in addition to eliminating the root causes of conflict, the OSCE's application of conflict prevention targets violence as the means through which competing interests are addressed, leading the OSCE to be concerned as well with tensions that can escalate into violence. Thus, the twin objectives of the OSCE's application of conflict prevention are the elimination of the root causes of conflict and the prevention of violent expressions of differences when tensions occur.

For the OSCE, the causes of conflict are many, but one root cause has become central to many instances of the OSCE's application of conflict prevention: the violation of national minority rights, related to aggressive nationalism and xenophobia.

The participating states commit themselves to cooperate "to counter tensions that may lead to conflict. The sources of such tensions include violations of human rights and fundamental freedoms and of other commitments in the human dimension; manifestations of aggressive nationalism, racism, chauvinism, xenophobia and anti-Semitism also endanger peace and security."[6]

By framing the violation of national minority rights in terms of sources of conflict, the OSCE has also signalled it as a threat to European security. In this respect, security can be strengthened by promoting respect for the rights of national minorities in Europe, and "by attaining in particular full respect for human rights, including those inscribed in the CSCE provisions on national minorities" the root causes of tensions could be eliminated.[7] It is particularly noteworthy that the OSCE is unprecedented in recognizing the link between the protection of national minority rights and European peace and security, as "the rights of persons belonging to national minorities ... is an essential factor for peace, justice, stability and democracy."[8]

Ethno-national tensions in Estonia, Latvia, and Ukraine

This understanding of conflict and conflict prevention informed the OSCE's concerns with the potential for ethno-national conflict in Estonia, Latvia, and Ukraine and prompted its application of conflict prevention to these areas in 1992, 1993, and 1994, respectively. In the period prior to the OSCE's interventions, concerns were raised about possible violations of national minority rights in light of tensions arising between the Russian minority and the titular ethno-national groups. In Estonia and Latvia, these tensions revolved around the interrelated issues of language and citizenship. In essence, the political leaders in Estonia and Latvia adopted policies in these areas that sought to reverse the legacy of 50 years of Soviet rule and Russification, particularly its negative impact on their demographic and linguistic character.[9] Most importantly, both Estonia and Latvia adopted the policy of "reinstatement," thereby restoring citizenship to those who held it in 1940 and requiring all others to follow a severe process of naturalization.[10] However, these policies marginalized the sizeable Russian population in Estonia and Latvia, many of whom had been long-time residents of these countries and, given their support for independence, felt betrayed by the citizenship policy.

To this unpleasant mix were added other potentially destabilizing issues, such as the unsettled status of approximately 35,000 Soviet military pensioners who were prohibited by Estonian and Latvian law from ever obtaining citizenship and the continued presence of former Soviet and now Russian troops in Estonia and Latvia, which both governments wanted withdrawn to the Russian Federation. Furthermore, the Latvian government wanted the former Soviet radar station at Skrunda closed down and dismantled. For the Russian Federation's part, its insecurities and difficulties with readjusting its relations with former republics as those between independent, sovereign states raised concerns about a military intervention on behalf of Russian minority rights; indeed, in October 1992,

Russia suspended the withdrawal of Russian troops from the Baltics out of concern for the violation of Russian minority rights in the region, adding another element to an already unstable situation.[11]

Tensions in Ukraine revolved around two dynamics. First, Ukraine's territorial integrity was directly threatened by Crimean Russians who were pursuing secession of the peninsula from Ukraine and reunification with Russia.[12] Second, the Crimean Tatars were demanding recognition of their indigenous status in Ukrainian and Crimean political and legal documents and that they be granted the rights accorded by such a status, such as guarantees of representation and inclusion in the decision-making and political institutions of Crimea commensurate with their proportion of the Crimean population. The Crimean Tatars were also asking that returning deportees be assisted in overcoming legal, administrative, and financial obstacles to acquiring Ukrainian citizenship.[13] Taking note of the number of national minorities in Ukraine and the potential risk of setting a precedent for secession given that Ukraine's land was, in some cases as recently as World War II, formerly part of Russia, Poland, Czechoslovakia, and Romania,[14] the Ukrainian political leadership rejected all secessionist claims and pursued a policy of building a civic, territorial post-Soviet Ukrainian identity without privileging one ethnic group over others. In addition, the Crimean situation was complicated by the outstanding issue of the status of the Black Sea Fleet and competing claims of ownership by Ukraine and the Russian Federation. Nostalgia in Russia for the time when Ukraine was an integral part of the Russian empire was also raising concerns in Kyiv about Russia's intentions towards post-Soviet Ukraine, aggravated by periodic Duma resolutions which in effect challenged Crimea's status as part of Ukraine.

OSCE conflict prevention tools[15]

By eliminating the causes of conflict and preventing the escalation of tensions into violence, as exemplified by the situations in Estonia, Latvia, and Ukraine, the OSCE features not only an elaborate programme of commitments to uphold its principles and norms in these areas, but also tools, of which two will be examined in this chapter: the OSCE field mission and the High Commissioner on National Minorities.[16]

The OSCE field mission

The OSCE field mission is dispatched to participating states experiencing either the threat of or actual ethno-national conflict.[17] It is active on a long-term basis, for a renewable period of six months.[18] Established by the Senior Council or the Permanent Council of the OSCE,[19] its mandate is specific to the situation at hand, but in large part involves the facilitation of the political processes that are intended to prevent conflicts and to ensure that the OSCE community is kept informed of developments in the countries where missions are present.[20]

As part of its application of conflict prevention, the OSCE established field missions in Estonia, Latvia, and Ukraine in 1992, 1993, and 1994, respectively. The OSCE mission to Latvia is exemplary of the conflict prevention role and activities of the field mission. Established in September 1993, the mission received its terms of reference in October 1993 and became operational in November 1993.[21] Reflecting the tensions between the titular national group and the ethnic Russian minorities over language and citizenship rights, the OSCE mission's mandate was primarily concerned with addressing citizenship issues and other related matters: providing advice to the Latvian government and authorities on such issues; providing information and advice to institutions, organizations, and individuals with an interest in a dialogue on these issues; gathering information and reporting on developments relevant to the full realization of OSCE principles, norms, and commitments.[22]

To fulfil this broad mandate, the OSCE mission to Latvia was involved in several areas of activity. With respect to addressing citizenship and other related issues, the mission closely followed and advised the Latvian government on the drafting of specific relevant legislation (citizenship issues, language, education, employment, stateless persons) and the monitoring of its implementation, for example the issuing of non-citizen passports and naturalization testing.[23] Accordingly, the mission monitored and maintained a dialogue with Latvian authorities concerning the implementation of the 1994 Citizenship Law and the 1995 Law on Non-Citizens. Of particular concern regarding citizenship issues for the mission were the low levels of naturalization. In this respect, the mission travelled to towns and cities across the country in order to evaluate local attitudes to citizenship and registration issues and to observe what programmes are being implemented at the local level.[24] The mission was also actively involved in the preparation of a public opinion survey designed to make clearer the reasons for the low number of applications for naturalization and to encourage initiatives to promote the integration process.[25] Indeed, the mission also worked closely with the Latvian government on ways of promoting peaceful integration in Latvia and welcomed the outcome of the referendum of 3 October 1998, which favoured the implementation of the amendments to the June 1998 Citizenship Law, aimed at facilitating the acquirement of Latvian citizenship by the non-Latvian population.[26]

In addition, the OSCE mission to Latvia continuously played the role of a third-party facilitator with regard to the implementation of two June 1994 bilateral agreements between Latvia and the Russian Federation. In this respect, the Head of Mission served as OSCE Representative to the Latvian-Russian Joint Commission on Military Pensioners which handled problems connected with the retired Russian military personnel who stayed on in Latvia after the bulk of Russian forces was withdrawn in 1994.[27] Likewise, since it was established in May 1995, the Joint Committee on the Skrunda radar station features an OSCE Representative to assist in the implementation of the agreement to dismantle the station. On 31 August 1998 the Russian Federation fulfilled its obligation to switch off the Skrunda radar station and has since been dismantling it.[28]

Lesson learned no. 1: Importance of continual, on-site presence

The field mission provides the basis for identifying the first lesson learned from the OSCE's application of conflict prevention: the importance of a continual, on-site presence. Such a presence serves several valuable purposes of which only a few are listed here. One, it provides an early-warning service by constantly monitoring the local situation. Two, it provides first-hand, objective information to the international community that has not been filtered by any of the parties to the disputes.[29] Three, it provides a daily point of contact to which the parties may refer for immediate assistance and clarification of key issues. Finally, it offers an international presence and reassures the parties involved that the international community is regarding the situation closely and with great interest and concern.

Reflecting the value of the on-site presence, the OSCE mission symbolizes the intrusive quality of the OSCE's application of conflict prevention. So intrusive are these missions that they frequently develop a stake in the outcome of the situation, thereby inserting a positive influence into the process. By providing direct access, OSCE missions reinforce the dual message that issues regarding national minorities are of concern to the international community and that violations of national minority rights will not be neglected. As noted by the OSCE, "OSCE missions and field activities are the front line of the OSCE's work. They give the Organization an active presence in countries that require assistance and are the vehicle through which political decisions are translated into action."[30]

The positive contribution of the on-site presence to conflict prevention is illustrated by the OSCE missions to Estonia and Ukraine. In specific incidents, the OSCE missions' front-line position permitted them to identify immediately the crisis situation and to provide prompt assistance to defuse it. In Estonia, for instance, the OSCE mission was readily available during the June/July 1993 crisis over the draft Law on Aliens which the Estonian president refused to sign because of its controversial measures affecting the non-Estonian population.[31] The OSCE mission was approached by the Estonian president to advise on the diffusion of the escalating tensions principally among the non-Estonians and Estonian parliamentarians. Subsequently, the law was amended, the president established a Presidential Roundtable on minority issues and a procedure was adopted by which non-citizens were able to participate in subsequent local elections.[32]

Likewise, the OSCE mission to Ukraine organized roundtables in May 1995, September 1995, and March 1996 which had a positive effect and moved the Crimean situation away from a situation of tension and potential ethno-national violence. For instance, following Spring 1995 during which time tensions escalated over Crimea,[33] the May 1995 Locarno roundtable was noted to have developed among the participants a sense of belonging to a common political family, what the Head of the OSCE mission to Ukraine referred to as the "spirit of Locarno."[34] This spirit was represented in the unanimous recommendations produced by the participants that were considered to offer practical proposals to begin constructive work on a new Crimean constitution.[35]

However, the contribution of the on-site presence to the prevention of conflict is affected by several factors, some of which were evident with respect to the OSCE missions to Estonia, Latvia, and Ukraine. Of particular importance in this regard are the quality and skills of the mission personnel in terms of knowledge of human rights issues, training in human rights monitoring, diplomatic experience, and language skills. For instance, the Estonian and Latvian missions were generally staffed by diplomats from the Nordic countries who have extensive practical experience and knowledge of human rights issues.[36] Although interpreters were available as necessary, the independence and effectiveness of the mission personnel was also amplified by their knowledge of English (the working language of the OSCE), Russian, and, in some instances, even Estonian, Latvian, and Ukrainian.

Other factors pertaining to the missions have negatively affected their contributions. For instance, mission personnel were assigned for six-month rotations. This constant change in personnel disrupted the mission's activities and seriously weakened the institutional memory of the mission. It also affected the mission's ability to make any extensive long-term planning, and to establish processes and infrastructure within countries that encourage long-term dialogue and transformation of potential conflict. The potential damage of this inconsistency in staff is evident where the actual development and refinement of the mission mandate is done on site because the mission mandates are deliberately vague and lack operational specificity in order to allow for a range of activities and mission involvement. As a result, activities end up being designed and implemented by either non-specialists or temporarily assigned staff.[37] Notwithstanding that the short-term rotations are less of an issue now because mission personnel increasingly extend their assignments for at least a year, these longer rotations have not been formally adopted as personnel policy. At the same time, however, the OSCE faces competition with other organizations and international bodies and at times encounters difficulties in staffing the missions with suitable, skilled officers; indeed, OSCE missions themselves compete amongst each other for qualified staff. The onus is on the participating states to supply and compensate its nationals, generating another area of weakness and imbalance in the quality of personnel that only now is receiving the attention of the OSCE.[38]

Another factor has been the on-site facilities from where the missions operate. Although they are modestly supplied with adequate transportation, communication, and administrative equipment by the OSCE Secretariat in Vienna, the larger issue has been the insufficient cooperation from the host state in providing and locating suitable accommodation. In Ukraine, for instance, the operation of the mission and branch office from hotel rooms for a period of a year considerably hampered their productivity and effectiveness. The branch office personnel in Simferopol spent a considerable amount of time and effort on establishing a permanent office; time and effort that could have been better spent on the mandate of the mission. At the same time, the hotel accommodation suggested a temporary, short-term presence and an indication of a less than serious approach by Kyiv and Simferopol to the activities of the OSCE.

A final factor that complicates the activities of the OSCE and that negatively affects its efforts to prevent conflict is the negative perception attributed to it by the host state. Specifically, the presence of the OSCE mission is often unfavourably perceived as an indication of an unstable area, thereby warding off necessary foreign investment and weakening the country's economic development in these areas.[39] While this negative perception has not been found to affect the extent to which the host government and local disputants cooperate with the mission, it has put pressure on the OSCE mission to withdraw prematurely from a situation which it feels warrants its continued attention and assistance.[40]

The High Commissioner on National Minorities

The High Commissioner on National Minorities (HCNM) is exclusively concerned with the implementation of commitments pertaining to national minorities and violations of national minority rights. Established at the 1992 Helsinki Summit in order to enhance the OSCE's capacities of early warning where ethno-national tensions were concerned, the HCNM's mandate is to

[p]rovide "early warning" and, as appropriate, "early action" at the earliest possible stage in regard to tensions involving national minority issues which have not yet developed beyond an early warning stage, but, in the judgement of the High Commissioner, have the potential to develop into a conflict within the CSCE area, affecting peace, stability or relations between participating States, requiring the attention of and action by the [Ministerial] Council or the [Senior] Council.[41]

The HCNM is the only agent of the OSCE specifically involved in preventing ethno-national conflict. He/she plays a key initial role in beginning a process of action that would avoid an escalation of tensions and prevent ethno-national conflict from erupting at the sub-state level.[42] The HCNM is invited by the participating state experiencing such situations to use good offices, to play an advisory role, to mediate and to make recommendations that generally reflect the principles, norms, rules, and decision-making procedures of the OSCE regime in order to defuse tensions arising from issues involving national minorities. The HCNM's solutions emphasize the need for the protection of minority rights to be seen as a direct interest of the majority population and the state. Furthermore, he/she supports those solutions that work within the framework of the state, such as harmonized relations between majority and minority ethnic groups. The HCNM serves to remind states that violate human dimension commitments that stability and harmony are best served by ensuring the rights of national minorities. At the same time, members of a minority are reminded that, in addition to rights, they also have duties to society in the sense of refraining from actions or positions that can exacerbate tensions.[43]

For the most part, the HCNM's efforts to prevent conflict are manifested through personal visits and correspondence with the government in question. These efforts are exemplified in his involvement in Ukraine. Since his first visit to Ukraine in February 1994, the HCNM has played a particularly active role in the OSCE's efforts to prevent ethno-national conflict in Ukraine in his capacity of pursuing conciliation and mediation among the parties as well as by making recommendations on Crimea's constitutional status in Ukraine and on facilitating the citizenship process for formerly deported Crimean Tatars. The HCNM has visited Ukraine frequently and has met with relevant officials and authorities in Kyiv and Simferopol.[44] He has also corresponded steadily with the Minister for Foreign Affairs of Ukraine about the status of Crimea and the Crimean Tatars.[45]

In light of his mandate, the HCNM's recommendations strongly supported Crimean autonomy at a level that respects the territorial integrity of Ukraine. In one specific instance, the HCNM recommended that the 1 November 1995 Crimean constitution be amended so that references are made to the "Autonomous Republic of Crimea," not "Republic of Crimea," and to "citizens of Ukraine residing in Crimea," not "citizens of Crimea."[46] The HCNM also continuously recommended that Crimea end its pursuit of Crimean citizenship.[47]

Regarding the Crimean Tatars, the HCNM has urged Ukraine to facilitate citizenship acquisition for the Crimean Tatars, in particular focusing on the bureaucratic and costly difficulties surrounding the renunciation of another citizenship, thereby allowing them to participate in elections and benefit from other rights granted to citizens of Ukraine, such as employment and housing. Furthermore, he has recommended that the Crimean constitution provide the Crimean Tatars with the right to use their language with local authorities in areas where they make up at least 20 per cent of the local population. Regarding political representation for the Crimean Tatars, the HCNM has recommended, (1) a proportional representation electoral system that would give the Crimean Tatars "near certainty" for representation in the Crimean parliament "broadly commensurate to their percentage of the total population of Crimea," (2) changes to the Ukrainian election law that otherwise discriminates against Crimean political parties and Crimean Tatar political parties by requiring registration in at least 13 oblasts, (3) formal and legal recognition of the Mejlis as the supreme representative college of the Crimean Tatars and protector of the Crimean Tatar identity, and (4) the Mejlis being given responsibilities regarding Tatar culture and schools.[48]

Lesson learned no. 2: The value of a non-institutional, confidential, and flexible approach

The second lesson learned stems from the largely positive experience of the HCNM as another of the OSCE's applications of conflict prevention: the value of a non-institutional, i.e., personal, confidential, and flexible approach to the prevention of conflict. There are several advantages to this approach. One, it removes the constrictions otherwise found in formal, official negotiations that can corner parties and reduce their level of cooperation. Two, it increases the level of trust between the parties and the intervenor. Three, complications and unforeseen developments can be attended to immediately. Finally, it ascribes to non-state parties the same degree of attention and respect as state parties, thereby including them and their concerns in the process.

The experience of the HCNM personifies this lesson. He personally meets with the disputants concerned, promotes dialogue between them, and offers recommendations through which the parties themselves resolve the situation. The HCNM's informal meetings and consultations with the affected parties are held not on an interstate basis and with only government representatives, but also with opposition parties, representatives of key minority groups, religious leaders, and key individuals. He employs a "pragmatic political approach, trying to identify, first, the main causes of tension and, including through an analysis of existing and draft legislation, policies and administrative practices, second to explore the possibilities for mutually acceptable first steps to removing this causes."[49] He uses persuasion and cooperation rather than coercion to ensure durability based on consent. In addition, he "makes conscious efforts to show that he is aware of the many sensitivities involved in the situation under scrutiny, those of minorities as well as of majorities."[50]

The case studies of this chapter illustrate this second lesson. The HCNM's frequent travels to the areas of concern assured the parties involved that they have not been marginalized. Indeed, the HCNM's first visit was paid to the Baltic regions in January 1993; in the cases of Latvia and Ukraine, his visits precipitated the establishments of the OSCE missions to these countries. In Latvia, the HCNM had met with the Prime Minister, the Minister for State Reform, the Speaker of the Latvian parliament and the Chairpersons of the Legal and Human Rights Commissions of the Latvian parliament in order to promote integration and a dialogue between the titular nation and the Russian minority. In addition, the HCNM maintained regular correspondence with the government concerned, making recommendations and advising on matters at hand.

In essence, the HCNM's recommendations focus on the elimination of the root causes of conflict and promote respect for the rights of national minorities. Accordingly, in Latvia his attention focused on the draft law on citizenship and, in particular, on the provisions concerning naturalization, expressing reservations in 1994 with those that appeared to violate the rights of national minorities (such as the proposed system of annual quotas). In this instance, the HCNM's suggestions to introduce a gradual system of naturalization, which would provide non-citizens with more certainty regarding their chances of acquiring citizenship, were accommodated and the law was subsequently changed to make it compatible with international norms and principles. In addition, the HCNM stressed the need to promote Latvian language training to facilitate the naturalization process of non-Latvians as well as to inform the affected populations about programmes in this respect.[51]

As illustrated by his experience in Estonia, the HCNM has established a reputation of impartiality and serious knowledge of the local situations:

"Thus, the Estonian government was reassured that the HCNM would not be an 'Estonian-basher' or be focusing exclusively on protecting the human rights of persons belonging to national minorities."[52] In this respect, the HCNM has informed the OSCE that serious human rights violations do not occur in Estonia, at the same time sending a message to the Russian Federation that claims of human rights violations of non-Estonians and non-Latvians were not supported.[53] Likewise, the HCNM's activities have reassured the non-titular populations that they were not going to be expelled from Estonia or Latvia.[54]

As valuable as the HCNM has been to the prevention of conflict, concerns must be raised about the extent to which this favourable outcome relies almost exclusively on the individual occupying the position. More specifically, the first occupant, Max van der Stoel, served as HCNM for nine years when his term ended on 30 June 2001. His lengthy tenure raises valid questions about the extent to which the position is distinct from the occupant, thereby, and perhaps unfairly, setting unrealistically high expectations for his successors. Such questions will only be answered after a proper evaluation of the current HCNM, Rolf Ekens, who, since his appointment in July 2001, brings to the position his own skills and perceptions.[55]

Likewise, the achievements of the HCNM have generated higher expectations without a comparable increase in the resources available to support his activities. The success of the HCNM has generated more work than an individual could reasonably be expected to manage, placing unrealistic demands on his limited agenda and resources. Indeed, it is impressive that the HCNM has been able to accomplish what he has, given the limited staff and financial resources available to him. While the HCNM's office has expanded in an effort to cope with the increasing demands, there is a serious lag between resource allocation and the demands that are increasingly placed on the position.

Assessment and conclusion

At first glance, the OSCE's application of conflict prevention (here limited to the OSCE field mission and the HCNM) in Estonia, Latvia, and Ukraine has achieved its objectives: ethno-national tensions have not escalated into violence since the OSCE's intervention and arguably have receded. In Estonia, for instance, legislation concerning naturalization for non-Estonians has been amended to facilitate the process and to make it and its language requirements less restrictive. In addition, the Estonian government has been working at facilitating language training in order to assist naturalization applicants in their efforts to meet the language requirements and in improving its efforts to inform affected residents of the procedures. As well, non-citizens were allowed to participate in the October 1993 local elections if they met the five-year residency requirement. In February 1998, the Estonian government adopted a National Integration Policy, which lays out guidelines for implementation of the government's integration policy.[56] Above all, Estonia concluded agreements in July 1994 on the withdrawal of Russian troops and on social guarantees for Russian military pensioners in Estonia; the withdrawal was completed on time in August 1994. Finally, in November 2001, the Laws on National and on Local Elections were amended and approved by the OSCE mission.

Similar positive developments are evident in Latvia. More specifically, the Latvian government passed amendments to its citizenship law in June 1998, which aimed at facilitating the naturalization process for non-Latvians; these amendments were supported by the population in a referendum held in October 1998. Moreover, the Latvian government passed a law on non-citizens in April 1995, essentially confirming that former Soviet citizens will have all basic rights as spelled out in Latvia's constitutional law and permitting non-citizens to choose freely a place of residence in Latvia, as well as to leave the country and return by way of non-citizens' passports.[57] As in Estonia, Russian troop withdrawal was completed in August 1994 and agreements were signed in 1994 between Latvia and Russia over social guarantees for military pensioners residing in Latvia as well as over the dismantlement of the Skrunda radar station which, as per the agreement, began in August 1998.

Likewise, the overall potential for sub-state ethno-national conflict in Crimea has receded since the intervention of the OSCE in February 1994. In the first case, the potential for conflict over the status of the Autonomous Republic of Crimea in Ukraine involving the Crimean Russians and the Ukrainian government in Kyiv has diminished. In essence, Crimea's status in Ukraine as an autonomous republic with its own constitution, parliament, flag, and symbols has been legally formalized in the Ukrainian constitution adopted June 1996. Notwithstanding the delays by the Crimean parliament to bring the Crimean constitution into accordance with the Ukrainian constitution and legislation, ultimately, secession is no longer an issue.[58]

In these instances, the OSCE is regarded to have played an effective and influential role in obtaining these positive results. Indeed, the OSCE missions to these countries are now closed (Ukraine since March 1999, Estonia and Latvia since December 2001) and the HCNM pays fewer visits. In place of the OSCE mission to Ukraine, an OSCE Project Coordinator was established in Kyiv to coordinate various projects pertaining to the human dimension.

However, it must be noted that the closures of the missions were not without controversy. In contrast to the perceptions of the governments involved, a perception that was translated into repeated and longstanding requests to close the missions, the OSCE kept the missions operational in light of considerations that the situations were not yet stable enough to permit disengagement. For example, in both Estonia and Latvia, serious concerns remained about the slow progress of integrating the non-titular populations into the political, legal, and social aspects of these newly independent states. Knowledge of the titular languages remained at low levels, negatively affecting the extent to which these populations could contribute effectively to the political and economic development of Estonia and Latvia. In addition, the slow registration for alien status and the low rates of naturalization among the non-titular populations sustained concerns about the presence of large numbers of the population without a legal status. Ultimately, this situation raised questions about the extent to which both the government authorities and the Russian minorities favour integration in Estonia and Latvia.

Tensions remain in Crimea over perceived threats to ethno-national identities.[59] For instance, Crimean Russians continue to resist policies viewed as "forced Ukrainianization." In addition, the Crimean Russians are feeling threatened by the Crimean Tatars' demands, the increasing number of Crimean Tatars and their high birth rate; in their view, the Crimean Russians are becoming a minority group in their historic homeland.[60] As a result, they are concerned about protecting and preserving Russian rights "against Crimean Tatar nationalism and Islamic fundamentalism" and have been pursuing the establishment of an unofficial Russian parliament to overcome these concerns.[61] In October 1997, the Crimean parliament passed legislation making Russian the only official language of the peninsula.[62]

Furthermore, serious concerns remain about the Crimean Tatar situation since the intervention of the OSCE. In essence, their situation has not improved and remains problematic, involving difficulties surrounding their resettlement efforts, their unsuccessful pursuit of political recognition as an indigenous people, and obstacles to their acquisition of Ukrainian citizenship. Any lands that they are granted for settlement are not agriculturally sustainable or suitable for housing.[63] The Kurultai faction[64] of the Crimean parliament abstained from voting on Crimea's November 1995 constitution because it did not include guaranteed parliamentary representation for the Crimean Tatar community and then launched a hunger strike to denounce it.[65] Both the Ukrainian and Crimean constitutions fail to make specific reference to the Crimean Tatars as indigenous people of Crimea. Difficulties persist with respect to the acquisition of Ukrainian citizenship. As the Crimean Tatars are a very well-organized and disciplined ethno-national group, able to act on their organizational abilities, they present a great challenge for Crimean stability.

Thus, given the reduced presence of the OSCE in these three cases of conflict prevention, other valuable lessons emerge in addition to those already outlined, specifically with respect to the role of the field mission and the HCNM. These include the added benefit of inter-instrumental cooperation and coordination as exemplified by the close working relationship between the OSCE field missions and the HCNM. While this chapter was limited to these two tools, other OSCE instruments raise additional lessons to the application of conflict prevention, such as the advantage of providing regular fora for consultations (the weekly meetings of the OSCE's Permanent Council in Vienna), the value of a comprehensive membership to assure that all interests are considered, and the availability of different entry mechanisms by which the organization is able to exert influence on potential members' political, economic, and cultural transition processes.

However, the OSCE is aware of the limits of its conflict prevention activities and, since it first began the institutionalization process, has continuously sought ways for improving these measures and adding new ones. Indeed, its flexibility has been a critical feature allowing for its evolution in this regard. This chapter will conclude with two general recommendations for overcoming some of the key areas of weakness regarding the OSCE's application of conflict prevention. The first recommendation concerns increasing the OSCE's financial resources. As was alluded to in the previous pages with respect to the HCNM's activities, the OSCE as a whole suffers from a lack of sufficient resources to meet the expectations and responsibilities allocated to it by the international community. This affects in particular the human resource element of the OSCE. In other words, too few OSCE staff members are expected to carry out the duties and responsibilities of a regional organization with at least 19 field missions (as only one area of expense) in the region on a limited budget. Indeed, some increases in the budget have taken place, but there is a strong contingent among the participating states that has regularly opposed substantial and appropriate increases to the OSCE's budget. In large part, this contingent is opposed to any efforts that might bureaucratize the OSCE unnecessarily.[66]

The second recommendation addresses the need for greater advance planning by the OSCE to prepare, as much as is reasonably possible, and respond to situations requiring its attention. Of course, this recommendation is strongly related to the previous: only with sufficient finances can the OSCE undertake advance planning rather than overuse the resources it has for dealing with only the most urgent matters. One area requiring advance planning is that of an exit strategy for the field missions. Having an exit strategy in place that includes indicators or expected results that would prompt the field mission to begin disengagement would greatly ease the relationship between the OSCE and the host state, thereby avoiding the unnecessary and prolonged process that took place, for instance, in disengaging the OSCE missions in these three cases. Indeed, the problems arising out of the absence of a clear exit strategy are related to differences in views over the purpose of the OSCE's presence. More specifically, Estonia, Latvia, and Ukraine have admitted to turning to the OSCE to strengthen their ties with the West and securing their independence in the face of Russia's potential interference into their matters, rather than for the purpose of preventing conflict; in fact, they all claimed that there was no conflict to prevent.[67]

To conclude, it appears possible that the OSCE's application of conflict prevention can be replicated in other regions. However, it must be noted that the OSCE itself recognizes the limits to its conflict prevention activities and does not claim to have the answers to how situations featuring an incompatibility of differences can be prevented from escalating into violent conflict. In any assessment of the OSCE's effectiveness in conflict prevention, the context of the situation is often more influential to preventing conflict than the actual activities of the OSCE. It is unlikely that violent conflict would have erupted if the OSCE had not intervened in Estonia, Latvia, and Ukraine. This does not diminish in any way the OSCE's role in facilitating dialogue among the disputants and reducing the level of tensions that are evident, but the context needs to be included in any assessment of the effectiveness of certain applications of conflict prevention. In other words, as much as the tools of conflict prevention might be replicated in other situations, the context cannot be and the tools can only be as effective as the context allows.

Notes

1. Prior to December 1994, the institution was known as the Conference on Security and Cooperation in Europe (CSCE). For the sake of easier reading, this chapter will refer throughout to the OSCE; references will be made to the CSCE only in the notes for the sake of accurate documentation of sources.
2. "Building on its status as a regional arrangement of the United Nations, States confirmed the OSCE's role as a primary instrument for conflict prevention, crisis management and post conflict rehabilitation in the OSCE area. Never before have the OSCE participating States engaged their organization so actively as their vehicle in so many issues relevant to their common security." *1997 Copenhagen Council Document*, p. 1.
3. Although the OSCE was harshly criticized for its poor performance in preventing conflict in Yugoslavia in the early 1990s, its activities during this episode reflected its inexperience and nascent and immature institutions. This chapter is devoted to another, later period in the OSCE's existence and, in this respect, promises to provide a more valuable analysis of the OSCE's application of conflict prevention.

4. These instruments are primarily of an operational nature where conflict prevention is concerned. Although the OSCE also features structural conflict prevention measures, such as those pursued by the Office of Democratic Institutions and Human Rights (ODIHR), these will not be considered here for lack of space.

5. Luc Reychler, "The Art of Conflict Prevention: Theory and Practice," in Werner Bauwens and Luc Reychler, eds., *The Art of Conflict Prevention*, New York: Brassey's, 1994, p. 4. In contrast to Reychler who treats these two aspects as separate, this paper attributes both to conflict prevention.

6. *1994 Budapest Document: Towards a Genuine Partnership in a New Era*, p. 14.

7. *1992 Prague Council Document*, p. 2.

8. *1990 Document of the Copenhagen Meeting on the Human Dimension*, p. 40.

9. Toivu Raun, "Estonia: Independence Redefined," in Ian Bremmer and Ray Taras, eds., *New States, New Politics: Building the Post-Soviet Nations*, New York: Cambridge University Press, 1997, p. 405; Erika Schlager, "The Right to Have Rights: Citizenship in Newly Independent OSCE Countries," *Helsinki Monitor*, Vol. 8, No. 1, 1997, p. 25; A. Kirch and M. Kirch, "National Minorities in Estonia," in Kumar Rupesinghe, Peter King, and Olga Vorkunova, eds., *Ethnicity and Conflict in a Post-Communist World: The Soviet Union, Eastern Europe and China*, New York: St. Martin's Press, 1992, p. 98. For instance, by 1989, ethnic Estonians comprised almost 62 per cent of the total population, a significant decrease from the pre-Soviet level of 88 per cent; in contrast, the proportion of ethnic Russians rose dramatically, from pre-1940 levels of 8 per cent to 30 per cent by 1989. The predominance of the Russian language in Soviet Estonia combined with the domination of ethnic Russians politically, economically, and socially in the republic as well as in Union-level institutions aggravated the sense of vulnerability of and threat to the ethnic Estonian identity. Kirch and Kirch, "National Minorities in Estonia," p. 100.

10. For instance, according to Estonia's February 1992 post-Soviet Citizenship Law, Estonian citizenship is granted automatically to anyone who was an Estonian citizen in June 1940 and to their descendants. Others seeking Estonian citizenship would have to follow a naturalization process and meet legislated requirements, including a set period of residency and knowledge of the Estonian language. Raun, "Estonia: Independence Redefined," *ibid.*, p. 429; Vello Pettai, "The Situation of Ethnic Minorities in Estonia," in Magda Opalski and Piotr Dutkiewicz, eds., *Ethnic Minority Rights in Central Eastern Europe*, Ottawa: Canadian Human Rights Foundation, Forum Eastern Europe, 1996, p. 42.

11. Schlager, "The Right to Have Rights," note 9 above, p. 25. In February 1992, Russia agreed to withdraw its troops from the Baltics.

12. By 1989, Russians formed 68 per cent of the population of Crimea. The 1954 transfer of Crimea from Russia to Ukraine marked the 300-year anniversary of the union between the two entities and, in effect, retracted Russia's almost 200-year control over Crimea during which the peninsula developed a strong political and ethnic identification with Russia. Indeed, ethnic Russian migration to the region increased during the Soviet period due in part to the development of the tourist industry in Crimea and to Crimea's city of Sevastopol serving as the base of the Black Sea Fleet. As part of Ukraine, Crimea had the lower-administrative status of an *oblast* within Ukraine until it was promoted to an "autonomous republic" in 1991. Denis Shaw, "Crimea: Background and Aftermath of its 1994 Presidential Election," *Post-Soviet Geography*, Vol. 35, No. 4, 1994, pp. 223–7; *The Crimea: Chronicle of Separatism, 1992–1995*, Ukrainian Centre for Independent Political Research, Kyiv, Ukraine, 1996.

13. Only those Crimean Tatars who were in Ukraine in November 1991 when Ukraine's citizenship law was passed were immediately granted Ukrainian citizenship together with other residents of Ukraine. However, the approximately 100,000 Crimean Tatars

who arrived after November 1991 have had to undergo a complicated, expensive and prohibitive process to acquire Ukrainian citizenship. Without Ukrainian citizenship, Crimean Tatars are unable to find gainful employment, buy land, find or build shelter, and, most importantly, participate in the electoral process. At that time, Crimean Tatars and other applicants of Ukrainian citizenship are legally obliged to renounce their current citizenship before they can apply for Ukrainian citizenship. However, in the aftermath of the collapse of the Soviet Union, the successor countries, such as Uzbekistan from where the majority of Ukraine's Crimean Tatars were arriving, did not pass their own citizenship law until after some of the Crimean Tatars had already returned to Crimea. As a result, the affected Crimean Tatars have no citizenship to renounce and, holding only the citizenship of the Soviet Union which no longer exists, have been considered stateless persons. At that time, Ukraine had not adopted a law on stateless persons. Those Crimean Tatars who are interested in renouncing their Uzbek citizenship are told that the process would take an unreasonable period of six months and that they must pay the US$100 fee, which is out of the reach of the majority of Crimean Tatars. In their opinion, these obstacles are unwarranted and unreasonable given the unique situation in which they find themselves. Specifically, but for the forced deportation in 1944, they would have remained in Ukraine at the time of independence and would have been Ukrainian citizens. Presentations made at the Conference on Problems of Migration and the Resettlement of the Deported Peoples in Ukraine, Kyiv, Ukraine, March 1997; Presentations made at the Conference on Managing Diversity in Pluralistic Societies, Kyiv, Ukraine, Simferopol and Yalta, Crimea, May 1997; Interviews with Nadir Bekirov, Deputy, Supreme Soviet of Crimea, member of the Kurultai faction of the Crimean Parliament, Kyiv, Ukraine, Simferopol and Yalta, Crimea, May 1997.

14. Parts of this territory, especially in the west, were attached to the Ukrainian SSR from Romania, Czechoslovakia, and Poland as part of Stalin's World War II policies. Other parts were considered to be historically part of Russia but formed the basis of the Ukrainian SSR when it was established in 1922.

15. Given the large sample of appropriate demonstrations of the OSCE conflict prevention tools in Estonia, Latvia, and Ukraine, only a small sample will be demonstrated.

16. The OSCE's post-Cold War institutionalization from the CSCE featured the addition of other conflict prevention tools, including the proliferation of fora for consultations in the Ministerial Council, the Senior Council (successor to the Committee of Senior Officials), and the Permanent Council (successor to the Permanent Committee) as well as the Chairman-in-Office, the Conflict Prevention Centre in Vienna, the Forum for Security and Cooperation, the Office for Democratic Institutions and Human Rights, the Human Dimension Mechanism and the Emergency Mechanism. For accounts of the institutionalization process, see Rob Zaagman, "Helsinki-II and the Human Dimension: Institutional Aspects," *Helsinki Monitor*, Special Issue: Helsinki II, Vol. 3, No. 4, 1992; Alexis Heraclides, *Helsinki II and its Aftermath: The Making of the CSCE into an International Organisation*, London: Pinter Publishers, 1993; and Walter Kemp, *The OSCE in a New Context: European Security Towards the Twenty-First Century*, London: Royal Institute of International Affairs, 1996.

17. The 1990 Copenhagen document first mentions the use of missions as measures for improving implementation of human dimension commitments, including the protection of national minority rights. There are many types of OSCE missions other than the field mission, such as fact-finding, rapporteur, and expert. Fact-finding, rapporteur, and expert missions are generally active for only a few weeks and have a very specific and limited mandate. The reports drafted by such missions are submitted to the Chairman-in-Office of the OSCE and discussed by the Senior Council or Permanent Council which then decide on what, if any, future action is to be taken. Primary attention in this chapter will

be focused on the long-term field mission. The more accurate term to be used is "field presence" since not all forms of long-term field missions are called missions, but also "offices." In essence, the activities of all of them are similar and bear no real distinction. The different terms used reflect instead the politics of having a mission on one's territory, suggesting or implying a greater level of intervention and activity than an "office." Nonetheless, reference in this chapter will be made to "missions" since Estonia, Latvia, and Ukraine have had OSCE missions established.

18. Recently, there has been some discussion to provide missions with a longer-term period so as to avoid the constant renewing of mandates. Mandates are renewed by consensus decision of the Senior Council or the Permanent Council.

19. The Senior Council and the Permanent Council are two of the most regular decision-making bodies of the OSCE. Their decisions, including those establishing missions, are made by consensus. Whereas the Senior Council's purpose and level of activity has been reduced over the course of the last few years, the Permanent Council continues to meet weekly in Vienna and has evolved into the regular forum for discussion and political consultation of the OSCE.

20. *OSCE Handbook*, 1999, p. 45.

21. The OSCE Mission to Latvia was established at the 23rd CSO Meeting. Its terms of references were drawn up at the 31st CSO-Vienna Group Meeting. Until December 1994, the Senior Council functioned as the Council of Senior Officials (CSO) which met in Prague every three months to take decisions on the OSCE's activities. The CSO-Vienna Group was the precursor of the Permanent Committee, later the Permanent Council, which met weekly in Vienna as an OSCE decision-making body. It was established at the 1993 Rome Ministerial Council.

22. 31st CSO-VG Meeting, 7 October 1993, Annex 1.

23. *OSCE Handbook*, 1999, p. 75.

24. *OSCE Newsletter*, Vol. 3, No. 12, December 1996.

25. *OSCE Annual Report 1998*, p. 11.

26. http://www.osce.org.

27. *OSCE Annual Report 1998*, p. 11.

28. http://www.osce.org.

29. As a former Head of the OSCE Mission to Estonia has noted, "honest and straightforward presentation of the problems – rather than the customary exchange of diplomatic courtesies – is an important part of the Mission's terms of reference." Timo Lahelma, "The OSCE's Role in Conflict Prevention: The Case of Estonia," *Helsinki Monitor*, Vol. 10, No. 2, 1999, pp. 32–3.

30. *OSCE Handbook*, 1999, p. 45.

31. In June 1993, the Estonian parliament adopted a Law on Aliens that the non-Estonian population found highly objectionable, requiring non-citizens to register for residency permits within one year and to do so every five years notwithstanding that they have been long-term residents of Estonia. Gershon Shafir, *Immigrants and Nationalists: Ethnic Conflict and Accommodation in Catalonia, the Basque Country, Latvia and Estonia*, New York: State University of New York Press, 1995, p. 191.

32. *CSCE Newsletter*, Vol. 1, No. 2, March 1994. One important amendment was the provision of an appeals process for residence and labour permits. Megumi Nishimura, "The OSCE and Ethnic Conflicts in Estonia, Georgia and Tajikistan: A Search for Sustainable Peace and Its Limits," *European Security*, Vol. 8, No. 1, Spring 1999, p. 30. In addition, non-Estonians were allowed to vote in the October 1993 local elections if they met the minimum five-year residency requirement; they were still prohibited from standing for office. Raun, "Estonia: Independence Redefined," note 9 above, p. 419.

33. Specifically, the Ukrainian parliament abolished the separatist 1992 Crimean constitu-

tion as well as the Crimean presidency and the Crimean government is made directly answerable to the Ukrainian government until an acceptable Crimean constitution is adopted. Furthermore, Russian parliamentary officials visited Crimea ostensibly in support of Crimean separatism and a Russian consulate was established in Simferopol to prepare dual citizenship for Crimean citizens, which is prohibited in Ukraine.

34. Speech by the OSCE Head of Mission to Ukraine, Andreas Kohlschutter, to the Parliament of Crimea, 31 May 1995.

35. These recommendations included the following: avoid at all possible an escalation of tensions and therefore no referendum on the Crimean 1992 constitution; status of the autonomous republic of Crimea to be set out in the constitution of Crimea and so respected in Ukrainian constitution; action on Ukrainian citizenship that would encourage Crimean Tatar involvement in elections. Letter from the HCNM to the Minister of Foreign Affairs for Ukraine, 15 May 1995.

36. Estonian mission staff normally includes a human rights expert. Lahelma, "The OSCE's Role in Conflict Prevention," note 29 above, p. 26.

37. Diana Chigas, "Preventive Diplomacy and the Organisation for Security and Cooperation in Europe: Creating Incentives for Dialogue and Cooperation," in Abram Chayes and Antonia Handler Chayes, eds., *Preventing Conflict in the Post-Communist World: Mobilizing International and Regional Organizations*, Washington, D.C.: The Brookings Institution, 1996, pp. 46, 71.

38. At the Istanbul Summit Meeting in November 1999, the participating states agreed to pursue the implementation of a recruiting roster that would input qualification standards on to recruits as well as hasten the process of establishing and staffing the missions.

39. Interviews with government officials, Tallinn, Estonia and Riga, Latvia, December 1999.

40. Interview with Maria Beaulne, former official with the OSCE Mission Staff, Vienna; Ottawa, 23 November 1999.

41. *1992 Helsinki Document: The Challenges of Change*, p. 8.

42. Max van der Stoel, "The Role of the CSCE High Commissioner on National Minorities in CSCE Preventive Diplomacy," in Staffan Carlsson, ed., *The Challenge of Preventive Diplomacy*, Stockholm: Ministry of Foreign Affairs, Sweden, 1994, p. 37.

43. Chigas, "Preventive Diplomacy and the Organization for Security and Cooperation in Europe," note 37 above, p. 55. It is notable that the HCNM plays an independent role in the OSCE regime. While accountable to the political head of the OSCE, the Chairman-in-Office (CiO), the HCNM acts without the need for approval from the CiO and shares information about situations involving national minorities with the CiO when deemed necessary.

44. The HCNM visited Ukraine on average three to four times a year. During his various visits, the HCNM in Kyiv has met with, among others, the President of Ukraine, the Minister for Foreign Affairs, the Speaker of the Ukrainian Parliament, Deputy Prime Minister of Ukraine, the Foreign Minister, the Minister for Minorities and Migration, Minister of Justice, the Deputy Speaker of the Parliament, the Acting Minister of Justice, the Chairman of the Ad Hoc Parliamentary Commission on the Legal and Political Aspects of the Crimean Crisis, the Chairman of the Parliamentary Commission on Legal Policy and Law Reform, the Chairman of the State Committee on Migration and National Policies, the Head of the Parliamentary Commission on Human Rights, the Special Political Adviser to the President, and the Deputy Minister of Education. In Simferopol, the HCNM met with, among others, the Acting Prime Minister of the Autonomous Republic of Crimea, the Speaker of the Crimean Parliament, and three Deputy Speakers of the Crimean Parliament. He also met with leaders of the Russian and Tatar factions of the Crimean Parliament and with the Chairman of the Crimean Tatars' Mejlis. (The Mejlis is the representative political group of the Crimean Tatars.) *The Role of the High*

Commissioner on National Minorities in OSCE Conflict Prevention, The Hague: Foundation for Inter-Ethnic Relations, 1997, pp. 74–5.

45. A sample of the correspondence between the HCNM and the Foreign Minister of Ukraine includes letters dated 15 May 1994, letters reporting on the Locarno Round Table, 11–14 May 1995 dated 15 May 1995, 30 June 1995, 12 October 1995, 14 November 1995, 30 June 1995; *The Role of the HCNM*, p. 76. Recommendations made by correspondence with the Ukrainian Minister for Foreign Affairs are requested to be passed on to the appropriate Ukrainian and Crimean authorities.

46. Letter from the HCNM to the Minister for Foreign Affairs of Ukraine, 19 March 1996. After several previous failed attempts, the Crimean parliament adopted a constitution on 1 November 1995; although this constitution contained articles which contradicted the more supreme Ukrainian laws, it was deemed to be acceptable enough for consideration by the Ukrainian parliament. This occurred in April 1996 on the condition that certain articles of the Crimean constitution be amended to harmonise with the Ukrainian constitution.

47. Letter from the HCNM to the Minister for Foreign Affairs of Ukraine, 12 October 1995; letter from the HCNM to the Minister for Foreign Affairs of Ukraine, 5 April 1996.

48. Letter from the HCNM to the Minister for Foreign Affairs of Ukraine, 15 May 1995; letter from the HCNM to the Minister for Foreign Affairs of Ukraine, 12 October 1995; letter from the HCNM to the Minister for Foreign Affairs of Ukraine, 5 April 1996. In February 1997, the HCNM recommended specifically that, to facilitate the process, affected Crimean Tatars could submit an application requesting Ukrainian citizenship accompanied by a formal declaration of renunciation of citizenship of the country from which they had returned to Crimea, rather than renounce their other citizenship first. The Ukrainian government could then send a list of those who have renounced citizenship to the appropriate state. Letter from the HCNM to the Minister for Foreign Affairs of Ukraine, 14 February 1997.

49. Rob Zaagman, "Conflict Prevention in the Baltic Area: The OSCE High Commissioner on National Minorities in Estonia, 1992–1999," *Helsinki Monitor*, Vol. 10, No. 3, 1999, p. 31.

50. *Ibid.*

51. *Annual Report 1994*, p. 13.

52. Zaagman, "Conflict Prevention in the Baltic Area," note 49 above, p. 34.

53. *Ibid.*

54. Lahelma, "The OSCE's Role in Conflict Prevention," note 29 above, p. 35.

55. The process of finding a successor to van der Stoel proved exceedingly difficult and led to several extensions of his term over the course of this three-year long search.

56. *ECMI Report*, No. 2, March 1999, p. 11.

57. *OSCE Newsletter*, Vol. 2, No. 4, April 1995.

58. Interview with Roman Lishchynski, OSCE Head of Mission to Ukraine, Kyiv, Ukraine, February 1997.

59. Interview with Victor Krizhanivsky, Ukrainian Delegation to the OSCE, Vienna, Austria, February 1997.

60. *Ibid.*

61. Interview with Sergei Shuvaynikov, Chairman of the Executive Committee, Congress of Russian Communities in Crimea, Simferopol, Crimea, May 1997.

62. This law directly contradicts Ukrainian legislation.

63. Meeting with Mustafa Djemilev, Chairman, Crimean Tatar Mejlis, Conference on Managing Diversity in Pluralistic Societies, Simferopol, Crimea, May 1997. These settlements are often located away from any infrastructure support and the Crimean govern-

ment has shown itself to be unable to correct the situation, for financial and political reasons.

64. The Kurultai consists of the Crimean Tatar deputies of the Crimean parliament.
65. John Packer, "Autonomy Within the OSCE: The Case of Crimea," unpublished manuscript, p. 24.
66. Chigas, "Preventive Diplomacy," note 37 above, p. 71.
67. Schlager, "The Right to Have Rights," note 9 above, p. 34.

Part Three

Information and response

9

Early warning and prevention of violent conflict: The role of multifunctional observer missions[1]

David Last

We seem never to learn. Time and again differences are allowed to develop into disputes and disputes allowed to develop into deadly conflicts. Time and again, warning signs are ignored and pleas for help overlooked. Only after the deaths and the destruction do we intervene at a far higher human and material cost and with far fewer lives to save. Only when it is too late do we value prevention. (Kofi Annan, Secretary–General of the United Nations[2])

Introduction

United Nations Military Observer (UNMO) missions and civilian fact-finding missions have been deployed by the United Nations and by regional organizations at various stages in the escalation and de-escalation of conflicts. Are they effective components of an early warning and prevention system? Can they enhance early warning and response to incipient violent conflict? I believe that they can do more than they have in the past if they go beyond flying diplomatic visits and simple military observation. If they incorporate effective analysis of all the dimensions of a conflict, and communication in the broadest sense, then balanced multifunctional observer missions can help to prevent conflict.

This chapter begins with a look at the sort of information that is needed if prevention is to have a chance. The limitations and strengths of traditional fact-finding and observation missions suggest expanding the concept of observer missions to include political, social, economic, and psychological dimensions of the conflict. By collecting the right sort of information and interpreting it accurately, we might link resulting knowledge of potential violence directly to the international community's ability and will to respond to it. Even after the violence starts, prevention efforts continue. Giving observer missions a voice through liaison and public affairs resources can help them to spur appropriate regional and international responses, whatever stage the conflict has reached.

Information for early warning

Since its earliest days, the UN has used fact-finding and military observer missions authorized by the Security Council as instruments to manage international conflict, but they have not always been focused on early warning and prevention. This is evident in the review of missions that follows. The nature of the conflicts to which these missions have been deployed has also changed over the last five decades. They are less likely to be interstate and more likely to be internal conflicts. They are driven not only by the top-down processes of state decision making, but by the more pervasive bottom-up dynamics of intercommunal conflict. Shaping new missions for early warning and prevention must begin with an understanding of the most likely kinds of violence and their precursors. With appropriate knowledge about how conflicts escalate and spread, we can link missions more effectively to warning and action.

We can begin with the well-established notion of stages in the escalation of conflict.[3] There is nothing inevitable about the progression of a conflict through stages. Protracted social conflicts like those in Lebanon, Cyprus, and Ireland show repeated crises and remissions. Stages are simply a useful way of describing the nature and intensity of violence in order to indicate the appropriateness of different responses.[4]

The UN's programme on the use of military and civil defence assets in disaster relief operations (MCDA Field Manual) lists four stages in the progression of vulnerability to humanitarian disasters. Underlying causes include poverty, limited access to resources, flawed economic systems, and ideology. Dynamic pressures compound these underlying factors. They include the lack of institutions, education, training, appropriate skills, investment, markets and press freedom, and macro level forces such as population increase, urbanization, and environmental degradation. The third stage is entered with unsafe conditions and a fragile local economy. Finally, trigger events include war or civil conflict and natural disasters.[5]

In a similar vein, Jean-H. Guilmette identifies five stages in the evolution of a conflict, during which different forms of intervention are appropriate. Guilmette suggests that effective development initiatives during malaise, crisis, and denied conflict might forestall the violence of "open conflict." During open conflict and war, diplomatic and military action strives to control and resolve the conflict, while humanitarian aid takes the place of development aid. With settlement comes a period of reconciliation and reconstruction and a return to development activities.[6]

From a sociological perspective, Acheson describes three stages in the breakdown of social order, which leads to the threat of genocide. In the first stage, there are isolated individual threats, attacks, and prejudice. The second stage is characterized by sporadic, often cyclical outbursts of unplanned violence. Shop smashing, looting, arson, and riots are typical incidents. The third stage is entered with the active participation of the state, the leadership of individual politicians, the use of police, armed forces and possibly the misuse of social welfare records to identify groups.[7]

Each of these stages suggests indicators of rising violence, turning points in the early warning process, and increasing risks for the first-hand observers and analysts in a country. The stages do not indicate proximate and underlying causes of the violence they describe. Understanding causes would help observers to estimate the probability of rising violence, and to describe the likelihood in ways that might galvanize international action. Table 9.1 summarizes Michael Brown's four sets of relevant factors. These can serve as a checklist for the sort of information we need to collect in order to identify the likelihood of progression through various stages of conflict. External affinities, stereotypes, and competition for power within groups are linked to the severity of a conflict, and should also be assessed.[8]

Few of these causes fall within the sphere of military competence. Most cannot be observed on a short fact-finding visit. Most are difficult to assess outside the country affected. For example, changing ethnic geography, the rise of exclusionary ideology and perceived economic inequities all characterized the tensions between Muslims and Serbs in Northwest Bosnia between November 1990 (the release of the national census) and April 1992 (the referendum result). Muslims and Serbs living in Prijedor and Sanski Most who lived through these events saw plenty of danger signs. First-hand knowledge not only provides a more comprehensive and accurate picture of risk, but also might help to reinforce restraint and undermine extremists.

What balance is an early warning mission trying to achieve? Flying diplomatic visits give high-level access, but not local knowledge and understanding. Military observers focus on military facts, omitting the most important social and economic dimensions. Although different sorts of information are necessary at different stages in the escalation or de-escalation of a conflict, the mission must be balanced in at least three ways. First, it

Table 9.1 Underlying and proximate causes of internal conflict

Factors	Underlying causes	Proximate causes
Structural	Weak states	Collapsing states
	Intrastate security concerns	Changing intrastate military balances
	Ethnic geography	Changing demographic patterns
Political	Discriminatory political institutions	Political transitions
	Exclusionary national ideologies	Increasingly influential exclusionary ideologies
	Inter-group politics	Growing intergroup competitions
	Elite politics	Intensifying leadership struggles
Economic/ Social	Economic problems	Mounting economic problems
	Discriminatory economic systems	Growing economic inequities
	Economic development and modernization	Fast-paced development and modernization
Cultural/ Perceptual	Patterns of cultural discrimination	Intensifying patterns of cultural discrimination
	Problematic group histories	Ethnic bashing and propagandizing

Source: Michael E. Brown, "The Causes and Regional Dimensions of Internal Conflict," in Michael E. Brown, ed., *The International Dimensions of Internal Conflict*, Cambridge, MA: MIT Press, 1996, p. 577.

should include assets for the collection of information at the national and international levels likely to shape a conflict, but it must also have a local presence. Second, it must balance military and civilian skills; the closer a situation moves towards violence, the more important military observation will become. Finally, it is not enough to know the storm is coming. Early warning missions need tools to spur the international community to appropriate action.

Fact-finding and military observers

More than 40 UN missions since 1947 have included military observers or expert fact-finding teams around the world. Observer missions have typically been composed of military officers, usually unarmed, and deployed in multinational teams for six months to a year at a time.

Fact-finding missions have usually been comprised of civilian experts who visit an area for no longer than is necessary to answer specific questions within their mandate – a matter of days or weeks. Fact-finding missions have often been sent to areas of rising tension to investigate allegations and provide the necessary background information for diplomatic efforts to resolve the dispute. They are a basic tool of preventive diplomacy and routinely employed in the resolution of disputes between states.[9]

The first example of UN fact-finding was typical of the genre. A mission was sent to the Balkans in 1947 at the request of the Greek government. Its mandate was to investigate the Greek government's claim that Albania, Bulgaria, and Yugoslavia were supporting insurgents in Greece. The commission consisted of officials representing 11 Security Council members. Between January and April 1947 it visited the region and reported that there was some evidence of support for the insurgency, and that Greece's territorial claims were aggravating the situation. The Security Council was unable to adopt the recommended resolution over Soviet objections. The General Assembly called for restraint and established the UN Special Commission on the Balkans (UNSCOB). UNSCOB worked mainly in Greece, without the cooperation of Yugoslavia, Albania, and Bulgaria. It reported growing refugee problems and arms trafficking until 1951, when the UN Peace Observation Commission replaced it, until disbanded in 1954. These missions were deployed in a way that permitted them to verify Greece's accusations, but not its neighbours' denials. It seldom had a local physical presence on the frontiers or areas in question, relying on the aggrieved party to direct it to evidence.[10]

Fact-finding missions have typically made a single report (often behind closed doors), then dissolved. They have not been well placed to influence decision making or build a constituency for preventive action. Recent examples include the special envoys to Burundi in 1993 and 1995, the Special Mission and Good Offices Missions to Afghanistan in 1994 and a mission to Rwanda in February 1995.[11] Yet special envoys and fact-finding missions have far greater access to decision makers during the brief span of their reporting period than do observer missions. The latter are impeded not by their duration, but by their limited ability to collect information.

Observer missions have typically been deployed after a cease-fire. When the cease-fire is unstable, they may find themselves in the midst of a conflict of uncertain duration and intensity. The information that individual military observers provide to their headquarters, perhaps at considerable personal risk, often adds little to the international community's will or ability to respond to or prevent violence. Understanding some of the ways in which fact-finding and military observer missions have been used in the past gives an impression of their utility and limitations.

Table 9.2 is a partial list of UN military observer missions. Since the end of the Cold War, military observer missions have increasingly been used to monitor conflicts within state boundaries, although these often have an international dimension. Many of the missions listed have witnessed successive bouts of violence. Sometimes they have taken the form of

Table 9.2 UN observer missions

Mission	Location	Dates	Composition	Outcome
UNTCOK	Korea	1947–48	Observers	Completed
UNTSO	Lebanon-Syria-Israel	June 48–	Observers	Continues (52 years)
UNMOGIP	India-Pakistan	Jan. 49–	Observers	Continues (51 years)
UNOGIL	Lebanon	June 58–Dec. 58	Observers	Concluded
ONUC	Congo	July 60–June 64	Force and observers	Combat operations
UNSF and UNTEA	West Irian (New Guinea)	Oct. 62–Apr. 63	Force, police, civil administration, elections	Concluded
UNYOM	Yemen	July 63–Sept. 64	Observers	Concluded
DOMREP	Dominican Republic	May 65–Oct. 66	Observers	Regional intervention (US-led Inter-American Peace Force)
UNIPOM	India-Pakistan	Sep. 65–Mar. 66	Observers	Concluded
UNDOF	Syria-Israel (Golan)	June 74–	Observers	Continues (26 years)
UNIFIL	Lebanon	Mar. 78–	Observers	Continues (22 years)
UNGOMAP	Afghanistan-Pakistan	May 88–Mar. 90	Good offices	Concluded
UNIIMOG	Iran-Iraq	Aug. 88–Feb. 91	Observers	Concluded
UNAVEM I	Angola	Jan. 89–May 91	Observers	Repeated missions with dubious outcome, fighting continues
UNTAG	Namibia	Apr. 89–Mar. 90	Force, observers, police, civil administration, elections	Concluded
ONUCA	Central America	Nov. 89–Jan. 92	Observers	Concluded
UNIKOM	Kuwait	Apr. 91–	Observers	Continues (9 years)
UNAVEM II	Angola	May 91–Feb. 95	Observers	Second in a series with dubious outcomes, fighting continues
ONUSAL	El Salvador	July 91–Feb. 95	Observers	Concluded, banditry
MINURSO	Western Sahara	Apr. 91–	Observers	Continues, awaiting referendum (9 years), sporadic fighting

162

Mission	Location	Dates	Type	Outcome
UNAMIC	Cambodia	Oct. 91–Mar. 92	Observers/good offices	Precursor mission to UNTAC
UNPROFOR	Former Yugoslavia	Mar. 92–Dec. 95	Force and observers	Degenerated to combat operations, transition to NATO
UNTAC	Cambodia	Mar. 92–Sep. 93	Force, observers, police, civil authorities, elections	Concluded, fighting continues
UNOSOM I	Somalia	Apr. 92–Mar. 93	Force	Repeated missions with dubious outcomes
ONUMOZ	Mozambique	Dec. 92–Dec. 94	Force and observers	Concluded, some fighting continues
UNOSOM II	Somalia	Mar. 93–Mar. 95	Force	Second in a series with dubious outcomes
UNOMUR	Uganda-Rwanda	June 93–Sep. 94	Observers	Concluded
UNOMIG	Georgia	Aug. 93–	Observers	Continues (7 years)
UNOMIL	Liberia	Sept. 93–Sept. 97	Observers	Concluded, regional missions continue
UNMIH	Haiti	Sept. 93–June 96	Force and observers	Concluded, unable to halt genocide
UNAMIR	Rwanda	Oct. 93–Mar. 96	Force	Concluded
UNASOG	Aouzou (Sudan/Libya)	May 94–June 94	Observers	Continues (6 years)
UNMOT	Tajikistan	Dec. 94–	Observers	Third in a series of missions with dubious outcomes
UNAVEM III	Angola	Feb. 95–June 97	Force and observers	Degenerated to combat operations, concluded, regional missions continue
UNCRO	Croatia	Mar. 95–Jan. 96	Force and observers[1]	Continues (5 years)
UNPREDEP	Macedonia	Mar. 95–	Force and observers	Regional mission continues
UNTAES	E. Slavonia, Croatia	Jan. 96–	Force, observers, civil affairs, elections	Continues (4 years)
UNMOP[2]	Prevlaka, Croatia	Jan. 96–	Observers	

163

Table 9.2 (cont.)

Mission	Location	Dates	Composition	Outcome
MONUA	Angola	July 97–Feb. 99	Observers	Fourth in a series of missions with dubious outcomes
MONUC	DR Congo	Nov. 99–	Observers	Continues (1 year)
UNOMSIL	Sierra Leone	July 98–Oct. 99	Observers	Concluded, degenerated into conflict
UNTAET	East Timor	Oct. 99–	Civil affairs, observers, elections	Continues
UNMIK	Kosovo	June 99–	Civil affairs, police, elections (with OSCE)	Continues

Sources: *The Blue Helmets: A Review of United Nations Peace-Keeping*, 3d ed., New York: United Nations Department of Public Information, 1996; and UN websites. Those that are currently deployed or who have worked with a UN force (armed military units) have been omitted.
1. The Office of the High Commissioner for Human Rights (UNHCHR) was established in 1994 and by 1995 routinely sent observers to field missions.
2. Most recent entry in *Blue Helmets*, 1996.

organized military fighting, but in many other cases low levels of inter-communal and internal violence have been endemic. The table shows that such instances have been more common in the last decade.

Many missions have included civilians, although usually in administrative and support roles. The first truly multifunctional mission was the UN Transitional Executive Authority (UNTEA) and UN Security Force (UNSF) in West Irian (New Guinea) in 1962–63, which combined civil administration, military observers, a police-training mission, and a security force. The UN, Indonesia, and the Netherlands credited UNTEA's many-faceted efforts for the conflict-free transition from colonial rule.[12] Such positive, multidimensional transitional missions were not to appear again until the end of the Cold War. The UN Transition Assistance Group (UNTAG) in Namibia and the UN Observer Group in Central America (ONUCA) set new standards for the integration of civilian and military components in missions that were designed to facilitate transition from conflict to peace. They were not early warning missions, but like UNTEA they helped to prevent potential violence.

Many purely military observer missions have met with less success. The UN Observer Mission in Liberia (UNOMIL) and the UN Observer Mission in Sierra Leone (UNOMSIL), for example, have witnessed recurring violence. Observers have been dispatched and withdrawn repeatedly, sometimes without even filing reports. They have found themselves confined to small areas around the capitals, while aid agencies and non-governmental organizations continued to work in the hinterland. In several missions, however, military observers have worked closely with civilians to enhance monitoring and analysis. In Croatia in 1995, they formed "Human Rights Assessment Teams" with civilian police, human rights observers of the Office of the UN High Commissioner for Human Rights (UNHCHR), and civil affairs officers. In Central America, they worked with local government and development officials to facilitate demobilization and with election officials and civilian police to support a peaceful transition.

The Organization for Security and Cooperation in Europe (OSCE) has a shorter record of field missions than the UN. From the outset, these missions have been more completely integrated than the UN military observation missions, with military observers in a supporting role (normally out of uniform) in only nine cases. Missions to Belarus, Estonia, Latvia, and Ukraine are purely civilian and operate from capital cities. Missions in the wake of conflict (Croatia, Bosnia, Georgia, and Chechnya, for example) or its margins (Macedonia and Albania, for example) rely more heavily on military presence, and operate closer to the sources of potential violence, with a broader mandate.

Both the OSCE and the UN appear to be moving towards a concept of continuous presence in areas of interest. In 1997, Sir Marrack Goulding (formerly of the UN Office of Special Political Affairs) described efforts to bring all UN agencies in a country within a single "UN house." Under normal conditions the head of the household would be the representative of the United Nations Development Programme (UNDP). If the country or region emerged as a threat to international peace and security, a Special Representative of the Secretary General would be appointed for as long as the Security Council remained seized of the matter.[13] The broad and flexible mandates of groups like the "OSCE Presence in Albania" allow their officials to move seamlessly from monitoring borders to supporting institutional development, depending on the stage that a conflict has reached. In fact, OSCE missions seem to have the capacity to combine high-level fact-finding and diplomatic contact with grass-roots presence and technical expertise appropriate to a variety of circumstances.

How can early warning and prevention work?

With hindsight, what might an early warning and prevention mission in Bosnia have detected in 1990? With the approval of the Federal Government of Yugoslavia, it might have had a regional office in Banja Luka or Bihac responsible for the Northwest. If constituted like the European Community Monitoring Mission (ECMM) or the OSCE observers deployed later, it might have provided information of impending violence as early as 1990,[14] and certainly would have yielded a much more accurate picture of events by 1991. Interviews at local level would have revealed that the economic downturn in the late 1980s had led to attempts by several groups, not all ethnically based, to gain control of worker-managed factories. Factory committees controlled housing and job allocation, and discrimination on ethnic grounds was evident as early as 1990, although the victims and perpetrators varied. Talking to local politicians and analysing local radio and newspapers would have yielded a clear picture of the formation and expansion of nationalist parties. People travelling in the area might have noted the appearance of nationalist symbols on police uniforms (lilies for Muslims and chequered shields for Croats, neither worn by Serbs on the same police force). The Serbian takeover of Radio Prijedor in March 1992 would have been a clear watershed.

A police component to the early-warning team might have been able to discern the isolation and expulsion of non-Serbs from the local police forces. This culminated in early 1992 as Serbs expelled from Croatian police forces in Sisak and Zagreb came to towns like Prijedor and Nova Gradiška and were given police jobs there.

The municipal defence departments charged with civil defence in cities like Prijedor, Banja Luka, and Nova Gradiška had taken on a more militant character by November 1991, and played an active role in the municipal coups of April–May 1992. Military observers might have noted this changing role, as well as the decreasing control of the Yugoslav National Army (JNA) and the military reaction to defeat in Croatia.[15] Much of this information might have come too late to constitute "early warning" but might still have led to more effective early intervention using all means at the disposal of the international community.

As the conflict in Bosnia progressed, the most useful reports for spurring action were often those that provided specific examples of a general problem, such as treatment of minorities.[16] The implication is that observers at field level need to be familiar with the mechanisms that might be used to take action. For example, the Vienna Mechanism on Military Developments, the Moscow Mechanism on Human Dimension Developments, and the Berlin Mechanism on Serious Emergency Situations, are not always understood by those who are collecting information from local mayors, chiefs of police, and garrison commanders. These mechanisms were used to establish the missions that eventually did provide some early warning of the conflict in Kosovo:

One of the operational advantages of the mechanisms is comprehensive, impartial, on-the-spot fact-finding. This leads relatively easily to concrete recommendations for specific CSCE involvement, including the application of other CSCE instruments. The fact-finding mission to Kosovo in 1992, undertaken in the context of the unusual-military-activities mechanism, prepared the ground for a further CSCE involvement, which resulted in the decision to establish CSCE missions of long-duration in Kosovo, Vojvodina and Sanjak.[17]

The CSCE mission in Kosovo in particular was structured to provide local information that would warn of the spread of the violence. Yugoslavia's refusal to renew its mandate in 1993 served as a warning that merited a Security Council resolution.[18] It was not until 1998 that the OSCE was able to return observers to Kosovo to verify the 16 October cease-fire, reduction of security forces and respect for human rights. The Kosovo Verification Mission (KVM) included military and civilian members with diverse backgrounds, but found itself reacting to breaches of the cease-fire, and unable to engage in democratization and human rights tasks envisioned in its mandate. It was effective, however, at defusing many local fights and confrontations. It established a presence in ethnic Albanian villages like Racak when these came under attack by security forces. Such presence is credited with slowing the destruction. It negotiated the return of hostages, assisted humanitarian agencies, monitored court appearances, and investigated incidents and allegations of human rights abuse.[19]

The detailed local information from KVM monitors was frequently referred to in negotiations leading up to the air strikes and deployment of NATO's Kosovo Force (KFOR).[20]

The international community did not have the tools it needed to provide effective early warning of impending violence in Bosnia in 1990. KVM, with its local presence and mix of backgrounds, provided such a tool in Kosovo, but arrived too late in the process to provide "early warning." Despite this, it was a crucial link in the escalating response of the international community to internal violence, and demonstrably reduced the rate of destruction in the areas in which it was present. Its use of the international media, and direct liaison with NATO and the OSCE offices in Vienna were instrumental in connecting its reports to international action.

Collecting information

Only at a late stage of internal conflict, and with considerable international pressure do states consent to the sort of monitoring regimes described above. At earlier stages, benign and collaborative missions represented by UNDP programmes or the OSCE country offices can serve as a starting point for monitoring and a platform for developing trust. The contrast between international involvement in Bosnia in 1992 and 1996 illustrates several aspects of the gap in information collection. This gap has to be filled if the mission progresses from presence in a stable country to monitoring incipient violence. As the potential for violence increases, the mission will need more effective collection and analysis of political, social, economic, military, and perceptual information. Liaison and use of the international media can help translate that information and analysis to shape preventive action by regional and international organizations.

Political and social information

International involvement in domestic conflict may stem from altruism or self-interest. Hegemonic ambition, a desire to restore or preserve regional stability, ethnic sympathy with the oppressed, a sense of national or international responsibility, and humanitarian concern are some of the reasons identified by Cooper and Berdal.[21] Not all of these are sound bases for preventive action. Some may exacerbate conflict.

The OSCE has five mechanisms which can be related both to collection of political and social information for early warning purposes, and to early response to problem areas. These are: (1) intensive political consultation; (2) implementation debates within the OSCE framework; (3) Confidence and Security Building Measures (CSBMs) and their continuation through, for example, inspections and verification; (4) the activities of the High Commissioner on National Minorities; and (5) the Office for Democratic Institutions and Human Rights.[22] Because each of these mechanisms creates its own flow of information and contacts, an early warning mechanism needs some access to them. In the case of the ECMM, informal links between the mission headquarters and the Centre for the Prevention of Conflict in Vienna helped in this regard. But the higher level mechanisms also need detailed information about regions of concern. Thus, EC monitors were sometimes commissioned to provide information on local political, economic, and social questions.[23]

Knowledge of politics and society at the local level is essential if observers are to understand the accelerators and decelerators of violence. In practical terms, this means that observers must be able to talk to municipal politicians, understand local politics and social pressures, and have the trust and confidence of local people to collect information about the changing dynamics of domestic tensions. In my experience, it is often difficult to interpret simple statements; the difficulty increases with translation, lack of familiarity with the local context and the complexity of the problems political leaders are dealing with. After several months in a community, some things which appeared clear begin to seem less so, and much of the information previously gathered begins to take on new meaning as knowledge is gained of personalities, personal backgrounds, and local agendas.

The OSCE code of conduct forms a basis for expanding the concept of early warning and conflict prevention, by providing a means of measuring deviation from accepted norms.[24] In practice, this means either international observation at local level, or alliances with local groups dedicated to monitoring the standards of free speech, media access, electoral fairness, human rights, and minority protection which are included in the OSCE code. The dilemma is that local groups may be the targets of reprisals and restrictions just as their information is most needed for early warning and preventive action. International observers may be restricted or expelled, but this in itself constitutes a warning signal that might not come with the tightening of access to local groups.

Economic information

The relative deprivation hypothesis linking economic hardship to violent conflict is widely accepted, though not well supported.[25] It is likely that the impact of macro-economic indicators on inter-ethnic conflict is ambiguous, but probably marginal. Micro-economic indicators and distribution issues are more likely to be related to the sort of intercommunal violence seen in the Balkans and former Soviet Union. The problem for

early warning missions is that neither macro nor micro-economic indicators are likely to be readily available. The figures available at a distance
are probably unreliable (as were IMF and World Bank figures for Yugoslavia in 1991). Figures on inter- and intra-ethnic distribution may have
convoluted implications.[26] Collecting and analysing economic information might be better done in the country than at a distance. If distribution
is a key element in early warning, then observers should understand factors affecting distributive politics in ethnically diverse countries. These
include ethnic patterns, regime type, and institutional context. Regime
strategies for accommodating the economic power of ethnic minorities
also need to be assessed.[27] In practice, this means understanding how
local authorities respond to shortages, how distribution networks function, and how this affects individuals. Collective response to frustration
and inequity may be rioting and violence in some circumstances and
meek acceptance in others. This level of detail is difficult to judge from a
distance.

Measuring return to normality after a conflict helps provide early warning of impending breakdown. We have good examples from the ongoing
mission in Bosnia. Objectives may include: measuring housing reconstruction to assess repatriation and resettlement; examining food security
and food prices; comparing morbidity and mortality rates to historic figures; and assessing the restoration of markets and economic activity.[28]
"Normality indicators" collected in Bosnia in 1996 included such indicators as the price of bread, oranges, and underwear, and the frequency
of truck and bus transport on particular routes. Aggregated at regional
level, these indicators gave a rough impression of the return to normalcy,
measured against events in the country as a whole. Collecting them,
however, was time-consuming and manpower intensive.

Information about the media

As with economic factors, the relationship between public information
and violence is not precise. Domestic media in the local language has the
greatest impact on the evolving conflict. Surveys of groups that seek to
use the media can indicate public and special interest access. Impartiality of access may vary or be set by national policy. Limiting access may
actually help to prevent incitement to violence. If the government is the
problem, it will exacerbate matters.

A second problem is assessing broadcast material. Sampling is an option, but parochial sources may be more virulent than the media, which
is easily monitored in capital cities. The quality and speed of translation
will influence media transparency to observers. Contact with independent journalists and international networks may no longer be viable as the

situation deteriorates. Even the ability of an observer mission to use local help may be undermined by pressure on translators or their families. There are non-governmental groups with expertise in monitoring and assessing media. OMRI, the Soros Foundation, and Broadcasters without Borders are examples of organizations that might assist with some aspects of media monitoring.

Military information

Military observers tread a fine line between information gathering and activities perceived as hostile spying. The key to monitoring effectively without being accused of spying is liaison. Colonel Peter Williams, a former Chief Military Observer for UNPF, argues that liaison is an essential function of observation.[29] Observers maintain communications with military units, build trust between commanders, and assure parties that information will be treated in confidence. Information should be collected about armed movement, irregular troops, clandestine arming or training, changing intrastate military balances, mobilization of reservists, new restrictions on movement near bases or training areas, paramilitary activity by the police or plain-clothes units, and so on. These are useful indicators of rising tensions or preparation for armed conflict.

After a conflict, military observers might be deployed to provide early warning of breakdown of cease-fire arrangements. Cease-fires are normally stable when one side is completely defeated, when the parties have effective governments which have agreed to the cease-fire and can control all the elements under their authority, and when there are few advantages and some costs to violating the cease-fire. An integrated military approach might include establishing a buffer zone, limiting forces in a particular area, and enforcing or monitoring air exclusion zones.[30]

As a situation deteriorates, military observers find their activities increasingly restricted and risky. Political influence might help retain access to military information. But the value of military information should be assessed. If the information is not going to be acted upon, then it makes little sense to risk lives to collect it.

Establishing a multifunctional mission

If an early warning mission is to collect information on all the indicators that might be relevant for the prevention of violent conflict, it cannot be limited to a short-term fact-finding mission, nor to a military observer mission. A combination of military, economic, political, and media expertise is required. A mission must remain long enough to secure the trust of local leaders. Alliances with local groups can help. But as tension increases, relying on locals will bring increasing restrictions. Given the types of expertise required, what would an early warning and prevention mission look like? The mission should be structured to collect and analyse information. Beyond that, it should have means of ensuring that the information is effectively used. A third consideration is the preventive role that a field mission might serve.

The alternatives

The UN has seven main instruments to influence conflicts. Fact-finding missions, traditional peacekeeping missions (including both forces and observers), multifunctional peacekeeping missions (such as UNTAG in Namibia and UNTAC in Cambodia), and humanitarian assistance.[31] These four instruments are authorized under Chapter 6 of the UN Charter and their effective use hinges on the consent of the parties. Sanctions and embargoes, judicial enforcement and military force are imposed on parties to a conflict, and have repercussions for use of the first four instruments.

Some conclusions about the effective management of multinational military interventions are relevant to multifunctional observation missions. General Andrew Goodpaster concludes that the UN has three basic alternatives for organizing missions: under UN command; under the control of regional organizations; or with ad hoc arrangements. Common doctrine within the framework of a regional organization (perhaps only NATO at present) affords the greatest coherence to a military mission. Command and control arrangements form the vital link between forming a mission and employing it effectively. Intelligence about the disposition and intent of parties to the conflict must be used to guide the mission, and comprehensive contingency plans should be prepared to respond to sudden changes in the mission's environment.[32]

Adding dimensions to observer missions

The limitations of purely military observer missions and diplomatic fact-finding have been mentioned. The ECMM represents a different sort of observer mission. It had many of the characteristics desirable in an early warning and prevention mission. EC monitors were geographically dispersed in teams with responsibility for defined political boundaries. They had diplomatic status, and represented a range of military and civilian skills and backgrounds. They had a broad mandate to talk to local authorities, police, community leaders, in fact anyone in their area. They lived in local communities, paid for good quality translators, and were readily accessible to locals. The willingness of some teams to help individuals opened the door to sources of information and insight at the local level. Teams reported daily via secure satellite links. Their consolidated reports were on desks in the foreign offices of European capitals the following morning. Regional offices provided summaries and assessments based on multiple reports and the headquarters in Zagreb included a sophisticated analysis and assessment branch with regional and functional experts, considerably larger than the Analysis and Assessment Unit attached to UNPF Headquarters. The mission was responsive to questions asked at higher levels to support the development of plans; monitors received direction to address specific issues (opportunities for micro-investment to employ demobilizing soldiers in May 1996, for example). All of these characteristics make the ECMM a useful model for an early warning and prevention mission.

Collecting information

Although many of the EC monitors were serving or retired military officers, their mandate was primarily political and social. As the situation stabilized with the introduction of IFOR, economic information was increasingly important and some observers were unprepared for this. Teams also had to cover very large areas. Typically, a two-person team covered four or five major municipalities, in an area that might take a day just to drive across – five municipal governments, five police forces, dozens of major economic enterprises and public utilities, minority communities, non-governmental organizations and so on. Given the constraints of travel time and poor telecommunications, collecting detailed information was a slow process.

With the arrival of the OSCE Human Rights Monitors, the Office of the UN High Commissioner for Human Rights, the International Police Task Force (IPTF) and UN Civil Affairs, much closer monitoring of the police, judicial, and minorities situation became possible. Without the assistance of other organizations, police monitors could not observe the whole judicial process. Police monitors can effectively supervise community policing, investigations, arrest, and detention. Human rights and civil affairs monitors were more effective at monitoring the passage of cases through the courts and the handling of judicial rulings, such as the right to establish commercial radio stations, complaints about property rights, and so on. These are all valid indicators.

Missions work best when there is systematic cooperation between all the components at regional and local level. In Bosnia in 1996, information was shared at local level and passed up separate information "stovepipes" to each of the mission headquarters. Sometimes it was less effectively shared at higher levels; others argue that only at higher levels was it properly fused. The advantage of having several organizations collecting information is that it spreads the risks for the international community. An organization can be deprived of resources or lose the confidence of participants, and others can pick up its functions. The Office of the UN High Commissioner for Human Rights, for example, did not have the resources to execute its mandate at regional level in Bosnia in the Spring of 1996, and the OSCE was able to fill in.[33] The disadvantage is that the mission may absorb far more resources than necessary, and may expend a lot of energy coordinating disparate parts.

Analysing information

There is already a lot of information without launching expensive monitoring missions to collect more. Ideally, having observers at local level allows information collection for specific purposes. It is analysed, and action taken as a result. One example illustrates how this might work in practice for an early warning mission. Changing demographic patterns can be a source of conflict. After the Dayton Agreement, the Inter-Entity Boundary Line became a focus for intercommunal tension, as Otis suggests is commonplace in divided societies.[34] As settlement of the final boundary line approached, tensions increased around the town of Otoka in northwest Bosnia. A physical confrontation between Muslim and Serb crowds occurred on 19 April with little warning, and deaths were narrowly averted. It was clear from the 19 April incident that further mass demonstrations were likely in two volatile corridors in northwest Bosnia: at Otoka and between Prijedor and Sanski Most.[35] A concerted effort was launched to identify the timing and location of the next disturbance, and reduce the risk of violence that might derail the fragile progress towards return of refugees. UNHCR contacts with refugee leaders identified organizers. On about 6 May, British troops on the Federation side of the IEBL received information that the demonstrations were scheduled for 12 May, with the participation of up to eight bus-loads of Bosnian refugees residing in Germany. US Information Teams distributing the *Herald of Peace* heard of the involvement of a German NGO called "Society for the Preservation of Threatened Peoples." Its agenda was to expose the continued presence of war criminals in Prijedor and their role in preventing the return of refugees. In meetings, Muslim refugee leaders revealed a strategy of highlighting Serb obstruction, by storming the IEBL with large numbers.[36] Civilian Police and EC monitors identified preparations on the Serb side of the IEBL for a violent reception, including piles of rocks along the anticipated route. The local Serb and Muslim radio stations in Prijedor and Sanski Most were used to inflame public sentiment on the issue of return throughout April and May.

Putting this information together from diverse sources, and interpreting it to allow a clear picture of upcoming events was a challenge for all concerned. Authorities on both sides had some interests vested in a confrontation. They were apprehensive, but also reluctant to cooperate in de-escalating tensions because of fear that the other party would thereby gain an advantage. A series of meetings at local and regional level, under the chairmanship of IFOR and UNHCR, were the forums in which the information was first interpreted and then acted upon. In the context of the IFOR mission, the G2 or intelligence cell was the focus for "assembling" a coherent picture of likely events. EC monitors and particular UNHCR field officers had a clearer idea of likely events, because of their privileged communications with refugees and local authorities.

Although demonstrations occurred on both sides of the IEBL on 12 and 18 May 1996, direct confrontations were avoided. This was achieved through a series of escalating meetings with officials and police on both sides, and with Muslim refugee leaders. After the inflammatory role it played in the 12 May event, pressure was successfully exerted in Europe to prevent the German NGO from participating in the 18 May event. These modest tactical successes illustrate some of the complexity of collecting the right sorts of information to permit short-term action to head off violence.

In the larger picture, there are situations that are the aggregate of many small incidents like this, and there are larger events that originate in the strategic designs of the parties to the conflict, or players outside the affected country. One of the most important roles for systematic analysis is to attempt to identify chains of causality, trends and actions that might lead to violence, and those which are susceptible to external influence.

From information to action

Alexander George and Jane Holl make the case that marshalling timely and effective responses to warnings of violent conflict requires an integrated strategy that develops potential responses with anticipated warnings. "The need to do so will only increase as publics grow increasingly expectant that their governments will do something to deal with the crises that they surely see coming."[37] This is the heart of prevention.

Drawing an analogy from perception experiments, George and Holl list the three factors likely to influence ability to distinguish a warning in a stream of other information. These are: the strength of the signal relative to the strength of confusing or distracting background; the expectations of observers evaluating signals; and the costs and rewards associated with recognizing and correctly appraising the signal.[38] If the analogy is correct, then early warning missions might be more effective at prevention if they could achieve two things. First, they might attempt to screen out confusing signals and shape information available. Without accurate analysis, there is a risk that attempting to screen and shape information will add to confusion or result in erroneous actions. Second, they need access to decision makers or their advisers. Early warning and prevention missions might therefore be concerned with two sorts of messages: comparatively simple public messages conveyed through the international media; and sophisticated private messages conveyed to key decision makers and their advisers.

Direct personal liaison by trusted colleagues is the most effective way of passing relevant information between large and complex organizations. There are many examples. The International Conference on the Former Yugoslavia (ICFY) had an ambassador to UNPF in Zagreb. Starting in 1993 NATO attached high-ranking liaison officers to UNPROFOR in Zagreb and Sarajevo. Ambassador Holbrooke placed a liaison officer in UNPF headquarters in Zagreb in October 1995 to help coordinate his initiatives with UN actions, and to keep him informed of developments. Choosing the right people for these posts, and ensuring that the "target" organization has sufficient confidence in the contact to use the information and advice is essential if an early warning mission is to use this vehicle to influence decision makers or their advisers.

Examining the international media's influence on decision makers, Nic Gowing has concluded that the "CNN factor" is only suggestive rather than directive, and is often seen by leaders as trite and crude.[39] International mass media, however, remain an effective way of reaching large audiences with a simple message. The practice of joint, multi-agency press conferences ("speaking with one voice") in Sarajevo prevents discord or contradiction in the mission from becoming the story. An early warning and prevention mission needs to have an accurate assessment of current media presence and media coverage (host-nation, regional, and international) and should be prepared to adjust its information strategy to use available information effectively. IFOR, for example, ran an information campaign on at least three different levels. The affected population was one target audience. Local media were a related target audience. International audiences were reached through both the international media and coordinated press releases from contributing nations' national media outlets. Readily available video imagery, satellite hook-ups, and transport attract the international media, but they are not natural allies.[40]

The most important target to overcome international inertia is decision makers. They might be reached directly or through liaison with their advisers. A second vehicle is the pressure of public opinion, mobilized through the international media, guided by a careful information pro-gramme. Our experience in Bosnia should lead us to be cautious about both. The parties to the conflict will have their own interests at stake, and will use the same means to influence *their* international environment. The international community was often unable to match the sophistication or the resources deployed by Milosevic, Izetbegovic, and Tudjman to manipulate public opinion at home and abroad.

In the effort to instigate action, participants in a mission should beware the hubris of assuming that they know best. There seems to be a natural tension between headquarters at different levels that stems partly from different perceptions of risk.

Early warning mission as precursor to preventive action

The Balkan experience, although not an early warning and prevention mission, has been used to provide examples of ways in which one might function. This may extend to taking direct action within the scope of the mission to help forestall violence or mitigate its impact. Providing warn-ing, taking direct action, and acting as a vanguard may be related func-tions which an early warning mission should be prepared to undertake as the situation changes.

Direct economic action might include identifying development oppor-tunities, assisting worthwhile causes to secure international funding, help-ing to prepare proposals, and acting as project officers for programmes run by development agencies. This sort of activity is likely to increase the stature of the mission and the cooperation of local authorities, making it easier to gain access and information. Direct political and social action is more likely to be perceived as meddling in internal affairs, particularly once officials have become involved in discrimination or oppression. Ob-serving without offering any hope of assistance, however, makes infor-mation collection difficult. People will be reluctant to expose themselves to official retribution for the benefit of "voyeuristic" observers who report to some distant centre, with no evidence of any result.[41] There is even scope for direct military and police action in the early warning stages. Sending each faction's officers out of country for training and professional development, holding seminars and workshops in-country, and building professional relationships would all be useful steps on which to build later. In each case, one of the functions of the early warning mission is to bring greater resources from outside the mission to bear at an early stage and in places where they will have a positive impact. This argues for a mission with many organizational links.

Should it be necessary to escalate from an early warning mission to one that takes direct action, a multifunctional mission might help the deployment of a larger mission. In military terms, observers can function as liaison, reconnaissance, and advance parties.[42] The same functions are required for political, economic, and social aspects of a mission. One of the most important functions is simply preserving and transferring information. Many wheels were reinvented by IFOR, the High Representative's Office, and UNMIBH, having been lost without a trace in the ashes of UNPF and UNPROFOR.

Conclusion: The right balance

We have not yet achieved the right balance for effective early warning and prevention. UN fact-finding missions have been conducted at high level over short duration. UN observer missions have been predominantly military, conducted at low level, often over long duration. Multifunctional missions under regional auspices have sometimes been deployed too late to exert a galvanizing or preventive role. The new forms of missions under the OSCE, however, show great potential.

There are three steps to using observer missions to provide effective early warning and prevention. The first is to get the missions into the right place at the right time, with appropriate mandates and freedom of action. Even if they arrive late, they can always hope to prevent matters from getting worse. The second is to ensure that they are appropriately structured and prepared to detect vital signs, interpret them correctly, and communicate that information. The third is to ensure that they are linked into the international community in such a way as to maximize the impact of the warning they can provide. This last step is key to preventive action. It might include a media strategy, liaison to international and regional organizations, and personal links to key decision makers.

Achieving these three steps to effective warning and prevention requires the right balance. Missions must balance high-level access and low-level input. They must balance military presence with specialized civilian expertise. This balance will vary depending on the stage of escalation that the conflict has reached. Finally, at each level, the mission must balance the functions of collecting and analysing information, and taking action to prevent violence locally while galvanizing the international community to broader preventive action. Prevention is multidimensional and continuous – relevant at every phase of intervention in a conflict.[43] Multifunctional observer missions with a culture of proactive collection, analysis, and action, can help to spur regional and international actors to do the right thing for prevention.

Notes

1. An earlier version of this chapter was published in Susanne Schmeidl and Howard Adelman, eds., *Early Warning, Early Response*, CIAO, Columbia University Press, 1998, https://wwwc.cc.columbia.edu/sec/dlc/ciao/bookfrm.html. A version translated and edited by Robert Bussière has been published in *l'Europe et la prevention des crises et des conflits: le long chemin de la théorie à la pratique*, Paris: L'Harmattan, 2000.
2. Address to the Presentation of the Final Report of the Carnegie Commission on Preventing Deadly Conflict, New York, 5 February 1998 (SG/SM/6454).
3. Christopher R. Mitchell, "Problem Solving Exercises and Theories of Conflict Resolution," in Dennis J. D. Sandole and Hugo van der Merwe, eds., *Conflict Resolution Theory and Practice: Integration and Application*, Manchester: Manchester University Press, 1993, p. 88.
4. On the utility of a contingency approach to third-party intervention, see Betts Fetherston, *Toward a Theory of United Nations Peacekeeping*, London: St. Martin's Press, 1994, pp. 115–21.
5. United Nations, *The Use of Military and Civil Defence Assets in Disaster Relief Operations: MCDA Field Manual*, Draft Version 3, 16 November 1995, pp. 1–2, 1–8.
6. Jean-H. Guilmette, "Beyond Emergency Assistance: Early Warning, Conflict Prevention and Decision-Making," Discussion Paper, July 1995 (CIDA/ACDI), pp. 18–19.
7. Donald Acheson, "Preventing Genocide: Episodes must be Exposed, Documented and Published," *British Medical Journal*, Vol. 313, 7 December 1996. Other descriptions of the process are found in Cynthia Brown and Farhad Karim, eds., *Playing the Communal Card: Communal Violence and Human Rights*, New York: Human Rights Watch, 1995 and Edward L. Nyankauzi, *Genocide: Rwanda and Burundi*, New York: AAIC International, 1994.
8. Donald L. Horowitz, "Making Moderation Pay: The Comparative Politics of Ethnic Conflict Management," in Joseph V. Montville, ed., *Conflict and Peacemaking in Multiethnic Societies*, New York: Lexington Books, 1991, pp. 455–6.
9. Office of Legal Affairs, Codification Division, *Handbook on the Peaceful Settlement of Disputes Between States*, New York: United Nations, 1992, multiple entries deal with different applications of fact-finding by the various bodies charged with the resolution of disputes.
10. Indar Jit Rikhye, Michael Harbottle, and Bjørn Egge, *The Thin Blue Line: International Peacekeeping and its Future*, A Study Sponsored by the International Peace Academy with the Support of the Charles F. Kettering Foundation, London: Yale University Press, 1974, pp. 143–7.
11. Chantal de Jonge Oudraat, "The United Nations and Internal Conflict," in Michael E. Brown, ed., *The International Dimensions of Internal Conflict*, Cambridge, MA: MIT Press, 1996, pp. 528–31.
12. United Nations, *The Blue Helmets: A Review of United Nations Peace-keeping*, New York: Department of Public Information, 1996, pp. 641–8, and Secretary General's *Report on the United Nations Transitional Executive Authority*, A/5501, April 1963.
13. Sir Marrack Goulding, Discussions at the Pearson Peacekeeping Centre, Cornwallis, Nova Scotia, 27 November 1997.
14. The stories collected by Zdenko Lešic, ed., *Children of Atlantis: Voices from the Former Yugoslavia*, Budapest: Central European University Press, 1995, include several which reflect the sudden turn to ethnic identity and militant support for ethnic parties after the summer of 1990.

15. Interviews conducted in Prijedor, Banja Luka, Sanski Most, and Novi Grad from January to July 1996.

16. Discussions with EC monitors in Mission Headquarters, Zagreb in August 1995, and in Team Bravo Headquarters in Banja Luka in April–May 1996.

17. Wilhelm Höynck, "CSCE Capabilities for Contributing to Conflict Prevention and Crisis Management," speech at the NATO Seminar on Crisis Management, Brussels, 7 March 1994, in *From CSCE to OSCE: Statements and Speeches of Dr. Wilhelm Höynck, Secretary General of the OSCE*, 1993–1996, Vienna: Secretariat of the OSCE, 1996, p. 106.

18. Security Council Resolution 885, 1993. S/RES/885.

19. Brigadier General Michel Maisonneuve, "The OSCE Kosovo Verification Mission" typescript, and interviews with other participants in the mission. Some of the most perceptive analyses of the situation in Kosovo have come from NGOs like International Crisis Group, which employs academics with local knowledge. The ICG Report of 2 November 1999, "Security Shortfall in Kosovo," lists five different groups with separate motivations behind the continued violence. Private communication to author.

20. Interviews with participants, December 1999.

21. Robert Cooper and Mats Berdal, "Outside Intervention in Ethnic Conflicts," in Michael E. Brown, ed., *Ethnic Conflict and International Security*, Princeton, NJ: Princeton University Press, 1993, pp. 197–8.

22. Höynck, "CSCE Capabilities for Contributing to Conflict Prevention and Crisis Management," note 17 above, pp. 102–4.

23. Discussions with European Community Monitoring Mission (ECMM) analysts and Head of Analysis and Assessment Unit in Zagreb, Croatia, November 1995.

24. Michael R. Lucal, "The OSCE Code of Conduct and Its Relevance in Contemporary Europe," *Aussenpolitik*, Vol. 111, 1996, pp. 223–35.

25. Stephen G. Brush, "Dynamics of Theory Change in the Social Sciences: Relative Deprivation and Collective Violence," *Journal of Conflict Resolution*, Vol. 40, No. 4, December 1996, pp. 523–45.

26. Milton J. Esman, "Economic Performance and Ethnic Conflict," in Montville, ed., *Conflict and Peacemaking in Multiethnic Societies*, pp. 481–9. Esman describes how Israeli hegemony has benefited the lowest economic class of Palestinians, who have taken menial employment in Israel; landed Palestinian gentry, a traditionally privileged group, have lost status and power; middle classes excluded from the new prosperity have become radicalized. Thus the impact of economic change has varied by socio-economic group, and the impact on potential for violence depends on intra-ethnic dynamics, pp. 485–6.

27. Peter Lewis, "Ethnic Accommodation, Distributive Politics and Economic Growth in Developing Countries: The Cases of Indonesia and Nigeria," paper presented at the 1996 Annual Meeting of the American Political Science Association, San Francisco, 1996, p. 25.

28. Andrew S. Natsios, "Commander's Guidance: A Challenge of Complex Humanitarian Emergencies," *Parameters*, Vol. 26, No. 2, Summer 1996, pp. 61–2.

29. Colonel P. G. Williams, OBE, "Liaison – A Capability Gap in Current Peacekeeping Doctrine: A Lesson Learned from Operation in the Former Yugoslavia," unpublished paper received from author. Williams lists 12 components or characteristics of a monitoring and liaison mission.

30. E. D. Doyle, "Verification in the Sinai – An Integrated Approach," *International Peacekeeping*, Vol. 1, No. 3, Winter 1994, pp. 336–48.

31. de Jonge Oudraat, "The United Nations and Internal Conflict," note 11 above, pp. 489–90.

32. Andrew J. Goodpaster, "When Diplomacy Is Not Enough: Managing Multinational Military Interventions," report to the Carnegie Commission on Preventing Deadly Conflict, July 1996.

33. In some cases, human rights observers from the Commission for Human Rights transferred to the UN Civil Affairs at local level, and none of the local expertise was lost.

34. Pauletta Otis, "Boundaries and Ethnic Conflict," paper presented at the 92nd Annual Meeting of the American Political Science Association, San Francisco, 28–31 August 1996.

35. This reflects a Canadian perspective. The British Multi-National Division South West was concerned about IEBL crossings at Kljuc, Mrkonic Grad and other sites as well as Otoka and Sanski Most. In the other divisional areas, there were similar flashpoints. What follows is a simplified description of a complex sequence of events; others in possession of different information would perceive it differently. It is provided here as an illustration, not a historic picture of events.

36. Meetings with Adem Šahinovic at Otoka on 20 April 1996, and with Sead Cirkin in Sanski Most, 27 May 1996, and near Koprivna on 28 May 1996. In reality, individual traffic across the IEBL continued during this period.

37. Alexander George and June Holl, "The Warning-Response Problem and Missed Opportunities in Preventive Diplomacy," paper presented to the 92nd Annual Meeting of the American Political Science Association, San Francisco, 28–31 August 1996, p. 36.

38. *Ibid.*, p. 7.

39. Nik Gowing, "Media Coverage: Help or Hindrance for Conflict Prevention?" diagnostic paper for the Carnegie Commission on Preventing Deadly Conflict, unpublished draft, 3 November 1996.

40. Pascale Combelles Siegel, *Target Bosnia: Integrating Information Activities in Peace Operations*, Washington: Department of Defense Command and Control Research Program, 1998; and Ingrid A. Lehmann, *Peacekeeping and Public Information: Caught in the Crossfire*, London: Frank Cass, 1999.

41. This was the feeling some minorities expressed about the Commission for Human Rights observers in northwest Bosnia in spring 1996, after they repeatedly emphasized that they could only report but could take no action. The OSCE Human Rights monitors, taking a more assertive approach with local authorities, received more reports because there was some hope that something would come of the information, and it was worth the risk.

42. David Last, "Co-operation between Units and Observers," *News From The Front!*, The Centre for Army Lessons Learned, September/October 1994, pp. 1–2, 5, 7.

43. Carment and Schnabel, this volume.

10

Early warning analysis and policy planning in UN preventive action[1]

John G. Cockell

Introduction

Is there anything inadequate about current ways of framing the problem of effective preventive action, both within and outside the organizations called upon to produce concrete operational results? Organizational constraints are one of the most commonly cited problems when conflict prevention fails. The objective in this chapter is to examine the organizational and informational constraints on conflict prevention within the UN Secretariat. The UN reform process, with its system-wide emphasis on decentralization and coordination, is the organizational context in which the Secretariat is seeking to address these constraints and to translate its policy development on conflict prevention into a proactive operational capacity for preventive action. Against this context of constraints and reform the concept and practice of early warning, and its role in initiating conflict prevention operations, will be examined.

Drawing upon recent project research, the basis for an organizationally specific redefinition of conflict prevention will be outlined, focusing on the need for its strategic and proactive application in situations of protracted internal conflicts. A large measure of this redefinition involves the building of UN capacity to conduct early warning analysis in a manner that facilitates the applied planning and implementation of preventive action strategies. Reframing the early warning problematic in this way reverses the logic of much recent research on early warning methods, and thus a related objective of this chapter is to contest the assumptions underlying that logic. Finally, in outlining the basic elements of a composite analytical method for UN early warning, certain features of conflict analysis theory which either facilitate or hinder the contemporary need to evolve pragmatic strategies and instruments for the prevention of protracted violent conflict will be highlighted.

UN institutional transformation and reform

With internal conflicts demanding increasing attention from the international community, there has been a corresponding jump in the expectations of many UN member states that the organization will move to address these conflicts (and their human impact) in a proactive manner.[2] In most intrastate conflicts, the UN has found itself facing situations of protracted violence, in which the only external role feasible (by that stage of conflict escalation) is that of humanitarian assistance and/or multidimensional peace support operations. The deployment of such operations in conflict zones, always fraught with risk, has of late damaged the credibility of the UN in the high-profile disasters of Bosnia, Somalia, and Rwanda. Member states, largely responsible for imposing unrealistic and under-resourced mandates on the UN for such operations, have called on the UN Secretariat to upgrade its capacity to monitor and prevent such protracted situations from arising.[3]

In addition to being confronted with field situations of complex and protracted violence in which options are relatively circumscribed and chances for success are limited, the UN Secretariat's capacity to conduct such monitoring and prevention has also been constrained by the general paucity of resources. A 1996 study by the Clingendael Institute in the Netherlands found that many key international organizations, including the United Nations, were unable to engage in effective conflict prevention due to the demands they faced from existing conflicts and crises. They were oriented for the most part towards responding to the symptoms of full-blown conflicts and wars, and thus had done little to develop a repertoire of conflict prevention strategies.[4] While part of this dilemma relates to the need for enhanced organizational resources (human, diplomatic, and budgetary) it also involves the manner in which conflict early warning and prevention are managed within a larger strategic vision for the United Nations.[5] The current process of UN reform, which began with the arrival of Kofi Annan as Secretary-General in January 1997, has opened up new opportunities to make effective connections between improved early warning and preventive action. One of the primary reasons for this has been the initiation of new Secretariat practices to deal with actual and potential crisis situations. Notable among these are the new Executive Committee on Peace and Security (ECPS), and the restructured interdepartmental Framework for Coordination.[6] These internal reforms within the Secretariat have led to a heightened impetus for the development of new working methods for conflict analysis and intra-UN coordination.

Reframing the early warning problematic

Early warning is pursued in a variety of contexts, both national and international, both research and policy. Its content and practice tend to be shaped by at least six factors: subject (e.g. conflict, famine, human rights violations), operational purpose (e.g. defence, prevention, preparedness), method (e.g. quantitative, qualitative), user, target recipient, and format. For the policy practitioner, the issues of user (i.e. the person conducting the analysis, and his or her organizational setting), target recipient (i.e. the organizational arrival point for the warning produced), and format (i.e. the manner in which the warning is explained and presented) all loom large. The practitioner is confronted with the operational reality that warning and analysis do not constitute preventive measures in and of themselves, and that there is a "process connection" which has to be explicitly made between analysis and the application of preventive measures to a particular conflict. All of the factors mentioned above are central to effecting this "process connection" between early warning and preventive action.

Advocates of early warning are often faced with the cynicism of those who believe that preventive action is typically eschewed because of a lack of "political will." The critics argue that key decision makers in major governments and organizations are unwilling to take the risks associated with committing political and financial capital to a situation that either may not require such outlays or may not in fact respond positively to such actions. In fact, the gap between warning and action has often been discussed in the context of organizational constraints on governments and international organizations to take action on the basis of warning.[7] Such reasons for the gap include: (1) the traditional governmental separation between analysis/intelligence and policy/operations; (2) the difficulty of planning multisectoral responses to complex causes of conflict; (3) the dilemma that dealing with immediate operations tends to crowd out strategic consideration of future issues and potential problems; (4) lack of a structured model for systematic, rather than *ad hoc*, early warning analysis; and (5) deficiencies in the manner in which warnings are transmitted to decision makers, and the consequent difficulty in deriving assessments of the operational implications of these warnings.[8] The "political will" charge often fails to acknowledge these constraints. Instead, by addressing the last two constraints, organizational perception of the other three may be significantly reframed as being less problematic, at least within the organizational context of the United Nations.

Recent studies on early warning generally note the importance of the relationship between warning and action, but for the most part they neglect to view the issue as a gap that needs to be closed. Instead the relationship is viewed as a question of will, perception, and/or understanding on the part of policy makers. Either warnings were ignored or the preventive measures taken were inadequate for the crisis. In this context, policy makers may consider early warning to lack enough "credibility" to serve as a convincing basis for action.[9] They may also appear to lack sufficient knowledge of the range of possible options for preventive measures. For George and Hall, the essence of the problem lies in the lack of "receptivity" to warnings on the part of policy makers, and the resulting failure of those policy makers to seize the opportunities provided by warning for the initiation of timely preventive measures.[10] In short, the warning-response gap is most often characterized by the research community as one of receptivity, credibility, and/or knowledge. All of these explanations point to three important aspects of the warn-response relationship: the timeliness of the warning, the relationship of warning with decision making and/or planning, and the development of specific forms of action on the basis of warning. While doing so, they all avoid the central question of how, in concrete terms, early warning analysis could support the planning of and decision on preventive action.

Early warning needs and capacity in the United Nations system

Many Secretariat officials involved in the work of the Office for Research and the Collection of Information (ORCI, from 1987–92) concluded that the effective link between early warning and preventive measures was a direct function of the proximity of the analyst to senior decision makers, particularly the Secretary-General. As Tapio Kanninen has argued, "[e]arly warning is linked to possible immediate action by an actor who is close to one giving the early warning, e.g. belonging to the same organization." This, he asserts, calls for early warning to be "practice-oriented, dynamic, and geared to the possibilities of the actor to intervene purposefully."[11] Similarly, Jim Sutterlin continues to argue that analysts must have "direct access to the person or organization that is capable of taking preventive action." He, too, sees UN early warning as having three necessary components: information, analysis, and a "communication channel" to the decision level, ideally within the EOSG itself.[12] Thus, arising from the ORCI period, there was a clearer impression of the importance of the relationship between early warning and decision-making.

The weakness of ORCI, however, was that its process connection to the decision level in the EOSG did not make a direct analytical link to broader preventive action strategies on the basis of structured analysis. The emphasis was more upon the drafting of early warning alerts for the Secretary-General in the specific context of his good offices and Article 99 roles, i.e. analysis for alert rather than planning.[13] But with the post-1992 devolution of early warning to the new Department of Political Affairs (DPA), such a relationship could no longer be effected through proximity to the Secretary-General. A different approach would have to be built into the ordinary decision-making processes of departments and agencies.[14] As Jürgen Dedring argued in 1992, the role of the desk officer is, on the basis of conflict analysis, to recommend possible courses of action to decision-making organs. In his view, an integrated approach to early warning would comprise "consolidated advice ... including early warning signals, a specific situation assessment, and options for preventive action."[15] In short, political early warning activity (for the purposes of conflict prevention) is now primarily pursued by DPA desk officers, with more limited conflict-related information and analysis also being conducted by the Department of Peacekeeping Operations (DPKO), the Office for the Coordination of Humanitarian Affairs (OCHA), and by UN humanitarian field agencies such as the UN High Commissioner for Refugees (UNHCR) and the UN Children's Fund (UNICEF).

This apparent diffusion of early warning has not met with universal acclaim. A 1995 Joint Inspection Unit (JIU) report on conflict prevention called for a specialized unit within the DPA to conduct "action-oriented analysis of situations," provide "anticipatory planning" of "appropriate actions" to the Secretary-General, and thereby "facilitate early action." The report also called for greater interdepartmental coordination of early warning information within the UN.[16] Similarly, the multi-donor Rwanda evaluation also noted that early warning analysis within the UN did not do enough to integrate different sources of information (e.g. human rights with political) into a "larger information and analytic structure that can process the information in terms of complex social conflict and communicate the analysis to policy planning levels."[17] This reality militates in favour of the kind of interdepartmental coordination of *decision* now conducted by the ECPS, and coordination of working-level early warning *analysis* now being pursued in the widened Framework for Coordination.

Thus, there has been a growing perception of the need for increased capacity in both decision mechanisms and planning processes for conflict prevention.

The importance of building an interdepartmental, working-level capacity for early warning analysis was emphasized recently by former Under-Secretary-General for Political Affairs Sir Marrack Goulding in his comprehensive evaluation of the UN's peace and security departments. Recommending that early warning and policy analysis be consolidated as part of a set of centralized common services for the Department of Political Affairs (DPA), DPKO, OCHA, and the UN High Commissioner for Human Rights (UNHCHR), Goulding suggested that operational action requires both interdepartmental input and access to early warning analysis, as well as a process of policy development derived from such analysis which will feed into decision-making at the senior management level.[18] What is common to the assessments of UN early warning by former and current Secretariat officials such as Goulding, Kanninen, Ramcharan, Sutterlin, and Dedring, is a shared perception that further progress will be dependent on addressing three related organizational needs: the need for standardized methods of action-oriented analysis; the need for greater interdepartmental coordination on such analysis; and the need for improved decision-making utility of the results of such analysis. As we have noted earlier, these needs reveal an operational concern with issues of method, user, recipient, and format.

Recent consultations with Secretariat officials confirm that there is a strong preference for new early warning methods that will be both action-oriented as well as practical, and reflect the new focus on the role of the desk officer in providing analysis.[19] The consultations, which were based on an extensive needs assessment conducted in 1998, generated seven broad conclusions on required characteristics of future early warning within the UN system: (1) practical to use in terms of its method, (2) decentralized from the decision-making level in terms of its location, (3) devolved to the desk officer level in terms of its user, (4) interdepartmental in terms of its process, (5) coordinated across the departments concerned with peace and security, (6) targeted at supporting decision makers in terms of its recipients and, thus, (7) actionable in terms of its format, making explicit recommendations on options for preventive measures. Rather than looking at early warning as information for exchange (raising credibility and receptivity issues), the UN tends to view it as analysis that informs decision-making processes. In addition, however, *applied* early warning should be viewed as a *process* that connects the content of analysis directly to the operational assessment and implementation of options for action.

In other words, the problematic of applied early warning is not that its outputs should somehow be closely linked to, or received by, the procedure that decides on possible response measures. It is, rather, that the practice of early warning should itself be understood to be part of the process of determining and executing preventive action. As Kuroda has argued, this means viewing early warning as being integrated into a "management cycle" comprised of "early warning, preparedness, action, and post-action evaluation."[20] Similarly, Adelman notes that "[e]arly warning goes beyond the collection and sharing of information to include both analysis of that information *and* the formulation of appropriate strategic choices given the analysis."[21] Our thinking about early warning thus needs to be reframed: it should be viewed as an integral element in the very process that supports the operational planning and implementation of conflict prevention.

Closing the warning-action gap: Towards a planning approach

Recent efforts of the UN to assess and develop its internal early warning needs and practices point to the fact that early warning must have both analysis and a connection to options for preventive measures. Second, this UN practice shows that the connection between analysis and response options must support decision-making procedures in a single, integrated process. Finally, a process-based approach means that the method and format of applied early warning is shaped directly by the operational focus of the process itself, in this case preventive action as opposed to preparedness. All of these elements point to the relevance of basic policy analysis and planning methods to closing the warning-action gap. Such methods incorporate the structuring of problems, the application of appropriate analytical tools to solve those problems, and the communication of analysis and recommendations in a format useful to decision makers. In short, policy planning is a type of decision-support procedure. A definition of early warning consistent with a planning approach would thus be: the process of collecting and analysing information for the purpose of identifying and recommending strategic options for preventive measures.[22]

As noted above, recent UN reforms have made manifest the organizational need for improved decision support in early warning. Building-related capacity for working-level analysis and planning began in earnest in 1998–99. With initial support from the British government, a project was initiated by the EOSG in March 1998 to address the needs which Goulding had identified, and which were required by the new reform process. The Early Warning and Preventive Measures (EWPM) project has since developed an early warning methodology which can serve as a common analytical language for those UN departments and agencies responsible for the joint planning of preventive action.[23] Drawing upon the work of the EWPM project, the following discussion presents the connection between UN early warning analysis and the implementation of preventive action as one of applied policy planning. This process involves nine basic steps, beginning with early warning and ending with strategic action:[24]

1. Analyse key causes of conflict and conflict dynamics.
2. Prioritize sectors for strategic and comprehensive responses.
3. Define specific operational objective(s).
4. Identify range of potential preventive measures for each operational objective.
5. Assess UN comparative advantage.
6. Determine required combination of preventive measures.
7. Integrate participation of key UN departments and agencies.
8. Coordinate operational implementation of preventive measures.
9. Monitor preventive action and determine exit criteria.

In sum, a planning approach to applied early warning views its function as that of operational decision support, such that recommended options for the strategic application of preventive measures may be considered and (if necessary) approved in the shortest possible timeframe.

Policy planning and action-oriented early warning analysis

The challenge of coordinating the input of multiple UN departments and agencies into conflict early warning (as the Framework for Coordination seeks to do) is to get them to think in terms of what analysis they can structure and contribute to the specific but shared objective of conflict prevention. This is an objective which requires the coordinated input of various departments and agencies, such as OCHA and UNDP, but it is also an objective which will be less central to their core mandates than it is to the DPA's. The preventive action planning process calls for analytical steps that will identify operational measures specific to the prevention of conflict.

Analysing conflict causes and dynamics (Step 1)

Problem structuring is the preliminary step taken in most forms of policy planning. It is important for the analysis of causes and the mapping of possible objectives.[25] The manner in which one defines and structures a problem influences – both implicitly and explicitly – the range of possible alternatives and the evaluation of those alternatives. Problem structuring for preventive action planning is both empirical as well as normative. The process is concerned with analysing the objective causes of conflict escalation, and with prescribing what should be done to prevent such escalation (i.e. what does or will exist? (facts) and what should be done? (action)). While conflict is a normal condition of human societies, there is a general sense that the focus of preventive action must be on those conflicts that have the potential to generate long-term instability, violence, and insecurity for human populations. But rather than assuming that such violent conflicts are driven by one particular cause, such as ancient ethnic hatreds or resource scarcity, effective analysis will survey a broader and more comprehensive range of potential causal factors. In most cases of protracted internal conflict, a range of basic human needs is being denied to one group, producing a complex condition of deprivation and marginalization. The imposition of such complex deprivation may be understood as an indirect form of violence, one which is not manifested as direct physical violence, but also in the situational or "structural" conditions of that deprivation.[26] We may thus speak of two preliminary points of departure: (1) protracted social conflicts are not mono-causal in nature; and (2) such conflicts are not characterized simply by the manifestation of direct violence. We will now consider briefly two different ways of analysing conflict causes: sectoral and temporal.[27]

Sectoral analysis of conflict causes

How can desk officers best assess the importance of various human needs as structural conditions of potentially violent conflict? In the context of UN efforts to explore alternative approaches to conflict analysis, that of human security (as developed by UNDP and explored by Schnabel in this volume) bears the closest correspondence to the discussion of basic human needs outlined above.[28] By using human security as a preliminary framework of reference for conflict analysis, causes of social conflict can be interpreted as potential threats to human security. One can thereby begin to determine whether some threats are more significant for protracted conflict that others, and isolate the complexities of the conflict's internal dynamics. Some human security components that are important for conflict analysis are:

- Governance and political security;
- Societal and communal security;
- Human rights and personal security;
- Economic and resource security.

Human security also offers a useful framework for the interpretation of conflict causes because of its implicit recognition of the importance of group (i.e. collective) as well as individual perceptions of identity, values, and security. Such collective (e.g. ethnic) perceptions of difference over fundamental, non-negotiable values tend to be more central to the intractability of internal conflicts than instrumental interests by any one conflict actor. In short, human security provides a foundation for analysis. But, as a point of departure, it must also be adjusted for contextual specifics and also for temporal change, particularly during periods of rapid social transformation.

Temporal analysis of conflict causes

The causes of protracted social conflict may also be understood in temporal terms. Causes vary over time, as the conflict situation develops. This begins to take the analytical process from the static identification and classification of causes towards a more dynamic analysis of those causes and their interaction. Most early warning models distinguish between long-term (structural) conditions and more near-term (proximate) events and actions.[29] The discussion above mentioned the importance of structural conditions of deprivation in protracted social conflict. In such situations, multiple sectoral causes (e.g. political exclusion, intercommunal hostility and polarization, economic deprivation) combine over the passage of time to form an interlocking web or "structure" of human insecurity. Minorities in multi-ethnic societies (e.g. Kashmiri Muslims, Sri Lankan Tamils, Kosovar Albanians) are particularly vulnerable to the progressive accumulation of such systemic conditions of group insecurity. As collective perceptions of threat and fear build, political elites can use this popular sentiment to promote strategies of militancy and confrontation. These can be made manifest in specific policies and acts, either by the government or by an opposition group, and are thus often found in the governance/political security sector of human security. They may also result in specific instances of gross human rights violations, such as massacres. Such near-term or proximate events can exacerbate the volatility of the structural conditions and cause the situation to escalate towards protracted levels of violence. They are thus relatively more dynamic, and usually involve the discrete acts of specific actors.

In spite of the fact that conflict phases do not necessarily proceed in a linear fashion, it is possible to argue that external preventive measures should be adjusted to take into account a particular identifiable phase of the conflict.[30] Certain types of preventive measures, such as human rights monitoring, will be more effective if employed during the phase of non-protracted confrontation than during the phase of high-intensity, protracted violence. This means that in order to maximize the possibility of early action and the timely application of phase-sensitive measures, early warning analysis should identify the phase of escalation and its central features. As well, such analysis would note the change in actor dynamics in different phases: moderate leaders and factions tend to play a central role only in early phases of escalation, whereas warlords and criminalized factions tend to define conflict dynamics only after a sustained period of protracted high-intensity violence. The nature of the dominant actors at any given phase, and the dynamic shift of their perceptions and agendas over time, clearly affects the types of preventive measure external actors might employ during that period. Measures that presume the primacy of economic agendas may not, for example, be effective in lower stages of conflict escalation where political security issues and values are of central importance to moderate leaders. Similarly, the impact of prolonged human rights violations at higher phases of escalation will make justice and retribution more salient as structural issues for group security than at earlier phases.

Prioritizing causal sectors for strategic responses (Step 2)

Since conflicts are both dynamic and multi-causal, it follows that an effective preventive response will have to address both the particular phase of a conflict and the particular conjunction of conflict causes that characterize that phase. An effective response, in other words, must be strategic: engaging all the primary conflict factors in an integrated fashion, so that their preventive management results in successful de-escalation, rather than a narrowly focused intervention which leaves certain key causes unresolved. This is the core of action-oriented early warning, since it allows the practitioner to move from a simple checklist of unrelated causal factors to the basis for an operationally relevant explanation of their interaction dynamics.[31] As conflict causes grow in salience for the groups and elites in society, they also affect each other and mutually influence their further formation and development. Disaggregating and relating such key causal factors is a crucial element in effective analysis, since this will present the basis for a plan to prevent any further escalation of the situation. While a single effort to address one or two key causes may have the effect of de-escalating the conflict dynamic, it is much more likely that effective prevention would entail the integrated engagement of all relevant conflict causes.

So far the discussion has emphasized the range of conflict causes in both sectoral and temporal terms, and the importance of dynamic analysis of the interactive conjunction of those causes. How does this combination facilitate the planning need to prioritize causal sectors for preventive strategy? Drawing on a human security perspective, one could argue in favour of six basic categories of causal preconditions for protracted social conflict:

• Governance and political process;

- Societal and communal stability;
- Human rights and personal security;
- Economic and resource security;
- Military and arms;
- External factors.

This is to argue that the most important basic causes of protracted conflict are the breakdown or paralysis of a contested political process; the
polarization of social divisions along communal identity (ethnic, religious,
tribal) lines; the systematic violation of human rights and endemic personal insecurity; the presence of differential economic underdevelopment,
deprivation, and possibly resource scarcity; the militarization of political
action and availability of small arms; and the presence of regional and/or
international support for one or more conflict actors.[32] This can be dis-
played as a composite schema that highlights various causal interactions
(see Fig. 10.1). The manageable number of categories allows for analysis
to focus on the key causal factors present in each, while retaining a broad,
macro-level picture of the situation as a whole as it moves along the
conflict life cycle.

Of these six categories, however, there is a growing body of research
which suggests that bad governance and collapse of a contested political
process are frequently and centrally indicated in conflict escalation.[33] Indicators of political process breakdown are thus at the centre of the dy-

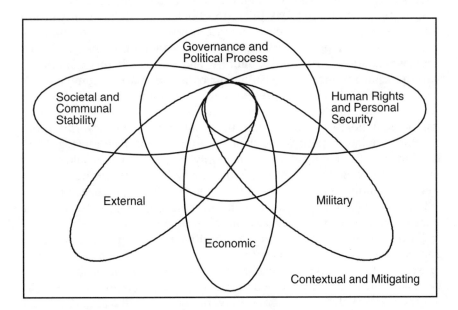

Figure 10.1 Composite format for early warning analysis

namic analysis of protracted social conflict. As UNDP's Sam Amoo argues in his study of conflict in Africa, political structures and dysfunctional governance arrangements are central to causal interaction:

Contrary to commonly held impressions, often it is not perceived inequitable distribution of national wealth and authoritative positions which precipitate internal conflicts; the issue at stake invariably devolves on the *processes* by which resources are allocated, and these processes relate to such needs as recognition, identity, and participation. *The process may be more important than the actual allocation; and the process is a political issue.*[34]

This is also the category, as noted earlier, in which most of the proximate acts and events of state and non-state actors will be found. It is important to note here that economic or other instrumental factors that may appear to be driving the specific agendas of conflict actors may in fact be either symptomatic of or derived from the more fundamental and antecedent breakdown of processes of legitimate governance and political participation. Governance breakdown is also most often caught in a spiral of interactive escalation with social polarization between identity groups (the majority group often controlling the institutions and definition of political process) and group fears of communal insecurity and even extinction.[35]

On top of the conjunction of governance and societal polarization factors may be laid targeted violations of civil and political liberties, intended (for example) to break the support of an alienated minority group for its nationalist elites. Such deliberate use of human rights violations and threats to personal security are a key precondition in many cases of conflict escalation.[36] Economic, military, and external factors can also be part of this increasingly combustible mix of factors. Various combinations of causal preconditions will present, depending on the nature and phase of the conflict, moderate to high potentials for conflict escalation. The risk of escalation would depend on the number, type, and severity of the categories in interaction. While the composite format diagram (Fig. 10.1) is a rather artificial representation, in reality the causal ovals would change shape and size as the conflict situation moved through various conflict stages, expanding and receding as the dynamics developed over time.

Early warning analysis should focus on the central point of concurrent interaction, at which the largest number of preconditions are coalescing. It is by outlining the key factors in causal interaction that early warning analysis will provide an action-oriented conflict profile, in which these causes will be the top priorities in a proactive, structurally oriented preventive strategy. Finally, in examining such broad categories, one must always acknowledge that there are invariably local political and cultural dynamics that can act as unusual causes or mitigating factors in situations of potential escalation. In the case of such mitigating factors, it is important for analysis to highlight these features as potential anchor-points for indigenous coping strategies that could be supported by an external preventive strategy. The composite format diagram indicates contextual and mitigating factors as a consideration relevant to the analysis of all six sectors.

Defining operational objectives (Step 3)

In order to make early warning analysis truly action-oriented, a series of explicit operational objectives must be stated, which derive clearly and concisely from the content of the situation profile. To do this, each objective will state the specific goal, or outcome, which preventive action is intended to achieve in each key causal sector. What has to be done in order to address effectively each key cause of conflict? For example, a governance objective for a proximate cause might be to re-establish access by minority group political formations to the parliamentary process. A societal objective for a structural cause might be to reduce overt expressions of communal hostility and intolerance between the minority and majority communities.

Context-specific planning for preventive action is crucial. This requires that specified objectives derive from the composite analysis of the conflict situation, and are not objectives imposed by institutional mandates or goals. As the conflict situation develops, objectives will also necessarily have to shift to reflect the changing contextual conjunction of causes and actors. This "goal displacement" is not only inevitable, but desirable, given the complex dynamism of conflict escalation.[37] Finally, objectives should be measurable, such that their achievement (or not) may be tracked within a specified period of time.

Policy planning and preventive action strategy

Success in the preventive engagement of multiple causes of conflict clearly rests upon cross-sectoral coordination of the relevant operational measures. Preventive action, in fact, should be understood to mean the strategic integration and application of a range of preventive measures, as opposed to such measures being applied in a disconnected and *ad hoc* manner. As Kofi Annan observes in his 1999 annual report: "To address complex causes we need complex, interdisciplinary solutions." He further notes that "implementing prevention strategies ... requires cooperation across a broad range of different agencies and departments" and that "cross-sector cooperation ... is a prerequisite of successful prevention."[38]

Making such cooperation work in practice, in practical and effective strategies, is the essential thrust behind the concept of preventive action. With conflict prevention as the overarching strategic logic or concept of operations, the idea of preventive action also demands that each part of the UN system examine its own programmes' possible relevance to prevention in light of such a broader strategic approach.

Integrating preventive measures (Steps 4 to 6)

The complexity of preventing (as with analysing) the interaction and escalation of a multiple number of causal factors virtually ensures that the operational task of prevention will also be beyond the capacity of any single department or agency. In fact, it will often be the case that the totality of the situation's requirements will fall outside of the capacity of the UN itself, requiring the sort of inter-organizational cooperation we now witness in the UNMIK operation in Kosovo. Beyond this widened operational agenda, preventive action also implies a more proactive approach to the causes of protracted social conflict. As argued earlier, proximate forms of prevention (or "light prevention") tend to be more reactive to the specifics of actor analysis. Structural forms of prevention (or "deep prevention") require a more proactive approach. This would involve a desk officer thoroughly engaged in situation analysis, in search of possible opportunities to address the underlying causes of sociopolitical instability.[39] Finally, a wider agenda, the need for proactivity, and the imperative of context-specific planning on the basis of situation analysis all call for preventive action to be practised in as innovative a manner as possible.

This leads us to the fourth step in the planning process: the identification of a range of *options for preventive measures* for each operational objective identified in the previous step. Options analysis is another key element in the policy planning process, as effective decision support requires that recommendations for action be based on a considered survey of the available measures, both from within the organization and from without.[40] Each potential option, or means, for achieving a specific sectoral objective should be examined for its situational advantages and disadvantages. Again, given the process imperative for context-specificity, an option may be advantageous at one phase of conflict escalation, but less so at a later phase. Alternatively, an option that appeared to be successful in an entirely different conflict may be unsuited to the specific causal conjunction involved in the situation at hand, even if the two conflicts appear to be at roughly the same phase of escalation.

In examining the advantages and disadvantages which attend any potential option, it is also important for there to be some form of risk assessment. This will ascertain the degree to which any particular option is consistent with its corresponding objective, and the relative potential for each available option to successfully produce the desired goal. As argued above, the dynamic analysis of the situation is key, for it points to the combination of elements which must be brought together into a strategic and concerted response. In such cases, the specific means (preventive measures) must be tailored to address the nature of the situation (conflict factors). Preventive measures cannot simply be replicated from past cases, and knowing that one particular measure worked at one time tells the decision maker little since it has been abstracted from the important contextual factors in which that success took place.

The fifth step in the planning process is a direct complement to the analysis conducted in Step 4, and is the assessment of UN *comparative advantage*. Where can the UN contribute successfully to the promotion of a sustainable peace? Where and when does the UN enjoy an operational advantage in such roles in comparison with other possible external actors? As Anthony Lake has remarked, international engagement in conflict situations cannot simply amount to a "summons to every possible task."[41] If key conflict actors are unwilling to entertain a role for the UN, it is very unlikely that the organization could do anything to address the dynamics of the conflict in the strategic manner necessary. Comparative advantage analysis has two important elements, both of which are captured by the concept of *triage*. Triage is an assessment of whether the UN system, in whole or part, has both the capacity and the opportunity to implement its preferred preventive measures in a strategic manner for a given situation. In light of a consolidated options analysis as discussed above, triage assesses the net potential for UN engagement to be successful, and places priority on those situations that offer the greatest potential for success.[42] If a composite analysis of causal interaction suggests that such an opportunity exists for a positive UN role, the second consideration is that of feasibility. Feasibility analysis assesses the availability of and constraints on UN political, diplomatic, human and financial resources in relation to the effect their allocation would have on the calculation of options and risks.

The sixth planning step in the process of integrating a range of preferred options for preventive measures is to determine the *required combination* of measures for optimal strategic impact. The preferred measures, as determined by options and comparative advantage analysis, must address the sectoral objectives identified in Step 3 in an accurate and sustainable manner, and must be mutually complementary in their support of a sustainable peace process. The effective prevention of different types of causes will involve the cooperation of a range of different actors and agencies, from both within and outside the UN system. While some will be best placed to engage conflict actors in the preventive management of proximate causes such as specific policies or acts, others will be better suited to the longer-term amelioration of the structural conditions of human insecurity present in society.

Recent UN policy statements on conflict prevention point to the emergence of six basic categories of UN preventive measures. Three of these are considered to be more short-term measures directed primarily at *proximate* causes of conflict: preventive peacemaking (including preventive diplomacy); preventive deployment; and preventive humanitarian action. The other three are viewed as longer-term measures designed to address the *structural* causes of conflict: preventive peacebuilding; preventive disarmament; and preventive development.[43] While space limitations preclude an extended discussion of specific forms of preventive measures for each category, their most important elements are noted here:

Proximate prevention

Preventive peacemaking:

- Preventive diplomacy: to prevent the possible collapse of non-violent modes of conflict resolution through the use of indirect and *ad hoc* diplomatic contacts;
- Consultations: to prevent the possible collapse of non-violent modes of conflict resolution through the use of direct and *ad hoc* missions to the conflict area;
- Good offices/mediation: to prevent the collapse of, or to re-establish, a stable political process and dialogue between contending conflict actors, by providing various forms of direct third-party facilitation.[44]

Preventive deployment:

- Military: to prevent the threat or potential use of armed force, or to prevent the spread of existing armed conflict to new areas, through pre-emptive positioning of peacekeeping and civilian police (CIVPOL) forces;
- Political: to prevent the threat or potential use of armed force, or to prevent the spread of existing armed conflict to new areas, through pre-emptive positioning of political and/or human rights observers.[45]

Preventive humanitarian action:

- Refugees: to prevent the causes of forced migration (with particular reference to support for national protection capacity) in potential or existing crisis situations;

- Relief: to prevent the presence of conflict and violence from causing humanitarian disasters, and to prevent the further violation of humanitarian norms in conflict situations.

Structural prevention

Preventive peacebuilding:

- Governance: to prevent the paralysis or breakdown of political process and legitimate governance in the regulation of non-violent confrontation and conflict between groups;
- Human rights: to prevent the systematic violation of human rights (with particular reference to civil and political rights) as a form of conflict escalation, and to protect and promote respect for human rights in conflict situations;
- Societal stability: to prevent the polarization of social relations between different groups within a society (particularly between an ethnic/ religious majority and minorities) from leading to political crisis and violence;
- Economic: to prevent the impact of economic crisis and dislocation/ transition from contributing to political violence and the rise or return of armed violence; and to prevent the escalation of conflict through war economies.[46]

Preventive disarmament:

- to prevent the easy recourse by conflict actors to armed violence by reducing or circumscribing their access to and/or deployment of weaponry.

Preventive development:

- Social: to prevent the emergence of intergroup polarization and hostility within society through the promotion of norms and practices of tolerance for plural social identities;
- Economic: to prevent the sudden impact of economic crisis and dislocation/transition from contributing to social unrest and instability.[47]

The political, social, economic, human rights, and military measures referred to above are all supported by extant frameworks for operational planning and implementation within the UN system. Recommendations for preventive action strategies which make this "process connection" are thus more likely to constitute the essence of a compelling case for such action to senior decision makers. But one should not draw the conclusion that most of the sectoral programmes of the UN system have simply been cast in newly fashionable "preventive" garb. Ismat Kittani has argued that it is important not to define preventive action so broadly that it captures most of the activities of the organization: "While development, democratization, and the promotion of human rights are all worthy goals and can contribute to political stability, they do not necessarily constitute preventive action. It is the context and purpose of the activities that matter, that is, whether they are implemented as part of a deliberate strategy to prevent the outbreak of violence."[48] Thus, the test of whether a specific operational option will be preventive in practice is the extent to which it strategically addresses a specific conflict cause in the situational context of the larger causal interaction in the conflict dynamics, the phase of the conflict, and the broader strategic requirements of a sustainable peace.

Implementing preventive action (Steps 7–9)

The final three steps in the planning process make the connection between the formulation of integrated implementation strategies and the tasks related to the actual translation of strategy into action. For our purposes, the most important of these three steps is Step 7, the collective participation of key UN departments and agencies in *joint consultations*. In the final planning stage before recommendations are forwarded for decision, it is essential that there is working-level contact between those departments and agencies with a potential contribution to make to a larger, multi-sector strategy. At this stage, a country- or conflict-specific Secretariat task force may be established to make such integration more formal. The current Framework for Coordination can also provide an effective means for the interdepartmental discussion of collective UN efforts to prevent conflict escalation in a given situation. Once agreement is reached on the strategic objectives and preventive measures needed, the concerned parts of the UN system can move towards decision by finalizing implementation arrangements, clarifying mandates, initiating operational mechanisms, obtaining clearances, and other such transactional requirements. To the extent that working-level consultations have addressed all major analytical, planning and administrative issues relating to interdepartmental coordination, final decision at the Executive Committee and/or EOSG level on the recommended strategy will be correspondingly facilitated. Where such working-level consultations have not been completed, decision at the senior level can be blocked by the fact that not all USGs or agency heads will be familiar with the nature of the crisis and the potential role their department or agency should play.[49]

When the ECPS, EOSG, Security Council or other relevant decision-making body has approved the recommended strategy, actual implementation (Step 8) will entail the *coordinated application* of all measures to the key conflict causes, facilitating a sustainable process of de-escalation. In this active implementation period, it will be important not only to maintain strategic coordination between UN actors, but also to forge partnerships with those regional organizations, member states, contact groups, NGOs and other actors that may have greater comparative advantage in addressing certain aspects of the conflict than any single UN department or agency. Finally, the last step (Step 9) in the planning process entails the ongoing *monitoring and evaluation* of the impact of preventive measures on the conflict situation. Desk officers in the relevant departments and agencies should continue to consult jointly in the evaluation of the strategy's success in achieving the key operational objectives, and in the evaluation of any unforeseen negative outcomes. Where necessary, such assessments can act as a basis for the iterative adjustment of the objectives or implementation strategy. In the event that certain UN programmes, missions, and/or agencies depart, follow-on arrangements for long-term development programmes will be important to determine in collaboration with local actors.

Conclusions

Four arguments therefore highlight the difficulties involved in forging a connection between warning and action on conflict prevention in the UN system. The first is that the manner in which early warning is conceptualized, both in theory and practice, often provides little value for the real-time pursuit of policy-oriented conflict analysis (see Ampleford, Carment, and Joseph, this volume). As a result, and driven by the reform-related need for a common language of analysis, there is a need for structured and systematic guidelines on the causes of internal conflict and conflict escalation, which will be oriented towards addressing those causes. Second, for such guidelines on a composite format for dynamic early warning analysis, the diagnosis of the concurrent interaction of conflict causes is of central importance. This conclusion derives from the complex and multi-causal nature of internal conflict, the capacity-related need for improved UN conflict analysis methods, and the planning-related need to specify operational objectives for the targeted application of preventive measures. The third major argument, and the one central to addressing the warning-action gap, is that applied early warning within the UN system must directly support the bureaucratic decision-making bodies responsible for authorizing the deployment of preventive measures. This calls for reframing the manner in which we think about applied early warning: not just as an analytical product which somehow has to capture the attention of policy makers, but as an integral part of the very process which supports the operational planning and implementation of conflict prevention. With an eye to the promotion of standardized guidelines, nine specific steps which comprise the planning connection between analysis and operational action within the UN have been proposed here. Fourth and finally, effective prevention by the UN has to be designed to match the specific nature of the conflict situation, as well as operationally strategic in its engagement with the key causes of protracted internal conflict. This speaks not only to the need for proactive innovation as part of an organizational culture of prevention, but to the reform-driven imperative for improved interdepartmental coordination on the analysis of and responses to conflict-related threats to human security.

Notes

1. This chapter is an overview of background research and content development conducted for the joint UN Department of Political Affairs-UN Staff College project on Early Warning and Preventive Measures (EWPM). For their thoughtful comments on various aspects of the material discussed here, I wish to thank the editors of this volume and my fellow Design and Development Team members Derek Boothby, George D'Angelo, and Mark Hoffman. Several individuals outside the team also provided invaluable input, particularly Sir Marrack Goulding, Bertie Ramcharan, Andrew Mack, Tapio Kanninen, Udo Janz, Jürgen Dedring, Jehangir Khan, Connie Peck, and Andrei Dmitrichev. Finally, I would like to express my deep appreciation for all those UN staff who have participated in the various workshops and meetings conducted under this project. I remain, of course, wholly responsible for the content of the chapter itself.
2. On the authority of the UN to engage in preventive action, apart from the general terms of Art. 1(1) of the Charter, see the General Assembly resolution "Declaration on the Prevention and Removal of Disputes and Situations Which May Threaten International Peace and Security and on the Role of the United Nations in this Field," UN Doc. A/Res/43/51, 1988. On early warning see General Assembly resolution "Declaration on Fact-Finding by the United Nations in the Field of the Maintenance of International Peace and Security," UN Doc. A/Res/46/59, 1992.
3. See, for example, the General Assembly resolution arising from Boutros Boutros-Ghali's An Agenda for Peace: "An Agenda for Peace: preventive diplomacy and related matters," UN Doc. A/Res/47/120, 18 December 1992; and the more recent statement by the President of the Security Council, "Role of the Security Council in the prevention of armed conflicts," UN Doc. S/PRST/1999/34, 30 November 1999.
4. See Klaas van Walraven, "Intergovernmental Organizations and Preventing Conflicts: Political Practice Since the End of the Cold War," in van Walraven, ed., Early Warning and Conflict Prevention, The Hague: Kluwer, 1998, pp. 19–44.
5. See B. G. Ramcharan, "Early Warning in United Nations Grand Strategy," in Kumar Rupesinghe and Michiko Kuroda, eds., Early Warning and Conflict Resolution, London: Macmillan, 1992, pp. 181–93; and Ramcharan, The International Law and Practice of Early Warning and Preventive Diplomacy: The Emerging Global Watch, Dordrecht: Martinus Nijhoff, 1991, pp. 18–22.

6. United Nations EOSG, Inter-Office Memorandum, "Policy Coordination Group," 29 January 1997; United Nations, "Renewing the United Nations: A Programme for Reform – Report of the Secretary-General," UN Doc. A/51/950, 14 July 1997, paras 28–30; United Nations, Inter-Office Memorandum, "Reorientation of the Framework for Co-ordination mechanism toward more responsive early warning and preventive action," 11 September 1998. Also interviews with DPA, DPKO, and OCHA officials, March 1998.

7. See Howard Adelman and Astri Suhrke, *Early Warning and Conflict Management*, Vol. 2 of *The International Response to Conflict and Genocide: Lessons from the Rwanda Experience*, Joint Evaluation of Emergency Assistance to Rwanda, Copenhagen, Chr. Michelson Inst., 1996, pp. 66–71; Andrei Dmitrichev, "The Role of Early Warning in the Office of the UN High Commissioner for Refugees," in John L. Davies and Ted R. Gurr, eds., *Preventive Measures: Building Risk Assessment and Crisis Early Warning Systems*, Lanham, MD: Rowman and Littlefield, 1998, pp. 219–29.

8. In addition to Adelman and Suhrke, *Early Warning and Conflict Management*, *ibid.*, see Ruddy Doom and Koen Vlassenroot, "Early Warning and Conflict Prevention: Minerva's Wisdom?," *Journal of Humanitarian Assistance* (www-jha.sps.cam.ac.uk), July 1997, section II.2; Alexander L. George and Jane E. Holl, *The Warning-Response Problem and Missed Opportunities in Preventive Diplomacy*, Washington, DC: Carnegie Commission on Preventing Deadly Conflict, May 1997, pp. 10–12; and Howard Adelman, "Difficulties in Early Warning: Networking and Conflict Management," in van Walraven, *Early Warning and Conflict Prevention*, pp. 56–7.

9. Ted R. Gurr and Barbara Harff, *Early Warning of Communal Conflicts and Genocide: Linking Empirical Research to International Responses*, Tokyo: United Nations University, 1996, p. 5; Sara Rakita, "Early Warning as a Tool of Conflict Prevention," *NYU Journal of International Law and Politics*, Vol. 30, Nos. 3–4, 1998, p. 541.

10. George and Holl, note 8 above, p. 10. The authors go on to assert that "[e]arly warning of a possible crisis is desirable not in and of itself but insofar as it provides decision-makers with an opportunity to make a timely response of an appropriate kind" (p. 13).

11. Tapio Kanninen, "The Future of Early Warning and Preventive Action in the United Nations," Occasional Paper No. 5, Ralph Bunche Institute on the United Nations, New York: CUNY, May 1991, p. 2.

12. James S. Sutterlin, "Early Warning and Conflict Prevention: The Role of the United Nations," in van Walraven, *Early Warning and Conflict Prevention*, note 4 above, pp. 122, 125.

13. Needs assessments and interviews with ex-ORCI and DPA staff, New York, March and October 1998. See also Ramcharan, *The International Law and Practice of Early Warning and Preventive Diplomacy*, note 5 above, pp. 47–51; and Rakita, "Early Warning as a Tool of Conflict Prevention," note 9 above, p. 577.

14. As Dmitrichev notes in the context of UNHCR. See Dmitrichev, "The Role of Early Warning in the Office of the UN High Commissioner for Refugees," note 7 above, p. 220.

15. Jürgen Dedring, "Early Warning and the United Nations," *Journal of Ethno-Development*, Vol. 4, No. 1, 1994, pp. 102–3.

16. United Nations, Joint Inspection Unit, *Strengthening of the United Nations System Capacity for Conflict Prevention*, UN Doc. JIU/REP/95/13 (also as Annex to A/50/853, 22 December 1995), paras 113, 120–1 at pp. 25–7.

17. Adelman and Suhrke, *Early Warning and Conflict Management*, note 7 above, p. 80. The report specifically cites the DPA as having no systematic link to strategic planning, and also argues that the absence of a central unit for early warning meant that in practice the great range of field-based information gathered by various UN agencies was not collected for structured political assessment.

18. Sir Marrack Goulding, Practical Measures to Enhance the United Nations' Effectiveness in Peace and Security: A Report Submitted to the Secretary-General of the United Nations, internal UN document, New York, 30 June 1997, paras. 12.15–12.18 at 97–8.

19. Needs assessments and interviews with UN Secretariat officials in DPA, DDA, DPKO, OCHA, OHCHR, UNHCR, EOSG, and UNDP, Geneva and New York, March and September-October 1998.

20. Michiko Kuroda, "Early Warning Capacity of the United Nations System: Prospects for the Future," in Rupesinghe and Kuroda, *Early Warning and Conflict Resolution*, note 5 above, p. 216.

21. Adelman, "Difficulties in Early Warning," note 8 above, p. 57. Emphasis in original.

22. This view is shared by Goulding in his internal study. He recommends that the departments concerned with the prevention and management of complex political emergencies evolve an integrated policy analysis method to integrate such planning needs. See Goulding, Practical Measures to Enhance the United Nations' Effectiveness in Peace and Security, note 18 above, para. 3.14 at p. 17 (see also Boothby and d'Angelo this volume).

23. Early Warning and Preventive Measures Project, *Mission Statement*, 2 September 1998. The stated aim of the project is "to build institutional capacity by significantly improving professional and analytical skills and awareness of UN staff in the area of early warning and preventive action and, as a corollary, by promoting greater mutual exchange and coordination within and between departments and offices dealing with policy and practical aspects of preventive action" (para. 4).

24. This approach is drawn from my *Policy Planning for UN Preventive Action: Nine Step Process Outline*, Turin: UN Staff College, Early Warning and Preventive Measures Project, May 1999. As a process framework approach to the planning of public policy, it is based roughly on the nine steps outlined in Brian W. Hogwood and Lewis A. Gunn, *Policy Analysis for the Real World*, Oxford: Oxford University Press, 1984, p. 24. On decision support, see Peter G. W. Keen and Michael S. Scott Morton, *Decision Support Systems: An Organizational Perspective*, Reading, MS: Addison-Wesley, 1978.

25. See the discussion of problem framing and structuring in Hogwood and Gunn, *Policy Analysis for the Real World, ibid.*, pp. 119–24; see also International Training Centre of the ILO, *Policy Analysis and Planning*, Turin: ITCILO, 1995, Unit 2.

26. This of course owes much to Johan Galtung's theory of structural violence. See for example his "Violence, Peace, and Peace Research," *Journal of Peace Research*, Vol. 6, No. 3, 1969, pp. 167–92. On relative deprivation, see Ted R. Gurr, *Why Men Rebel*, Princeton: Princeton University Press, 1970; or, more recently, Gurr, *Minorities At Risk: A Global View of Ethnopolitical Conflicts*, Washington, DC: US Institute of Peace Press, 1993, pp. 123–38.

27. The following discussion of sectoral and temporal approaches to the causes of conflict is drawn from my "Human Security and Preventive Action Strategies," in Edward Newman and Oliver P. Richmond, eds., *The United Nations and Human Security*, London: Palgrave, 2001, pp. 17–21.

28. See United Nations Development Programme, *Human Development Report 1994*, Oxford: Oxford University Press, 1994, pp. 22–40.

29. See for example Ted R. Gurr, "Testing and Using a Model of Communal Conflict for Early Warning," *Journal of Ethno-Development*, Vol. 4, No. 1, 1994, pp. 20–4; and Alex P. Schmid, "Indicator Development: Issues in Forecasting Conflict Escalation," in Davies and Gurr, *Preventive Measures*, note 7 above, pp. 47–9.

30. See Loraleigh Keashley and Ronald J. Fisher, "A Contingency Perspective on Conflict Interventions: Theoretical and Practical Considerations," in Jacob Bercovitch, ed., *Resolving International Conflicts*, Boulder, CO: Lynne Rienner, 1996, pp. 235–61. See also

the comparable use of this approach in Louis Kriesberg, "Preventing and Resolving Destructive Communal Conflicts," in David Carment and Patrick James, eds., *Wars in the Midst of Peace: The International Politics of Ethnic Conflict*, Pittsburgh: University of Pittsburgh Press, 1997, pp. 240–6.

31. As Kanninen argues, action-oriented early warning is about "identifying ominous trends, factors involved and their interactions, and ... the impacts and outcomes of sectoral approaches on the whole and other sectors." See Kanninen, "The Future of Early Warning and Preventive Action in the United Nations," note 11 above, p. 11.

32. Former ORCI officer Jüergen Dedring, drawing on ORCI methodology, suggests the following five comparable categories of causal indicators: governance, particularly oppressive, weak or corrupt government; social unrest and divergence of principles between groups; human rights violations; ethnic polarization, particularly in combination with discrimination; and environment. See Juergen Dedring, "Socio-political Indicators for Early Warning Purposes," in Rupesinghe and Kuroda, *Early Warning and Conflict Resolution*, note 5 above, pp. 206–11. See also the discussion of causal interaction in my "Human Security and Preventive Action Strategies," note 27 above, pp. 21–4.

33. See I. William Zartman, "State Collapse Under Ethnic Conflict: Models and Remedies," *Journal of Ethno-Development*, Vol. 4, No. 1, 1994, pp. 83–7; Hugh Miall, Oliver Ramsbotham, and Tom Woodhouse, *Contemporary Conflict Resolution*, Cambridge: Polity, 1999, pp. 84–87: "For many analysts who take a governance-oriented view of the sources of contemporary social conflict this is the key sector, since social and economic grievances are in the end expressed in political form" (p. 86).

34. Sam G. Amoo (Senior Advisor, UNDP), *The Challenge of Ethnicity and Conflicts in Africa*, New York: Emergency Response Division, UNDP, 1997, pp. 9, 31. Emphasis in original.

35. United Nations, "The Causes of Conflict and the Promotion of Durable Peace and Sustainable Development in Africa: Report of the Secretary-General," UN Doc. A/52/871-S/1998/318, 13 April 1998, para. 12: "The nature of political power in many African states, together with the real and perceived consequences of capturing and maintaining power, is a key source of conflict across the continent ... A communal sense of advantage or disadvantage is often closely linked to this phenomenon, which is heightened in many cases by reliance on centralised and highly personalised forms of governance."

36. See B. G. Ramcharan, "Reforming the United Nations to Secure Human Rights," *Transnational Law and Contemporary Problems*, Vol. 4, No. 2, 1994, pp. 527–9: "If there is to be effective early warning systems within the United Nations, there will need to be a bridge between the political and human rights sectors" (p. 528).

37. On the importance of definition of objectives and the pitfalls involved in realizing them, see Hogwood and Gunn, *Policy Analysis for the Real World*, note 24 above, pp. 150–70. The authors suggest that the key questions for any organization are: "What are we trying to do? How will we know when we have done it?" (p. 158).

38. United Nations, "Report of the Secretary-General on the Work of the Organization," UN Doc. A/54/1, 1999, paragraphs 24–25; JIU, "Strengthening of the United Nations System Capacity for Conflict Prevention," para. 156 at p. 33.

39. On light vs deep prevention, see Miall, Ramsbotham, and Woodhouse, *Contemporary Conflict Resolution*, note 32 above, p. 97.

40. On options analysis see Hogwood and Gunn, *Policy Analysis for the Real World*, note 24 above, pp. 171–83.

41. Anthony Lake, "After the Wars – What *Kind* of Peace?," in Lake, ed., *After the Wars*, New Brunswick: Transaction for ODC, 1990, p. 16.

42. See Goulding, Practical Measures to Enhance the United Nations' Effectiveness in Peace and Security, note 18 above, paras 4.7–4.8 at p. 22; Marrack Goulding, "Obser-

vation, Triage, and Initial Therapy: The Role of Fact-Finding Missions and Other Techniques," in Kevin M. Cahill, ed., *Preventive Diplomacy*, New York: Basic Books, 1996, pp. 144–53.

43. See Boutros Boutros-Ghali, "An Agenda for Peace: Preventive Diplomacy, Peace-making, and Peace-keeping – Report of the Secretary-General," UN Doc. A/47/277-S/24111, 17 June 1992, paras 20–2; Boutros Boutros-Ghali, "Supplement to An Agenda for Peace: Position Paper of the Secretary-General," UN Doc. A/50/60-S/1995/1, 3 January 1995, paras 23–65; United Nations, "Strengthening of the United Nations System Capacity for Conflict Prevention: Note by the Secretary-General," UN Doc. A/52/184, 24 June 1997, Annex para. 10; United Nations, "Achievement of Effective Prevention is Testament to Succeeding Generations That Ours Had the Will to Save Them From the Scourge of War," Press Release SG/SM/6454, 5 February 1998 (Secretary-General's Address on the Final Report of the Carnegie Commission on Preventing Deadly Conflict); UN Doc. A/54/1, 1999, paras 36–47.

44. See Jentleson, this volume, for examples of state-based versions of this approach.

45. See Väyrynen, this volume, for examples of preventive deployment.

46. See Talentino, this volume.

47. See Rowlands and Joseph, this volume.

48. Ismat Kittani, "Preventive Diplomacy and Peacemaking: The UN Experience," in Olara A. Otunnu and Michael W. Doyle, *Peacemaking and Peacekeeping for the New Century*, Lanham, MD: Rowman and Littlefield, 1998, p. 105.

49. Needs assessments and interviews with UN Secretariat officials in DPA, DPKO, OCHA, EOSG, and UNDP, New York, March and September-October 1998.

11

The International Monetary Fund and conflict prevention

Dane Rowlands and Troy Joseph

Introduction

This chapter examines the role of the IMF in civil conflict.[1] It begins by reviewing the literature linking economic factors generally, and IMF programmes specifically, with civil conflict. A second section presents a statistical analysis of civil conflict with a focus on Fund activity. A review of IMF conditionality and its possible connection to conflict is then provided. Then the role of the IMF in conflict early warning, prevention, and resolution and reconstruction is discussed. A final section presents some preliminary policy lessons and outlines future research issues.

At the end of World War II, two international financial institutions were created in an attempt to promote economic development and international monetary stability. Of these, the World Bank (initially known as the International Bank for Reconstruction and Development, currently the Bank's main constituent part) is perhaps more commonly associated with conflict due to the "reconstruction" part of its mandate, an element that has been revived since the end of the Cold War. In contrast the International Monetary Fund (the IMF, or the Fund) was (and is) limited to a fairly specialized technical role as overseer of balance of payments problems generally, and the Bretton Woods fixed exchange rate system specifically.

After 1973, when most industrial countries adopted flexible exchange rate arrangements, the IMF quickly saw its role evolve into a quasi-lender of last resort for its less developed members. In exchange for providing financial assistance to troubled countries, however, the IMF extracted policy concessions designed to restore greater balance and stability in the borrower's external economic relations, primarily the current account. Some observers argued that the policy conditions required by the Fund were excessively harsh, and imposed severe hardships on a country's population. Furthermore, the policies were considered socially divisive and damaging to the pursuit of equitable income distribution. In addition, the adoption of austerity packages sponsored by the IMF has been directly linked to civil disturbances. Consequently, the Fund acquired a reputation for provoking conflict.

The IMF's sister organization, the World Bank, arguably has maintained its higher profile in dealing with situations of conflict. For the most part, however, its efforts have focused on post-conflict states, and it has not emphasized any role in conflict prevention. Conflict prevention is used here to refer to the conscious effort to minimize the likelihood that social tensions will escalate into violence. Conflict prevention requires an understanding of the factors that contribute to the onset of violence, how these factors interact with the policy environment to aggravate or ameliorate the situation, and how policies may be modified to reduce the emergence of violent conflict. Aside from its general goal of encouraging economic and social development, with concomitant pacific effects, the World Bank is generally perceived as playing a more subordinate role in dictating austerity programmes for its member states. Instead, it is the IMF's stabilization and adjustment programmes that seem to require more dramatic and austere policy initiatives, often at times of severe economic and social turmoil. Thus, in this chapter, we focus on the IMF as a possible contributor to conflict prevention.

The current debate

It is widely believed that economic factors are an important part of the set of conditions associated with the emergence of conflict. For example, Brown identifies high unemployment, high inflation, resource competition, inequality, and economic modernization as specific conditions that may contribute to the use of violence by some groups within a society.[2] Indeed, economic factors have retained the attention of analysts, such as those at the Carnegie Commission,[3] interested in the diminution of conflict propensities. More importantly, empirical research finds support for the general claim that economic conditions influence a variety of political and social events, including violence and government instability.

For example, economic equity issues are front and centre in many analyses. For example, Gurr and Duvall state that "greater social justice within nations in the distribution of economic goods and political autonomy is the most potent path to social peace."[4] Gurr cites further evidence of the link between minority rebellion and economic differentials, while Gurr and Duvall and Kpsowa and Jenkins, among others, draw out the link between external economic dependence and a heightened vulnerability to various forms of civil disorder.[5]

Mirroring this literature on general economic conditions and civil disorder are attempts to draw a specific link between IMF activity and civil conflict. One of the larger strands of this research focuses on the role of the IMF as a contributing factor in the emergence of civil conflict. In some circumstances the adoption of austerity measures associated with IMF programmes is seen primarily as the trigger of a conflict that may have far deeper roots. In other cases, authors have suggested that the Fund's policies have more profound implications, and may indeed be primary contributors to the emergence of violence.

The accusation that IMF programmes provoke domestic unrest and civil conflict has been a durable one. Negative reviews of the IMF are common, and are often linked to the adverse consequences for income distribution that are associated with Fund adjustment programmes. Payer is a key proponent of this view.[6] Siddell refers to this literature in motivating his examination of IMF agreements and political instability.[7] However, several authors note a more direct link between the Fund and civil conflict. Eckstein, Alves, and Walton all refer to a direct connection between the austerity programmes associated with IMF agreements and civil disturbances, which are often referred to as "IMF riots."[8]

The case linking IMF agreements with civil conflict is indeed compelling. First, there is a substantial number of cases in which protests immediately follow the implementation of IMF programmes. Furthermore, the precipitating or immediate causal factors that have been identified also seem reasonable, such as the removal of food subsidies in direct compliance with an adjustment programme. Finally there are cases in which the protesters have themselves identified the termination of an IMF programme as a key demand.[9] Boyce and Pastor also claim that the activities of the IMF (and World Bank) have often been less than helpful in defusing civil unrest, citing Guatemala, El Salvador, Yugoslavia, and Rwanda as cases in which their efforts were inadequate or counterproductive.[10]

Woodward goes further in identifying the IMF (and the World Bank) as key contributors to the disintegration of Yugoslavia and the emergence of civil war in Bosnia-Herzegovina.[11] According to Woodward, the IMF insisted that the Yugoslavian government repay debt as part of the conditions of receiving further IMF assistance. Being in a weak financial state, the austerity measures imposed on the government made it impossible to continue the sorts of interpersonal and interregional transfers that had maintained a degree of social cohesion in a state comprised of multiple groups with historical animosities. The economic decline associated with the IMF programme sparked unrest and dissension, which eventually exploded into civil war. There are, therefore, strong reasons for associating IMF programmes with civil violence.

There are also grounds for reconsidering the significance of this commonly held perception. The case for linking the IMF with civil disturbances relies heavily on case studies. While structured comparative case studies are a legitimate methodological approach, most sample selection is clearly biased (e.g. few of the authors refer to cases in which an IMF agreement did *not* spark protests). In addition, there is no counterfactual; few of the authors espousing the anti-Fund view appear to have considered what would have happened in the absence of an IMF agreement. Furthermore, as Walton points out, governments often use the IMF as a scapegoat for policies that it willingly implemented.[12] Finally, in the context of this chapter, the kinds of riot associated with IMF agreements are a relatively mild form of civil disturbance; Woodward's suggestion that the IMF-WB programme contributed substantially to the emergence of civil war in Yugoslavia is unusual. These objections should not be taken as refutation of the hypothesis that the IMF causes domestic political disturbances, but rather indicate that the hypothesis needs to be examined more carefully.

Some studies question the importance of specific elements of IMF programmes and their links to conflict. Thus Bienen and Gersovitz suggest that the removal of subsidies does not have much effect on civil violence and political stability.[13] Remmer suggests that the political importance of IMF programmes is limited, largely because they are mostly ineffective at changing fundamental conditions.[14] Among the more systematic analyses of the Fund-conflict hypothesis is Siddell's.[15] Siddell uses a variety of statistical techniques to investigate the potential relationship between IMF stand-by agreements and various forms of civil disturbance – coups d'etat, internal war, and collective protests. He concludes that any association between the IMF agreements and any civil disturbance is most likely the result of underlying structural economic problems that cause both to occur simultaneously. The causal link, he concludes, is spurious. The difficulty with Siddell's analysis is the timeframe of 1969–77, one that predates many of the relevant anecdotes (although Payer's research period is clearly covered by Siddell). The IMF's activities increased dramatically in number, magnitude, and controversy in the decade after Siddell's study period.

Auvinen examines the connection between IMF agreements and civil disturbances for 70 countries between 1981 and 1989.[16] In the study the

IMF's interventions are presented as triggers to conflict. The effect of the agreements is presumed to depend on the facilitating conditions of urbanization, political regime type, and level of economic development. In general, Auvinen's results support those of Siddell in the sense that IMF agreements do not seem to be systematically linked to civil conflicts. Indeed, for poorer less developed countries (LDCs) and lower levels of urbanization, the presence of IMF agreements were found to be associated with fewer incidents of disturbance, a result Auvinen links to the size of IMF funding. Indeed, Auvinen concludes that the "Fund's resources may generally alleviate economic problems and promote political stability," a statement that reflects closely the earlier views of Bienen and Gersovitz.[17] Auvinen does suggest, however, that IMF agreements may be more likely to induce conflict in more urbanized and democratic LDCs. Furthermore, a history of many IMF agreements may also be positively related to protest. Of further interest is Auvinen's observation regarding other potential causal factors in a model of conflict and protest. In general Auvinen finds that higher inflation rates and debt service are associated with political protest.

Auvinen's analysis is quite sophisticated in conception and execution. By going beyond the traditional anecdotal linkages between protests and IMF agreements, both Siddell and Auvinen provide insight into the nuances of IMF programmes and their effect on civil conflict as well as a focus on the more dramatic and dangerous forms of civil disturbance.[18] Both of these contributions assist policy formulation by analysing the causes of conflict and the associated signals. In the next section we discuss the results from attempting to extend these analyses in two directions. First of all we use data that include post-Cold War observations as part of the sample. Secondly, we attempt to include variables that reflect the economic factors most commonly associated with IMF conditionality.

Statistical results

Siddell and Auvinen review a substantial literature regarding the determinants of political conflict.[19] Among the hypothesized factors contributing to conflict for which there was some corroborating evidence are: the presence of IMF agreements, low economic growth, high inflation, high debt service-to-export ratios, high urbanization levels, high military spending, a history of conflict, and ethnic competition or dominance. The level of economic development and the degree of authoritarianism were also linked to political disturbances, but researchers found different effects: in some cases low levels of development were linked to higher levels of conflict, while others found the opposite relationship.[20]

The model outlined in Auvinen provides the starting point for the statistical analysis presented here. The dependent variable is coded on the basis of indicators of crisis from several sources (see the data appendix on p. 186 below for details) supplemented with a review of each country's recent history as described in the *Europa World Yearbook*. The dependent variable measures the intensity of conflict on a scale of 0 (no conflict) to 3 (full-scale civil war). A dependent variable of 1 indicates the presence of minor civil conflicts such as riots or violent protests, while a code of 2 indicates an intermediate level of conflict involving more organized opposition to the government.[21]

First, a quick review of the data indicates that the frequency of IMF agreements was much higher for countries involved in conflict than for the sample as a whole. Prior to the beginning of internal unrest the mean number of high-conditionality IMF agreements in either the year the conflict started or the preceding year was 0.44, compared to 0.27 for the full sample. For countries experiencing the onset of civil unrest this mean rose to 0.82 when the previous three years were considered, and 1.2 when extended back to five years. The equivalent means for the full sample were 0.53 and 0.8. Standard t-tests suggest that these means are significantly different.

The preliminary analysis uses ten independent variables. The first of these reflects the history of the country's relations with the IMF by indicating the number of higher conditionality agreements a country has had in the year of a conflict and the three preceding years.[22] This variable's sign will be taken as an indication of whether or not the presence of the IMF is correlated with civil conflict.

The level of economic development is represented by the GNP per capita of the country, and the expectation is that the estimated coefficient will be negative. In other words, general economic performance is reflected in the average growth rate for the previous three years, with the lag being used to avoid the correlation that would emerge from the civil conflict causing a decline in economic activity. This variable is also useful for evaluating the effect of the IMF since a common observation is that IMF programmes cause a decline in immediate growth, although they may lead to higher growth in the longer run.[23]

Openness to foreign trade is measured by the sum of exports and imports as a ratio of GNP. It is postulated that more open societies may be less prone to civil conflict, and so the expected sign of the coefficient is negative. The variable is lagged to avoid the problem of conflict disrupting international trade. A second international variable is the rate of currency depreciation or devaluation. A rapid fall in the value of a nation's currency makes imported goods expensive and has been linked anecdotally to civil disputes. If these arguments are correct, then the coefficient on the devaluation variable should be positive. Both variables are also relevant to IMF conditionality. The IMF has long pushed countries to open up their current account procedures and promote international trade. One of the mechanisms of doing so, and one of the key specific elements of many IMF programmes, is the devaluation of the currency.

The currency value is also linked to the next explanatory variable: inflation. Average inflation performance over the preceding three years is included for several reasons. In and of itself, inflation causes economic disruption when it reaches sufficiently high levels. Historically, high inflation rates have also been considered as symptomatic of social tension and a weak government. Specifically, weak governments may find themselves forced to make expenditures to mollify disgruntled elements of their country while being unable to raise the revenue to cover the payments through taxation. The result is that the government is forced to rely on inflation financing. The expected sign of the estimated coefficient is positive, indicating that high inflation leads to more intense internal conflict. The average inflation in the previous three years is used to avoid any simultaneity problem in which the conflict itself provokes the government's adoption of inflationary policies.

While inflation reflects in part the inability of the government to raise revenues to match its expenditures, the ratio of government spending to GDP measures the overall involvement of the government in the country's economic life. It is expected that a government may be better placed to reconcile conflicts within its society if it is able to allocate more of the country's resources itself. The expected sign of the coefficient would therefore be negative. Of course it may also be true that the larger the government, the more intense the competition may be to rule. In this case the coefficient would be positive.

Following Auvinen, measures of urbanization are also included.[24] Auvinen's contention is that its influence is non-linear.[25] Urbanization is measured as the percentage of the population living in an urban area. Although Auvinen uses a more complex interaction term as well, the initial hypothesis is that more urbanized societies are more prone to conflict.

Finally, a variable measuring military expenditures as a ratio of GNP is included. This variable is lagged, since conflict may provoke an increase in expenditures. The expectation is that more militarized societies are more likely to experience civil violence. Four sets of regressions were conducted on 90 countries between 1986 and 1995.[26]

Table 11.1 shows the results of the estimation for two slightly different equations.[27] The differences in the results of the two equations, therefore, may represent both the change in sample as well as the possible introduction of multi-collinearity and the adoption of a more appropriate estimating equation.

In general, the results are surprisingly strong. In both estimations the level of economic development (GNP per capita in constant dollars) has the expected negative estimated coefficient, both of which are statistically significant. Similarly, both regressions indicate that inflation, government expenditure levels, growth, and openness have the expected signs (positive, negative, negative, and negative respectively) for their statistically significant estimated coefficients. In the first equation without military expenditures, the measure of currency devaluation has a significant positive coefficient (as expected), while the level of urbanization has no apparent significant effect on the intensity of internal conflict. In the second equation, the estimated coefficient for the devaluation variable is statistically insignificant, while the coefficient estimates for both the linear and squared measures of urbanization become significant and indicate that the relationship with conflict is U-shaped and suggests that the minimum level of violence occurs when the urban population represents around 72 per cent of the population.

The estimated coefficient for the ratio of military expenditures to GNP is positive and statistically significant, as expected. Finally, of particular interest to this chapter, the estimated coefficient for the variable indicating the frequency of IMF conditional agreements in the past four years (including the year of the dependent variable) is negative and statistically significant, suggesting that the presence of the IMF in the past reduces the intensity of civil conflict.

In column three of Table 11.1, the statistical significance of many of the variables declines dramatically, and only three of the explanatory variables appear to have any statistically significant effect on the intensity of internal conflict.[28] The estimated coefficients for the level of international trade and the ratio of military expenditures to GNP remain statistically significant and with the correct predicted sign. Similarly, the negative estimated coefficient for the presence of past IMF agreements remains quite robust in terms of magnitude and statistical significance. While the coefficient estimates of the explanatory variables themselves show some robustness, the marked change in their variance suggests that the results are quite sensitive to the model structure.[29] Therefore some attention must be paid to deriving a suitable functional form for estimation.

The Probit estimation on the initiation of conflict is still very preliminary, and considerable refinement is still required. Of note, however, is that with one notable exception the preliminary estimations generated no statistically significant coefficient for any of the explanatory variables. The one exception was that in the equation that used the three-year history of IMF agreements, the effect of past IMF involvement had a significant positive estimated coefficient.

This result suggests that the presence of the IMF may contribute to the

Table 11.1 Results of the estimation for different equations (estimation results with intensity of internal conflict as the dependent variable)

Variable	Equation 1, OLS-White	Equation 2, OLS-White	Equation 2, Tobit
Constant	0.834***	1.692***	1.38***
	(8.69)	(9.34)	(3.61)
GNP per capita	−0.000033***	−0.0000289***	−0.0000835
	(5.48)	(2.32)	(1.47)
Average inflation	0.000225***	0.00017	0.000294
	(3.89)	(1.21)	(1.21)
Average growth	−0.0166***	−0.0044	0.0246
	(3.93)	(0.49)	(1.00)
Trade/GNP	−0.0528***	−0.334***	−2.05***
	(4.16)	(7.44)	(7.08)
Government/GDP	−0.014***	−0.028***	−0.0301
	(5.95)	(5.14)	(1.52)
Devaluation	0.00000697***	−0.000237	−0.000737
	(7.73)	(1.27)	(1.57)
% Urban population	−0.00312	−0.020***	−0.00352
	(1.08)	(3.57)	(0.24)
(% urb. pop.)^2	0.0000272	0.000138***	−0.000105
	(1.04)	(2.71)	(0.64)
Military spending/GNP	–	0.0776***	0.170***
		(6.14)	(5.63)
IMF (3-year history)	−0.066***	−0.139***	−0.253***
	(3.97)	(4.53)	(2.69)
Observations	1723	771	771
R^2	0.08	0.20	–
Adjusted R^2	0.075	0.19	–
Log likelihood	−1843	−935	−781

Note: *** implies significant at the 1% level. The t-statistics appear in brackets.

onset of civil violence. Although the Probit equation clearly requires some modification, if this result holds true it partly contradicts the earlier results and indicates that the IMF may act as a trigger for civil unrest. Such an inference on the basis of the large sample analysis, however, would be premature at this time.

Finally, the regression was repeated to account for country-specific effects through the use of standard panel estimation procedures. The F-test makes it clear that significant country-specific effects are present, while the Chi-squared test suggests that the random-effects model may be the most appropriate.

These results confirm the significant positive relationship between the military-to-GNP ratio and civil conflict, and the significant negative relationship between the openness of the economy and civil conflict. In addition the U-shaped effect of urbanization on civil unrest is apparent,

Table 11.2 Results of the panel data estimation (random effects model)

Variable	Random effects model estimated coefficients
Constant	1.38***
	(4.79)
GNP per capita	−0.0000415
	(1.24)
Average inflation	0.00013*
	(1.61)
Average growth	−0.0138*
	(1.60)
Trade/GNP	−0.304***
	(2.92)
Government/GDP	0.000984
	(0.12)
Devaluation	−0.000156
	(1.11)
% Urban population	−0.0247**
	(2.17)
(% urb. pop.)^2	0.000196*
	(1.67)
Military spending/GNP	0.0448***
	(3.13)
IMF (3–year history)	−0.032
	(0.99)
Observations	771
R^2	0.057
Adjusted R^2	−0.082

while the estimated coefficients for inflation and growth are weakly significant with the correct predicted sign. Of interest is the lack of robustness of the openness variable, which appears with a statistically significant but negative estimated coefficient. The IMF indicator variable also appears to have no statistically significant effect when country-specific effects are taken into account. The lack of robustness again suggests that some care is needed in formulating the estimation equation. The results are presented in Table 11.2.

The results in Table 11.2 are helpful in indicating certain robust connections within the data. In conjunction with the results presented in Auvinen, these estimations allow us to make some observations regarding the propriety of IMF conditionality and the implications for civil unrest.

The likely effects of IMF conditionality

A recent paper by Ul Haque and Khan describes the higher-conditionality IMF programmes as "complex packages of policy measures that include, among other things, monetary and exchange rate policies, fiscal measures, policies to raise investment and improve its efficiency, trade liberalization, wage reforms, and financial sector reforms."[30] They go on to suggest that due to the weak theory connecting the policy reforms to outcomes, "the adjustment package is not necessarily guaranteed, at least from a theoretical viewpoint, to achieve the desired outcomes."[31] Despite the complexities of evaluating the success of IMF programmes, some general observations have been made about their effects.[32]

One of the first observations is that the current account deficit does tend to decline in response to an IMF programme. As no strong reason exists for supposing that the current account is linked to civil conflict, such an observation is not particularly useful. It should be noted, however, that a decline in the current account that is brought about by contractionary demand policies could be correlated with civil unrest, but the intermediating variables would be government and personal expenditure.

Ul Haque and Khan also conclude that inflation tends to fall as a result of IMF intervention, although the change is not generally found to be statistically significant. The results reported by Auvinen as well as those presented in the previous section indicate that inflation may be positively correlated, and perhaps even causally related, to the level of civil conflict.[33] What implications should be drawn for IMF conditionality? This remains a difficult question to answer. If inflation represents a means by which the government reconciles competing social demands with limited resources, then it may be more of a symptom of social tensions within the country than a cause. Forcing the government to reduce inflation may eliminate one policy option for containing – or perhaps avoiding – these social pressures.

Requiring a reduction in inflation may also force the government to come to terms with any such underlying social conflicts. For example, in Brazil, inflation reflects in part the constitutional arrangements that pit state governments against their federal counterparts. The price and currency stabilization programmes have forced the Brazilian government to recognize and to some extent begin to deal with these fundamental constitutional problems. If the observed correlation between inflation and civil conflict is valid and is causal, then support for the anti-inflationary measures of the IMF would seem to be warranted.

Such support, however, must be cautious. One of the crucial dimensions of the IMF's anti-inflationary policy is the restraint of aggregate demand brought about primarily through cutbacks in government expenditure. The preliminary evidence from the previous section suggests that states with higher levels of government expenditure (relative to GNP) are less likely to experience civil conflict. The state may be able to use its expenditures to build social cohesion and defuse sources of tension. Again, care must be taken in inferring causality, as it is also possible that states with greater social cohesion accept higher levels of state expenditure. If there is indeed a causal link running from expenditure to civil harmony, then the anti-inflationary programme of the Fund should perhaps be emphasizing an increase in taxes as a means of accommodating higher government spending while removing the budget deficit and consequent inflationary pressures. Certainly the IMF may need to take some care in requiring budget cuts in states which are predisposed towards violence, and should consider more fully the social and political consequences of the cuts being contemplated. According to the argument of Woodward and others, this dimension of the adjustment packages may have contributed to the onset of civil violence in past cases such as Yugoslavia.[34]

Policies that suppress growth may contribute to conflict. The data suggest that there is a weak negative correlation between economic growth and civil unrest. The implications for IMF conditionality are complex, however. Ul Haque and Khan conclude that while there may be an immediate decline in output, growth eventually resumes, and possibly at a higher rate.[35] Such a contention, however, is likely to provoke some controversy. Earlier studies concluded that the high interest rates that frequently result from the strict monetary policies prescribed by the IMF discouraged investment and therefore harmed future growth. The evidence linking growth rates to IMF programmes has traditionally been thought of as being weak at best, negative at worst.

Two issues seem important here: to what extent does the sharp contraction of output trigger unrest in the short run, and to what extent can Fund programmes foster growth in the long run. It seems that there may well be a crucial trade-off here that needs to be recognized in the determination of Fund conditionality. Economic models are not well equipped to deal with political discontinuities, and the emergence of civil conflict could well jeopardize any prospective economic gains believed to be associated with restructuring. The IMF will clearly have to consider the social context more fully in order to determine what the appropriate trade-off is between short-term pain and long-term gain. Otherwise it may end up with short-term pain and long-term political and social catastrophe.

The devaluation of currency is also among the policy requirements normally associated with IMF agreements. The evidence presented in the previous section suggests that no firm conclusions can be drawn regarding the effects of devaluation on civil violence. In the first estimation in Table 11.1, a devaluation is significantly associated with the emergence of civil conflict. When military expenditures were added to the equation, however, the effect disappears.

Devaluations are one of the key instruments for promoting the export sector of a country as well. The IMF's clear preference is for more liberalized trade regimes and enhanced integration into the international economy. All of the estimations indicated that openness was significantly associated with lower levels of conflict. By encouraging countries to become more integrated into the international economic system the IMF may also be helping to suppress civil violence. The possible causal mechanisms linking openness with harmony include the exposure to international norms of behaviour that discourage violence, and the fear that civil conflict will discourage trade links or lead to the imposition of trade sanctions. In any case, there do not appear to be any grounds for suggesting that the IMF delete this policy element from its list of conditions for fear of exacerbating tensions in a country.

Finally, there is a clear and very strong link between military spending and civil conflict. Again, assigning causality is awkward at this stage of the investigation, as societies that are more prone to violence may also tend to have larger militaries. If the causal relationship runs the other way, however, there are some clear policy implications for the IMF. Both the Bank and the Fund have begun to include more intrusive, some would say more political, elements of conditionality in their agreements.[36] Prior to the end of the Cold War such policy prescriptions were deemed inappropriate on the grounds of political interference, with both institutions claiming to be apolitical in nature. Whether such claims were justified or not, meddling in certain details of a client's budget was considered improper.

Since 1990, however, both institutions have been using their influence to try and promote "good governance." The Fund has traditionally interpreted this concept rather narrowly to include such things as corruption, which is strongly believed to compromise the economic growth prospects of a country. The Bank has a wider definition that encompasses aspects of civil society and government structure, although it has not gone as far as some of its wealthier shareholders in making the promotion of democracy a condition for receiving their development assistance. Whether or not such policies are politically or morally acceptable from a philosophical perspective, the evidence suggests that the pursuit of such goals will be likely to have a positive effect in dealing with civil conflict. Both the Bank and Fund, as well as bilateral donors, have been willing to make military budget cuts a condition of assistance. The evidence here suggests that such a policy may indeed help to discourage the emergence of violence. At least the link is plausible. Auvinen also suggests that authoritarianism is also linked to protest, although in a non-linear fashion.[37] Thus some care is required in using governance conditionality to bring about certain policy goals, as the effect depends on the initial conditions of the country. In some cases undermining an authoritarian regime may lead to more violence, as such structures may actually be able to suppress conflict. Here it is necessary to consider whether civil unrest is a price worth paying to remove a repressive regime.

While some of the standard conditions of the IMF agreements appear to be consistent with the objective of diminishing civil conflict, there appear to be adverse social effects associated with others. Of specific concern is the requirement that governments restrict aggregate demand through reductions in public expenditure. The policies may reduce the capacity of governments to build social cohesion and maintain buoyant economies. There may be circumstances in which it would be preferable for the IMF to sacrifice some speed in the adjustment process in order to diminish the possibility of inducing civil strife. The identification of when a country may be predisposed to lapse into conflict requires further analysis, however, and a brief overview of the Fund's role in any early warning process is provided in the next section.

The IMF and conflict prevention

There are some interesting issues about how the IMF might assist in conflict prevention. To the limited extent that its policy conditionality will affect resolution and reconstruction, the relevant discussion will largely reflect those concerns. A conflict prevention role for the IMF would have two dimensions to it. First of all, the IMF could adopt a general, non-country specific, policy approach to conflict prevention. In this case the analysis of specific conflict likelihood is unnecessary. The second dimension requires the use of forward-looking risk assessments to determine when conflict is likely to emerge in specific countries, followed by appropriate modification of the IMF's programme to diminish any of its adverse effects and to reinforce other conflict prevention efforts within that country.

With respect to the first idea, the general modification of IMF programmes to facilitate conflict prevention does not seem particularly appealing for two reasons. First, it must be kept in mind that the IMF has a very different mandate from traditional conflict-oriented institutions. While integrating it into a more "holistic" approach to conflict management might be appealing at one level, it risks compromising the narrow macro economic and financial goals of the Fund. Asking the IMF to serve two masters is inappropriate, and would obviously meet with resistance from amongst its staff. The IMF has developed its own approach to handling the balance of payments and structural economic problems that fall within its purview. Although some may question the effectiveness or appropriateness of these approaches, it must nonetheless develop its policies with primary reference to its central purpose. Diluting the economic content of a stabilization programme to satisfy conflict prevention imperatives is hardly sensible if most recipient countries are not at risk of immediate violence.

Second, the large sample analysis suggests that IMF programmes do not, in general, have an adverse effect on civil order. Identifying the specific elements of the programmes that should be changed as a general method of alleviating conflict pressures is therefore somewhat contentious. Even the modification of something as basic as the speed of adjustment is problematic; rapid adjustment might restore economic growth more quickly and defuse longer-term societal pressures, but may provoke short-term tensions. Therefore there can be no general conclusion that adjustment be accelerated or slowed down, as it clearly requires a judgement to be made about the relative risks of current and future violence. Therefore it may be advisable to adjust IMF programmes when there are concerns about provoking civil conflict, but otherwise allow the Fund to concentrate on the economic requirements of stabilization and adjustment.

With respect to the second idea, a country-specific approach to programme modification requires that the IMF establish a method for spotting future trouble spots. While it might do so on its own or in cooperation with the World Bank, inexperience in conflict forecasting suggests that it does so as part of a larger alliance of conflict management institutions. In addition to inexperience, the IMF does not have a particularly inspiring record of predicting financial or political crises. For example, a review of the relevant IMF annual reports shows that Mexico's financial crisis at the end of 1994 was not foretold (or at least not publicly identified) by IMF staff in their written appraisal, nor was there any mention of Yugoslavia's impending civil war. At least on the basis of these public documents there are grounds for questioning the capacity of the IMF to identify – or at least interpret – early warning signals with any reasonable degree of accuracy. To some extent, therefore, the IMF will need to rely on the greater in-country exposure and expertise of personnel from the World Bank and other institutions for an assessment of the social and political conditions in a member state. In collaboration with other institutions the Fund may be able to provide a useful source of data and analysis relevant to the early warning of both financial and civil disturbances. In this way the IMF may contribute to the improvement of the early warning and conflict forecasting efforts developed elsewhere.

Early warning systems, of course, are less likely to be useful to the IMF than risk assessment procedures. Early warning relies on clear indications of imminent violence, and as such really constitutes "late warning."[38] While the IMF may be able to come up with some additional money to try and "bribe" combatants to the negotiating table, the ability to modify or introduce a useful programme will be severely limited or redundant, "since conflict presumably means that the affected government will abandon any pretence of following Fund conditions."[39] Furthermore, IMF conditions operate with some delay and rarely affect economic and social conditions immediately, to the extent that they are beneficial at all. To contribute to conflict prevention there must be considerable lead-time between Fund involvement and the potential emergence of violence. Thus the trade-off between accuracy and timeliness simply renders an early warning approach – as opposed to a risk assessment approach – less appropriate as a guide for IMF or World Bank activity.

Indeed, the tailoring of IMF programmes to deal with rapidly emerging conflicts may even be counterproductive. For example, one of the few instruments at their disposal to deal with such a problem in short order is the injection of financial resources, the distribution of which may provide yet another source for conflict within a country. The excessive reliance on financial resources to "buy" peace also raises the potential problem of moral hazard, in which countries or factions are rewarded for behaving inappropriately. Therefore, IMF strategies for conflict prevention are probably best seen as long term in outlook and associated as much with policy conditionality as with resource provision.

Since neither a universal programme adjustment nor a crisis-response approach seems appropriate, the role of the IMF in conflict prevention will probably have to be limited to one of addressing longer-run issues in conflict-prone countries. To facilitate a longer-term approach to programme modification, the IMF first needs to establish a risk assessment procedure. This may include, for example, a checklist of characteristics that tend to be associated with the eventual emergence of conflict. While not exhaustive, it is possible to think of factors such as ethnic cleavage, inequitable resource distribution, emerging social, economic, and political transformation, poor governance, weak institutions, and past episodes of violence as being potentially indicative of higher conflict propensities. Reinicke essentially argues for such a conflict risk assessment process to be included in the IMF and World Bank country consultations and reviews, although he focuses on the ethno-nationalist tensions that he suggests are the primary cause of conflict in transition economies.[40] Additional research will hopefully lead to a more comprehensive list that provides a sense of the relative importance of these factors. Furthermore, the previously discussed drawbacks to a general approach to programme modification notwithstanding, it is not essential that the forecasting be held to exacting standards. Erring somewhat on the side of anticipating violence in marginal cases is unlikely to compromise the general thrust of IMF programming.

Anticipating when to modify programmes is only the first step of a conflict prevention strategy for the IMF. It is also important to determine an appropriate response. Many conflicts have their roots in the competition over resources either in the past or present. Even if the initial conflict was not over resource competition, war creates interest groups with an economic incentive to prolong the conflict.[41] In many cases economic deprivation has interacted with weak political systems to create a situation in which violence is likely to occur. Thus Shearer characterizes the civil war in Sierra Leone in the following manner: the underlying causes of the outbreak of conflict in 1991 centred on corrupt and unaccountable government, where "[p]oor economic performance, bad management, and a patrimonial system of favours ... characterized [the] regime."[42]

The situation in Sierra Leone can hardly be considered unique. Economic structures and management of the economy clearly play important roles in conflict. To the extent that these general patterns of conflict are repeated, there is room to identify some associated IMF programme reforms. An emphasis on governance reform, attention to the livelihood of marginalized but potentially violent groups within a society,[43] or greater tolerance of expenditures that are needed to compensate disaffected elements of society may be some common programme adjustments that the IMF might consider when dealing with countries identified as being at risk of civil violence. Again, a basic approach to conflict prevention requires an awareness of the sources of conflict and an understanding of contributing factors. Just as the IFIs have begun to target policies relating to the environment and governance, so too do they need to develop an arsenal of policies aimed at reducing civil conflict.

Each conflict, however, is also likely to have important idiosyncratic elements. Therefore any programme review must incorporate considerable sensitivity to the particular case at hand. For example, in a country with a frustrated and politically neglected urban population the role of food subsidies might be found to be of greater importance from a conflict-management perspective than in a country where ethnic differences are the dominant source of tensions. Woodward's description of the collapse of Yugoslavia is rich with case-specific detail with which to inform conflict prevention strategies.[44] For example, there is some emphasis on the importance of balance between the central government and regional administrations. According to Woodward, policies as economically focused as the reform of the central bank amounted to significant modification of the relative powers of the central and regional governments. Two lessons should perhaps be drawn here. First, the idiosyncratic dimensions of conflict mean that there is not likely to be a one-size-fits-all approach to accommodating conflict prevention into IMF activity, an accusation often directed at the Fund in terms of its seemingly undifferentiated approach to balance of payments problems. Second, considerable caution must be used to ensure that all elements of a programme are scrutinized for potential impact on civil violence, as even fairly mundane and technical policy suggestions might have an adverse effect, depending on the specific circumstances of a country.

Finally, targeted programme adjustments of this nature should not be conceived as detracting from the IMF's effectiveness. On the contrary, social tensions generally undermine the effectiveness with which IMF programmes are pursued, and nothing can be as detrimental to the success of an IMF programme as a civil war. The explicit integration of conflict prevention into the IMF's activities should instead be seen as a critical aspect of its mandate. Political and social events are inextricably linked to economic conditions, and focusing on the latter at the expense of the former constitutes an inexcusable simplification. Economic stabilization and restructuring requires that careful attention be paid to the political and social context in which the reforms are taking place. The inclusion of governance conditions into IMF and World Bank programmes is a belated but clear recognition of these important linkages.

Conflict prevention as an element of IMF planning, however, must be viewed with uncertainty. It is highly unlikely that an IMF or World Bank programme would be sufficient, in and of itself, to prevent the emergence of violence. Indeed, as Carment and Harvey argue, international organizations seem relatively ineffective in dealing with conflict when compared to the efforts of nations. So at best, such a policy should be seen as a supplement to the more traditional state-based system of prevention and resolution.[45]

It should also be recognized that there is a substantial literature that would argue that long-term gains may not be forthcoming as a consequence of IMF policies, and that the adoption of IMF conditions may immiserise a country and make conflict more likely. Even in cases where aggregate production rises, many observers would argue that income inequality and social division are frequent companions of IMF policies. Furthermore, some critics suggest that the IMF (and the World Bank) are inherently malevolent institutions under the direct control of wealthy industrialized countries and uninterested in the welfare of the inhabitants of poor countries. Unfortunately these arguments are either empirically contentious or mired in ideological debate, although the second point about inequality has appeared to hold up fairly well over time. In any case, the proposition that the IMF can be harnessed in the interests of global welfare generally, and in the interests of conflict prevention specifically, will not meet with universal acceptance.

The anecdotal evidence provides some support for the sceptics. Past practices of the IMF have been reported as being inconsistent with the minimal requirements for conflict prevention or resolution. Chayes *et al.* suggest that while the IMF staff have acknowledged the need to have its programmes facilitate conflict prevention and resolution, the Fund's activities in El Salvador were counterproductive due to their focus on austerity.[46] Their claim clearly echoes the views expressed by Woodward.[47]

As noted earlier, however, the case studies may suffer from sample selection bias. Such bias does not invalidate the specific observations of Fund policies damaging conflict management objectives. However the associated conclusion that the IMF's activities are generally and necessarily incompatible with conflict management seems premature. The analysis presented here suggests that the IMF may well have a useful role to play within a wider conflict management mechanism.

Research and policy implications

The empirical results do not yet provide a sufficient foundation for making strong policy recommendations. While some general connections have been made regarding specific elements of standard IMF conditionality and their connection to civil conflict, the implications of these linkages require further refinement. Therefore, in lieu of stronger conclusions, the following observations are offered.

First of all, on the research side, both large sample and case study analysis is required to answer two basic questions. The first question is: what underlying factors predispose a country to develop situations of civil conflict? Answering this question goes to the heart of understanding conflict and is the key to developing models for both early warning and risk assessment. From the perspective of deploying IMF resources, effort directed at risk assessment and conflict forecasting appears to be of particular importance. The second question is: how can IMF policy conditionality be modified, and resources deployed, to alleviate the tensions that may give rise to civil conflict? Answering this question requires both an understanding of the economic factors that contribute to the emergence of conflict, an appreciation of the effects of IMF programmes, and a comprehension of the constraints and requirements of IMF programme development. This research agenda is advancing within several institutions, and the IMF and World Bank should become more closely involved with this effort. The World Bank has set up a unit dedicated to problems of conflict, and the IMF should arguably have a similar one.

Second, on the policy side, there appear to be sufficient grounds for recommending that the IMF routinely incorporate an evaluation of the conflict potential of member states in their country review process. In terms of implementation, the IMF needs to align itself with the more traditional conflict-management institutions in order to gain expertise in conflict risk assessment, and in order to contribute to the effort through the provision of data and analytical capacity. The fact that civil disturbances and tension may well compromise the effectiveness of their programmes means that such efforts are entirely consistent with their current mandate. Exposure to these other institutions may well provide the Fund with additional information on what policy adjustments might be useful from the perspective of conflict management, although presumably the flow of information and expertise will also flow in the other direction as well.

Anticipating conflict situations must entail a response as well. Making specific policy recommendations on this aspect of conflict prevention is more difficult. While the financial equivalent to a sort of Hippocratic "do no harm" principle might serve as a general guide, research has not progressed far enough to be able to specify general responses. Instead, for the moment at least, case-specific analysis will be required to identify the social cleavages that may lead to violence. Policy modifications to minimize the frictions along those social fault lines must then be developed for each situation. As a first step, however, the IMF must acknowledge that flexibility is required in dealing with conflict-prone states, and that it will need to consider slowing down the pace of restructuring and providing supplementary finance in cases where social divisions are likely to lead to violent conflict.

Appendix 1: Measuring internal conflict

In recent years, researchers have constructed a number of conflict lists and data sets describing international conflicts and several of their key characteristics (type of dispute, levels of violence, type of mediation, etc.). Though many, and perhaps even all, of the data sets lack comprehensiveness, they have nonetheless proven quite useful to the research and policy communities for analysing similarities, differences and the root causes of conflict worldwide. The present study constructs an analogous list of *internal* conflicts throughout the world since 1980. A copy of this can be obtained from Dane Rowlands at Carleton University,

Developing a list of internal civil conflicts and disturbances was especially challenging given the reluctance of national and international statistical agencies to report situations of this kind. Both the instances and intensity of internal conflict are not particularly easy to track nor quantify, partially since there is no strong motivation to publicize internal disturbances by governments or the international institutions to which member countries belong.

As a starting point in constructing an index of domestic disturbance, instances of internal conflict were drawn from the following nine sources (see references). Though most of the data sets focus primarily on international conflicts, many of the most notable internal conflicts were included (civil wars, coups, etc.). Hence these sources furnished a preliminary list of internal conflicts which were further investigated and supplemented through an examination of the written accounts provided in the Europa Year Book.

After examining the historical record for over 100 countries from 1965 to 1995, a four-unit index of civil conflict was developed.

0 – no domestic conflict, or routine domestic conflicts with minor violence and no or few fatalities

1 – mass protest, or protest with significant casualties or some fatalities

2 – large-scale domestic turmoil or conflict producing significant fatalities

3 – mass unrest or civil war

The threshold of observance for the conflict index was fairly high. A zero value was assigned for years in which a country experienced no substantial domestic conflict, or disturbances were confined to the political realm (e.g. a government non-confidence vote, a routine non-violent political protest, a sporadic assassination). The least intense instances of domestic disturbance were assigned a value of 1. These included sizeable political protests or protests resulting in significant injuries and/or only a handful of deaths. Instances of significant turmoil or several fatalities were assigned a value of 2, while a value of 3 was reserved for cases of mass unrest or civil war.

The internal conflict index was employed as the dependent variable in the regression analysis of this study. Although the indicator would benefit from further refinement and more specific denotation, it is already surprisingly highly correlated with several of the intuitive causes of internal conflict and provides insight into the influence of the Fund in intensifying domestic disturbances.

Notes

1. The discussion is limited to the IMF chiefly because the World Bank's Structural Adjustment Loans, which also impose policy conditions on restructuring economies, tend to have IMF programmes as prerequisites. Furthermore the IMF's conditions are generally perceived to be more harsh and more binding, even though they are generally less intrusive and less numerous than those required by the Bank. For an excellent discussion of the World Bank's role in conflict situations see John Stremlau in Francisci Sagasti, "Preventing Deadly Conflict: Does the World Bank Have a Role?" *Carnegie Commission on Preventing Deadly Conflict*, 1998, available from the CCPDC website: www.ccpdc.org/pubs/worldbanl/worldframe.htm

2. Michael Brown, "The Causes and Regional Dimension of Internal Conflict," in Michael Brown, ed., *The International Dimensions of Internal Conflict*, Cambridge: M.I.T. Press, 1996.

3. Carnegie Commission on Preventing Deadly Conflict, *Preventing Deadly Conflict*, New York: Carnegie Corporation of New York, 1997.

4. Ted Robert Gurr and Raymond Duvall, "Civil Conflict in the 1960s: A Reciprocal Theoretical System with Parameter Estimates," *Comparative Political Studies*, Vol. 6, 1973, p. 160.

5. Ted Robert Gurr, "Why Minorities Rebel – A Global Analysis of Communal Mobilization and Conflict since 1945," *International Political Science Review*, Vol. 14, No. 2, 1993, pp. 161–201; Gurr and Duvall, "Civil Conflict in the 1960s," *ibid.*; Augustine Kpsowa and J. Craig Jenkins, "The Structural Sources of Military Coups in Postcolonial Afrika, 1957–1984," *American Journal of Sociology*, Vol. 99, No. 1, 1993, pp. 126–63.

6. Cheryl Payer, *The Debt Trap: The IMF and the Third World*, Harmondsworth: Penguin, 1974.

7. Scott Siddell, *The IMF and Third-World Political Instability: Is There a Connection?* Houndmills: Macmillan, 1988.

8. Susan Eckstein, "Power and Popular Protest in Latin America," in Susan Eckstein, ed., *Power and Popular Protest: Latin American Social Movements*, Berkeley: University of California Press, 1989, pp. 1–60; Maria H. M. Alves, "Interclass Alliances in Brazil," in Eckstein, ed., *Power and Popular Protest*, pp. 278–98; John Walton, "Debt, Protest and the State in Latin America," in Eckstein, ed., *Power and Popular Protest*, p. 308.

9. Walton, "Debt, Protest and the State in Latin America," *ibid.*, p. 300.

10. James Boyce and Manuel Pastor Jr., "Aid for Peace: Can International Financial Institutions Help Prevent Conflict?" *World Policy Journal*, Vol. 15, No. 2, 1998, pp. 42–9.

11. Susan Woodward, *Balkan Tragedy: Chaos and Dissolution after the Cold War*, Washington D.C.: The Brookings Institution, 1995.

12. Walton, "Debt, Protest and the State in Latin America," note 8 above, p. 319.

13. Henry Bienen and Mark Gersovitz, "Consumer Subsidy Cuts, Violence and Political Stability," *Comparative Politics*, Vol. 19, No. 1, 1986, pp. 25–44.

14. Karen Remmer, "The Politics of Economic Stabilization: IMF Standby Programs in Latin America, 1954–1984," *Comparative Politics*, Vol. 19, No. 1, 1986, pp. 1–4.

15. Siddell, *The IMF and Third-World Political Instability*, note 7 above.

16. Juha Auvinen, "IMF Intervention and Political Protest and the Third World: A Conventional Wisdom Refined," *Third World Quarterly*, Vol. 17, No. 3, 1996, pp. 377–400.

17. Bienen and Gersovitz, "Consumer Subsidy Cuts," note 13 above; Auvinen, "IMF Intervention and Political Protest," *ibid.*, p. 395.

18. Auvinen's piece is based on an earlier and more extensive paper that examines various types of conflict ranging from protests to rebellion to irregular executive transfers. See Juha Auvinen, "Socio-Political and Economic Indicators for Conflict Early-Warning," paper presented at the 1995 Annual Meeting of the International Studies Association (ISA), Chicago, 1995.

19. Siddell, *The IMF and Third-World Political Instability*, note 7 above; Auvinen, "Socio-Political and Economic Indicators for Conflict Early-Warning," *ibid.*

20. See Auvinen, "Socio-Political and Economic Indicators for Conflict Early-Warning," note 18 above, for a review of the hypotheses investigated by other researchers.

21. The dependent variable is not ideal. There is necessarily an element of subjectivity in both the assignment of ranks and the consequent relative magnitudes. While the absence of a comprehensive data set on internal conflict is a serious constraint on the analysis, some effort was made to ensure a degree of consistency in the rankings used here. Future work includes a refinement of the dependent variable, and the use of econometric techniques to minimize the potential effect of improperly assigned relative magnitudes.

22. The high conditionality agreements are the Stand-by Arrangements, Extended Financing Facility, and the Enhanced Structural Adjustment Facility.

23. Nadeem Ul Haque and Moshin Khan, "Do IMF-Supported Programs Work? A Survey of the Cross-Country Empirical Evidence," *IMF Working Paper*, 98/169, 1998.

24. Auvinen, "IMF Intervention and Political Protest," note 16 above.

25. Despite the sophistication of the analysis, Auvinen (*ibid.*) does not provide a very compelling justification of the actual functional form used in his estimations. This should

not lead us to reject his conclusions, but it does invite an analysis of the robustness of his results to the form of the variables used. It is in this spirit that we hope to continue the research presented here. Besides refining the dependent variable and expanding the set of explanatory variables, more work needs to be done in terms of identifying the appropriate functional form for the equation and identifying the appropriate data correction procedures.

26. Unfortunately, missing data reduced the sample to an unbalanced panel of as few as 771 observations in some cases, with some of the countries appearing for only two years. The regression methods used included a standard robust estimation (using White's procedure for consistent coefficient estimates even if the error terms are heteroscedastic), a Tobit procedure to take into account the censoring of data on the lower bound of zero, a Probit procedure using a binary indicator of the onset of internal conflict as the dependent variable, and a panel estimation procedure to take into account the possible presence of fixed country effects.

27. In the first regressions, White's procedure was used to generate heteroscedastic-consistent coefficient estimates for the model in which the dependent variable took on the value of 0 to 3. There was no correction for the fact that the data are censored on the lower bound. In the first case the military expenditure to GNP ratio was not included because the data were not widely available and its inclusion reduced the sample size by more than one-half.

28. The next estimation uses a Tobit procedure to reflect the fact that a dependent variable value of 0 may represent a significant censoring of the data, i.e. that the intensity of conflict has fallen below a critical threshold. Auvinen suggests that the Tobit procedure does not significantly affect the results of his model. In this case the results prove to be highly sensitive to the estimating procedure. The third column of Table 11.1 presents the results of the Tobit procedure.

29. Auvinen may not have this difficulty because the model is already log-linear prior to being estimated with a Tobit procedure. *Ibid.*

30. Ul Haque and Kahn, "Do IMF-Supported Programs Work?" note 23 above, p. 5.

31. *Ibid.*

32. *Ibid.*

33. Auvinen, "IMF Intervention and Political Protest," note 16 above.

34. Woodward, *Balkan Tragedy*, note 11 above.

35. Ul Haque and Kahn, "Do IMF-Supported Programs Work?" note 23 above.

36. Devesh Kapur, "The New Conditionalities of the International Financial Institutions," *International Monetary and Financial Issues for the 1990s*, Vol. VIII, New York: Group of Twenty-Four and the United Nations, 1997, pp. 127–38.

37. Auvinen, "IMF Intervention and Political Protest," note 16 above.

38. David Carment and Karen Garner, "Early Warning and Conflict Prevention," *Canadian Foreign Policy*, Vol. 6, No. 2, 1999, pp. 103–18.

39. *Ibid.*

40. A. Reinecke, "Can International Financial Institutions Prevent Internal Violence? The Sources of Ethno-National Conflict in Transitional Societies," in Abram Chayes and Antonia Handler Chayes, eds., *Preventing Conflict in the Post-Communist World: Mobilizing International and Regional Organizations*, Washington D.C.: The Brookings Institution, 1996, pp. 281–337.

41. Mats Berdal and David Keen, "Violence and Economic Agendas in Civil Wars: Some Policy Implications," *Millennium: Journal of International Studies*, Vol. 26, No. 2, 1997, pp. 795–818.

42. David Shearer, "Exploring the Limits of Consent: Conflict Resolution in Sierra Leone," *Millennium: Journal of International Studies*, Vol. 26, No. 2, 1997, p. 849.

43. This is not to suggest that such concerns are irrelevant in cases where violence is not perceived as likely, or that other moral arguments are not sufficient justification for placing greater importance on them.
44. Woodward, *Balkan Tragedy*, note 11 above.
45. David Carment and Frank Harvey, *Using Force to Prevent Ethnic Violence*, Westport, CT: Praeger, 2000.
46. Antonia Handler Chayes, Abram Chayes, and George Raach, "Beyond Reform: Restructuring for More Effective Conflict Intervention," *Global Governance*, Vol. 3, No. 2, 1997, pp. 117–45.
47. Woodward, *Balkan Tragedy*, note 11 above.

Part Four

Building capacity at the regional level

12

Conflict prevention in Africa: Establishing conditions and institutions conducive to durable peace

Rasheed Draman

Introduction

Africa is the most violent continent in the world. In the last couple of decades, it has been home to some of the world's most atrocious armed intrastate conflicts.[1] According to Wallensteen and Sollenberg, in 1999, out of 37 armed conflicts around the world, 16 (or 43 per cent) of these conflicts were located in Africa.[2] In addition, some experts have rightly concluded that, while the prevalence of armed conflict declined significantly in the 1990s, "Africa ... will continue to experience serious warfare in the future."[3]

It is fair to point out that not all is bleak and lost in the continent. Whilst it shoulders the heaviest burden of intrastate conflicts currently underway around the globe, there are some countries that are showing signs of development, democracy, and positive change. Democracy is consolidating in places like Botswana, Benin, Senegal, and Mauritius; and there have been very peaceful electoral transitions in places like Ghana, Mali, and Burkina Faso. The two giants of Africa – South Africa and Nigeria – have also witnessed transitions albeit with still very difficult racial, ethnic and religious problems to grapple with.

The end of the Cold War unleashed opportunities for both the UN and regional organizations to play a key role in conflict prevention.[4] But this opportunity has evaded Africa thanks to weak and wildly inconsistent international efforts, venal leadership and failed democratic transitions. In fact there is ample evidence to suggest that conflict prevention in Africa has been ad hoc, and if this trend continues, Africa's future threatens to replicate its past; a past of violent conflict, hunger, and disease.

Admittedly, conflict prevention has remained difficult and elusive to both academics and policy makers. Typically, a conflict evolves through five stages: pre-violence, escalation, endurance, de-escalation, and post-violence. Sadly, the common approach to handling conflicts in Africa focuses beyond the pre-violence stage. In fact, international and domestic actors engage themselves in the uphill task of managing crises instead of the relatively easier job of anticipating and preventing these crises.

This chapter makes a case for conflict prevention in Africa. It argues that two issues are important for conflicts to be effectively prevented. First, regional and sub-regional organizations and their initiatives should be supported, nurtured and strengthened; and second, good governance and responsible leadership should be encouraged and rewarded. These strategies should not be ad hoc. They should be carefully planned and executed over a long period of time if any meaningful progress is to be achieved. We will begin by examining the nature and sources of conflicts in Africa. This discussion is very important in order to put the discussion on prevention in perspective and to understand exactly what has to be prevented. The second section discusses the challenge of prevention. It will be argued that conflicts in Africa, although distant and posing no immediate threat to the national interests of "big powers," disturb international stability in the long run if left unattended. The third section examines some of the African regional and sub-regional initiatives for conflict prevention. The fourth section puts forward some recommendations for more effective preventive action in Africa.

Nature and sources of conflict in Africa

A close look at the nature of conflicts in Africa reveals certain patterns. First, the conflicts, which normally assume communal forms, are characterized by military hostilities between rebel groups, mostly organized, and the incumbent government. For example, in the former Zaire, now Democratic Republic of Congo (DPC), Laurent Kabila organized rebels to launch an incursion against the government of Mobutu Sese Sekou in Kinsasha; similarly, Charles Taylor led the rebels of the National Patriotic Front of Liberia (NPFL) to fight the government of Samuel Doe in Monrovia. Thus, there is, as Douglas Anglin observed, "the widespread acceptance of force as an appropriate dispute settlement procedure." Since most of the incumbent governments came to power through the barrel of the gun, there is a tendency among them to react to challenges to their power with further force.[5]

The rebel groups often succeed in mobilizing several different groups against the government, which is usually made up of people of the same ethnic group. Thus, the nature of most of these conflicts, as already mentioned, is communal and calls into question not only the legitimacy of specific regimes but also the essentials of state power. Most states in Africa are colonial creations with large numbers of sub-national groups. Ted Robert Gurr writes that in 1994, about one-sixth of the world's population, or 989 million people, belonged to some 292 groups whose members either have experienced systematic discrimination or have taken political action to assert their collective interests against the states that claim to govern them.[6] According to Gurr's breakdown, of the world's 190 countries, 120 have politically significant minorities. Sub-Saharan Africa has 81 groups – the greatest concentration; Europe has 59; Asia, Latin America, and the Western democracies have the smallest proportions, between 11 and 13 per cent each.[7] If these statistics are right and bad governance continues to be the order of the day in most of sub-Saharan Africa, the region will continue to be characterized by widespread turmoil unless decisive and workable measures are put in place.

Another pattern, aside from the use of force to settle disputes in Africa, is the fact that most conflicts in Africa take the form of "irregular warfare" in which, for strategic reasons, civilians instead of professional soldiers are subjected to the most heinous atrocities. As Secretary-General Kofi Annan has pointed out, in domestic conflicts, "the main aim, increasingly, is the destruction not just of armies but of civilians and entire ethnic groups" with the prime targets being women and children.[8] Indeed, the "rules of war" have now given way to sheer bestiality, especially in Africa.[9] The Revolutionary United Front (RUF) of Forday Sankoh in Sierra Leone is one group that is particularly notorious for perpetrating crimes against innocent civilians – the group has been accused by victims of hacking hands and arms of civilians in a reign of terror that has put Sierra Leone in the spotlight since 1991. Rebel movements in other parts of Africa are guilty of similar crimes. But as Douglas Anglin reminds us, these gross abuses of civilians are not confined to undisciplined rebel movements; governments too are guilty.[10]

A third pattern is the extent to which almost all conflicts in Africa have been commercialized. According to Anglin, "war has become big business in which the major motivation of an emerging class of military entrepreneurs is the accumulation of wealth, either to finance the war effort or, all-to-often, personal enrichment."[11] Annan notes that in Liberia, for example, the control and exploitation of diamonds, timber, and other resources was the motivating factor driving the warring factions.

Since the protagonists are those who benefit most from controlling these strategic resources, they have much interest in prolonging the war.[12] It is not only these organized groups that struggle to control and exploit these resources. Smaller groups, such as those characterized as "rebels without a cause," found in the dense forest area bordering Liberia, Sierra Leone, and Guinea, are driven to a life of extortion, looting, and plundering in order to make a living. This is also true of the remnants of the Rwandan *interahamwe*.

Whatever patterns conflicts assume in Africa, the sad fact remains that they have exacted and continue to exact a high toll on the lives of civilians and the economic and social potentials of the continent – a continent blessed with more resources than any other continent, yet immersed in deep poverty and profound misery. The obvious question to ask at this point is "why do people in Africa resort to violent means of addressing their differences?" Several explanations have been offered for the conflicts in Africa. The following section examines some of the causes and contributing factors.

The ethnic argument

First, in an attempt to unearth the roots of civil conflicts in Africa, there is the tendency for scholars to view these conflicts as being precipitated by communal and ethnic factors.[13] The usual argument put forward by scholars like Claude Ake is that, given the multiplicity of ethnic groups, and the absence of permanent national institutions within each African state to address historical grievances adequately, the resort to conflict becomes the route for seeking redress. The problem with this view (linking civil conflict with ethnicity and structural problems) is that it relegates to the background the significance of political, economic, and a complex web of other factors.[14]

By itself, ethnicity is not a cause of violent conflict, as most groups, most of the time, pursue their interests peacefully through established political channels. Ethnicity only emerges as one of the fault lines along which societies fracture when it is linked with acute social uncertainty and the fear of what the future might bring.[15] Having said that, it is however difficult to deny the fact that in many conflicts in Africa, highly emotive, ascriptive and powerful group bonds, bonds which do not seem to be fading from the African scene, are a principal factor in conflict.[16] In fact, ongoing lower-level violence in Nigeria, Uganda, and many other places in Africa, testifies to this fact. Thus, even though nothing can be done about the existence of ethnic groups in Africa, since any attempt to recognize and give every single group autonomy will only lead to further chaos, it is important to recognize the powerful mobilizing effect of ethnicity.

Closely linked to the ethnic factor is the emergence of modern states with expansionist tendencies, a factor that has been blamed for most conflicts in Africa.[17] According to Gurr and Harff, the emergence of the state system since the seventeenth century as the dominant form of social organization has created tensions between the state and other forms of large-scale organizations resulting eventually in wars within and between states.[18]

Poverty, economic inequality, and conflict

According to Stephen Ryan, even though there is no general agreement about the extent of the influence of economic factors on conflict, little doubt exists that inter-ethnic stability can be affected by such factors.[19] A common feature of multi-ethnic societies, whether in Africa or elsewhere, is an uneven distribution of wealth, leading in most cases to claims of unfair treatment and exploitation by those who do not have access to political and economic power.[20] Ironically, however, Ryan observes, sometimes these claims emanate from well-off areas, where they can be an important factor in secessionist demands. Examples of such cases include the Basques in Spain, the oil rich Ibo region of Nigeria, mineral rich Bougainville in Papua New Guinea, and Slovenia and Croatia in the former Yugoslavia.[21]

A close look at some of the hot spots in Africa will reveal that there is a very high correlation between poverty and conflict. In Sudan for instance, the acute poverty of the South compared with the North, as well as the feeling that the Northern-based government was exploiting the region's resources without any returns to the region, contributed to the outbreak of conflict in 1983.[22] Similarly, in Angola and Mozambique, the resentment of the rural people toward an urban elite of partly mixed race that controlled economic and political power, contributed to the emergence of conflict in the two countries.[23] Some analysts believe that the participants in many of Africa's violent demonstrations and wars in recent years have been moved by the poor economic conditions under which they live. Copson, for instance, argues that when guerrillas join a rebel group, they may obtain food and clothing as well as opportunities for recognition and advancement that are normally unavailable to them in an urban slum or a farming village.[24] The situation becomes especially precarious when poor economic conditions are accompanied by poor government policies. The next section will examine the relation between governance and conflict.

Governance and conflict in Africa

There is little doubt about the relationship between bad governance and conflict in Africa. The way a country is governed is an indicator of social unrest – or the lack thereof. Zartman was right when he observed that "governing a state is not only the prevention of violent conflict from destroying the country; it is the continual effort to handle the ordinary conflicts among groups and their demands which arise as society plays its role in the conduct of normal politics."[25]

At the root of many conflicts in Africa are the repressive and political excesses on the part of some African governments. When a system of governance does not allow the full and equitable participation of citizens, especially when certain groups are systematically excluded, the seeds of discord and conflict are being planted, and will grow. As Michael Brown reminds us, the prospects for conflict in a country depend to a large extent on the type and fairness of the political system in place. Closed as well as authoritarian systems are likely to generate considerable resentment over time, especially if the interests of some ethnic groups are served while others are trampled.[26]

Brown's observation has great relevance for Africa, where most countries are made up of several hundred different ethnic groups. For instance, Nigeria has about 300 and Tanzania about 150 ethnic groups. One can argue that if a "test of fairness" is conducted on all regimes in Africa today, there is the likelihood of all of them failing the test. In many African countries, as Raymond Copson observed, "the tendency of many African governments to rule through arbitrary and repressive means has provoked violent and armed resistance in many instances."[27] Not only do African regimes cultivate a "politics of exclusion," they design mechanisms that stifle civil societies. The consequences of such vicious policies are the numerous killing fields on the continent.[28]

Regional causal factors

Today, regional politics is an important causal factor in most of the conflicts that are underway in Africa. In fact, it will not be an exaggeration to assert that the collaboration of nearby states in war-torn regions in Africa – West Africa and the Great Lakes for example – has played an important role in destabilizing these regions. The case of Liberia can be used to illustrate this point.

Charles Taylor's incursion against the government of Samuel Doe, initially dismissed as an attempt by a small group of disgruntled rebels who could be smashed with little resistance by government forces, succeeded eventually in not only claiming the life of Doe, but also those of several thousand Liberians. This would not have been possible without the support of some countries in the region. The two leading francophone countries in West Africa – Burkina Faso and Côte d'Ivoire – supported Taylor's NPFL (National Patriotic Front of Liberia) in many respects. Burkina Faso is alleged to have supplied arms to Taylor's rebels while Côte d'Ivoire had allowed the rebels free transit across its border into Nimba County in Liberia.[29] According to David Wippman, attempts made in 1990 to place the Liberian crisis on the Security Council's agenda failed, partly because of Côte d'Ivoire's opposition and partly because the Council's members shared the US view that the problem should be solved by Africans themselves.[30]

Not only did they support Charles Taylor's cause, the francophone countries in the region initially rejected the idea of ECOMOG's intervention in Liberia. In a message to ECOWAS Chairman Dawda Jawara, reported on 13 August 1990 by Radio Burkina, President Blaise Compaore of Burkina Faso declared his country's "total disagreement" with the intervention. He stated that the Standing Mediation Committee (SMC) had "no competence to interfere in member states' internal conflicts, but only in conflicts breaking out between member countries." He warned of "an eventual expansion of the internal conflict, which could break out among member countries if an intervention force is sent to Liberia against the will of the Liberian people."[31]

Evidently, regional interference is one of the biggest contributory factors in most of Africa's killing fields. Most rebel forces use neighbouring states that support them as a conduit for weapons coming from abroad. Not only that, they also use those territories as headquarters in the conduct of their foreign relations.[32]

It is important to note that none of the factors discussed above are by themselves sufficient to trigger a conflict. Most of the conflicts underway in Africa are the result of a combination of many of these factors. Thus, any preventive regime must be multifaceted and must address most of these causes if it is to have any impact. For instance, whilst designing a preventive regime that is aimed at addressing the structural causes of conflict and changing the nature of societies that are prone to conflict, serious attention has to be paid to stopping arms flows and encouraging African leaders to stop giving rebel leaders safe havens.

The challenge of prevention in Africa

Since the American debacle in Somalia, most Western nations have become casualty-sensitive and reluctant to risk the lives of their soldiers in intrastate conflicts in Africa – conflicts that take place in distant lands without any immediate threat to their national interests. Against this background, it would of course be wiser if conflict is prevented in the first place. Bruce Jentleson captures the essence of preventive action when he argues that:

The basic logic of preventive diplomacy seems unassailable. Act early to prevent disputes from escalating or problems from worsening. Reduce tensions that if intensified could lead to war. Deal with today's conflicts before they become tomorrow's crises. It is the same logic as preventive medicine: don't wait until the cancer has spread or the arteries are fully clogged.[33]

Conflict prevention is not a new phenomenon[34] but as already noted already, because of the absence of superpower competition, the post-Cold War era provides opportunities especially in Africa for acting preventively. During the Cold War, structural defects in international cooperation have been blamed for the lack of efforts to stop wars before they escalated.[35] Thus, the retreat of the superpowers from Africa has created the space for regional and international actors to take on the challenge of maintaining peace and security. Michael Barnett has noted that during the Cold War most regional organizations were imprinted by superpower competition, but since its demise many regional organizations are capitalizing on the power vacuum to create new mechanisms to foster regional security and to fulfil the spirit of Chapter VIII.[36] Connected to this is the fact that in Africa today, the politics of traditional statecraft, which since the early 1960s found expression in the Charter of the OAU, which upholds state sovereignty and non-interference in the internal affairs of member states, has clearly disappeared with the Cold War.

In recent times, African regional and sub-regional organizations have crossed the threshold of sovereignty in a bid to bring order to neighbouring states where conflicts are taking place – the ECOWAS initiatives in Liberia (1990–97), Sierra Leone (1993–2000) and Guinea Bissau (1998–99) are clear cases in point. These kinds of initiatives demonstrate the fact that the political will needed to intervene in conflict situations is very much alive in Africa – what is lacking is the economic means. This is where the support of the international community becomes crucial.

Critics of conflict prevention will question both the value and viability of prevention;[37] and by extension, they will argue against the involvement of "big powers" whose national interest is not threatened by these "distant conflicts." However, it is an illusion to assume that conflicts in Africa will have no bearing on security outside the region. As Jan Eliasson notes:

Prevention of conflicts is a moral imperative in today's world. It is a humanitarian necessity in order to save innocent lives. It is an economic necessity both for the countries immediately involved and for the international community, because of the exorbitant price of war and postwar reconstruction. It is a political necessity for the credibility of international cooperation, in particular for the United Nations.[38]

Indeed, it is morally imperative on the part of the international community, especially the United Nations, to act and in a timely manner to prevent conflicts before they erupt, irrespective of where they erupt. Once they start, they are like, in the words of Eliasson, "the genie escaping from the bottle – it is almost impossible to put it back."[39] It is important to note, however, that even though the United Nations is a very important actor in the field of conflict prevention, the world body is by no means the only or always the most important actor engaged in preventive action. Even though the United Nations remains engaged in Africa, in the last couple of years the continent is witnessing a shift towards more local involvement in conflict prevention through the activities of regional and sub-regional organizations. This shift is more out of necessity than choice. African leaders have realized that they have to wake up to the realities of the post-Cold War world and rise to the challenge of managing security on the continent. The next section examines the activities of the Organization of African Unity (OAU), the Economic Community of West African States (ECOWAS), and the Inter-Governmental Authority on Development (IGAD) in the area of conflict prevention.

African regional and sub-regional conflict prevention initiatives

The Organization of African Unity (OAU)

The OAU is a continent-wide organization, which was formed in 1963 by the first group of post-independent African leaders to foster the political and economic integration of the continent. For much of its history, the organization has not been able to achieve the goals for which it was set up thanks to the numerous problems that plague the continent. The 1990s have been particularly difficult for the organization, as it had had to watch helplessly whilst most of its member states crumbled because of the instability that afflicted them.

Even though the founding fathers of the OAU had clearly expressed their desire to work collectively to prevent and manage conflicts, in order to place the continent on a path to sustainable development, the organization could not perform this role because of lack of resources and the fact that its Charter prohibits the violation of the sovereignty of member states.[40] Developments on the continent after the end of the Cold War compelled African leaders to take a critical look at the Charter and to come to the realization that the organization needed to play an active role in managing security on the continent. As a result, an institutional framework for the prevention and management of conflicts was created.

The Mechanism for Conflict Prevention, Management and Resolution

The OAU Assembly of Heads of State and Government, in its 1993 Session held in Cairo, Egypt for the first time in the history of the organization adopted the Cairo Declaration, a unique declaration giving the organization the legal competence and legitimacy to intervene in internal conflicts falling within the jurisdiction of member states. Through the Cairo Declaration, African leaders created the Mechanism for Conflict Prevention, Management and Resolution.

The primary objective of the Mechanism is to anticipate and prevent potential conflicts from developing into full-blown conflicts. This objective will be achieved through peacemaking and peacebuilding which will obviate the need to resort to complex and resource-demanding peace-keeping operations which are mostly beyond the financial capability of member states. In the event that the Mechanism fails to prevent conflicts from escalating into full-blown crises, it empowers the organization to engage in peacemaking and peacebuilding in order to prevent the re-emergence of conflicts which may have been resolved.

It is evident that the key motivation of African leaders for putting together this Mechanism is to develop a "preventive culture" towards the handling of conflicts in Africa. An evaluation of the Mechanism a decade later reveals that this desire by African leaders has not progressed much beyond verbal commitments. To be sure, since its inception, the mechanism has undertaken a number of initiatives: in Rwanda, by deploying a Neutral Military Observer Group (NMOG) to monitor the implementation of the Arusha Peace Agreement; in Burundi, by deploying an OAU Observer Mission (OMIB) to monitor the peace process in that country; in Liberia and Sierra Leone, by supporting the sub-regional efforts of the ECOWAS countries; in the Central African Republic, by supporting the initiatives undertaken by the four African heads of state (MISAB), aimed at defusing the crisis in that country. In the Great Lakes region the OAU worked closely with countries of the region in the search for a peaceful solution to the crises in the Democratic Republic of Congo and the Republic of Congo.[41] But in almost all these cases, the organization has been involved in the prevention of a re-emergence of conflicts, as most of these conflicts were underway before the Mechanism came into effect. What the organization has failed to do is anticipate and prevent conflicts that erupted into violence after 1993. The conflicts in the Democratic Republic of Congo, the Central African Republic, Burundi, and Guinea were test cases for the organization's proactive approach.

The New Partnership for Africa's Development (NEPAD)

Apart from the proactive role envisaged under the Mechanism for Conflict Prevention, African leaders have put together an initiative aimed at ensuring sustainable development on the continent. The New Partnership for Africa's Development (NEPAD) came into effect in July 2001. Under NEPAD, African leaders pledged to eradicate poverty in Africa by ensuring that the continent is placed on a path of sustainable growth and development. To make NEPAD a reality, African leaders pledged to take responsibility for:

- Strengthening mechanisms for conflict prevention, management, and resolution at the regional and continental levels to ensure that these mechanisms are used to restore and maintain peace;
- Promoting and protecting democracy and human rights in their respective countries and regions by developing clear standards of accountability, transparency, and participatory governance at the national and sub-national levels.[42]

With the end of the Cold War, it became evident that without peace in Africa there can be no sustainable growth and development. Consequently, the priorities of NEPAD include human security, good governance, and democracy, necessary steps if the vision for sustainable development is to move beyond rhetoric. The core of NEPAD's objectives is to build and enhance the capacity of African institutions for early warning, regional conflict prevention, and management. Specifically, the Peace and Security initiative of NEPAD has three elements:

- Promoting long-term conditions for development and security;
- Building the capacity of African institutions for early warning as well as enhancing African institutions' capacity to prevent, manage, and resolve conflicts;
- Institutionalizing commitment to the core values of the New Partnership for Africa's Development through leadership.[43]

The OAU has come a long way since its inception. In fact, the organization has made much more progress in the last ten years as compared to its first 30 years of its existence. In particular, it has made significant progress in the area of managing conflicts on the continent, even developing some commonly accepted norms and practices. These two important initiatives by the continental organization are very laudable and should be supported and nurtured in order to help stabilize the troubled continent.

The Economic Community of West African States (ECOWAS)

In 1990, ECOWAS, which was originally formed to foster sub-regional economic integration, was transformed into a security organization when sub-regional leaders took on the challenge of intervening in the Liberian conflict. The outbreak of that conflict coincided with the end of the Cold War and the heightening of tensions in the Gulf in the early 1990s. This phenomenon had two effects on the West African sub-region. First, it resulted in a neglect of the region by the international community; and second, it created the space for regional actors to take on the challenge of maintaining peace and security.

The case of Liberia is an interesting one, particularly as the United States had "special" ties with the country and was so greatly involved there during the Cold War. Liberia was a major African recipient of US aid, with the Doe regime receiving about US$500 million between 1980 and 1985 alone. Also the US had strategic interests in Liberia, including the Omega navigation station and the Voice of America's largest transmitting station in Africa.[44] Thus, when the conflict broke out, there was an expectation that at least the United States would intervene. ECOWAS took on the Liberian challenge when the conflict was five months old. Salim Ahmed Salim, the Secretary-General of OAU, justified ECOWAS's intervention as follows: "Africans are one people. It is hence unacceptable that a part of that people should stand in silence and in seeming helplessness when another part is suffering."[45]

ECOWAS put together a monitoring group – ECOMOG – to intervene in Liberia from 1990–97. Since its creation, ECOMOG has intervened in other conflicts in the region – in Sierra Leone (1993–2000) and Guinea Bissau (1998–99). The creation of ECOMOG represents, on the one hand, a credible African initiative to maintain regional peace especially at a time when some African countries that are engulfed in conflict no longer enjoy the support they used to receive during the Cold War. In fact, ECOMOG is the first sizeable peacekeeping force to be controlled and financed by a sub-regional organization in Africa. On the other hand, because of its ad hoc nature, ECOMOG has been accused of illegality, bias, corruption, brutality directed against ordinary citizens of the host states, and above all, it was seen as not sufficiently multinational because of the dominant role of Nigeria.

In 1998, ECOWAS's leaders took the initiative to transform the ad hoc, Nigerian-dominated force into a permanent standby force. Like the OAU, the leaders endorsed a proposal to create a Mechanism for Conflict Prevention, Management, Resolution, Peace-Keeping and Security.[46] The Mechanism, which was finally established in December 1999 in Lome, Togo, replaced previous protocols such as the 1978 Non Aggression Protocol and the Protocol on Mutual Assistance on Defence. By doing so, ECOWAS institutionalized norms and processes with structures that would ensure consultation and collective management of regional security concerns. Recognizing the destructive nature of conflicts once they start, ECOWAS, like other regional and sub-regional organizations is placing more emphasis on prevention instead of reaction.

ECOWAS has made some progress since the Mechanism for Conflict Prevention was put in place. For instance, in January 2002, ECOWAS and US officials held a discussion in Abuja, Nigeria with the aim of setting up a regional communication system for early warning to monitor threats to regional security. According to a statement issued by the ECOWAS secretariat, "the regional communication system will facilitate peace-keeping operations in West Africa by providing vital communication links for the subregional peace and security observation system."[47] Under the observation system, the 15 ECOWAS states are divided into four zones coordinated from Banjul, The Gambia; Cotonou, Benin; Monrovia, Liberia; and Ouagadougou, Burkina Faso. An observation and monitoring centre is located at the ECOWAS secretariat in Abuja.[48]

Even though ECOWAS has come under much criticism, it represents by far the most successful attempt of a sub-regional group to manage security in its backyard. This security management initiative has been a rapid but positive learning experience for the peacekeeping nations of West Africa. It has also brought about increased regional stability and an emerging regionally based conflict prevention capacity.

The Inter-Governmental Authority on Development (IGAD)

IGAD evolved from the Inter-governmental Authority on Drought and Development (IGADD), which was formed in 1986 by countries in East Africa and the Horn of Africa – Djibouti, Ethiopia, Kenya, Uganda, Sudan, and Somalia. Eritrea, the newest member, was admitted to the group in 1993. The original aim of the organization was to coordinate member states' efforts in the prevention of drought and desertification. When the organization was renamed IGAD, its mission was broadened to include regional political and economic integration. Recognizing the importance of peace and security in fostering economic and political integration due to the prevalence of conflicts in most member states, one of the specific aims of IGAD is "to promote peace and security in the sub-region and create mechanisms within the sub-region for the prevention, management and resolution of inter and intra-state conflicts through dialogue."[49]

Since 1998, IGAD leaders have decided to take a more proactive role by putting in place a programme on Conflict Prevention, Resolution and Management (CPMR).[50] Recognizing its limitations in playing an active role in conflict prevention, IGAD commissioned the Forum on Early Warning and Early Response (FEWER) to undertake a feasibility study on the design of a conflict early warning and response mechanism (CEWARN).[51]

The CEWARN project evolved through three different stages. The first stage was linked to a workshop that brought together participants from the sub-region to provide them with an opportunity to identify how IGAD could effectively engage in early warning and response activities. Phase two of the project was devoted to identifying in-state systems in early warning and conflict management by assessing their strengths and limitations and examining ways of linking them with other early warning systems at the sub-regional, regional, and international levels. The final phase concentrated on developing the principles that should govern CEWARN's operations.[52]

At the Ninth Summit of Heads of Government of IGAD in Khartoum, Sudan, in January 2002, IGAD leaders adopted the "Protocol on the Establishment of a Conflict Early Warning and Response Mechanism for IGAD Member States."[53] With this Protocol, CEWARN has officially come into effect. But like both the ECOWAS and OAU mechanisms, the easiest part is the verbal commitment. It remains to be seen whether this Protocol can move beyond rhetoric.

From the preceding discussion, it is evident that the discourse on conflict prevention, which previously focused on international capacities for preventive action, is gradually beginning to shift towards local capacities for conflict prevention. This shift is important and should be encouraged for three important reasons. First, regional and sub-regional organizations in Africa are close to conflict spots and can therefore respond at short notice. Second, they have a greater understanding of issues within the various sub-regions. Third and most importantly, they have a large stake in preventing conflicts in their backyards because of the potential destabilizing effects of such conflicts on stable countries in the region. Against this background, one of the most effective ways of preventing conflicts in Africa is to strengthen the capacities of regional and sub-regional organizations throughout the continent.

Recommendations for more effective preventive action

As mentioned earlier, this chapter adopts a focused approach to conceptualizing conflict prevention, which is action that is taken to address the roots of conflict and turn the resort to violence in addressing disputes into resort to peaceful ways of coexistence.

This section will put forward strategies that are useful in addressing the roots of conflicts. It must be emphasized that for these strategies to be successful anywhere they are applied, they must be sustained and concentrated. Indeed, what is needed is a focused, sustained, and consistent programme of conflict prevention. Approaches that make attempts only to abandon them soon after for some reason, exacerbate rather than alleviate the poor plight of most hot spots in Africa.

Since the causes of conflicts in Africa are multiple, so must be the strategies designed to prevent their occurrence. One strategy that requires urgent attention is the strengthening of African regional and sub-regional conflict prevention initiatives whose mere existence can have a deterrent effect. In fact, if a sub-regional organization is well equipped and trained, and is able to deploy troops within days, it will send a signal to rebel groups that their actions would be met with decisive force should they attempt to destabilize governments in the sub-region. Such a strategy has both a short and long-term effect. Other long-term preventive strategies include the promotion of good governance and responsible political leadership. This is based on the realization that the political management of the continent since independence has been disastrous.

Strengthening regional and sub-regional organizations

As a short-term operational measure, there is the need for strengthening the OAU (Organization of African Unity), ECOWAS (Economic Community of West African States), IGAD (Inter-Governmental Authority for Development), SADC (Southern African Development Council) as well as NGOs[54] actively involved in conflict prevention efforts to raise their capacity for preventive deployment. In addition to strengthening these organizations, a long-term measure, there is the need for some form of integration of these activities with those of other actors engaged in preventive work (such as the UN, the European Union and donor countries). As Ciru Mwaura has noted, for conflict prevention to be effective, the "forging of synergies between actors at different levels of involvement in the conflict management nexus" is very important.[55]

Not only is there a need for forging synergies, these regional and sub-regional initiatives have to be nurtured and supported by the international community so that they can continue the task of taking the burden of intervening in Africa off the shoulders of the international community. There is clear evidence, at least from the efforts of ECOWAS in West Africa, that in Africa political will is not as much a problem as economic means. The logistics and financial resources to sustain preventive deployment are demanding and often beyond the means of most African countries. Operating within such constraints impairs preventive action. It will be an understatement to say that most of these organizations are as poor and weak as their continent. Africa is not blessed with organizations like the OSCE. Most of these organizations which are struggling to transform themselves into security organizations simply lack the capacity to perform such a role. ECOMOG was blessed with the presence of Nigeria in West Africa – but as has recently become evident, there is a limit to which countries like Nigeria can go, especially given its own internal turmoil. Recently, when an OAU observer mission was deployed in the DRC at a critical stage of the peace process, officials had to pack themselves (they sat two to a seat) in a military jet borrowed from the Zambian government after they had waited for support that was promised, but not delivered, by the UN. Not only do these organizations need resources to build their capacity, they also need training in handling complex emergencies, and they need skills in conflict resolution. The story of ECOMOG soldiers in Liberia and Sierra Leone, accused not only of partiality, but also of various malpractices (bullying of civilians, corruption, profiteering, extortion, and outright looting) are very good lessons.[56]

Improving governance

One of the biggest challenges facing the international community is to develop innovative ways of improving governance systems in Africa. In general, when international policy makers are dealing with the issue of governance in Africa, the usual prescription is to insist on multi-party elections and democracy. Should the type of democracy practised in the United States, England, or France be the same type of democracy that has to be practised in Nigeria, Liberia, or Sudan? We are well aware that most countries in Africa are colonial creations and federations of ethnic groups. For this reason, politics is usually played out along ethnic lines where the ruling group(s) exclude(s) all other groups from sharing power.

Africa needs a system of governance that is fair and accountable, and which does not necessarily have to mirror the Western concept of democracy. It could build upon pre-colonial structures of inclusive government – a real form of democracy in which everyone had a say in the way society was governed. In pre-colonial Africa, there was a form of consensus democracy which allowed all adults to take part in discussions on issues affecting a community. Discussions were usually long and could last days until a consensus was reached.

If people are poor and hungry, but live in a society where there is justice and accountability and under responsible leadership, there can be a big difference. We understand that it is very difficult to come up with strategies to prevent internal conflicts, but as Stephen Ryan reminds us, it is because such conflicts are difficult to deal with that we need enlightened, flexible, and imaginative responses from good leaders as well as good policies that can make a substantial difference.[57] The Yugoslavia of Tito and that of Milosevic and the South Africa of de Klerk and that of Mandela are very instructive here.

Responsible political leadership

If conflict is to be prevented in Africa, we urgently need responsible political leadership on the continent. African leaders must demonstrate a commitment to building a stable and peaceful Africa. They must set very good examples and then we can call on the international community to help. Any effort at creating conditions and institutions conducive to durable peace in Africa will be a "mirage" if African leaders do not unite to say "no" to rebel movements no matter their cause and to condemn irresponsible government takeovers. This is probably a difficult thing to achieve, but it is not impossible, given that in recent times, African leaders who, many years ago, were deeply engaged in armed conflicts, are today sticking their necks out and condemning military takeovers.

At the thirty-fifth summit meeting of the OAU heads of government in Algiers in July 1999, the numerous conflicts that beset the continent crowded the agenda. Recognizing the negative impact of these conflicts on the much-needed development on the continent, the heads of state resolved that coups d'état will no longer be tolerated.[58] While this looks like mere rhetoric, it signals the beginning of a norm that is slowly taking root within African political circles.

By this declaration, African leaders have recognized the fact that they need to be responsible if the continent is to get out of the mess in which it finds itself today. Interestingly, most of the leaders who signed the declaration came to power through coups d'etat and "legitimized" their rule through controversial elections. A few years ago, such a declaration would have been unthinkable. In commending the leaders for taking such a giant step, some of them need to be rebuked in their conduct of regional politics. They must not only say no to coups d'état, they should resolve their regional differences and stop supporting rebels to destabilize their neighbours. They should put aside the differences that exist between them as leaders and consider how their behaviour affects innocent civilians in Africa – because of their selfish interests, many younger generations in Africa may never have a normal life.

The duty of the international community in this regard is to use "carrots and sticks"[59] to enhance the establishment, support, and respect of norms of peace and responsible leadership at the sub-regional and regional levels. This will mainly be in the form of withdrawing support for rebel movements fighting legitimate neighbouring governments. West Africa and the Great Lakes region would have been stable regions in Africa today if some African heads of state had not lent their support to rebel movements. In fact, regional leaders have to be encouraged to embrace what is acceptable political behaviour, practise accountable political leadership, and support peace efforts. The international community can achieve this by rewarding the leaders who behave responsibly with development and other forms of aid and taking a tough stance against such leaders as Robert Mugabe of Zimbabwe, and Yoweri Museveni of Uganda.

Conclusion

Three issues have been addressed in the preceding pages. First, we have examined the sources of conflict in Africa, which include the problems of ethnicity, poverty, and economic inequality, bad governance and bad neighbours. We have also examined the challenge of conflict prevention in Africa and argued that conflicts in Africa, although distant and posing no immediate threat to the interests of big powers, disturb international relations in the long run if left unattended. We have also outlined the African regional and sub-regional conflict prevention initiatives. This was followed by some recommendations for effective preventive action.

Conflict prevention is not a new phenomenon. However, the post-Cold War era provides opportunities, especially in Africa, for acting preventively. As noted, the retreat of the superpowers from Africa has created the space for regional and international actors to take on the challenge of maintaining peace and security. And most importantly, there is a need for responsible political leadership on the continent if conflicts are to be prevented. African leaders must demonstrate a commitment to seeing a stable and peaceful Africa. They must set very good examples and then the international community can be called upon to help.

It is true, as demonstrated at the beginning of this chapter, that in the last couple of decades, Africa has been home to some of the world's worst armed intrastate conflicts. This makes the task of conflict prevention in Africa a difficult, but not an insurmountable one. If proper attention is paid to regional and sub-regional conflict prevention initiatives in Africa, violent conflict can be eliminated in the long term.

Notes

1. We define intrastate conflicts as situations in which there is a contest between the state (the incumbent government) and group(s), mostly organized, which assume communal forms and are characterized by armed military hostilities. Such conflicts usually take the form of "irregular warfare" in which civilians, instead of professional soldiers are subjected to the most heinous atrocities and have at least 1,000 deaths in a single year.
2. See Peter Wallensteen and Margareta Sollenberg, "Armed Conflict, 1989–98," *Journal of Peace Research*, Vol. 37, No. 5, 2000, p. 638.
3. Ted Robert Gurr, Monty G. Marshall, and Deepa Khosla, *Peace and Conflict 2001: A Global Survey of Armed Conflicts, Self-Determination Movements, and Democracy*, University of Maryland: Center for International Development and Conflict Management, 2000, p. 13.
4. Numerous definitions of the term "conflict prevention" abound in the literature. These definitions range from the Carnegie Commission's focus on both operational and structural aspects of prevention to Boutros-Ghali's focus on prevention before, during, and after conflict. While some of these definitions are useful in giving direction to preventive efforts, they are too broad for a study such as this one. For the purpose of this chapter, a focused approach to conceptualizing conflict prevention is adopted. Conflict prevention is defined as action that is taken to address the root of conflict and turn the resort to violence in addressing disputes into resort to peaceful ways of coexistence.
5. Douglas G. Anglin, Conflict in Sub-Saharan Africa, 1997–1998, Carleton University, Ottawa, Canada, July 1998, p. 5, unpublished article.
6. Ted Robert Gurr, "Communal Conflicts and Global Security," *Current History*, May 1995, pp. 212–17.
7. *Ibid.*
8. UN document S/1998/318, 13 April 1998, p. 21.
9. Anglin, note 5 above, p. 6.
10. *Ibid.*
11. *Ibid.*
12. UN document S/1998/318, 13 April 1998, p. 5.
13. See for example, Claude Ake, "Why Is Africa Not Developing?" *West Africa*, No. 3538, 17 June 1985, p. 1213; Alexis Heraclides, *The Self-Determination of Minority in International Politics*, Portland, OR: Cass, 1991; William Bloom, *Personal Identity, National Identity and International Relations*, London: Cambridge University Press, 1990; Michael E. Brown, "The Causes and Regional Dimensions of Internal," in Michael E. Brown, ed., *The International Dimensions of Internal Conflict*, Cambridge: MIT, 1996, p. 583.
14. See for example George Klay Kieh, Jr, "The Political and Economic Roots of Civil Conflicts in Africa: Implications for US Foreign Policy," *Small Wars and Insurgencies* (special issue), Vol. 7, No. 1, 1996, pp. 41–54. Kieh makes a strong argument against the tendency for scholars to associate civil conflict in Africa to the issue of ethnicity.
15. See for example, Kathleen Newland, "Ethnic Conflict and Refugees," in Michael E. Brown, ed., *Ethnic Conflict and International Security*, Princeton, NJ: Princeton University Press, 1993, p. 161.
16. Raymond W. Copson, "Peace in Africa? The Influence of Regional and International Change," in Francis M. Deng and I. William Zartman, eds., *Conflict Resolution in Africa*, Washington, D.C.: The Brookings Institution Press, 1997, p. 25.

17. Markakis makes a strong argument in this regard especially for the Horn of Africa where he argues among other things that the emergence of the state system is to some extent responsible for conflict in the region. See John Markakis, "Ethnic Conflict and the State in the Horn of Africa," in Katsuyoshi Fukui and John Markakis, eds., *Ethnicity and Conflict in the Horn of Africa*, London: James Currey, 1994, p. 220.
18. Ted Robert Gurr and Barbara Harff, *Ethnic Conflict In World Politics*, Boulder, CO: Westview Press, 1994, p. 8.
19. Stephen Ryan, "The Structural Aspects of Conflict Prevention," paper presented at The United Nations Global Seminar 1995, Tokyo, 4–8 September 1995 p. 11.
20. See for example, *ibid*.
21. *Ibid.*
22. Copson, note 16 above, p. 25.
23. *Ibid.*
24. *Ibid.*, p. 26.
25. I. William Zartman, "Introduction," in I. William Zartman, ed., *Governance as Conflict Management: Politics and Violence in West Africa*, Washington, D.C.: The Brookings Institution Press, 1997, p. 1.
26. Michael E. Brown, "Introduction," in Brown, ed., note 13 above, p. 16.
27. Copson, note 16 above, p. 20.
28. For a similar view, see Donald Rothchild and Letitia Lawson, "The Interactions Between State and Civil Society in Africa: From Deadlock to New Routines," in John W. Harbeson, Donald Rothchild, and Naomi Chazan, eds., *Civil Society and the State in Africa*, Boulder, CO: Lynne Rienner, 1994, p. 271.
29. See for example, Herbert Howe, "Lessons of Liberia: ECOMOG and Regional Peace-keeping," *International Security*, No. 21, pp. 1996–97, pp. 145–76.
30. David Wippman, "Enforcing the Peace: ECOWAS and the Liberian Civil War," in Lori F. Damrosch, ed., *Enforcing Restraint: Collective Intervention in Internal Conflicts*, New York: Council on Foreign Relations, 1993, p. 165.
31. BBC Monitoring Report, 15 August 1990, "Report: Taylor to Visit Banjul; Burkinabe Leader Rejects ECOWAS Intervention, 13 August 1990," cited in M. Weller, ed., *Regional Peace-Keeping and International Enforcement: The Liberian Crisis*, Cambridge International Document Series, Vol. 6, Cambridge: Cambridge University Press, 1994, p. 85.
32. *Ibid.*
33. Bruce W. Jentleson, "Preventive Diplomacy: A Conceptual and Analytical Framework," in Bruce W. Jentleson, ed., *Opportunities Missed, Opportunities Seized: Preventive Diplomacy in the Post-Cold War World*, New York: Rowman & Littlefield, 2000, p. 3.
34. Writers on preventive diplomacy such as Michael Lund argue that the notion of conflict prevention is not new since history, especially that of the nineteenth and twentieth centuries is replete with examples of efforts to discourage the use of force as a means of dealing with international disputes. In spite of the fact that the basic idea of conflict prevention is not new, Lund argues that the concept was first used in 1960 by Secretary-General Dag Hammarskjöld. For a discussion on the origins and evolution of the concept, see Michael Lund, *Preventing Violent Conflicts: A Strategy for Preventive Diplomacy*, Washington, D.C.: USIP Press, 1996, pp. 32–4.
35. Janie Leatherman, William Demars, Patrick Gaffney, and Raimo Väyrynen, *Breaking Cycles of Violence: Conflict Prevention in Intrastate Crises*, West Hartford, CT: Kumarian Press, 1999, pp. 4–5.
36. Michael Barnett, "Partners in Peace? The UN, Regional Organizations, and Peace-keeping," *Review of International Studies*, Vol. 21, 1995, pp. 411–33. For a similar discussion, see I. William Zartman and Saadia Touval, "Mediation: The Role of Third

Party Diplomacy and Informal Peacemaking," in Sheryl J. Brown and Kimber M. Schraub, eds., *Resolving Third World Conflict: Challenges for a New Era*, Washington, D.C.: USIP Press, 1992, pp. 246–7.

37. Jentleson, note 33 above, p. 5.
38. Jan Eliasson, "Establishing Trust in the Healer: Preventive Diplomacy and the Future of the United Nations," in Kevin M. Cahill, ed., *Stopping Wars Before They Start: Preventive Diplomacy*, New York: Basic Books, 1996, p. 318.
39. *Ibid.*
40. Article II of the Charter establishing the OAU. See *The Charter*, available at www.oau-oua.org.
41. See Conflict Management Division of OAU at www.oau-oua.org.
42. New Partnership for Africa's Development (NEPAD) at www.dfa.gov.za/nepad.
43. *Ibid.*
44. Holly Burkhalter and Rakiya Omaar, "Failures of State," *Africa Report*, Nov.-Dec. 1990, in Funmi Olonisakin, "UN Co-operation with Regional Organizations in Peace-keeping: The Experience of ECOMOG and UNOMIL in Liberia," *International Peacekeeping*, Vol. 3, No. 3, 1996, p. 28.
45. In *West Africa*, 22–8 October 1990, p. 2714.
46. David O'Brien, "The Search for Subsidiarity: The UN, African Regional Organizations and Humanitarian Action," *International Peacekeeping*, Vol. 7, No. 3, 2000, pp. 57–83, p. 67.
47. See "West Africa: ECOWAS, US discuss early warning system," 31 January 2002, at www.irinnes.org.
48. *Ibid.*
49. See "IGAD – General Information," available at www.igadregion.org.
50. See, "Towards a Conflict Early Warning and Response Mechanism (CEWARN) for the Inter-Governmental Authority on Development (IGAD)," Summary Report by FEWER, 15 October 2000, p. 7.
51. *Ibid.*
52. *Ibid.*, pp. 9–11.
53. See "IGAD Protocol on Conflict Early Warning Mechanism," available at www.igadregion.org.
54. The two most important of these NGOs are the West Africa Network for Peace-building (WANEP) which leads the FEWER network's early warning and response efforts in West Africa covering Liberia, Sierra Leone, Guinea, Senegal, Gambia and Guinea Bissau; and the Africa Peace Forum (APFO) which leads the FEWER network's efforts in the Great Lakes.
55. See Ciru Mwaura, "Local conflict prevention initiatives and regional frameworks: Prospects for integration in Africa," paper presented at the All Africa Conference on African Principles of Conflict Resolution and Reconciliation, Addis Ababa, Ethiopia 8–12 November 1999, available at www.fewer.org/research/artun.htm.
56. See for example, Klaas van Walraven, *The Pretence of Peace-keeping: ECOMOG, West Africa and Liberia (1990–1998)*, The Hague: Clingendael, 1999; David Carment and Rasheed Draman, Managing Chaos in Sub-Saharan Africa: Assessing the Role of ECOMOG in Liberia, unpublished manuscript.
57. Ryan, note 19 above, p. 13.
58. Africanews.com, "To hell with coups, say presidents," available at www.africanews.com/daily/inews01.htm.
59. They should encourage African leaders, especially those currently involved in the Democratic Republic of Congo, to behave responsibly. Those who fail to do that should have travel and other punitive sanctions placed on them, their families and cronies.

13

Conflict prevention in the Americas: The Organization of American States (OAS)

Osvaldo Kreimer

Introduction

There is a well-established set of mechanisms in the Americas working towards conflict prevention and resolution. Most of these mechanisms are organized within the inter-American system, the web of institutions developed within or deeply connected with the Organization of American States. Five areas of the OAS are involved in conflict prevention, and while autonomous in their action, they have an interconnected effect and have been a major factor in the relatively good performance of the Americas in conflict prevention and resolution.

At the end of a century in which conflicts abounded in the Americas, three sources of conflict still predominate. First, these are leftovers from the Cold War: conflicts among nation states, guerrilla and paramilitary groups. While these conflicts are still active in Colombia, and minimally in Peru, their potential in other countries is negligible. Second, they are old controversies about boundary issues. They are usually dormant and do not threaten peace, but have the potential to escalate.[1] In 1977 the existence of 10 territorial disputes building up as conflict in Latin America and the Caribbean were estimated as the most probable sources of interstate conflict.[2] Just in early March of 2000, three disputes over territorial rights were under active efforts by the OAS to prevent them from becoming hotter disputes: between Costa Rica and Nicaragua; between Honduras and Nicaragua; and between Belize and Guatemala. Third, these are new conflicts with transnational characteristics; among them illicit drug traffic, international terrorism, arms smuggling, and migratory pressures.

Since the Cold War, as recent data clearly demonstrate, the great majority of conflicts in the region have been among states.[3] Social conflicts, however, of internal nature still abound, and may become more intense due the increased negative income distribution in the region. Such movements over time have shown that governments' responses have played a significant role in determining outcomes. In situations where governments recognize, listen to, and accommodate dissatisfied groups, grievances tend to be lessened or resolved. Problems arise when governments ignore or repress these concerns.[4]

The OAS and its role in conflict prevention

Peaceful solution of conflicts between countries has a long and respected tradition in the Americas, pre-dating the OAS.[5] The OAS predecessors go back to 1890 with the Continental Commercial Bureau, which developed into the Pan-American Union in 1910, and into the present OAS structure established in 1948. Since its origins, the inter-American system worked under the principles of non-intervention, juridical equality of the states, and the peaceful solution of controversies. Inter-American international law was built and agreed to with those goals in mind. These bindings help to create a multifaceted network of friendships in the regions, a network in which tensions tend to be received and solved.[6]

Different conflict prevention mechanisms operating within the OAS

When analysing the inter-American system, it is possible to identify at least five main mechanisms, which are significant in terms of conflict prevention in the region:[7]
- The hemispheric security system;
- Mechanisms related to the application of Resolution 1080 and the Washington Protocol concerning breaches against democracy and constitutional continuity;
- The "good offices" capacity of the Permanent Council and of the Secretary General;
- The work of the Unit for the Promotion of Democracy; and
- The inter-American system on human rights.

These mechanisms have been built to work towards different objectives (e.g. the preservation and strengthening of democracy, human rights, or constitutional law), but their action has often resulted in the reduction and prevention of conflict and its causes.

Hemispheric security

A series of agreements, mechanisms, and institutions are in place in the inter-American system under the general label of hemispheric security. They can be clustered in two collaborative areas, those under the direct purview of the Commission on Hemispheric Security of the Permanent Council; and those established among the ministries of defence and armed forces of the region.

The Committee on Hemispheric Security has as its goal, set by mandate of the General Assembly, to revamp the agreements and norms for regional security "under the light of a changing international context."[8] In an effort to prevent military conflicts, this committee facilitates exchanges of information including budgets, prior notice of military exercises, documents on security doctrines, and inventory of weapons among the countries of the region. Efforts are also made to ensure greater transparency in weapons procurement.

Among the trust measures the inter-American system has put in operation in last years under the direct action of this committee are:

- The Inter-American Conferences for Strengthening of Security;
- The Inter-American Convention Against the Illicit Manufacturing and Trafficking in Firearms, Ammunition, Explosives and Other Related Materials (September 1997) that establishes, among other actions, intelligence data compilation and the improvements of techniques and personnel responsible for the search and capture of smuggled arms, as well as the strengthening in the region of the international system to trace arms and explosives via Interpol;
- The Inter-American Convention on Transparency in Arms Acquisitions (adopted on 6 July 1999), providing reciprocal and common measures to monitor the strength of the national armed forces;
- The creation of a peace zone in the region; and
- The development of a Western Hemisphere Mine-Free Region; and the Program of Mine Removal.

Present doctrine on hemispheric security considers not only interstate conflict, but also threats to nation states and their constitutional structures by transnational criminality, in particular the illicit drug and arms traffic. As an ambassador to the OAS stated:

Today, a new concept of security is taking shape, going beyond states' territorial security and the defence of the classical principles of sovereignty ... Phenomena like the Cold War and ideological conflict do not justify a paradigm forged in the

post-World War II period ... Today organized crime has technological and financial resources that allow for actions that may put in jeopardy the systems for crime
prevention and repression, especially in countries of less relative development.[9]

The role of the armed forces in the region is still a factor to be considered
in reviewing the regional mechanisms for conflict prevention. While their
pre-eminent role in conflicts has been highly reduced after the dissipation
of Cold War tensions, they are still important actors. As noted, parts of
their budgets are growing, such as in Mexico, and their role is significant
in transitional periods after internal conflicts, as in Nicaragua.[10] Cooperation and mechanisms for conflict prevention have been established among
ministries of defence and armed forces in the region. As a result of the OAS
Declarations of Santiago and San Salvador on "Confidence and Security
Building Measures in the Americas" the General Assembly approved
resolutions 1409 (XXVI-0/96), 1494 (XXVII-0/97), and 1566 (XXVIII-
0/98), recommending that these countries adopt specific measures. Several agreements and cooperative actions have been put in operation in
fulfilling those mandates. Among them are:
• Gradual adoption of agreements regarding advanced notice of military
  exercises;
• Participation of all member states in the UN register of conventional
  arms and reporting of military expenditures;
• Exchange of information concerning defence policies and doctrines;
• Invitation of observers to military exercises, installations, and person-
  nel exchanges;
• Activities to prevent incidents and increase security for transport by
  land, sea, and air;
• Cooperation programmes in natural disasters and their prevention;
• Development of communications among civilian or military authorities
  of neighbouring countries;
• Seminars and courses on mutual confidence and security; and
• Development of a cooperation programme to address maritime trans-
  port of nuclear and other waste.
Many bilateral or multilateral activities take place within these goals. The
Inter-American Defence Board, an organ of the OAS, is an important
forum contributing to the development of these measures. The Inter-
American Defence College,[11] site of year-long courses for civilian and
military personnel of the member countries, is also an important arena
for exchanges on the reconceptualization of the role of the armed forces
and its constitutional responsibilities. One of the most significant technical gatherings is the Ministerial Meeting on Defence, where civilian and
military authorities from all member countries are invited to exchange
opinions and proposals about common interests and problems, and to

create a process of permanent interaction geared at cooperation. These ministerial meetings began in Williamsburg, Virginia, in 1996 and have been held regularly since.

Mechanisms for preserving democracy and constitutional regimes – General Assembly Resolutions 1080 and the "Washington Protocol"

Probably the most important mechanism for preventive diplomacy at the OAS is Resolution AG 1080 (XXI-0/91) adopted in Santiago de Chile in 1991. Already utilized in several cases, the resolution has undoubtedly played a preventive role in others. Resolution 1080 has been reinforced by the "Washington Protocol" to the OAS Charter, in force since 1999.[12] Like Resolution 1080 the Protocol calls for immediate action when democracy is threatened, but in this case the action is predetermined: when a member state becomes undemocratic ("breaches of power by illegal or undemocratic means") it can be suspended from the Organization.

Entering a period in which elected civilian governments had become virtually the norm throughout the Americas, coups in Haiti and Peru during 1991 and 1992 presaged difficult items for democracy and human rights. Coup attempts in Venezuela in 1992 and 1993,[13] the imposition of emergency measures and the suspension of liberties there in mid-1994, and the then recurrent hints of coups elsewhere in Latin America contributed to the sense of instability at the time (i.e. in February 1992 a group of officers threatened a coup in Honduras; later in 1992 rumours developed of a coup in Paraguay as it prepared for its first real presidential election since the fall of General Stroessner).

In 1991 the OAS adopted the "Santiago Commitment to Democracy and the Renewal of the Inter-American System." On 5 June 1991 the General Assembly approved a resolution entitled "Representative Democracy" that included a trigger mechanism for collective reaction to attempts to breach constitutional rule: as soon as possible the OAS Secretary-General must implement a process by which the OAS will respond within 10 days to any occurrences giving rise to the sudden or irregular interruption of the democratic political institutional process or of the legitimate exercise of power by the democratically elected government in any of the Organization's members states.[14] The same Commitment of Santiago called for the promotion of human rights through specific existing agencies, in a clear understanding that defence of human rights and defence of democratic and constitutional processes go together as ongoing mechanisms of conflict prevention (see below).

Resolution 1080 has been applied in situations in Peru, Guatemala, Haiti, and Paraguay. Secretary-General Gaviria noted that "in all these cases, Resolution 1080 has been shown to be broad enough to enable the nations of our Organization to examine the crisis and adopt a solution appropriate to the circumstances and the context of the situation." The Resolution 1080 mechanism has several advantages.

First, it defines clearly the situations that could activate its use, on the basis of objective criteria agreed upon, and free of the distorting effect of ideological decisions ("any circumstance giving rise to the sudden or irregular interruption of the democratic political institutional process or the legitimate exercise of power by the democratically elected government of any of the OAS member-states"). As the Secretary-General noted in reference to the Haitian case, "[using Resolution 1080] the inter-American system returned a president [Aristide] to office without regard for his political background, his ideas, or the standing of his country; solely because he had been removed by unlawful means."[15]

Second, additionally, Resolution 1080 gives the SG the immediate possibility to act either by examining the situation and bringing information to the Permanent Council or the Meeting of the Foreign Affairs Ministers, or by following specific recommendations of resolutions issued by one of these bodies. It allows for prompt action, as the Permanent Council is available to be convened in Washington within hours.

Third, a valuable condition for the use of this mechanism is that it does not interfere with parallel actions by other bodies or entities. On the contrary, it offers additional legal foundations to third parties' diplomatic actions. In the case of Paraguay, for instance, MERCOSUR[16] had its intervention facilitated by the previous agreement to react unanimously decided by the OAS. It is important for the OAS to maintain close communication with the relevant UN bodies in these cases to activate their complementary powers under Article 7 of the UN Charter, as was done in the Haitian case.

The Resolution 1080 mechanism operates through peaceful means of solution (persuasion, mediation, and good offices); economic sanctions can be recommended but their adoption are not mandatory under the OAS Charter. As shown by the Paraguayan case, additional pressures by relevant parties (in this case the Brazilian and Argentinean presidents on behalf of MERCOSUR) can coincide and complete the effect of regional pressure under Resolution 1080. On 11 September 2001, the Democratic Charter was approved unanimously by resolution of a Special General Assembly in Lima, reinforcing Resolution 1080. The Charter widens the options for activation of the intervention of the OAS: (a) "when the government of a member state considers that its democratic political institutional process or its legitimate exercise of power is at risk, it may request assistance from the Secretary General or the Permanent Council ..." (Art. 17); (b) "when situations arise in a member state that may affect the development of its democratic political institutional process or the legitimate exercise of power, the Secretary General or the Permanent Council may with prior consent of the government concerned, arrange for visits or other actions in order to analyze the situation (and report to the Permanent Council ... [that] where necessary, may adopt decisions for the preservation of the democratic system and its strenghtening." (Art. 18); (c) "In the event of an unconstitutional alteration of the constitutional regime that seriously impairs the democratic order in a member state, any member state or the Secretary General may request the immediate convocation of the Permanent Council to undertake a collective assessment of the situation and to take such decisions as it deems appropriate." (Art. 20).

The unconstitutional removal of the elected Haitian president in 1991

Just a few months after the approval of Resolution 1080 on 29 September 1991, a military coup that overthrew elected President Aristide of Haiti put the OAS resolve under test. An ad hoc meeting of the Permanent Council was called and met within 24 hours of the coup. The Permanent Council condemned the coup and convened an ad hoc meeting of Consultation of Ministers of Foreign Affairs on 3 October 1991. Days before, on 1 October, the Inter-American Commission on Human Rights had also issued a stern condemnation. Not too long after, a similar condemnation was pronounced by the UN General Assembly, but the Security Council met only informally, citing the "principle of non-interference in the internal affairs of Member States" and heard an appeal for assistance by Aristide.

The ministers' meeting at the OAS on October 3 agreed to recognise Aristide's government and its representatives as "the only legitimate representatives of the Government of Haiti." They also asked the IACHR "to take immediately all measures within its competence to protect and defend human rights in Haiti and to report thereon to the Permanent Council." They recommended: (a) suspension of all diplomatic relations with the military government; (b) an end to economic and military aid to Haiti; and (c) a break with all commercial ties.

The OAS Secretary-General was requested by the ministers to visit and inform Haiti's military rulers of the OAS's demand that they relinquish power. Facing their rejection to the request, the foreign ministers urged member countries to "freeze the assets of the Haitian State and to impose a trade embargo except for humanitarian aid." The request was quickly obliged by most member countries. Despite the apparently vigorous efforts and measures taken by the OAS members, after a year and a half and numerous initiatives the military rulers were still in charge. Only after the UN[17] imposed a worldwide embargo on June 1993 on oil and arms shipments to Haiti was an agreement reached for the reinstatement of President Aristide by 30 October 1993; still the military rulers decided not to uphold it. After a series of failed attempts to resolve the situation and parallel moves by the military regime to avoid Aristide's return as president, a Tripartite Agreement was achieved within Haiti by the military, parliament and other authorities, not including representatives of the Aristide supporters. The OAS foreign ministers immediately rejected the agreement. Both the UN General Assembly and the OAS condemned the sham parliamentary elections called by the military in January 1993.

In September 1992, 18 OAS "democracy monitors" were sent to Port au Prince, but confined in that city their action was ineffective. In February 1993 40 UN human rights monitors arrived in Haiti, but their effectiveness was also marginal. Former Foreign Minister of Argentina, Dante Caputo, was appointed as joint OAS-UN envoy, but his efforts at that point were not enough to reach a successful agreement to dislodge the military regime.

On 23 April 1993, a joint UN/OAS human rights monitoring force was approved. Only after a UN Security Council embargo on "petroleum or petroleum products or arms and related materials of all types" was imposed, did the Haitian military accept negotiations. Finally on 3 July 1993 an agreement (the Governors Island Agreement) was achieved by the joint envoy, and accepted by the military under the threat of the incoming invasion by a US-led military force. The Governors Island Agreement included measures to reinstate the power of President Aristide, removal of the major leaders of the coup from Haiti, and full amnesty for coup leaders and supporters. An international police force would be stationed in Haiti, and an international aid programme amounting to US$1 billion over five years would be instituted.[18]

The sending of international armed personnel was delayed and timidly enforced until the Haitian army prevented the USS Harlan County bringing 200 US troops and 25 Canadian military trainers from docking at Port au Prince, and international monitors were stopped at gunpoint in the city. New condemnations by the UN and OAS followed, and again they failed in getting the illegal regime to resign.

On 18 October 1993, the UN embargo took effect, with the support of the OAS. The US froze the assets of 41 individuals and 31 Haitian organizations, and imposed a ban of trade with Haiti, invoking the OAS embargo that (unlike the UN embargo) covered all trade, and not just oil and military goods. Deadlines passed and the Governors Island Agreement also failed to resolve the situation. All along the process, human rights violations were denounced against Aristide supporters or people the local police or paramilitaries considered "enemies." In March 1994, an increase in human rights violations was reported, as well as the use of rape as a weapon of political intimidation. On 4 May 1994, the Security Council imposed a full trade embargo on Haiti, effective 21 May, essentially converting the OAS embargo into a worldwide one.[19] It also banned non-scheduled airline flights and urged member states to freeze the assets of members of the Haitian military, and ordered all states not to grant entry visas to top military leaders and their civilian supporters.

On 7 June 1994 the OAS foreign ministers approved a resolution urging all members to ban commercial flights to and from Haiti, and all financial transactions with Haiti. As the member states imposed the ban, the military reacted, expelling the OAS/UN human rights observers from Haiti. Increased refugee outflow from Haiti trying to reach the coasts of the US in the thousands accelerated the pressure to reinstate the constitutional government. Finally, on 31 July 1994, the Security Council authorized military intervention by a multinational regional force.[20] The police mission to be sent to Haiti, originally created in September 1993, was increased from 1,200 members to 6,000. Under deteriorating conditions in terms of human rights abuses, and under the imminence of a military invasion by a multinational force led by the US, the military agreed to relinquish power to new US envoys.[21] The foreign military mission would enter Haiti "with the close cooperation" of the Haitian military and police, under "conditions of mutual respect." Amnesty was negotiated and granted, and sanctions were lifted. On 10 October 1994, General Cedras retired, leaving three days later for exile in Panama.

These Haitian events have shown the capacity of Resolution 1080 to activate inter-American action to restore constitutional rule, but also the complexities of that action and the need for additional support and actions.

The army was dissolved, and a new national police put in place to maintain order. Afterwards, the OAS continued its role in Haiti mainly through the good offices of the Deputy–Secretary–General Luigi Einaudi. The re-election of President Aristide in 2000 and a contested allocation of seats in the Assembly increased the confrontation between the Lavalas, the major national party and most other political and elite economic groups. International financial support and aid was suspended until an agreement is reached.

In this continuous confrontation, intensified by economic duress and violent incidents, the OAS intervention continues to play a restraining role, but has been unable to achieve a more or less permanent solution. Even the skilful mediation of veteran diplomat Einaudi and the suspension of the delivery of already assigned international aid are not sufficient to achieve a stable political solution, showing the limitations of this type of intervention when the parties involved are adamantly set in their positions. Still, at least the OAS intervention has been a major factor in avoiding a coup, and in keeping the violence from exploding into open civil war.

Peruvian President Fujimori's suspension of Articles of the Constitution

On 5 April 1992, President Fujimori, in the words of his Minister of Foreign Affairs, "was forced by the situation to take a dramatic and historic decision. He suspended several articles of the Constitution, ordered the reorganization of the Judicial System that had turned corrupt, as well as infiltrated by the narco-traffic. He also decided to reorganize the Tribunal of Constitutional Guarantees, the National Council of Judicial Magistrates and the Office of the General Controller of the Republic."[22] He installed a government of unity, emergency, and national reconstruction. He explained that terrorism (mainly the action of Sendero Luminoso), drug trafficking, institutionalized violence and poverty pushed him to take those actions, more concretely the dissolution of the Peruvian parliament and judiciary by the Executive Branch.

The OAS, which had just a year ago approved Resolution 1080, had to face the challenge to apply it for the second time in less than a year. The Secretary-General convoked immediately an ad hoc Meeting of the Ministers of Foreign Affairs. On 13 April 1992, the OAS foreign ministers strongly deplored what many observers called a "presidential self-coup (autogolpe)" and demanded that Peru show progress by 23 May (the date of the next General Assembly meeting) toward the restoration of democracy.[23] International condemnation had some effect: Fujimori soon released some detained opposition leaders and journalists, and the Peruvian media appeared to be operating without restraint a few weeks after the autogolpe. Pursuant to the Foreign Minister's resolution, the Inter-American Commission on Human Rights made two visits to Peru in May 1992.

In the same month, the OAS foreign ministers urged "the effective return of the representative democratic system [in Peru] as soon as possible, within the framework of respect of the principle of separation of powers and the rule of law, thus expediting the full reinstatement of international assistance and aid." Fujimori made a personal appearance at the OAS meeting, and promised to convene an elected constitutional assembly within months. The new constitution was prepared and issued by the Constitutional Assembly and approved by popular referendum on 31 October 1993.

The milder OAS diplomatic pressure on Peru may have helped persuade President Fujimori in 1992 to abandon plans for a plebiscite to legitimize his *autogolpe* and instead to hold OAS-monitored elections for a constituent assembly to draft a new constitution.

President Fujimori's regime under the umbrella of his anti-guerrilla war and with the support of the armed forces, continued strengthening its grip on all state institutions and the media. During this period the OAS Inter-American Commission on Human Rights (IACHR) issued several reports denouncing these actions as violations of Peru's international commitments in terms of human rights, but the political bodies of the OAS did not follow up on these reports. Moreover in 1999, the government of Peru decided to withdraw from the jurisdiction of the Inter-American Court on Human Rights, denying that those court decisions were binding and enforceable. Even facing this action – that the same court declared invalid and without effects – the political bodies remained practically silent. New general elections were due in 2000, and as usual the Peruvian government requested international observations by the OAS. Secretary-General Gaviria appointed, as Chief of the OAS Electoral Observation Mission, the former Guatemalan Foreign Affairs Minister Eduardo Stein, who had just hosted the OAS General Assembly in 1999.

After an indecisive first electoral round, Stein criticized the election because of serious irregularities that made the official results favouring Fujimori, at least doubtful and probably fraudulent. After unsuccessful and heated negotiations to improve the authenticity of the next electoral round, the OAS mission decided to leave the country because there were no conditions in place that would guarantee the respect of the free and legitimate expression of the popular will.

Despite the international signals of mistrust about the election, the National Electoral Council (Jurado Nacional de Elecciones) approved the results of the second round and declare Fujimori the winner in June 2000. The OAS General Assembly in July meeting in Windsor, Canada, decided to appoint a high-level mission to review the situation and to propose appropriate measures. Headed by Secretary Gaviria and the Canadian Foreign Minister Lloyd Axworthy this high-level delegation had contacts in Lima with government, opposition, and civic organizations, which resulted in the creation of a Round Table for Dialogue and Concert (Mesa de Dialogo y Concertacion).

Despite these negotiations and diplomatic pressure, President Fujimori was inaugurated with the support of the armed forces and the Supreme Court. Days after the inauguration, the publication of a video showing Fujimori and Vladimiro Montesinos, leader of the intelligence services, discussing the bribing of congressmen, provoked a final crisis. Additional attempts by Fujimori to retain power were unsuccessful, and finally he left the country, and his regime crumbled. A transitional regime constitutionally headed by Congress leader Valentin Paniagua called for new elections, again observed by an OAS electoral mission. In those elections then candidate and now President Alejandro Toledo won the majority vote.

Over the decade of Fujimori's presidency, there were clear weaknesses and hesitations in the OAS intervention in confronting the continuous and systematic thwarting of democracy and civil liberties by his regime. Originally when he dissolved Congress and put the judiciary under his own control by suspending judges and downgrading its stability, there was no clear resolution by the OAS Ad Hoc Meeting of Ministers of Foreign Affairs or the General Assembly condemning those actions and requesting full respect for the Peruvian Constitution.

When reports by the IACHR described the network of mechanisms that was increasingly violating human rights, including violations to the right to life, liberty, due process of law, right to privacy, and blatant breaches to freedom of expression, there were neither clear condemnations by the political bodies nor effective actions by the Secretary-General to try to revert those conditions.

Even when the Peruvian state refused formally to abide by a decision by the Inter-American Court on Human Rights and pretended to withdraw from its jurisdiction, the reaction of the Permanent Council was weak and conciliatory, merely requesting respect for international instruments and decisions of the court. It was only when Minister Eduardo Stein, chief of the electoral observation mission, took the courageous decision to leave the country and suspend the OAS electoral observation, that the OAS political bodies and its Secretary-General began to respond in a more effective and energetic way.

The importance of the personality and integrity of the chief of the OAS electoral observation missions is additionally underlined when we recall that the chief of the OAS mission to observe the 1995 election (in which Fujimori was re-elected) was Eduardo Gross Espiel, a Uruguayan jurist whose ties to the regime were denounced repeatedly and whose role as advisor to Chief Montesinos was confirmed by evidence surfacing after Fujimori's demise.

Guatemalan President Serrano's suspension of Articles of the Constitution

In 1986, Vinicio Cerezo became the first Guatemalan president in decades to be elected. He was succeeded by President Jorge Serrano Elias who, on

25 May 1993 suspended the constitution, dissolved the Guatemalan Congress and Supreme Court, and instituted rule by decree. He also detained several political figures and instituted censorship of the press and electronic media. He also promised to convene a Constitutional Assembly within two months. Both domestic and international repudiation of the coup ensued. The OAS condemned the coup two days later, on 25 May 1993, and called for immediate re-establishment of democratic institutions in Guatemala.[24] The Meeting of Foreign Ministers was convoked for 3 June, but on 1 June under internal pressure by a coalition of civilian leaders (including business leaders and human rights activists) Serrano was forced from office, and the Vice President, Espina Salguero, was to preside until Congress met, and then resign so that Congress could choose a new president. Vice President Salguero reneged from his agreement to resign.

On 3 June, the OAS foreign ministers met in Washington, D.C., convoked by the Permanent Council. They took no action, but sent the Secretary-General to Guatemala for a second report. The next day, the Constitutional Court, Guatemala's highest judicial body in matters relating to the Constitution, ruled Espina ineligible for the presidency on account of his support for Serrano's coup.[25] Following a procedure established constitutionally, on 6 June 1993 the Congress selected as new president the then-human rights ombudsman, Ramiro de Leon Carpio.

The unanimity of purpose shown by the OAS member states and the unequivocal and immediate message conveyed to the Serrano administration and other forces was that Guatemala would face political isolation and economic sanctions if constitutional rule remained disrupted.[26] The OAS and international pressure worked as rapidly as they did only because of the massive mobilization of Guatemalan civil society.

The Paraguayan crisis between the Executive and the Armed Forces Commander in-Chief, 1997

In 1996, the army commander, Major General Lino Cesar Oviedo, disobeyed orders from his Commander-in-Chief, President Juan Carlos Wasmosy, to step down, touching off a constitutional crisis from 22–25 April of that year. Oviedo was the commanding officer of a powerful mechanized regiment and had support among sectors of the military and among some political sectors, in particular the traditional Colorado Party, despite his crucial intervention to overthrow President Stroessner. Oviedo had already shown his interest in politics, and in becoming the Colorado national candidate for president he manoeuvred to prevent internal elections in that party, for fear of losing. Pressured by sectors of his own party and the opposition, President Wasmosy dismissed him, but decided to negotiate and arrange to name him Minister of Defence in exchange for his resignation from active duty and his post as army commander.

At that point, large segments of public opinion from the Colorado Party, students, and the press demonstrated against the agreement. President Wasmosy thus announced to the demonstrators that he had withdrawn his promise and had no intention of naming Oviedo as Minister of Defence.

Internal forces mobilized to avoid confrontation and to maintain constitutional order. Congress declared that a forced resignation (which Oviedo was trying to obtain from the president) is not a valid resignation. The political opposition carried that message to the rebellious commander in a private visit. It was delivered at noon on 23 April officially to the OAS in the hands of its Secretary-General.

Simultaneously, the ambassadors from MERCOSUR in Paraguay, following specific instructions by their presidents, who also played an active role at a distance, moved officiously to avert a breach of constitutional order. This coordinated action allowed the crisis to be averted. The prompt reaction of the international actors in concurrence with the swift political reaction inside Paraguay contributed significantly to the solution.

Secretary Gaviria explained later that from the moment the crisis began he was in touch all night with the Chairman of the Permanent Council; a meeting of the Council was called for the next morning, and hours after the initial event it was already adopting resolutions. It was decided to convoke a Meeting of Ministers of Foreign Affairs, but the quick solution to the crisis made it unnecessary. The reaction from MERCOSUR was an unprecedented intervention. Never had a regional economic and trade group come on to the domestic political stage of one of the member counties to ensure the continuity of the democratic system. Moreover, at the time, MERCOSUR lacked in its statutes the so-called "democratic clause" that was adopted two months after the Paraguayan crisis,[27] similar to the one formally embodied by the European Union in 1990 in its Charter of Paris.

This democratic clause may imply a collision between the democratic principle and the principle of non-intervention. Some voices have been raised noting that to avoid confusion in the future, it will be necessary to clarify the limits, forms, and requirements of such intervention.[28] Nevertheless, a former ambassador of the US to Paraguay interestingly remarked that,

[o]n the night of April 22 and 23 I had phone calls in the middle of the night from Paraguay reacting to old-fashioned threats in old-fashioned ways. They wanted to know what the Pentagon was going to do, what SOUTHCOM was going to do, where the helicopters were, and why, with our new cooperation on drugs, didn't a little SWAT team come down and do things the Cold War way.[29]

The presence of the OAS Secretary-General, the statements of the US government, and the support of MERCOSUR governments for constitutional order, overcame the resistance of the General (and his supporters) who abandoned his efforts and bowed to legitimate authority. In a similar case in Argentina, when the Carapintadas (a group of rebellious right wing army soldiers) attempted a coup against the constitutional order in Argentina in 1986, there are good reasons to believe that President Alfonsin made a secret agreement with some of the rebel forces to overcome the crisis. At the time, no official international network of solidarity reacted. As Domingo Laino, a well-known Paraguayan opposition figure noted,

[n]o such thing happened [in this Paraguayan crisis]. When the crisis may be said to have been at its peak, on the 23rd Mr. Gaviria showed up in my country and had lunch with us, together with members of the executive branch. During the actual military events of April, there appeared for the first time an international network of democratic solidarity.[30]

The "good offices" of the Permanent Council and the Secretary-General of the OAS

Prior to and beyond Resolution 1080 and the Washington Protocol to the OAS Charter, the Permanent Council and the Secretary-General had the mandate to monitor and assist in the peaceful settlement of disputes and in the maintenance of friendly relations among member states (OAS Charter Articles 84 to 89 for the Permanent Council and Articles 110 to 112 for the Secretary-General).

Article 85 states that "any party to a dispute in which none of the peaceful procedures provided for in the Charter is under way may resort to the Permanent Council to obtain its good offices. The Council, following the provisions of the preceding article, shall assist the parties and recommend the procedures it considers suitable for peaceful settlement of the dispute." The Permanent Council "may also, by such means as it deems advisable, investigate the facts in the dispute, and may do so in the territory of any of the parties, with the consent of the Government concerned" (Art. 87). "In case the procedure under the Permanent Council is not successful, it shall inform the General Assembly."

The "good offices" of the Permanent Council can be delegated in the Secretary-General, who additionally can "bring to the attention of the General Assembly or the Permanent Council any matter which in his opinion might threaten the peace and security of the Hemisphere or the development of the Member States" (Art. 110). The "good offices" of the

OAS Secretary-General are expressed in other roles, such as when he served as "witness of honour" to the technical talks over a boundary dispute between Belize and Guatemala in March 2000.

These "good offices" were put in operation in the Paraguayan case analysed above. They were also the legal and political framework for the Secretary-General's action during the two governmental crises in Ecuador, resulting in the replacement of President Bucaram in 1996 and President Mauad in 2000. In both cases, the Secretary-General, in close cooperation with the Permanent Council, was present in Ecuador and held consultations with members of the three constitutional powers. Under the same "good offices" mandate, the Secretary-General was an important actor in the resolution of electoral disputes between the two major candidates for the 1996 election in Peru, President Fujimori and former UN Secretary-General Perez de Cuellar.

The "good offices of the SG" and the Dominican Republic electoral conflict in 1994

While Resolution 1080 was ready in relation to the electoral conflict in the Dominican Republic in 1994, it was not used. A special envoy of the Secretary-General was sent and was able to achieve an agreement for constitutional continuity, which avoided a possibly violent confrontation.

In 1994 the government of President Balaguer invited the OAS to observe the coming elections. The opposition party had repeatedly accused the government of rigging the elections. Chances were that, as in the past, an unclear or irregular process could lead to overt clashes and social unrest, if not explosion, due to the class and racial undertones of the electoral confrontation. In fact, days before the elections, Secretary-General Baena Soares called attention to the climate of violence and the importance of allegiance by all to the Civility Pact signed by all parties on 14 May. Along with other international observers, 27 OAS observers monitored the election of 16 May. Right after the election, the OAS team indicated in its report that irregularities had been found in the electoral lists.[31] The communiqué went on to acknowledge the importance for the committee to follow up on the Civility Pact agreed upon by the different parties. Tensions grew during the counting and analysis of electoral irregularities.

As a result of a meeting between the director of the OAS mission, Ambassador John Graham, and President Balaguer, the latter accepted that a Verification Commission would monitor the counting. As the results showed, the difference (0.7 per cent of the votes registered) that had apparently re-elected President Balaguer, could very well have resulted from vote-counting irregularities – basically through significant disenfranchisement of voters in several areas, where voters were turned away because their names did not appear on the voter registration lists.[32]

On 2 August 1994 the electoral authorities proclaimed President Balaguer the winner of the presidential elections, despite the irregularities. The OAS immediately issued a press release expressing concern that the release of these results, without mention of the findings of the Verification Commission's report (that explained the irregularities and their crucial influence on the results) had raised tensions and he offered his good offices to seek a solution that would be satisfactory to all parties. Under the impending sessions of Congress to ratify the results (set for 11 August) and growing tension among the population, President Balaguer requested on 6 August that the OAS mission act as a facilitator of a meeting between his party and the opposition alliance. As a result of those meetings an agreement called "Pact for Democracy" was signed on 10 August, which reduced tensions and allowed for the continuity of the constitutional process. The signatories to the Pact for Democracy included all political parties, authorities of the major universities, churches, media, business, and labour organizations, and other civil organizations. The pact included the acceptance of the results as established by the electoral authorities by all parties; an agreement to reform the constitution so as to limit the next presidential period to two years (instead of four), to hold new presidential elections in 1996, inhibiting the re-election of the president and the vice president in two consecutive periods; and to establish a two-round electoral system in case the winning candidate did not reach more than half of the votes in the first round. It also agreed to reform the judicial system, the system to prepare the electoral lists, and to elect the electoral authorities with representation from different political parties. An agreement was also reached by the elected government to cooperate in its administration with the main political forces in the country.

A constitutional crisis had been averted, society accepted the agreement, and because constitutional continuity had not been breached it was not necessary to activate the mechanism of Resolution 1080. Nevertheless, the possibility of involving Resolution 1080 was present, when OAS Ambassador Graham met with the president and other parties to facilitate a solution.

The Unit for the Promotion of Democracy

This relatively new unit of the General Secretariat of the OAS has grown to be a very significant player in conflict prevention in the region. Its activities include projects in conflict prevention education and promotion, electoral observation, studies and proposals for conflict prevention and resolution in specific conflicts (e.g. the situation of Maroons in Suriname; the territorial and oil exploration dispute between the Colombian state and the Uwas indigenous peoples.)

The inter-American system of human rights

Juridically based in the American Declaration on the Rights and Duties of Man, and the American Declaration on Human Rights, the principal organs of this system are the Inter-American Commission on and the Inter-American Court of Human Rights, headquartered respectively in Washington, D.C. and San Jose de Costa Rica. While the processing of complaints about individual violations of human rights is the main function of both organs, the Commission mandate includes making specific recommendations to the member countries in favour of human rights and for their respect; as well as preparing and publishing reports on special situations threatening or violating human rights in all member states; and to request governments to take precautionary measures to prevent imminent and serious violations of human rights.

Numerous non-governmental institutions participate in the work of the system, by bringing petitions, providing information, requesting immediate precautionary measures and raising the visibility of violations of human rights, as well as frictions or dangers that threaten them. Numerous governmental institutions (including the judiciary, the public prosecutors, the ombudsmen and the government commissions on human rights) also play an active role in the system. The situations addressed by the system included attacks on civilian populations by armed forces or police; lack of due process and inadequacy of the judiciary to provide guarantees about violations to human rights; cases of discrimination for reason of race, gender, or other nature; the defence of the rights of indigenous peoples; electoral cases due to fraud, irregularities, and illegal prohibitions or obstacles to political participation; or asylum rights for individuals or groups of people. This is a mere list of their important role in the context of regional conflict prevention strategies.

But these human rights violations are not usually individual failures of the state apparatus in respecting and defending human rights. In many cases, they are part of an encompassing attempt to erode civil liberties and the rule of law, as well as democracy. Either stemming from a systematic plan of the central authorities (as in the military governments of several South American countries in the sixties and seventies), or by encroaching sectors of the security forces coalescing with political groups against democratic governments; or even by defiance of provincial semi-feudal authorities against central governments, these violations can be part of a systematic pattern affecting a whole country or region.

The IACHR in administering its mandate gives especial attention to these situations of systematic violations of human rights. By issuing special country reports, or including them in a particular chapter of its annual report to the General Assembly, by special in-situ visits and press conferences, and even confidentially by visits and communications with the specific authorities, the IACHR tries to call attention to and to reverse these patterns.

The delegations to the OAS political bodies are usually reluctant to mobilize the power of those bodies to reverse patterns of violation, being more attentive to the principle of non-intervention than to the full enjoyment of human rights and to the international commitments of the countries in that realm. Evidence of this is shown by the almost absolute lack of specific condemnations of countries by name both in the General Assembly resolutions about human rights, or in specific resolutions addressing systematic human rights violations in a particular country. This lack of response is especially inadequate given the fact that the human rights system in general and the inter-American one in particular are especially valuable early-warning mechanisms about failures in the rule of law and democratic process, and therefore for conflict prevention.

The inter-American human rights system provides in the Americas a major contribution in terms of conflict prevention. Among its contributions to conflict prevention are:
- The treatment of cases channelled through an international judicial process on failures of local authorities to legally solve violations, which unsolved become the source of conflicts;
- The international regime pressure on domestic authorities not to condone or to be lax before violations of human rights;
- The participation of local non-governmental institutions in this regime reinforces them and their leaders, increasing their effectiveness in obtaining legal and peaceful solutions to potentially conflict-detonating situations;
- It establishes an early warning system at the international level about situations usually hidden from the public view or outside the normal reach of the media;
- It allows the assessment of the calibre of local organizations capable of participating in conflict prevention. It also allows understanding of the leadership and specific organizational behaviour of sectors of the population that can become potential actors in conflicts;

- It permits the establishment of clear and legal standards for the behaviour of state agents, and for the duties and restrictions allowed by international standards in situations of conflicts or emergencies;
- It maintains a permanent, credible, and agile mechanism for promoting and mediating "friendly solutions" among the state and civilian actors or sectors;
- It motivates and supports central state authorities trying to intervene in conflict prevention and tension reduction by legal means in volatile but autonomous provinces;
- It maintains credible international institutions able to intervene and diffuse potential conflicts by balancing reporting of responsibilities and by their ability to recommend legal solutions; and
- It establishes a system of rewards and negative retributions to governments, depending on their ability to prevent or punish human rights violations by their agents, whose existence and impunity may generate further conflict.

It is not possible here to try to judge successes and weaknesses of the inter-American human rights system as such, but only in reference to its role as a mechanism for conflict prevention. Specific examples will shed light on its degree of effectiveness in this role:

- In Guatemala in 1995, more than several thousand indigenous peoples, organized as Communities of Population in Resistance, were confronting the army in the last stages of the civil war, demanding full recognition of their rights, their lands, and demilitarization of their areas. A visit and report by the IACHR was instrumental in minimizing open conflict, setting up a framework for agreement, and in several actions by the state that normalized the situation, pacified the area, and allowed for the orderly reinstatement of their rights.
- In Brazil, in the South of Para, growing tensions flared continuously so that the irregular bands armed by big ranch-owners confronted rural workers and their unions. The intervention of the IACHR making the issue visible at the international level, supported and gave additional strength to the action of Brazilian federal authorities and the local judiciary to reduce that serious source of violent confrontation and violation of basic human rights.
- In Bolivia, the IACHR was called by the government to make an immediate visit to a mining area where confrontations between Bolivian armed forces and organized miners had produced violent incidents that could escalate to major violence and political conflict. In three months the IACHR was able to visit the area and to issue a report that assigned responsibilities in an impartial way, providing the basis and space for the judiciary and the political system to carry out their duties in the matter.

- The harassment of people of Haitian origin or ancestry in the Dominican Republic has been a source of conflict between the two countries, and of course of exploitation and violation of the rights of these migrant workers and their families. The IACHR has intervened on several occasions denouncing these atrocities and calling publicly for redress of this difficult issue. While temporary relief has been achieved, and the problem as a whole has substantially reduced in these last years, still the IACHR was not able to make the political bodies of the OAS fully address this permanent source of conflict.
- On many occasions, the IACHR has requested and obtained the inclusion of candidates illegally banned from electoral contests, or inversely upheld constitutional provisions banning from major elective offices the candidacies of individuals who had been leaders of illegal regimes or coups. Its decisions and the prestige of its message released tension and allowed the confrontation to be peacefully resolved.
- The swift action of the IACHR Rapporteurship on Freedom of Expression (created in 1998) denouncing attempts in different countries to thwart the independence of the press and media in general, has energized international condemnation of those attempts and reduced potential internal conflicts that suppression of those independent voices could have provoked.

This is just a small sample of cases where the action of the inter-American system of human rights may have prevented major conflict. While the value of those achievements must be fully acknowledged and the agility and reach of the system has significantly increased in the last decade, there are weaknesses that have not been fully addessed. Insufficiency of human and material resources to respond to the different challenges to human rights in all countries of the region efficiently has been one weakness that the system still has to face. However, the reluctance of the OAS political bodies to assume and respond with their own political strength to the denunciations by the IACHR is probably the major obstacle to the full use of its value as a conflict prevention mechanism.

Conclusions

The Organization of American States has a system of organs and entities that can play a significant role in preventing or reducing conflict in the Americas. In the 1990s, with a growing regional push towards constitutionalism and rule of law, the system has been strengthened. It remains however timid and restrained by its need to reach consensus among 34 member countries with complex and contradictory relations with each other.[33] International frictions, boundary disputes, confrontations emerging from electoral processes, attempts to breach democratic rule, coup d'état attempts, and eventual social explosions as a consequence of systematic human rights violations, are some of the areas of conflict confronted and in many cases, solved. In general, the OAS works towards maintaining respect for democracy, human rights, and national sovereignty.

A review of results shows more successes than commonly known and credited, but also many opportunities lost. In comparison with other regions, a certain tradition of international action has been more predominant in the Americas in the last decades, but not systematic and assertive enough. On many occasions, inaction or timid action under the guise of respect for the principles of non-intervention, sovereignty, or just because of the complexity of the situation or the cross interests involved, has prevailed. The valid goal and pattern of decision by consensus has undoubtedly maintained the cohesion of the system, but has also lowered the firmness of its ideal leadership.

The strength of the OAS as a conflict prevention system is based on the simultaneous actions of its different organs: continuous monitoring and denunciations by the human rights system; coupled with growing commitments, harmonization and inter-American supervision about armaments and actions of the armed forces; plus the new "quick reaction" mechanisms for preserving democracy (Resolution 1080 and the Washington Declaration) act together in avoiding conflict escalation and eruption.

There has been a transformation of the principle of non-intervention, from a rigid formalistic conception towards a new balance with other inter-American principles, among them, the respect for human rights, democratic process, and the need for transparency in national actions dealing with areas of international friction (including boundary conflicts, armaments, drug traffic, or money laundering). The growing international impact of national decisions in those areas has helped to develop new agreements to reduce conflicts that tend to originate along those threats.

The human rights system in the Americas (the network created by national judicial systems, NGOs, and the Inter-American Human Rights Commission and the court) have proved to be a preventive early warning system, that can detect, expose, and, in many instances, dissolve or resolve areas of potential conflict. Its flexibility, autonomy, credibility, and ability to cut through different layers of bureaucracy and social tissue in the most diverse situations give the inter-American human rights system a major role in conflict prevention in the Americas.

Notes

1. The OAS Secretary-General outlined one century of conflicts in the Americas saying that "[e]xcept for the 'Guerra del Chaco' between Bolivia and Paraguay in 1932, and the

Malvinas war in 1982, more than inter-country conflicts, it should be called tensions and incidents between countries and internal conflicts. That is the case of incidents between Colombia and Peru in 1932, El Salvador and Honduras in 1969, of the internal conflicts during the eighties in El Salvador and Nicaragua; the one in Guatemala ended in 1997, the civil war in Argentina and Chile (from 1977 to 1984). Suriname at the early nineties; the internal conflicts still alive in Colombia and somehow in Peru; and more recently in 1995, the incident between Ecuador and Peru." For a more detailed listing of tensions and incidents see Jacob Bercovitch and Robert Jackson, "International Conflict. A Chronological Encyclopedia of Conflicts and their Management 1945–1995," *Congressional Quarterly Inc.*, Washington, D.C., that lists 36 conflicts in that period, including among others the US interventions in the Dominican Republic (1965) Granada (1983) and Panama (1989) and Cuba (1961) and the Cuban sponsored invasions to Haiti, Dominican Republic (1959), Panama (1958), and Venezuela (1967), as well as the incidents between Argentina and Chile (from 1977 to 1984).

2. Of course, there are other disputes remaining, e.g. Bolivia claims from Chile its rights to access to the Pacific; Argentina and the United Kingdom have frozen their differences over sovereignty on the Malvinas (Falkland) Islands while they negotiate other arrangements; Colombia and Venezuela have still unresolved issues over boundaries in the Caribbean sea. Many other boundary problems have been solved with external intervention, like the ones between Argentina and Chile over the Beagle Channel, or by bilateral agreements, like the ones Argentina had with Brazil about its northern border, and with Chile over Andean demarcation lines.

3. Connie Peck, "Strengthening Cooperative Approaches to Conflict Prevention: The Role of the United Nations and Regional Organizations," in Final Report Seminar, IDRC, 11–13 March 1998, Ottawa, Canada.

4. *Ibid.*, p. 4.

5. Ronald Scheman, *The Inter-American Dilemma*, New York: Praeger 1988, p. 51.

6. These principles have also been permanently sustained to maintain a balanced relation between the United States and its regional neighbours, both in general and in the inter-American bodies.

7. This list does not pretend to be exhaustive. In fact, it is possible to assert the potential for conflict prevention of the new multilateral mechanism for certification of the cooperation of the member states in the fight against drug traffic, developed under the CICAD (Inter-American Commission for Drug Abuse Control).

8. AG RES 1179/XX O-92, Cooperation for Hemispheric Security and Development: Regional Contributions to Global Security. This and other OAS documents can be retrieved from the OAS website at www.oas.org.

9. Chewning Fabrega, Panamanian representative to the OAS at the Democratic Forum on Paraguay, Washington D.C., 1997.

10. Riordan Roett, presentation at the Democratic Forum on Paraguay, OAS, Washington D.C., 1997.

11. This college, associated with the Inter-American Defense Board, is not to be confused with the "School of the Americas," associated with the US Army South Command.

12. The Washington Protocol was ratified in 1997 by two-thirds of member countries, the required number to amend the Charter, showing the strong support it obtained, and the new balance between the principles of "non-intervention" and "democracy." As the Ambassador from Panama said, "Before the Washington Protocol and Resolution 1080, the OAS was an inert OAS, where Ambassadors from democratic governments and from dictatorial regimes sat elbow to elbow." He reminded that during the Noriega regime in Panama, the OAS was ineffective in dealing with "the agony of the Panamanian people" and of all resolutions passed not one condemned General Noriega, or even named him.

13. The OAS condemned the coup (see Support for the Democratic Government of Venezuela, Permanent Council Resolution 576 (887/92) and General Assembly resolution, A.G. Resolution 2906/92) and sent the Chairman of the Permanent Council and the Secretary General to Venezuela after the coup attempt was put down. In November 1992, a second and more bloody coup attempt occurred in Venezuela. "It was notable for its failure to gain popular support, in contrast with the first." See Stephen Schnably, "The Santiago Commitment as a Call to Democracy in the United States: Evaluating the OAS Role in Haiti, Peru, and Guatemala," *The University of Miami Inter-American Law Review*, Vol. 25, No. 3, 1994, pp. 395–585.

14. Representative Democracy, A.G. Resolution 1080 (XXI-0/91).

15. Speech at the Tokyo International Conference on Preventive Strategy, 1997, p. 4.

16. MERCOSUR is a sub-regional agreement between Argentina, Brazil, Paraguay, and Uruguay.

17. The OAS Permanent Council on 10 November 1992 had urged the UN to become involved in OAS efforts to find a solution, see Resolution CP/Resolution 594, 923/92, and two weeks later the UN General Assembly approved a result directing the UN Secretary General to "take necessary measures in order to assist, in cooperation with the Organization of American States, in the solution of the Haitian crisis" (G.A. Resolution 47/20 UN GAOR, 47ty. Sess., UNDoc. A/RES/47/20 (1992).

18. For a well-documented and detailed analysis of the Haiti case see Schnably, note 13 above, pp. 418–60.

19. SC Resolution 917, UN SCOR, 3376 mtg.

20. SC Resolution 940, UN SCOR, 3413 mtg., para. 4.

21. President Clinton had requested former President Jimmy Carter, Senator Sam Nunn, and General Colin Powell to negotiate with the Haitian military.

22. Speech by Minister Arturo Blacker Miller to the Ad Hoc Meeting of the Ministers of Foreign Affairs of the OAS, 13 April 1992, OEA/Ser.F/V.2 MRE/Acta 1/92.

23. Support for the Restoration of Democracy in Peru, M.R.E. Resolution 1/92 OAS Ad Hoc Meeting of Ministers of Foreign Affairs, OEA/Ser.F/.V.2. Days before the OAS resolution, the US had suspended aid to Peru, and indicated that it would oppose any further loans from the World Bank, the Inter-American Development Bank, and the International Monetary Fund.

24. The situation in Guatemala, CP Resolution 605 (945/93) OAS Permanent Council.

25. See Schnably, "The Santiago Commitment as a Call to Democracy in the United States," note 13 above, p. 474. Art. 186a of the Guatemalan Constitution prohibits individuals that are leaders or the main supporters of a coup from running for the presidency.

26. Francisco Villagrán de León, "Thwarting the Guatemalan Coup," *Journal of Democracy*, Vol. 4., No. 4, 1993, p. 124.

27. The democratic clause states "the full effectiveness of democratic institutions is an essential condition for cooperation" and that "any disturbance of the democratic order constitutes an unacceptable obstacle to the continuity of the integration process." The sanctions provided for can include the suspension of agreements signed in the MERCOSUR framework. The Protocol signed in San Luis, Argentina, was also signed by the Presidents of Bolivia and Chile, countries interested in joining MERCOSUR; and this protocol includes not only agreements within MERCOSUR but also bilateral relations with its four founders Argentina, Brazil, Paraguay, and Uruguay. The importance of these agreements cannot be dismissed, intrazonal trade increased fourfold in less than five years, and its impact has reached areas of social policy, education, public health, and judicial cooperation.

28. Intervention of A. Mercader, Permanent Representative of Uruguay to the OAS, *Democratic Forum on Paraguay*, Washington D.C., 1997.

29. Timothy Towell, Intervention at the Democratic Forum on Paraguay, OAS, Washington D.C., 1997.
30. Speech at the Democratic Forum on Paraguay, 1997, Washington D.C., OAS.
31. OAS Electoral Mission, Preliminary Report, 18 May 1994.
32. As the Report of the Assistant Secretary-General indicated, those names appeared in the official lists that were given to the political parties before the elections. Moreover most political parties' poll watchers noted in response to inquiries by the OAS observers, that the majority of the voters turned away were supporters of the opposition party, OAS/Ser.G.CP/INF.3652/94, p. 3.
33. While this chapter was being reviewed, the irregular elections in Peru that allowed the Fujimori regime to stay in power showed the ambivalence of the countries to use the OAS mechanisms fully to disavow clearly fraudulent elections, in this case capping a series of infringements by the government of the Peruvian constitution and its international agreements. The OAS decided not to use the mechanisms of Resolution 1080 or to challenge elections that were deemed unacceptable by its own observer mission, and instead to send a high level delegation to negotiate with the Peruvian government measures towards future democratization and increased respect for the rule of law. The US, originally one of the more forceful complainants about this electoral fraud, withdraw its proposal to use Resolution 1080 when it did not get support from most governments. Critics maintained that this quick softening of the position was due to the collaboration Peru gave to the fight against international drug trafficking. Similar ambivalence influenced other countries' decisions.

Acronyms and abbreviations

ACC	Administrative Committee on Coordination
ACRI	African Crisis Response Initiative
APC	Armored Personnel Carrier
ASEAN	Association of South East Asian Nations
ASNDRM	African Symposium on Natural Disaster Reduction and Management
CAR	Central African Republic
CAR	Central Asian Republic
CARICOM	Caribbean Community and Common Market
CESDP	Common European Security and Defence Policy
CEWARN	Conflict Early Warning and Response Mechanism
CEWS	Conflict Early Warning System
CFSP	Common Foreign and Security Policy
CICAD	Inter-American Commission for Drug Abuse Control
CIFP	Country Indicators for Foreign Policy
CiO	Chairman in Office
CIPDD	Caucasian Institute for Peace, Democracy and Development
CIS	Commonwealth of Independent States
CIVPOL	Civilian Police
CJTF	Combined Joint Task Force
CP	Communist Party
CPMR	Conflict Prevention, Management and Resolution
CSBM	Confidence and Security Building Measure
CSCE	Conference on Security and Cooperation in Europe
CSO	Council of Senior Officials
CTEU	Consolidated Version of the Treaty on European Union

DDA	Department for Disarmament Affairs
DESA	Department of Economic and Social Affairs
DFAIT	Canadian Department of Foreign Affairs and International Trade
DPA	Department of Political Affairs
DPKO	Department of Peacekeeping Operations
DRC	Democratic Republic of Congo
EAPC	Euro-Atlantic Parnership Council
EBRD	European Bank for Reconstruction and Development
ECHA	Executive Committee on Humanitarian Affairs
ECMM	European Community Monitoring Mission
ECOMOG	Economic Community of West African States Cease-fire Monitoring Group
ECOWAS	Economic Community of West African States
ECPS	Executive Committee on Peace and Security
EIB	European Investment Bank
EISAS	Executive Committee on Peace and Security Information and Strategic Analysis Secretariat
EOSG	Executive Office of the Secretary-General
EPC	European Political Cooperation
ESDI	European Security and Defence Identity
EWPM	Early Warning and Preventive Measures
EWS	Early Warning System
FAFO	Forskningsstiftelsen Fafo (Fafo: Institute for Applied Social Science)
FAO	Food and Agricultural Organization
FAST	Early Recognition of Tension and Fact-finding
FEWER	Forum on Early Warning and Early Response
FIRST	Facts on International Relations and Security Trends
FMLN	Farabundo Marti National Liberation Front
FRY	Federal Republic of Yugoslavia
FUNCINPEC	National United Front for an Independent, Neutral, Peaceful, and Cooperative Cambodia
FYROM	Former Yugoslav Republic of Macedonia
GEDS	Global Event Data System
GIEWS	Global Information and Early Warning System
HCNM	High Commissioner on National Minorities
HEWS	Humanitarian Early Warning System
IACHR	Inter-American Commission on Human Rights
IBRD	International Bank for Reconstruction and Development
ICB	International Crisis Behaviour
ICFY	International Conference on the Former Yugoslavia
ICG	International Crisis Group
ICJ	International Court of Justice
IDP	Internally Displaced Person
IDRC	International Development Research Council
IEBL	Inter-Entity Boundary Line
IFI	International Financial Institution
IFOR	[NATO] Implementation Force

IGAD	Inter-Governmental Authority on Development
ILO	International Labour Organization
IMF	International Monetary Fund
IOM	International Organization for Migration
IPA	International Peace Academy
IPTF	International Police Task Force
ISS	Institute of Security Studies
JMC	Joint Military Commission
JNA	Yugoslav National Army
KLA	Kosovo Liberation Army
KVM	Kosovo Verification Mission
LDC	Less Developed Country
LDK	Democratic League of Kosovo
MAP	Membership Action Plan
MAPE	Military Advisory Police Element
MCC	Military Coordination Committee
MCDA	Military, Civil Defence and Civil Protection Assets
MCPMR	Mechanism for Conflict Prevention, Management and Resolution
MERCOSUR	Southern Cone Common Market
MONUC	UN Mission in the Democratic Republic of Congo
NAC	North Atlantic Council
NATO	North Atlantic Treaty Organization
NEPAD	New Partnership for Africa's Development
NGO	Non-governmental Organization
NMOG	Neutral Military Observer Group
NORDBAT	Nordic Battalion
NPFL	National Patriotic Front of Liberia
OAS	Organization of American States
OAU	Organization of African Unity
OCHA	Office for the Coordination of Humanitarian Affairs
ODIHR	Office of Democratic Institutions and Human Rights
OLMEE	OAU Liaison Officer in Ethiopia and Eritrea
OMIB	OAU Observer Mission
OMRI	Open Media Research Institute
ONUCA	UN Observer Group in Central America
ONUSAL	UN Observer Mission in El Salvador
ORCI	Office for Research and Collection of Information
OSCE	Organization for Security and Co-operation in Europe
PANDA	Protocol for the Assessment of Nonviolent Direct Action
PCIA	Peace and Conflict Impact Assessment
PCPB	Post-conflict Peacebuilding
PESC	La politique étrangère et la sécurité
PfP	Partnership for Peace
PIOOM	Interdisciplinary Research Programme on Root Causes of Human Rights Violations
PPEWU	Policy Planning and Early Warning Unit
PRK	People's Republic of Kambuchea
RGA	Rwandese Government Army

RPF	Rwandese Patriotic Front
RUF	Revolutionary United Front [Sierra Leone]
SAA	Stabilization Association Agreement
SADC	South African Development Council
SECI	Southeast European Cooperative Initiative
SFOR	[NATO] Stabilization Force
SMC	Standing Mediation Committee
SNC	Supreme National Council [Cambodia]
SRSG	Special Representative of the Secretary-General
TACIS	Techical Assistance to the Community of Independent States
UNAMIR	UN Assistance Mission for Rwanda
UNAMSIL	UN Mission in Sierra Leone
UNDP	UN Development Programme
UNEP	UN Environment Programme
UNFPA	UN Population Fund
UNHCHR	UN High Commissioner for Human Rights
UNHCR	UN High Commissioner for Refugees
UNICEF	UN Children's Fund
UNITA	Union for the Total Independence of Angola
UNMEE	UN Mission to Ethiopia and Eritrea
UNMIBH	UN Mission in Bosnia and Herzegovina
UNMIK	UN Interim Administration Mission in Kosovo
UNMO	UN Military Observer
UNOMIL	UN Observer Mission in Liberia
UNOMSIL	UN Observer Mission in Sierra Leone
UNPF	UN Protection Force
UNPREDEP	UN Preventive Deployment Force
UNPROFOR	UN Protection Force
UNSC	UN Staff College
UNSCOB	UN Special Commission on the Balkans
UNSF	UN Security Force
UNSG	UN Secretary-General
UNSRSG	UN Special Representative of the Secretary-General
UNTAC	UN Transitional Authority for Cambodia
UNTAES	UN Transitional Authority in Eastern Slavonia, Baranja and Western Sirmium
UNTAG	UN Transition Assistance Group
UNTEA	UN Transitional Executive Authority
WEU	Western European Union
WFP	World Food Programme
WHO	World Health Organization
WMO	World Meteorological Organization

Contributors

David **Carment** is an Associate
Professor of International Affairs
and teaches conflict analysis,
conflict mediation, international
organization, conflict resolution
and development at the Norman
Paterson School of International
Affairs, Carleton University, Ottawa.
In 2000–01, he was a Fellow with
the International Security Program
in the World Peace Foundation
Program on Conflict Prevention at
the Belfer Center, Harvard University. He was educated at McMaster
University, Carleton University, and
McGill University, where he received
his Ph.D. (Political Science) in 1994.
He was a lecturer at McGill and a
post-doctoral fellow at the Hoover
Institution, Stanford University.
His research interests include the
international dimensions of ethnic
conflict, the role of communication
technologies in conflict analysis
and resolution, early warning,

peacekeeping, conflict prevention
and peacebuilding. Recent articles
focusing on these subjects have
appeared in the *Journal of Conflict
Resolution, Journal of Peace
Research, International Politics,
Global Society, Third World
Quarterly*, and *Canadian Foreign
Policy*. His most recent books are
*Using Force to Prevent Ethnic
Violence* (with Frank Harvey, 2000),
*The International Politics of Quebec
Secession* (co-editor with Frank
Harvey and John Stack, 2001),
*Peace in the Midst of Wars:
Preventing and Managing
International Ethnic Conflicts* (co-
editor with Patrick James, 1998),
and *Wars in the Midst of Peace: The
International Politics of Ethnic
Conflict* (co-editor with Patrick
James, 1997).

John G. Cockell is currently a
Research Associate with the

Conflict Analysis and Development Unit (CADU) of the London School of Economics, and Technical Advisor on EWS for the UNDP Office in Kosovo. In 2000–01, he served as Political Affairs Officer with the United Nations Interim Administration Mission in Kosovo (UNMIK), where he managed democratization and political development programs. In 1998–99, he was a member of the design team for the Early Warning and Preventive Measures (EWPM) joint project of the UN Department of Political Affairs and the UN Staff College. In 1995–97, he worked as a policy advisor on conflict prevention for the Department of Foreign Affairs and International Trade Canada, and for the Canadian International Development Agency. Recent publications include "Human Security and Preventive Action Strategies," in Edward Newman and Oliver Richmond, eds., *The United Nations and Human Security: Beyond Peacekeeping*? (Palgrave/Macmillan, 2001); "Conceptualizing Peacebuilding: Human Security and Sustainable Peace," in Michael Pugh, ed., *Regeneration of War-Torn Societies* (Macmillan, 2000); and "Toward Response-Oriented Early Warning Analysis," in John L. Davies and Ted Robert Gurr, eds., *Preventive Measures: Building Risk Assessment and Crisis Early Warning Systems* (MD: Rowman and Littlefield, 1998).

Rasheed Draman is currently a Ph.D. candidate in Political Science at Carleton University, Ottawa, Canada. His research addresses early warning, conflict prevention, and public policy analysis. He is actively involved in research at the Security Defence Forum (SDF) at the Center for Security and Defence Studies, Norman Paterson School of International Affairs. He has presented his research at many academic forums including the 41st and 42nd International Studies Association Annual Conventions and at the Carleton University Mediation Center 9th Annual Symposium. His teaching experience includes a stint at the Harvard University Extension School, Cambridge, Massachusetts in November 2000; and as sessional lecturer on Politics of War in Africa at the Department of Political Science, Carleton University in winter, 2001. He has an MA in International Relations from the International University of Japan, Niigata, Japan.

Simon Duke gained his B.Sc. (Econ) from the University College of Wales, Aberystwyth and his M.Phil and D.Phil from Oxford University. He has held a variety of positions including: Head of the International Relations and European Studies programme at the Central European University, Budapest; Assistant Professor at Pennsylvania State University; a Postdoctoral Fellow at the Mershon Center, Ohio State University and a Research Fellow at the Stockholm International Peace Research Institute. Duke is currently an Associate Professor at the European Institute of Public Administration in Maastricht, the Netherlands. He has written extensively on security issues including, most recently, *The Elusive*

Quest for European Security: From EDC to CFSP (Macmillan/St. Martin's Press, 2000) and has contributed numerous chapters to books as well as many journal articles on various aspects of European and transatlantic security.

Hans-Georg Ehrhart is Senior Research Fellow and project leader of the "International Fellowship Progamme Graf Baudissin" of the Institute for Peace Research and Security Policy at the University of Hamburg (IFSH). He is also a member of the "Team Europe" of the European Commission's Representation in Germany. He received his M.A. and D.Phil. from the University of Bonn. He has held visiting research appointments at the Research Institute of the Friedrich Ebert Foundation in Bonn, the Fondation pour les Etudes de Défense Nationale, Paris, and the Centre of International Relations at Queen's University, Kingston, Canada. Ehrhart's research activities deal with the broad topic of peace and security. He has widely published on issues such as disarmament, peacekeeping, post-Soviet politics, German-French relations as well as German and European security politics.

Bruce W. Jentleson joined the faculty of Duke University on 1 January 2000 as Director of the Terry Sanford Institute of Public Policy and Professor of Public Policy and Political Science. He is a leading expert on a wide range of issues of American foreign policy, with a distinguished professorial record and extensive policy experience.

Jentleson stood as foreign policy adviser to Vice President Al Gore. In 1993–94 he was on the State Department Policy Planning Staff as Special Assistant to the Director, with a broad range of policy responsibilities, including serving as a member of the US delegation to the Middle East Multilateral Arms Control and Regional Security Talks (ACRS). In 1987–88, while a Council on Foreign Relations International Affairs Fellow, he served as a foreign policy adviser to then-Senator Gore. He holds a Ph.D. from Cornell University, and was recipient of the American Political Science Association's Harold D. Lasswell Award for his doctoral dissertation; a Master's from the London School of Economics and Political Science, and a Bachelor's degree also from Cornell. His publications include numerous articles as well as seven books including *American Foreign Policy: The Dynamics of Choice in the 21ˢᵗ Century* (W.W. Norton, 2000); *Opportunities Missed, Opportunities Seized: Preventive Diplomacy in the Post-Cold War World*, a project of the Carnegie Commission on Preventing Deadly Conflict (Rowman and Littlefield, 1999).

Troy Joseph is a Ph.D. candidate in the Department of Economics at Carleton University, Canada. He acted as Project Coordinator of the "Country Indicators for Foreign Policy" project, a study initiated by the Canadian Department of Foreign Affairs and International Trade (DFAIT) and the Norman Paterson School of International Affairs (Ottawa, Canada).

Osvaldo Kreimer is a special Advisor to the Inter-American Commission on Human Rights of the OAS (IACHR). Most recently he was a Principal Specialist lawyer at the IACHR, serving as desk officer for Brazil and Suriname, with responsibility for technical support to the Rapporteurships on indigenous rights, and on children's rights. He has worked as desk officer for the cases on Guatemala, Peru, Honduras, Panama, and Paraguay. Since 1989 he has been in charge of the preparation of the future American Declaration on the Rights of Indigenous Peoples that was approved by the IACHR in 1997, and is now under review by a Working Group of the Permanent Council of the OAS for future approval by the General Assembly. From 1977 to 1988 he was Specialist, Unit Chief, and later Director of the Inter-American Program for Educational Development (PREDE) and of Educational Affairs Department of the OAS. He taught at Rutgers University (1975–76), Boston University (1976–77), and published numerous articles on education, indigenous law, humanitarian and human rights law. Kreimer holds a Law Degree and a Sociology Degree (University of Buenos Aires), a Certificate of Studies (Ecole Pratique of Hautes Etudes and Université de Paris) and a Ph.D. from Stanford University.

David Last is a Major in the Canadian Armed Forces with both practical and academic knowledge of peacekeeping. He is a graduate of the Royal Military College of Canada, Carleton University, the London School of Economics (Ph.D.), and the US Command and General Staff College and has served with NATO and UN forces in Germany, Cyprus, Croatia, and Bosnia. The Canadian Peacekeeping Press published his book *Conflict De-escalation in Peacekeeping Operations* (1997), and recent articles have appeared in *International Peacekeeping, Canadian Foreign Policy*, and *Fletcher Forum*. Major Last teaches political science and war studies at the Royal Military College of Canada.

Natalie Mychajlyszyn is a Post-doctoral Fellow at the Norman Paterson School of International Affairs, Carleton University. She received her Ph.D. in Political Studies in 1998 from Queen's University, Canada. Her areas of interest include European security, civil-military reforms, international relations in the former Soviet Union, international regimes, ethnic conflict, and conflict prevention and settlement. Her current research project compares the enlargements of the OSCE and NATO and their impact on conflict prevention in Europe.

Dane Rowlands received his Ph.D. in economics from the University of Toronto in 1994, and is currently Associate Professor of International Affairs at the Norman Paterson School of International Affairs, Carleton University. In addition to his primary research in international debt and multilateral financial institutions, he has recently been involved in projects on third-party intervention and international migration. He has contributed chapters to various books and articles to such journals as the *Journal of International Economics,*

Journal of Conflict Resolution,
Review of International Economics,
Journal of Development Studies,
World Development, and *Canadian*
Foreign Policy.

Albrecht Schnabel is an Academic
Programme Officer in the Peace and
Governance Programme of the
United Nations University, Tokyo,
Japan. His work at UNU focuses on
conflict and security studies, with an
emphasis on conflict prevention and
post-conflict peacebuilding. He was
educated at the University of
Munich, the University of Nevada-
Reno, and Queen's University,
Canada, where he received his
Ph.D. (Political Studies) in 1995. He
was a lecturer at Queen's University
(1994), and an Assistant Professor
at the American University in
Bulgaria (1995–96) and the Central
European University (1996–98).
He served on OSCE election
monitoring missions in Bosnia-
Herzegovina, was a visiting fellow at
the Institute for Peace Research and
Security Policy at the University of
Hamburg and is currently a trainer
in Early Warning and Preventive
Measures for the UN Staff College
in Turin, and President of the
International Association of
Peacekeeping Training Centres. His
teaching and research focus on
international organizations, ethnic
conflict, refugee policy, peacekeeping,
conflict prevention and management,
and humanitarian intervention. He
has contributed articles on these
topics to numerous journals and
edited volumes. Recent books
include *The Southeast European*
Challenge: Ethnic Conflict and the
International Response (co-editor
with Hans-Georg Ehrhart, 1999),

Kosovo and the Challenge of
Humanitarian Intervention: Selective
Indignation, Collective Action, and
International Citizenship (co-editor
with Ramesh Thakur, 2000),
Southeast European Security:
Threats, Responses, Challenges
(editor, 2001), and *Recovering from*
Civil Conflict: Reconciliation, Peace,
and Development (co-editor with
Edward Newman, 2002).

Andrea Kathryn Talentino is an
Assistant Professor of Political
Science at Tulane University. She
has published previously on civil
conflict, and is completing a
manuscript on international
intervention in the post-Cold War
period. She received her Ph.D. from
the University of California, Los
Angeles in 1998. Her field of
specialization is international
relations, focusing on civil conflict as
both an intra- and international
issue and the role of institutions in
conflict resolution. In 1999 she was a
Sawyer Seminar Fellow at the
Center of International Studies at
Princeton University, where she
worked with a project studying the
origins and outcomes of civil
conflicts. She has published
previously on the ramifications of
civil conflict for the international
community, and is completing a
manuscript on international intervention in the post-Cold War period.

Raimo Väyrynen is Professor of
Government at the University of
Notre Dame where he served in
1993–98 as the Regan Director of its
Joan B. Kroc Institute for
International Peace Studies. In
1978–93 he was Professor of
International Relations and in 1990–

93 Dean of the Faculty for Social Sciences at the University of Helsinki. In 1972–78 Väyrynen directed the Tampere Peace Research Institute and served in 1975–79 as the Secretary-General of the International Peace Research Association. In the USA, he has held visiting appointments at MIT, Princeton University, Harvard University, and the University of Minnesota. He has chaired the Finnish Political Science Association, the Finnish Social Science Research Council, and the Board of the Copenhagen Peace Research Institute. In 1989–95 he was a member of the United Nations University Council. In 1992 Väyrynen was elected to the Finnish Academy of Sciences. His publications include 20 books and over 200 scholarly articles. His most recent books are *Breaking the Cycles of Violence* (Kumarian, 1999, co-author) and *Globalization and Global Governance* (Rowman and Littlefield, 1999, editor).

Index

Catalogue Request

Name: _____

Address: _____

_____

Tel: _____

Fax: _____

E-mail: _____

To receive a catalogue of UNU Press publications kindly photocopy this form and send or fax it back to us with your details. You can also e-mail us this information. Please put "Mailing List" in the subject line.

United Nations University Press

53-70, Jingumae 5-chome
Shibuya-ku, Tokyo 150-8925, Japan
Tel: +81-3-3499-2811 Fax: +81-3-3406-7345
E-mail: sales@hq.unu.edu   http://www.unu.edu